GROWING UP
IN A LAND CALLED HONALEE

GROWING UP
IN A LAND CALLED HONALEE

The Sixties in the Lives of American Children

Joel P. Rhodes

UNIVERSITY OF MISSOURI PRESS
Columbia

ISBN: 978-0-8262-2127-8
Library of Congress Control Number: 2017930378

∞™ This paper meets the requirements of the
American National Standard for Permanence of Paper
for Printed Library Materials, Z39.48, 1984.

Typefaces: Cardo, Cinzel

The author thanks Peter Yarrow and Lenny Lipton for permission to quote lyrics from "Puff (The Magic Dragon)."

To mom,

Gonna buy five copies for my mother . . .

CONTENTS

GROWING UP
IN A LAND CALLED HONALEE

CHAPTER ONE

Introduction

Puff, the magic dragon lived by the sea
And frolicked in the autumn mist in a land called Honalee

OH, I LOVED that rascal Puff. As a child during the Vietnam era, born in 1967, I remember so affectionately the wonderful story of his bittersweet friendship with little Jackie Paper sung as a lullaby in duet with my mother every night before bed. No other period is more intimately associated with its music as the sixties in our popular imagination and from my diminutive perspective Peter, Paul, and Mary's *Puff (The Magic Dragon)*—recorded in 1962 and number two on Billboard's chart in early 1963—was the absolutely essential song from that decade's musical catalogue. My mother, a baby boomer herself, was single, recently divorced, and bedtime at our home meant the two of us lying on the bed singing, either by memory or along with AM radio, she in an oversized football jersey and me in hand-made, fire-retardant footie pajamas covered with tiny green mice. We sang other favorites as well, anything from the Mamas and the Papas, the Beatles' "Yellow Submarine" (Ringo was my favorite), or Dr. Hook and the Medicine Show's "The Cover of 'Rolling Stone,'" the latter of which required the deepest bass tone a five-year-old could conceivably muster to really nail the line "I got a freaky ol' lady name of Cocaine Katy who embroiders on my jeans." And while I remained wholly oblivious to even those overt drug references, the Kingston Trio's bawdy "The Tattooed Lady" made me blush with such risqué lyrics as "all around her hips sailed a fleet of battleships" and "what we liked best was upon her chest / My little home in Waikiki!" Puff was always different, though, occupying a singularly elevated place in my young life, not only because of the charming fairy tale imagery and infectious folksy chorus, but something much more profound, a special

1

something that sets it apart from other cherished tunes we all nostalgically enshrine as the soundtrack to life's narrative. Only later when I became an historian did I come to fully appreciate why Puff resonates so deeply; as a child I had fashioned my understanding of 1960s America in large measure from Peter Yarrow and Lenny Lipton's enchanting ballad.

In mapping out the features and contours of a distinctive children's culture, historian Steven Mintz points out that "since the early twentieth century, children have constructed their identities and culture out of symbols, images, and stories from the raw materials provided by popular culture."[1] "Puff (The Magic Dragon)," indeed, provided many of those essential resources for imaginatively interpreting the adult world of the sixties while further socializing me in what my mother referred to as the "hippy-dippy" sensibilities her generation was experimenting with. And because children naturally blur any clear lines between fantasy and reality during this generational renegotiation, Puff's magical language helped to articulate a broad range of my otherwise quite confusing emotional development. While some single-minded adults mistakenly heard in the song a sly marijuana allegory, for me the lyrics nourished an enduring appreciation for mirth and whimsy along with a playful wonderment over life's more mundane *strings and sealing wax*, as well as its *other fancy stuff*.

Being raised by a working mother—who managed a clothing boutique offering countercultural-inspired commercial fashion to middle-class women—and with an absent biological father serving in Vietnam, I knew Puff to be at once a childlike playmate, yet somehow genuinely paternal. Unselfishly, the dragon guided another only child through an imaginative world of adventure. *Together they would travel on a boat with billowed sail. Jackie kept a lookout perched on Puff's gigantic tail.* Living truly in at least modest comfort, my mother tried rearing me as a pacifist, based on the conclusions she came to honestly during those last awful years of the Vietnam War, but that philosophy never really took root in me, which is why I appreciated Puff's peaceful nature residing easily within such a formidable fire-breathing presence. *Noble kings and princes would bow whene'er they came. Pirate ships would lower their flag when Puff roared out his name.* Consider that across the world in Vietnam the awesome firepower brought to bear by the AC-47 gunship earned that particular aircraft the nickname Puff, the Magic Dragon among admiring soldiers.

Looking back, though, probably more so than anything, "Puff (The Magic Dragon)" was steeped in a certain melancholia over what is lost when we grow up and reluctantly leave behind the seemingly simpler and more innocent time of our childhood. *A dragon lives forever but not so little boys. Painted wings and giant rings make way for other toys. One gray night it happened, Jackie Paper came no more. And Puff that mighty dragon, he ceased his fearless roar.* Even as a preadolescent child I sensed that the tears I shed while singing *His head was bent in sorrow, green scales fell like rain*, were already for me as much as for Puff, who was now *without his lifelong friend*. At some point soon as a grownup it would be I, not just Jackie, who *no longer went to play along the cherry lane.*[2] How much that wistfulness motivates my life's work reconstructing the history of the Vietnam era I cannot truthfully say.

Clearly my deep personal connections with that time are not so very different from those of the millions of Americans for whom the "sixties experience" is still recognized as a fundamental part of their individual lives. The ubiquitous era remains central to our nation's collective popular and political culture today, as evidenced by the ceremonial marking of each of its milestones with fiftieth-anniversary observations: John Kennedy's assassination, the eruption of Beatlemania, Lyndon Johnson's War on Poverty, the Civil Rights and Voting Rights Acts, and soon the Summer of Love, moon landing, and Woodstock. The dark specter of Vietnam tempts casual observers to see similar military quagmires in the Middle East, and candidates for even the nation's highest office can still be judged by what they did, or did not do, to serve the nation in Southeast Asia during that wrenching conflict. Since Richard Nixon's successful 1968 campaign demonstrated the value of framing electoral politics as a referendum on the sixties, savvy candidates keep looking to gain political advantage by associating their opponent—as Republican Meg Whitman did with Democrat Jerry Brown during the 2010 California gubernatorial race—with the loaded symbolism of peace signs, George McGovern posters, and free-lovin' hippies. That same obsession with countercultural craziness continues to rally the troops in our culture wars, fueling fervent jeremiads against the ceaseless erosion of traditional family values, sexual mores, and dutiful patriotism.

Yet, as a political and social historian of the Cold War years my scholarly interests extend well beyond the nostalgia, romance, or condemnation now generally associated with "the sixties," focusing instead on how that decade represents a profound sea change in American politics, society, culture, and foreign policy. Arguably these exhilarating years of hope and days of rage are the most important era in twentieth-century American history. Scholarship reflects this enduring significance as the proliferation of written and media works continues to come at such a pace that to keep up is a Sisyphean task indeed. And with each passing year the prevailing historiographical trends offer greater appreciation for circumstances and conditions outside the traditional sixties meccas of San Francisco and New York—recognizing that Ann Arbor, Chicago, and Madison were not the only places in between where political radicalism and social experimentation happened, while also, as Jacquelyn Dowd Hall has put it, exploring the more obscure "partial truths" in order to expand our historical perspective of the Vietnam era with a more textured and nuanced appraisal.[3]

It was in these particular pursuits that I became interested in William Tuttle's observation that historians might "understand the nature of social change, including the significance of culture, but they generally fail to recognize that social change has differential effects based on whether children, adolescents, or adults are affected." In his influential, interdisciplinary study of American home front children in World War II, *"Daddy's Gone to War,"* Tuttle focused on the intersections between the "shifting configurations of age, culture, and history" during another transformational period in American history to explore these three variables' impact on individual development and social change. This approach of studying children as historical subjects—still a relatively new discipline, but one embraced by the current generation of historians trained in social history—lends itself particularly well to the Vietnam era. Numerous and extensive studies, of course, have already accounted for the mammoth baby boom of the post–World War II era—crowned "the decisive generation in our history"—which dramatically transformed the demographic landscape of the United States with preadolescents in the 1950s and adolescents in the 1960s. Despite some quibbling on the exact parameters, it appears that in the nineteen years between 1946 and 1964, some 76,441,000 Americans were born. In terms of raw numbers, May 1946 marks the beginning of the boom in earnest, not coincidentally exactly nine months after V-J Day. Almost three and a half million babies arrived in 1946, one every nine seconds—a fertility record at the time—which gave the country its biggest one-year population gain to date and pushed the overall populace to 143 million. Unlike Europe, where the surge of pent-up war babies quickly evaporated, America pressed on, and, in fact, accelerated, with the birthrate outpacing India's for a time. Eventually reaching four million newborns a year in 1954, annual births did not dip below that staggering number—peaking in 1957 at 4.3 million—until 1964, which is generally accepted as the last real year of the boom. By the time of Lyndon Johnson's landslide victory over Barry Goldwater that year, the U.S. population stood at nearly 192 million. Four out of every ten Americans were under the age of twenty and there were more children under fourteen than there had been people in the country in 1881.[4]

Scholars tend to agree that whether referred to collectively as Spock babies, the Sputnik generation, the Pepsi generation, the rock-n-roll generation, the Emmett Till generation, the Love generation, the Vietnam generation, or the Me generation, the baby boomers remain integral to our understanding of the shifting national dynamics during the sixties as their immense demographic dimensions carried along and intensified the currents of that historical sea change. Yet for all the well-placed attention on adolescent and adult boomers as the agents and actors of such radical change, no one has ever considered the perspectives of their younger brothers and sisters who by virtue of age experienced the 1960s in profoundly different ways. So, inspired by William Tuttle's work, and embarking like him on a very personal endeavor, I am examining how the multiple social, cultural, and political changes between John F. Kennedy's inauguration in 1961 and the end of American involvement in Vietnam in 1973—the long view of the sixties—manifested themselves in the lives of preadolescent American children. These earliest years of childhood are the most formative and have significant life-span consequences, and thus I am focusing on the children born between 1956 and 1970—57.5 million in total—who have never been quantitatively defined as a generation, but whose child-centered preadolescent world was nonetheless quite distinct from the early baby boom cohort born prior to 1955, and who likewise contrasted significantly with children raised in more adult-oriented families after the mid-1970s. In adopting an interdisciplinary, age-specific perspective in my analysis of social change in the Vietnam era, I can examine how this cohort understood the historical forces of the sixties as children, and with the use of developmental psychology, how these children made meaning of these forces based on their developmental age. Ultimately, I am concerned not only with the immediate imprint of the historical sixties on the lived experience of children, but the causal developmental results which may have resonated across their life course—in short, how their unique perspective on the sixties has influenced them as adults.

Methodologically, my work is particularly informed by sociological developmentalist Glen Elder's pioneering application of this "life course perspective" to the study of children and families. The chapters are arranged around the general chronological framework of those phenomena which had the most immediate consequences for preadolescent children. In chapter 2, I begin the study by examining the presidency of John F. Kennedy, a central organizing principle in the process of political socialization for this cohort. Special emphasis is given to the idealistic energy radiating throughout Camelot from his 1960 election—especially for Catholic children—and two of the administration's initiatives most directly aimed at young Americans: the President's Council on Physical Fitness and the Maternal and Child Health and Mental Retardation law. Chapter 3 covers those exhilarating early years of the space race—NASA's Mercury and Gemini projects—and Kennedy's role in launching the nation on a rocket ride to the moon. These triumphs are juxtaposed with the terrifying prospect of nuclear holocaust, culminating in the thirteen restless days of the Cuban Missile Crisis. In chapter 4, the Kennedy presidency comes to an abrupt end with the painful flashbulb nature of the assassination, nearly inseparable from the shared mourning of the funeral, which left so many musing that even to this day, they still look for another JFK. In chapter 5, I discuss the Johnson presidency. Despite the Great Society's messianic spirit, the relationship between Lyndon B. Johnson and children was less emotive compared to Kennedy. Yet, as I argue, Johnson produced considerably more tangible change through his administration's sweeping health, education, and welfare policies, especially Medicaid, Head Start, and, indirectly, the television program *Sesame Street*.

Shifting away from politics, chapter 6 takes a new look at the African-American struggle for civil rights. Focusing on the complexity of race and racism in the lives of preadolescent children, I trace individual participation in school desegregation and other forms of social activism targeting Jim Crow segregation in the former confederacy. Understandably, the civil rights movement appears to have been a much more prominent feature in the childhood of those living in the South, while for preadolescents elsewhere across the United States the protracted war in Vietnam remained the era's prevailing national experience. Thus, in chapter 7 I discuss how, for this first generation raised in the era of televised combat, Vietnam effected numerous changes in the lives of children. Not only were children burdened with the emotional weight of anxiously watching the nightly televised "box scores" of death tolls and exposed to the divisiveness engendered by the war, but Vietnam also transformed familial relationships through wartime separations from fathers, which concluded with unforgettable reunions and emotionally taxing periods of family reformation.

Beyond Vietnam, the most recognizable images of the sixties involve the vast array of activism, in which millions of socially conscious Americans sought to communicate their stance on the war and other conflicts through public productions of political and cultural protest in what was understood as "the movement." Children's participation in this movement was relatively rare and, when it happened, quite controversial. Defenders of allowing pre-adolescents to join in public protest argued that it taught social responsibility and critical thinking, while critics derided the inclusion of children as nothing more than simple exploitation, if not abuse. Either way, there were really just two interrelated forms of activism which consistently and deeply impact-ed preadolescent children: the counterculture and women's liberation. In the search for alternatives to Cold War culture, both began with redefinitions of the middle class, suburban family, and motherhood. Accordingly, chapter 8 explores how living within a "hippie" lifestyle that hoped to create a more meaningful way of life influenced child rearing, socialization, and childhood, including the experiences of those growing up in communal living arrange-ments. Chapter 9 continues to follow many of these same themes by address-ing the much broader childhood implications of social changes in women's lives. These range from renegotiations of gender roles and increased wage employment of women to divorce and single-parent families, day care, and ideological changes in child rearing.

The study is concluded in chapter 10. After briefly revisiting that journey to the moon by Apollo 11 in 1969, I lay out the prominent changes in children's experiences and children's environments which took place in America toward the early 1970s. Rather than a fixed historical event such as Watergate, it was really these years, when the child-centered parenting dynamics of the early baby boom gave way to more contemporary adult-centered conceptions co-inciding with an age of narcissism, which mark the proper end of sixties child-hood. As such, the remainder of the chapter offers notes and observations on "the sixties" from the perspective of twenty-first-century adults looking back.

We can determine how these historical 1960s forces manifested themselves in the proximal world of children by locating the entry points where social and political changes from the broader adult society permeated the separate sphere of childhood to become changes in the reality of preadolescents. While in other studies of the sixties it is relatively easy to trace the various dialecti-cal conflicts and confrontations which produced the decade's sociopolitical transformations—whether in the halls of government, college campuses, or on the streets—it is much trickier to follow these paths into the lives of children because of how subtly and indirectly change is diffused at their level. With-in the physical and social environments of sixties children, this permeation played out in the cheerfully decorated classrooms where they learned and the undeveloped fields where they romped, sometimes facilitated by imaginative toys and games. Mass media—primarily television's commercial programming and news coverage—emerged as another chief thoroughfare and played an ever larger role with each passing year.

The most consistently reliable, yet elusive, socialization unfolded in the families, more often than not through the "imperial" practices of parents and "native" practices of the children. Imperial practices can be understood as any number of cultural narratives—bedtime stories, family lore, literature, games, and even songs like *Puff (The Magic Dragon)*—that parents purposefully recommended, and provided, to children in the hope that they would learn from, and internalize, their adult-sanctioned messages. As a Tennessee woman born in 1961 told me, "I think in retrospect I wasn't traumatized by the '60s so much as I was traumatized by adults' reaction to the '60s!"[5]

The native practices of preadolescents encompass the unique folkways in which some children—commonly older brothers and sisters—attempted to socialize other children to sixties realities through slang, humor, insults, pranks, games, songs, superstitions, and legends. Take, as an example, a story from that same Tennessee woman, whose older sister incorporated parental polemics against hippies into their preadolescent folk culture, using a time-honored method that made perfect sense to them. When they even thought about it, the children considered hippies to be harmless folks who, for all their eccentricities, were mostly interested in fun. But with adults expressing a variety of serious misgivings about these slackers, particularly condemning their dope use, the children came to understand that whatever "dope" was, it had to be horrible, something you needed to stay far away from lest you end up like those damned hippies. So the older sister invented a make-believe "evil" character who did everything bad around their home. If a vase had broken or something went missing, he was behind it. The imaginary fiend's name was Dope.[6]

The remaining component of my work is to consider the results and behaviors, or at least the implications, of these social and political changes on the lives of children, both the developmental significance at the time the events occurred and later on in the life course. Accordingly, I examined a broad range of children's experiences from the Vietnam era, relying heavily on firsthand accounts collected from two research strategies. Beginning in January 2010 I contacted hundreds of newspapers in all fifty states with a "Letter to the Editor"—an approach borrowed from William Tuttle—soliciting stories about growing up from the cohort born between 1956 and 1970. I received just over 400 responses from thirty-one states. In recalling what the decade meant to them as preadolescents, some respondents contributed paragraphs while others sent over thirty pages. To supplement these self-selected oral histories and address the inherent problem of sampling and memory distortion, I also surveyed preadolescent correspondence at the John F. Kennedy and Lyndon Baines Johnson Presidential Libraries in order to understand the process of political socialization and how young letter writers saw the era's historic presidencies. (Materials which might include children's letters have not been processed at the Richard M. Nixon Library and will not be open to researchers in the foreseeable future.)

Applying developmental and educational psychology where appropriate, this study recognizes the complexity of the sociohistorical phenomena which shaped these children's lives—helping define who they were and how they behaved—based on their age at the time the event took place and the adaptive resources, options, and explanations of life available to them at that age. The cognitive and moral heavy lifting in our lives is done prior to adolescence, between the ages of six and twelve, what psychologist Jean Piaget characterized as the "concrete operational stage" of development—or, as historian Howard Chudacoff says, the period when "children are really children." By the time young people reach high school, the essential bearings on which their identity rests are solidified to the point where little additional, substantive change can be expected. Extraordinary events can have the greatest impact on those traveling along these sensitive points of preadolescent development and socialization. Depending on the developmental stage at which they were absorbed—factoring in the intensity and duration of the historical moment as well—the impact of personalities and actions, such as John Kennedy's election or the war in Vietnam, molded this generation in a number of fundamental ways. Most immediately, the weaving of historical threads through the fabric of their young lives triggered ephemeral changes in behavior and habits, what Glen Elder recognized as "transitions." The most significant personal transitions in turn guided more permanent changes in children's "trajectory," leading them to consciously plot a course toward a particular lifestyle or career in adulthood.[7]

It is important to remain cautious about making grand and universal claims of direct causality between what happened to a child in the 1960s and explicit adult attitudes and behavioral outcomes like political party affiliation or voting patterns. Clearly, there is significant plasticity in our development as earlier childhood experiences are regularly modified when we encounter later events at numerous points along our unfolding life. However, there are tendencies and consequences which can be traced from the Vietnam era, often discernible only because, like the layers of an onion, the core ideologies forged in childhood are the last to be surrendered as adults. While the baby boomers born after 1955 share a great deal of common ground with the older boomers, the cohort is, as a woman born in 1957 describes them, "cuspers." "I always thought that we should have our own generation," she explained to me, "and not get lumped in with the baby boomers. It's amazing the effect that just a few years of age had on our perception of the world, compared to those people just a little bit older (or younger). It was as if we had just learned one set of societal rules when it was replaced by a new set." "For so long, people assumed that the older boomers were the most affected by the sixties," another woman, born in 1959, wrote, "but I have long had a theory that those of us who were children at the time were the most shaped by it all, because our *earliest* memories were formed at a time when the whole world seemed to be falling apart."[8]

As demographer Landon Jones observed, preadolescents in the sixties "had less agony—but also less ecstasy." Many look back with frustration, feeling cheated, having just missed out on the sound and fury of the sixties altogether or fated to crane their necks over adults for glimpses of the political and cultural whirlwind as "luckier" big brothers and sisters distilled news down to them. Being socialized during a time when so much of adult culture was in flux, they were prone to confusion and ambivalence, but with few resources available to them for making meaning of the events they saw transpiring in the adult world. Those who were politicized in such a polarized nation often followed politics with sincere interest, but were politely dismissed as cute, but not serious—just as their generational conflicts with their parents were more innocuous than their older siblings'. Their cultural rebellions were not part of a widely publicized youth quake, but rather manifested themselves in seemingly inconsequential little revolts such as reading *Mad* magazine past bedtime. As the older baby boomers moved through their demographic transitions like the metaphorical pig through a python, all the social celebration and scholarly attention that they churned up followed them, leaving the younger cohort in their wake and feeling as if their involvement in the country's most pivotal decade was minimal. If you remember the sixties, the saying goes, you were not really there. Since this cohort's only recollections are through the eyes of a child—not those of the proverbial "children *of* the sixties" famed in song and story, but just "children *in* the sixties"—they are hesitant to understand themselves as having been legitimate historical actors with agency. Thus, they remain less inclined to appreciate the validity of their experiences or the powerful developmental influences that make the sixties extremely relevant to our lives today.[9]

This, of course, does nothing to diminish the fond reminiscences and warm nostalgic glow of such a vibrant time to be a kid. After all, as Steven Mintz maintains, rightly or not, "a Cold War childhood remains the yardstick against which Americans access contemporary childhood." And while it is always risky to make too many generalizations about 57.5 million Americans, before delving into the historical permeation of large-scale events and personalities into the reality of preadolescents, it will be instructive to offer an abbreviated look at some of the common generational markers of childhood–inseparable from family dynamics–and children's culture in the sixties. As it was so affectionately captured in television's *The Wonder Years*–that sentimental ode to baby boomer upbringing which ran from 1988 through 1993–the family oriented, child-centered nature of middle-class suburban life associated with the 1950s "golden age of childhood" still largely defined growing up throughout the 1960s. Like so many who contacted the author, a Louisville, Kentucky, woman born in 1959 pointed out that while "I know you are interested in children growing up in the 'turbulent' 60's, I realize that most of my memories of the 60's are pleasant . . . a very innocent time for me and the other kids in my neighborhood."[10]

Indeed, sixties children were the last to be raised predominantly by youthful parents abiding by well-defined, traditional gender roles within the family: reliable, breadwinning fathers providing the necessary material support side-by-side with energetic and focused "stay at home" mothers. They are the final products of *Time* magazine publisher Henry Luce's grandiose notion of an "American Century," a time in which the nation's world leadership would be anchored in the nuclear family's idealized ability to perpetuate such democratic responsibilities as citizenship, the Protestant work ethic, and military honor. In these waning years of the largest economic expansion in the nation's history, for virtually every race, ethnicity, religion, class, and educational level, the good life remained predicated on the normative standards and values embodied in this therapeutic family pattern still holding sway from the earliest Cold War years.[11]

Cold War era children, in whom so much of their parents' identities and fortunes were laboriously invested, occupied the undisputed center stage in tightly bound households, a reality increasingly solidified by Madison Avenue's market positioning of youth as the straw that stirred American popular culture. And with society placing an ever higher premium on the value of children–both as the bedrock of the contemporary middle-class lifestyle as well as tomorrow's virtuous democratic citizens and anti-communist cold warriors–the pressures of child-rearing took on still more weight. Accordingly, baby boom mothers and fathers, eagerly following the guidance of recognized authorities on virtually everything from lawn care to fashion, relied heavily on the advice of child experts advocating more relaxed approaches to parenting, approaches that were based in part on the progressive era notion that children should be understood rather than managed. More specifically, this meant Dr. Benjamin Spock and his *Common Sense Book of Baby and Child Care*. First published in June 1946, on the front end of the baby boom, *Baby and Child Care* sold 4 million copies by the time Dwight Eisenhower was elected president in 1952 and annual sales remained over one million for eighteen straight years. When the first of the baby boomers reached thirty-years old themselves during the bicentennial year of 1976, Spock's virtual bible of parenting had sold 28 million copies over fifty-eight printings and several editions, making it America's second best-selling book in the twentieth century, behind only that actual sacred text.

In writing his popular owner's manual for baby boom children, the Yale and Columbia educated pediatrician followed in the psychological, educational, and anthropological traditions of Sigmund Freud, John Dewey, and Margaret Mead which were driving long-term liberalizing trends in child-rearing practices. But the real genius of Benjamin Spock rests in his ability to translate the developmental language of the Freudian into a chatty and constantly reassuring guide that any parent could understand. Essentially, from the simple encouragement which opens the book–"Trust yourself, you know more than you think you do"–Spock inspired parents to have faith in their instincts and love their babies. With gentle good humor, and not a little irony, Spock presented a compassionate case against the residual proscriptions for parental detachment and inflexible regimentation stubbornly left over from the Victorian era. To his reasoning, the misguided parenting of emotionally distant disciplinarians who imposed strict scheduling and generally refrained from rocking, tickling, or play had decidedly negative developmental consequences later in life for their children.[12]

Hence, Spock recommended the more permissive approach to handling kids. *Baby and Child Care* instructed parents to worry less about spoiling them and instead rely on common sense informed by their unique relationship with the child to determine such things as feeding times (when they were hungry), at what age to potty train (once they were ready), or how to discipline (without physical punishment). Moreover, Spock advocated a kinder, gentler style which broke down the psychic distance between parent and child, allowing moms and dads to be affectionate and fully vested in the lives of their children. By holding crying babies and attentively engaging them in conversation and play, Spock-oriented parents could get to know their kids as the reasonable, friendly little human beings they were. Doing so not only built trust, it also allowed parents to monitor the child's individual emotional needs and material interests so they might better facilitate them. In eschewing the application of a one-size-fits-all perspective on children, Spock encouraged parents to foster individuality and confidence. In the Cold War, this too was primarily geared toward perpetuating democratic society through new generations of children growing up to be strong-minded citizens, who, just as importantly, were at peace with themselves and society. The humanistic logic being that children reared to instinctively neither submit to authority nor dominate others would ultimately work to buttress a cooperative, consensus-oriented, and more stable America.[13]

While it remains problematic to claim a immediate causal relationship between Dr. Spock's writings and actual parenting practices, if as many mothers read Spock as bought the book, then at least one out of every five baby boomers, those born between 1946 and 1964, could be considered what was at the time called a "Spock baby." The number of "Spock babies" grows to one in four when taking into account only those later boomers born between 1956 and 1970, and realistically grows even further when factoring in parents who merely borrowed the paperback from friends. Even if it only seemed like every mother had a copy, the very ubiquity of *Baby and Child Care* suggests that a significant number of parents had a familiarity, or at least an acquaintance, with Spock's ideas. Again, while few would argue that mothers followed Spock word-for-word, there is ample evidence that, especially in the middle class, parenting trended away from the more rigid styles of previous generations toward Spock's more permissive model.

In most American homes, permissiveness and child-centeredness probably just meant that the family functioned more effectively for the mutual fulfillment of both parents and children, and that kids were afforded freer rein in the practice of childhood. Families did, in fact, spend a great deal of time together in the prefabricated built environment of what had by the sixties become a fully suburban-oriented country. Between 1950 and 1970, the nation's suburban population doubled from 36 million to 74 million and by 1960 nearly three out of every five white, school-age children lived in the suburbs. Fueled initially by the Veterans Administration's attractive new mortgage program, low inflation, cheap gas, and highways, 83 percent of the population growth in the peak baby boom years of the 1950s was along the periphery of American cities. In reality, more people arrived in the suburbs every year than had ever come through Ellis Island and by 1970 the United States became the first country in world history to have more suburbanites than city dwellers or farmers.[14]

Suburbia's architectural housing forms and interior space concepts further facilitated this togetherness. In the popular ranch style, for instance, the kitchen moved to the front of the house, positioned prominently to showcase the housewife while giving her clear lines of sight out picture windows to watch kids in either the front or back yards. Increasingly, new push-button, automated technologies in ovens, dishwashers, and assorted appliances, plus an expanding array of prefabricated foods, afforded a restaurant-style experience right there in mom's kitchen. So too did the "family room" evolve from a secondary recreational space, often relegated to a basement. By adding a television set and more durable furniture–frequently upholstered with virtually child-proof imitation leather Naugahyde–the homier family room emerged as both a home theater and less-formal locus of everyday rough-and-tumble household life, eclipsing the more traditionally furnished, and increasingly rarely used "living room." By the late 1960s, affordable air conditioning window units in nearly 70 percent of American homes tempted suburbanite families (especially in the South) to shut up the doors and windows altogether and never leave the comfort of their climate-controlled residence.[15]

Within these domestic spaces, television exercised an unprecedented capacity for shaping how children consumed all forms of culture, popular and otherwise. Many of the earliest and most cherished memories of a Cold War childhood involve television–programming, theme songs, and advertising jingles–whose dominating presence came to feel like a virtual family member, a sort of third parent. Since most American households featured just one television (and one telephone) in the family room, there was a campfire nature to congregating around its electric glow. Here adults and older siblings controlled the viewing habits of children, except on Saturday morning, which was basically a television world unto itself. The youngest audience members might be instructed to get up and change the channel (or adjust the rabbit-ears antenna for better reception), but preadolescents never of their own volition switched over to, say, a kid's favorite like the *Beverly Hillbillies* when everyone was already watching a more adult oriented western like *The Virginian*. Children either watched what their elders chose, digesting it and making meaning as best as they developmentally could, or went off to play. And through this perpetual series of repeatable experiences, television functioned as a chief entry point of the adult world into childhood. Moreover, by the 1960s the small screen was also quickly becoming a primary socializing agent whereby its mediated reflections of grownup reality (often augmented by parental commentary) were being enthusiastically discussed and disseminated amongst preadolescent peers, bonding kids together within a shared children's culture which transcended social class and region.[16]

Relative middle-class affluence also increasingly allowed children to have their own, or shared, bedrooms filled up and adorned with a wide array of store-bought kid's furniture, commercial amusements, and wall decorations. Yet, for all the familial closeness and creature comforts of home, preadolescents were perpetually pushed outside by bouts of boredom—which despite boomer recollections to the contrary were actually rather frequent—while at the same time being pulled toward the spectacular promise of adventure, risk, and discovery beckoning beyond the back door. In the suburban landscape of childhood, large numbers of neighborhood playmates laid claim to the small undeveloped universes of vacant lots, ditches, streams, ponds, marshes, trestles, and forests just beyond the subdivision's edge. Here was their refuge, an unsupervised and unhurried separate sphere where imagination and do-it-yourself creativity shaped the nature of play and social relationships—albeit mostly sex-segregated—that seem by today's parental standards to have been without pressure or much influence from adults. Those children remaining indoors were something of an oddity.[17]

While suburbia certainly remained the more natural habitat for childhood, the general trends toward unsupervised and "unsafe" play were equally prevalent in rural areas and cities. Even in metropolises the size of Chicago and New York, children roamed their neighborhoods by themselves over many square miles from one activity to the next, often after dark. Typically summer days and weekends unfolded naturally, first by briefing parents on the vague parameters of that particular day's agenda and then traveling by foot or bicycle (unencumbered by helmets) on reconnaissance missions around nearby houses, sandlots, or pastoral areas where a collection of parked bikes meant like-minded friends were already gathering. These days ended, and it was time to go home, only when the streetlights came on, or when preempted by mom's urgent shouting. During the school week, this routine was simply compressed to begin after homework or chores until dinnertime. Unwritten, but widely understood, rules dictated that children check in periodically at home to get a drink of water (from the garden hose), use the bathroom, or eat lunch, but otherwise the nearest parents were often blocks, if not miles, away. When problems arose–differences of opinions or rule disputes–aggrieved participants worked toward solutions without parental mediation. This is not to say that the world was completely devoid of grown-ups. Quite the contrary, children casually talked with neighborhood adults without fear–"The A-bomb might get you, but not your next-door neighbor"–and although parents customarily identified at least one person in each town as a "pervert" to be watched out for and avoided, preadolescents regularly incorporated men and women into their exploits, befriending the mailmen, following the garbage truck around hoping for an invitation to help, or chasing the mosquito truck in order to smell those toxic fumes.[18]

Here then, with good-natured brevity, are the fundamental child-centered underpinnings and broad parameters of childhood and children's culture in the 1960s. So prevalent were these normative preadolescent realities in the first postwar decades that such a middle-class childhood seemed, as Landon Jones also observed, "a permanent fixture of American life." Yet, by the early 1970s, when political and popular culture increasingly fixated on the presidential misdeeds collectively known as Watergate, the very nature of this childhood was already changing in subtle, but nonetheless fundamental ways with the emergence of more adult-oriented lifestyles which favored fewer offspring and deemphasized domesticity. Again, a fuller examination of those transitional shifts which impacted the experiences and physical spaces of modern childhood constitutes the more fitting conclusion to this study than does Watergate, which scholars generally recognize as the bookend of the long sixties. But these are stories for the following chapters. For now, consider that it was into this peaceable kingdom–of PF Flyers sneakers and the Sears "wish book" Christmas catalog, where pretend Captain Kirks and Robins imitated fantasy television shows *Star Trek* and *Batman* with wooden phasers set to stun, or jumped, bath towel capes around their necks, from porches to bat poles (sapling trees)–that the historical forces of the sixties permeated. It was from the perspective of these preadolescent eyes that the spectacle of the Vietnam era's dramatic social and political changes fairly exploded.[19]

CHAPTER TWO

John F. Kennedy

You must vote for Kennedy if you want Santa Claus to come this year.
Jonnie, a five-year-old boy from Stanley, New York

"THIS ELECTION IS really the first that I have been able to understand," a third grade girl in Louisiana wrote John F. Kennedy on the occasion of his inauguration. "You will be the first president I will remember."[1] That the torch had been passed to a new generation of Americans was an oft-quoted verse from the gospel of John Kennedy taken quite literally by those who considered themselves the nation's junior citizens. His iconic, snow-swept inauguration on January 20, 1961—"Ask not what your country can do for you . . . "—was a demarcation, laden with deliberately crafted symbolism, between the perceived inertia of Dwight Eisenhower's 1950s and the vigorous New Frontier of Kennedy's 1960s—the oldest president to leave office at the time yielding leadership of the free world to the youngest ever elected. Although a decidedly polarizing figure in the adult political arena, in a contest with Richard Nixon that had split the electorate down the middle, the youthful Kennedy enjoyed a genuinely affectionate and tight embrace from American children.

President Kennedy's soaring rhetoric offered them much to idealize, just as his carefully stage-managed image offered much to love and admire. For starters, there was the exciting newness of it all. The youngest baby boomers had never known anyone living in the White House other than the grandfatherly Eisenhower. Now the mansion sprang to life, housing a charming and lively first family with Caroline and John Jr., glamorous yet somehow familiar contemporaries whose own Sunday evenings in the *first* family room surely involved watching Walt Disney and whose letters to Santa probably also referenced the Sears Wish Book. From their first acquaintance with America's de

17

facto royal family in the fall of 1960, children almost naturally developed an intimate closeness with the Kennedys. It was as if, elementary school teachers across the country observed, youngsters actually knew the man from Boston personally, and had all their brief lives. Thus, every May 29ᵗʰ a crush of handmade birthday cards arrived at the White House, just as a green wave of Crayola-ed shamrocks and leprechauns came for St. Patrick's Day, even though most of what children knew of Kennedy's proud Irish heritage probably came from Disney's 1959 movie *Darby O'Gill and the Little People.*

Considering the casual and disproportionately idealized nature of children's political socialization, preadolescent adulation of John F. Kennedy was hardly unexpected. Yet the emotional bond between Kennedy and American youth in the first years of the 1960s is distinctive, and it is therefore appropriate that the unparalleled imprint of the Kennedy presidency on this cohort, and the centrality of Kennedy to their political socialization, is the first focus of this study. This topic generated a great deal of scholarship during the Vietnam era, led by political psychologist Fred Greenstein and behaviorist-inspired political scientist David Easton. From their postwar work on children's relationships to the American president, two schools of thought emerged. First, preadolescent Americans hold the president—easily the most recognizable public person in their diminutive view of the world—in unanimously high esteem, as an infallible and benevolent leader associated with inherently good paternal qualities. Moreover, political socialization—how we learn political attitudes and cognition—is a powerful determinant of political behaviors later in life.[2]

Although they are "political primitives," as Easton refers to preadolescents, children seem to acquire most of the fundamentals that will inform their adult politics prior to, and during, elementary school. No other period of life is comparable to these formative years in terms of the sheer volume of learning across the spectrum, from personality characteristics to basic acculturation. These are the first metaphorical layers of our cognitive and moral onion, the foundation on which our future worldview is built. Jean Piaget, the Swiss biologist and psychologist whose pioneering cognitive theories on the processes of childhood learning is still the discipline's standard, identified this period as the "preoperational" and "concrete operational" stages of intellectual growth. From roughly two to seven years of age, children make dramatic strides in language, basic classification of objects, and at least some symbolic thought. In their remarkably receptive minds, learning unfolds uncritically at the unconscious level, mostly through imitation and identification. The ability to work with concrete concepts like the presidency improves gradually, but they still stumble with more abstract concepts such as democracy and justice. By the same token, perceptions remain predominantly egocentric in nature, in that children instinctively assume that other people see the world from their vantage point. Yet, after increased experience, learning, and maturation, by approximately ages seven through eleven children experience the adaptive changes Piaget defined as the concrete operational stage. Here logical and abstract thinking become more prevalent and, while egocentrism certainly lingers, children progressively appreciate other perspectives—now able, for instance, to see through the eyes of such varied characters as the stoic Charlie Bucket and the eccentric Willy Wonka in Roald Dahl's classic children's book.

Equally, if not more, important is the trajectory of moral development coinciding with these determinative years. Harvard psychologist and educational philosopher Lawrence Kohlberg added several new layers to Piaget's work, positing that growing learners proceed through stages of ethical reasoning on their way toward a mature sense of morality. Kohlberg's levels and stages of "pre-conventional" and "conventional" ethics represent advancements in thinking about telling right from wrong and why a person should behave herself. Children functioning at the pre-conventional stage, until around age ten, are still reasoning egocentrically; their personal conduct is governed by concern over how external authority will punish or reward their actions. Corresponding to Piaget's concrete operational cognitive stage, Kohlberg's conventional level of moral development speaks to a more autonomous sense of self, where morality is grounded in mutual respect. Children accept, and follow, agreed upon rules and standards—as in cooperatively playing a board game such as Parker Brothers' Sorry!—because of a more fully formed grasp of abstractions such as fairness and justice.[3]

While children progress through these critical points of development, exceptional political characters and events can spur behavioral "transitions" which point toward more substantive "trajectories" in the later life course. This brings us back to the Kennedy presidency. For children, the president of the United States is the first public figure of which they are aware, the first point of contact with the notion of governmental authority, and by age nine, and in most cases much earlier, virtually every American knows the president by name. This sort of recognition appears quite naturally around the age of three with virtually no formal instruction, often nothing more than the child questioning his parents about obeying the law and the local police, thus setting the gears in motion toward developing ideas about a higher authority outside the family. Through mass media events such as news conferences and interaction with parents and older siblings during the preschool years, the emergent awareness of the president unfolds beyond name recognition to include a more general orientation toward the office. In the already larger-than-life adult world, the presidency is obviously a special category of grown-up. In a land of laws, the president is the chief lawgiver, the most important person in the land.[4]

Television, indirectly through parents, was Kennedy's chief point of entry into the world of children. That voice, instantly recognizable, obliged them to briefly put aside the Etch A Sketch and take a seat in the arena of adult television news programming whenever John F. Kennedy appeared on the family's twenty-three-inch black-and-white set. Although *Bonanza, The Andy Griffith Show,* and *The Flintstones* dominated prime-time ratings, nightly television news was steadily supplanting print media as the nation's chief public opinion shaper on domestic and foreign issues by the early sixties. Most children knew and admired Dr. Ben Casey, to be sure, but increasingly *The Huntley-Brinkley Report,* along with the *CBS Evening News* with Walter Cronkite, attracted their interest. "Good night, Chet. Good night, David," they mimicked at bedtime. In this realm, Kennedy dominated.

Like Franklin Roosevelt on radio a generation before, John Kennedy masterfully brandished the strategic power of television. After four decisive televised debates as a candidate in 1960, President Kennedy took up almost permanent residence on the nightly network newscasts, including occasional one-on-one interviews with Cronkite and others. The thoughtful and determined president addressed the nation live nineteen times during his brief administration, usually on grave subjects like Cuban missiles or Mississippi segregation. Specials such as NBC's first *JFK Report* programs in early 1961 and ABC's *Adventures on the New Frontier* that same spring offered viewers more intimate behind-the-scenes glimpses of the colorful Kennedy White House and family. At what should have been the halfway point of his first term in December 1962, the president projected the reassuring aura of a seasoned statesman (seven weeks away from making Nikita Khrushchev blink) in an hour-long conversation with newsmen from all three networks conducted from his rocking chair in the Oval Office.[5]

Yet, the president appeared at his most delightful, disarming best when engaging reporters in unscripted, live press conferences. Since the first such broadcast in January 1961, nine out of ten adults tuned in to at least one of the fourteen televised press conferences of the Kennedy presidency (out of sixty-four in total), and, with only one TV in the house, even the most disinterested children were exposed in some fashion, which experts believe may be one of the primary reasons why this form of communication has become such a staple of American political culture.[6] Without question, children were ignorant of any macroeconomic or geopolitical policy specifics Kennedy addressed. Nonetheless, it is evident that preadolescents absorbed his articulate and self-assured demeanor while chortling along with their parents at his almost effortless and off-the-cuff wit. Who cared about international trade or snarky partisan criticism when you could be routinely entertained by this bright and attractive man at the top of his game? To a query about a Republican resolution declaring his administration a failure, Kennedy offered the deadpan quip that he assumed the GOP vote was unanimous. He deflected reporters' observations that his promises often outpaced his accomplishments by politely and self-effacingly thanking them for constantly reminding him. When NASA launched Ham the chimpanzee into space in January 1961, the president relayed a fictive message from the primate that everything in his Mercury-Redstone rocket was perfect and working fine. Few stories played better than the one about a little boy asking the president how he became a war hero aboard PT-109, to which Kennedy responded that it had been completely involuntary . . . the Japanese sank his boat.

John Kennedy had long since unseated Little Joe Cartwright, Fabian, and even Mickey Mantle at the altar of children's hero worship by the time First Lady Jacqueline Kennedy invited CBS and NBC viewers on a videotaped tour of the White House on Valentine's Day 1962. "Dr. Spock is for my husband," Jackie Kennedy had said during the 1960 campaign, "and I am for Dr. Spock."[7] After the February telecast, children became even more obsessed with the familial details and daily routines of the cosmopolitan Kennedys. The president-as-father-figure (a developmental dynamic addressed shortly) emerged for countless children across the nation. Trick-or-treaters made the rounds in costumes from the Ben Cooper Company with a plastic mask bearing a resemblance to the president and a faux business suit reading "JFK" on one pocket and "Mr. President" on the other. Girls renamed their most cherished dolls John and Jackie. Schoolyard playmates earnestly speculated near the monkey bars about whether Caroline and John Jr. preferred Life cereal to Alpha-Bits for breakfast or the still novel Play-Doh to the trusty old Fisher-Price Chatter Telephone. Could a first-grader in Tennessee, they wondered, really be best friends with Caroline and even get a ride on her pet pony, Macaroni? And then there was the dizzying vision of landing a man on the moon before the end of the decade. In a word, cool!

Again, preschool and early elementary students possess very little factual information about politics or even the most rudimentary knowledge of government, although in this regard they are only a few steps behind the least informed adults. Other than important television appearances, presidential elections, space launches, and civil rights demonstrations, the vast majority of political news was, and is, simply not relevant to younger children, and, in fact, the words "politics" and "politicians" do not consistently appear in their vocabulary until eleven or twelve years old. Real life was about Coca-Cola in a glass bottle, oatmeal cooked on the stove, movie monsters, and riding in mom's Buick Riviera. As a Kentucky woman born in 1959 conceded, playing outside—four square, bat ball, jump rope, hopscotch, riding bikes, and frozen catchers—consumed the day: "the political aspects of my life were on the periphery, sort of background noise." That being said, political socialization was nonetheless under way. Every study conducted on this cohort indicates that well before entering kindergarten, the child's political world was already taking shape in preparation for even more dramatic understanding during the elementary school years.[8]

In Piaget's preoperational stage, children broaden their nascent political learning not through study or any rational process initially, but rather by egocentrically cultivating an emotional, and mostly imaginative, personal connection to the president. Little wonder that a three-year-old boy in Rhode Island concluded every one of the president's televised appearances with kisses on the screen because JFK was his "friend." In the mind of most children, the great and powerful president takes on a highly idealized character consisting of those benevolent qualities they find most satisfying about adults, only in a more heightened and fanciful sense that they already recognize from the depiction of royalty in children's literature or Disney movies. Three years before adults fashioned the Arthurian mythology of the Kennedy administration, Camelot was already quite literally real to preadolescents who, like an eight-year-old in Memphis, matter-of-factly concluded, "The president is our king. His wife is a queen." The parents of a three-year-old girl in Ohio finally fixed a photograph of President Kennedy on their daughter's headboard because she had taken to telling everyone that JFK was her boyfriend. A similar photograph was the prized possession of a five-year-old New York boy who said his prayers under it nightly, faithfully concluding with "And help the president. Amen." Just one week before the 1960 election, the opinionated lad had solemnly announced to his divided two-party household that "You must vote for Kennedy if you want Santa Claus to come this year."[9]

This romanticized tendency can be partially accounted for by the protective way adults communicate politics to children, distilling out all unpleasantness and applying a sugary coating. Young readers do not find any books in their school libraries criticizing the presidents, as children's literature is known for promoting patriotism. So too does psychoanalytic theory speak to a projection of ideal parental virtues onto the president. The affectionate imagery that younger children hold can resemble their overwhelmingly positive views about their own father. In a sense, the president is what is popularly understood as a "father figure" possessing a dad's unfailing authority, wisdom, empathy, and strength writ large. Predictably, then, preadolescents are uniformly uncritical of the commander in chief, demonstrating no inclination toward negativity or cynicism. Metaphorically speaking, *these*—not the skeptical adolescent boomers whose social activism sparked a movement—were truly Kennedy's children.[10]

A recently widowed Long Islander wrote the president that through her six- and nine-year-old daughters' vicarious relationship with Caroline they now "in a strange way . . . seem to respect you as sort of an 'adopted Daddy.'" Likewise, a Tennessee woman born in 1958 remembered pilfering her parents' *Life* and *Look* magazines for the pictures of the Kennedys in every issue. "He was always smiling and interacting with his kids," she fondly reminisced. "My favorite picture was of John-John underneath the president's desk. I thought JFK must be the best dad ever. I wasn't in school yet. I started school at age 5. Anyway, I had been told that the president was the father of our country. That's how my childish mind saw it. He was the father of us all in this country, so we shared him as a daddy, right?"[11]

By the time students took up their places with bright shiny faces in the first grade, they brought this measureable degree of political socialization from home as surely as they carried the requisite Big Chief tablet. Over the course of the next few years, as they transitioned from Piaget's preoperational to concrete operational stage, their friendly—albeit vague—association with the president matured toward a more sophisticated understanding of the president's executive and legislative functions, a deeper appreciation for the cultural attitudes and values attached to the office, and eventually a conceptual notion of the workings of government in general. Much of this political learning remained informal and ancillary—such as ritual patriotic observances—because state curriculum guides of the era did not recommend teaching what was then called "civics" until the sixth grade. Still, elementary students added specific details to their growing repertoire, increasingly able to articulate that the president makes the laws, runs the country, and assists the people. As eight-year-olds from Tennessee explained it to their teacher in 1963: "The president wurries with the cuntree." "The president is our friend. He is Good to us. He likes us. A president tries to help people. We love him very much." "The President helps us . . . takes care of us . . . plays football . . . loves us."[12]

The 1960 election made a compelling context for this cohort's learning sequence to unfold, as it coincided with their development of broader ideas about government. The vast majority of elementary schoolchildren know they are American, and, although they are unable to articulate how this differentiates from children in other countries, they are already thoroughly socialized toward unquestioning patriotism. Nearly seventy-five percent of seven- and eight-year-olds begin to use the presidency as a sort of developmental shorthand to sort out their confused sense of the government. As their central point of orientation toward the political system, the chief executive becomes a unifying symbol representing the vast array of governmental branches, levels, and the separation of powers. Essentially, the president is the entire political structure to young children. All political elements and players are understood in terms of their subordinate relationship to the chief executive: elections select him, the vice president serves him as an assistant, Congress and the courts work to carry out his orders, and so forth. In this way, an imagined personal bond with this singular politician affords children a manageable terrain from which to navigate government's complexity. Likewise, it provides the first opportunity for them to personally identify with American democracy by relating the impersonal functions of government to their favorite American.[13]

What better way to get those red, white, and blue juices flowing, and put this patriotism into practice, than to commit one's young body and spirit to a candidate in our quadrennial spectacle of participatory democracy? Elementary school students at all grade levels followed the 1960 election closely and to a remarkable degree took part. Teachers observed an unprecedented excitement about politics that fall, leading a first grade instructor in Denver to report that her class was "very keyed up for the election, perhaps as much or more so than most grown-ups."[14] Pupils from coast to coast followed the campaigns of Senator Kennedy and Vice President Nixon in *My Weekly Reader* and diligently cast their ballots in that publication's second-ever presidential poll, which Kennedy won. Election bulletin boards decorated classrooms and were updated daily with article and picture clippings brought from home. Class pets were named in honor of various members of the Kennedy clan. Many students staged their own mock debates (at least the boys did), which

Kennedy also usually won, and finally held elections, which tended to run fifty-fifty.

In response to Kennedy's declaring in the fourth televised debate that "we must give this country leadership and we must get America moving again," children across the land were thinking about the ways in which they and JFK could make that happen. A special education teacher in Washington State earnestly assured Kennedy that despite her nine- and ten-year-old students working at a first grade level, "they are still striving to be good Americans. Every child knows your name, where you live and who you are. They know about our flag and the Pledge of Allegiance. They also know," she grimly added, "Mr. Khrushchev's name and the location of Russia on the globe." Parochial and private grade-schoolers alike offered their faith and devout prayer. Catholic students in particular sought divine guidance and protection for Kennedy in his election bid and the inevitable confrontation with global communism he would face if elected. "Every day when the hour bell rings," a Catholic first grader from New York reported, "we say a Hail Mary for our Country and you."[15]

In the early grades of elementary school, religion often blurs with patriotism in the child's political world. Consider, for instance, the solemn morning ritual of reciting that Pledge of Allegiance. Many second and third graders approached it faithfully as a prayer to God to protect the United States and thanking for Him for having done so in the past; during the sixties public schools still routinely followed the Pledge with a prayer. Only by the fifth grade does politics eclipse religion as the central meaning behind the Pledge, as students begin to deliver the words as a promise of loyalty to their country's democratic principles and commitment to be good citizens.[16]

Party identification is also similar to religion in that children appropriate their family's affiliation with the Democrats or Republicans in much the same way spiritual beliefs are passed down. A couple of years before they can explain the parties' most basic stances on the issues, or even correctly use the term "political party," a substantial majority of children cast their lot with the party of their parents. In 1960, teachers said, children's support for both candidates was a reflection of what they were hearing from their parents at home, although it is likely that the opinions of those who broke hard for Kennedy were molded in some measure by their teachers' (mostly young and female) personal affection for JFK. Regardless, in the 1960 presidential election, thousands of children partook of the amplified partisan spirit by actively campaigning for John F. Kennedy. In fairness, many stumped for Nixon too

(Hanna–Barbera's Huckleberry Hound tossed his hat in the ring as well), and in catching the electioneering bug some were probably just engaged in a bit of social imitation. In the midst of what was obviously a major national event, they didn't want to be left out of the excitement they witnessed around them in the adult world, so they picked a candidate and joined the political fray. That being said, whether wearing Kennedy buttons, pedaling their bicycles (and tricycles) covered with Kennedy stickers around the neighborhood, or filling their rooms with "Leadership for the 60's" placards, children involved in this life course transition honestly felt they were making a real contribution to their man's victory.

A teenager wrote that despite living in Nixon's California, her nine-year-old sister "faithfully wore her many Kennedy buttons to school every day, even though her classmates harassed her at times." The commitment was heartfelt as the little girl "followed the campaign and debates very closely . . . and talked nothing but politics at the dinner table." "Although she is only a youngster," the sibling concluded, "she is very bright and extremely interested in what is going on in our changing world. She also has a scrapbook that is filled with pictures of her favorite movie and television actors; and in the middle of this mass of pictures is a candid photo of you, Mr. President." In the same way, a New Jersey father bragged that his eight-year-old son "was a staunch Kennedy fan." "Believe me," he wrote the White House after the election, "it took a lot of guts to go to school in Cranford, New Jersey—Republican for sure—with 7 or 8 Kennedy buttons on his shirt. But he did it *every day*, regardless of who liked it." This letter reinforces a truism about the most direct route through which history manifests itself in a child's daily life: parents. The dynamic parent-child relationship is intimately interlocked, with alterations in the life of one consistently impacting the reality of the other. "He naturally took his cue from me," the letter ends, "and I'm glad our faith was justified."[17]

Although Piaget's concrete operational children deal with their world in cooperative ways, they remain fairly uncompromising when believing themselves to be on the right side of an argument, and the smallest Kennedy workers were no less determined than adults as they routinely put in grueling hours at local campaign offices. "You would have thought," a Wisconsin mother mused in wonderment to the president, that her dedicated son's "very life depended upon your election." A twelve-year-old Kansan "worked hard and long both before and after the Democratic Convention," his Republican parents marveled, and although his "work of course probably led to no actual votes as it was done at the teenage and sub-teen level," they still wanted Kennedy to understand that it "was just as sincere and was certainly without hope of personal reward as was the work of your closest supporters." An eleven-year-old boy in Illinois fairly "haunted the Democratic headquarters" in his hometown "and brought home and distributed all the literature he could find," his aunt wrote to Kennedy. "Incidentally," she confided, "he is not above taking a poke at any of the kids that opposed you!"[18]

Another Garden State parent explained to JFK that his son "probably did more campaigning than I had done. (In his own way, of course.) He constantly speaks of you and without doubt is always thinking of you." The father concluded, "I sincerely mean this." The mother of an "A-Number-One Kennedy fan" relished how her seven-year-old son single-handedly turned the tide of public opinion in his first grade class after seeing Kennedy in person during a stop in Peoria, Illinois. In their solid Republican county, his teacher asked the class to raise their hand if they supported Nixon. All did, except the boy. "When the teacher asked who was for Kennedy," the mother explained, her boy, "in the face of overwhelming odds, still felt that he was for the right man, and proudly raised his hand. With equal determination he worked doggedly on his Kennedy banner while the other children scrawled their praises for Nixon on theirs." Because of his lone example, "the following morning a young Kennedy 'convert' showed up in the classroom with Kennedy buttons lined up solid on the front of his shirt." Before class was dismissed that afternoon, the two had distributed them all as "the fickle children departed for home and the inspection of their Republican parents, wearing their Kennedy buttons."[19]

Down in Florida a boy of ten made his own courageous stand in Nixon country. "During the election of last year all of his friends were for Nixon," his grandmother remembered. "He was the lone Kennedy man." Even in elementary school, "politics ran rampant among the children," and "as the one Kennedy supporter" in his classroom he "was called upon to speak for his candidate" during the fourth grade debate. This was quite an ordeal, she explained, because already "rather a shy child . . . he was heckled by the Nixon group." However, he considered public speaking "his duty" and confidently argued that "John Kennedy will make a great president because he loves children. I know this because I have seen him playing with his daughter, who is named Caroline. Some of you will not vote for him on account of his religion. What is wrong with being a Catholic? Everyone cannot be Presbyterian. So this is just plain stupid. Anyway we are going to beat your dopey Nixon."[20]

Although Nixon ultimately carried the Sunshine State, like so many others this timid little man firmly believed "that his speech won the election for Mr. Kennedy." However, for those with so much invested, November 8, 1960, proved to be an agonizingly long and anxious day whose outcome remained anything but certain. After school, children dashed past neighborhood playgrounds, forsaking friends and toys, on a single-minded mission to the Magnavox. This was the first presidential election in which television played a pronounced role in how Americans followed the action, and by the time mothers finished rinsing the dinner dishes, NBC's John Chancellor had begun explaining that while the race remained maddeningly close, early East Coast returns were giving Kennedy some breathing room in the popular and electoral vote. Those tuning into ABC during the early evening inexplicably found *The Bugs Bunny Show* (then still in prime time) running in its normal time slot instead of election coverage.

Fifty years later, a Missouri woman still remembered her first-grade perspective on that tense night as the nation held its collective breath (ABC viewers notwithstanding). "My mother was of the Democratic persuasion," she wrote, "my father was Republican." They had moved into a new house that day, and their furniture had not yet arrived. "My dad was lying on the hardwood floor with his elbow propped on a 25 lb sack of flour, and my mother was sitting on a 3 gal lard can, leaning forward in rapture as the votes were counted. Kennedy was winning," she recalled fondly, "and my dad was cursing. What a sight!"[21]

Then, as results started coming in from the Midwest and West, Nixon began to pull even. Adding insult to injury, it was already bedtime back East. The luckiest children were allowed to stay up after midnight. Those in stricter households went to bed not knowing who had won. Nixon gave an ambiguous, not-quite-concession speech near 3:00 a.m. Still there was no resolution to the closest election in U.S. history when children woke up for school the next morning or even after pledging allegiance to the flag. Finally, on Wednesday afternoon, while most children were still in the classroom, Nixon conceded defeat. The tally: Kennedy 34,220,984, Nixon 34,108,157.

Thirty-some hours of waiting had severely tried the patience of a demographic not known for that virtue to begin with. It was worth the wait, though. Students seemed to share an astute awareness of being eyewitnesses to history, with the accompanying exhilaration of knowing that this presidency would someday merit bold headings in textbooks. The inauguration on January 20, 1961, solidified this perception in dramatic fashion. The parade and ceremony were a big deal at school and many principals made a day of it. With a kinetic energy and vivid interest usually reserved for Halloween and Christmas parties, multiple grades crammed into already overcrowded classrooms vying for a view of the live proceedings on small, portable television sets (often brought from home by teachers). Some of the nation's coolest educators took the unprecedented step of allowing lunch to be brought back from the cafeteria and eaten right there at your desk. The smallest students howled when rodeo clown Buddy Heaton rode by on his buffalo Clyde, but got a little "wiggly" during all the talking and had to get out their crayons to capture the scene on construction paper. Even the wigglers paused respectfully when Kennedy placed his hand on the Bible, and, as a third grade teacher in Florida observed, "promised THEM that [he] would endeavor to protect and guide THEM."[22]

President Kennedy's majestic speech not only captured impressionable young imaginations with visions of a New Frontier, his words of inspiration also seared into their consciousness what a twelve-year-old girl from Yakima, Washington, called "personal and patriotic guideposts" for life.[23] "Let the word go forth from this time and place," Kennedy proclaimed, "to friend and foe alike, that the torch has been passed to a new generation of Americans, born in this century, tempered by war, disciplined by a hard and bitter peace, proud of our ancient heritage." Those words were without question powerful, but the line "Ask not what your country can do for you, ask what you can do for your country" resonated more deeply and struck a once-in-a-lifetime chord.

Consider the inaugural address within the context of moral development, and how Kennedy managed to speak to the varied sensibilities of those in the middle elementary grades, who were transitioning from Kohlberg's preconventional to conventional reasoning. In the last stage of preconvention, defined appropriately as the "market exchange" period by Kohlberg, preadolescents mainly base their behavioral decisions on reciprocity; what is in it for them? All actions that result in a net gain are morally justifiable. But John Kennedy's language of idealism challenged that way of thinking, introducing children to a less egocentric ethic accompanied by a myriad of opportunities to test drive the roles associated with Kohlberg's next stage of "interpersonal harmony." This initial stage of conventional moral thought, common in the middle to upper elementary grades, is characterized by more mature notions of loyalty, duty, and the desirability of living up to expectations. Appreciation for the concerns and opinions of others, especially those held in high regard, now progressively guide decision-making.

For these reasons, altruistic actions that strengthen the social fabric are intrinsically attractive to children in a two-fold, albeit still self-serving, way.

Not only does altruism hold out the promise of garnering highly sought after social approval, but the personal satisfaction derived from such behavior is also increasingly a central measure of self-worth and esteem. To put this new level of developmental reality in the spirit of one of Kennedy's economic observations, you might say that a rising tide lifts all boats. And what better catalyst for negotiating these new moral imperatives than the President of the United States, entrusting you with his critical directive?

Echoing the sentiments of many her age, an eleven-year-old New Yorker admitted that "at first I was baffled when I thought what I could do for my country," and some wanted the president to elaborate with specific ideas.[24] Yet once they put their minds to it, the possibilities for children seemed endless, and with almost sixty million preadolescent Americans doing their part, they pondered, how could the country fail? For many children, this epiphany—usually spurred by a school assignment—proved not only eye-opening but empowering, in that it got them thinking about citizenship in the context of childhood. Sixth graders in Los Angeles "picked out worthy vocabulary words" while watching the inauguration speech—words like *tyranny, anxiety, alliance, humility, affirmation, and allegiance*—and looked them up in the dictionary under their teacher's guidance. Later, of their own volition, they "all decided to remember at least two words out of the list."[25]

Commonly, teachers asked them to enumerate what they might do and instinctively students understood their limitations. Kennedy would tackle the big ticket items in the adult world: making the nation strong and keeping the world peaceful. "I could no more advise you than a baby," a young girl from Wisconsin admitted to the president, "for your decisions are far wiser than I could think of . . ." However, children would hold down the fort by obeying their parents, teachers, and local policemen, never lying to those adult authorities, sharing their toys with other children, and being good. After all, compared to leading the free world, a Chicago third grader admitted, "going to school and cleaning the house and watching my little sister isn't hard."[26]

Even so, there were a great many children who conceived of Kennedy's call in the much grander terms of paying any price, bearing any burden, supporting any friend, and opposing any foe. These loftier ambitions required boys and girls to be good citizens by—to co-opt a sentiment from the era's budding environmentalist movement—thinking globally and acting locally. "Every day when I leave for school," a fifth grader in Racine, Wisconsin, promised, "I will think of what I can do for my country." Her classmates contributed virtues like stewardship, keeping their neighborhood streets and playgrounds litter-free while planting trees and grass where needed. Other eleven-year-olds talked of setting goals, no matter how high, and striving to achieve them. Usually this included studying hard and going to college to pursue a chosen career, and learning about the country to become an intelligent voter someday. Boys spoke to their developing sense of masculinity in offering to do whatever it took to help America be the best in war and sports. Girls gravitated towards issues rooted in common experience by connecting with a pen pal overseas to learn about other cultures and spread positive information about America, a child's equivalent of the proposed Peace Corps. In what would soon become the most urgent domestic issue of their time, civil rights, a few recognized more chances to exercise Kohlberg's decentered conventional level thought. Another Wisconsin fifth grader solemnly vowed to "do my best to be friends with people of all races." "In the south," the student declared, "they're [sic] is a problem which I will try to stop. The whites don't want to eat, travel, and live with colored people at all. I want to stop this foolish thinking."[27]

More than one heard the call of public service and even higher office. "I have never thought about being a president," an eleven-year-old in Seattle confided to Kennedy, "but when I watched you those thoughts came out."[28]

Emotional fidelity to John Kennedy and the inspiration generated by his vision only accelerated after the inauguration as students followed his presidency, the older students in particular being better equipped to grasp the public policies of the New Frontier. Between the fourth and fifth grades, when the smell of mimeograph ink was well known to all, and again between sixth and seventh, students continued to make the most pronounced leaps along the various paths of political socialization. Cognitively, these are Piaget's years of "formal operations" where, having mastered the real and tangible, children logically work their way through higher levels of abstraction, even pondering the hypothetical and tantalizing "what if?" questions. At this point, their development is also facilitated by the formal introduction of social studies, civics, and history into the curriculum, which promotes a more sophisticated understanding of specific roles in government. Increasingly, the presidency is seen in a more realistic light, defined by the demands and expectations of the office instead of just the personal characteristics of any one occupant.

At school, *My Weekly Reader* introduced students to Kennedy's cabinet, a pluralist collection of the best and brightest, men such as Ford Motor Company's Robert McNamara, who would help define the president's liberal internationalism as secretary of defense, and Republican banker C. Douglas

Dillon, who provided a fiscally conservative flavor to the administration's "New Economics" as secretary of the treasury. The choice of the president's younger brother Robert F. Kennedy to lead the Justice Department made an impression as well, not so much for what the new attorney general might or might not bring to the table, but rather for the familial feelings it signified. Siblings could naturally relate to the pride of picking a younger brother or sister for your team. Moreover, they appreciated the instinctive protectiveness which comes with the territory of being the oldest when they heard about JFK deflecting criticism of Bobby's lack of legal qualifications with characteristic aplomb. The president saw nothing wrong, he said, with giving his little brother a bit of legal experience as the nation's highest law enforcement officer before he went out to practice law on his own.[29]

At this stage of socialization, children begin teasing out the president's foreign policy role as the nation's principal representative with other countries, including, but not limited to, commander in chief of the military. The Soviet Union, more specifically the perceived monolithic and expansionistic tendencies of communism, remained foremost in their minds as the dominant feature of geopolitical reality throughout the decade. While their default setting in making sense of the bipolar world order in which they lived remained the mano-a-mano relationship between the styles and personalities of John F. Kennedy and Soviet Premier Nikita Khrushchev, with each passing year they came closer to grasping what Cold War meant: a protracted political, cultural, and military struggle for world power between the capitalist "West" and communist "East."

So too do older preadolescents come to grasp the group character of government and the shared nature of governing our democracy. They even start to distinguish at least the broader ideological points of what makes a Democrat a Democrat and a Republican a Republican. "I like what Democrats believe," a California boy declared, further clarifying that the reasons for his own personal support of Kennedy in 1960 related to the political ethos Arthur Schlesinger, Jr. had termed "qualitative" liberalism. What the administration's resident historian meant was that at the dawn of the sixties liberalism would remain a vital force only insofar as it evolved beyond the largely obsolete "quantitative" focus of New Dealers on baseline economic necessities—jobs, wages, housing—toward a more complete agenda resulting in the "qualitative" enrichment of individual lives. Schlesinger encouraged other like-minded liberals then peopling the Democratic Party to utilize the instruments of government at their disposal in championing the causes of equal opportunity and civil liberty so that all Americans might achieve a higher sense of identity, dignity, and fulfillment.

Without articulating it as such, what the boy from California meant was that in identifying with Schlesinger's notion of qualitative liberalism children his age were developmentally becoming more eager collectivists by nature. Consequently, the domestic social policies they trusted to be benefiting the overall collective—initiatives to reduce poverty or eliminate racism—reverberated in harmony with budding ways of thinking that we recognize as humanitarianism. This ethic of empathy for human suffering goes a long way in explaining favorable preadolescent orientations toward the Kennedy years, and an even longer way when it comes to the Great Society. Not only did a burgeoning identification with the spirit of sharing and basic fairness, at precisely the historical moment when a liberal returned to the White House, convince some, like a ten-year-old from Pontiac, Michigan, that if children were allowed to vote "the Democrats would win all the time," it also contributed to the shaping of party identification in the future. Speaking for many of her cohort, a fifth grader in Atlanta pledged to Kennedy, "When I grow up I want to be a democrat."[30]

Education and healthcare were central to Kennedy's pragmatic notion of qualitative liberalism. The president had campaigned passionately on the critical need for reform in these key areas, specifically as they pertained to preadolescents, and here one can see the first intersections of New Frontier public policies penetrating the reality of children in tangible ways. Kennedy envisioned education as the preeminent domestic issue of his administration, and few other national topics dominated so many of his speeches and internal discussions. His commitment to excellence in elementary, secondary, and higher education combined a genuine interest in unlocking individual human potential with a domestic objective of investing in sustainable economic growth, but he also saw it as a direct means of reversing a perceived gap with the Soviets in scientific and military training. "Our progress as a nation can be no swifter than our progress in education," he began a special education message to Congress in February 1961. In maximizing the republic's awesome power, "The human mind is our fundamental resource."[31]

Except for a general hysteria over the prospect that the Department of Health, Education, and Welfare (HEW) might mandate year-round school, fifth and sixth grade students tended to concur wholeheartedly. "We hope that everyone knows that if the United States is to be secure in the next years, it must have good citizens," a Michigan girl observed. "By saying citizens, I don't mean grownups only. Children are also citizens. To raise good citizens, the United States must have good teachers and parents who are interested in their children's work. We must also have a good government which would build schools, libraries, universities, and get the best school books and equipment possible."[32]

Yet in 1961, despite the nation spending some $26 billion on educating the baby boomers, the resources of state and local governments were woefully outpaced by the demand of that generation's massive numbers. As the boom swelled throughout the 1950s, Americans had become increasingly concerned with the declining condition of the country's education system, in particular the outdated teaching methods and school overcrowding. There simply were not enough classrooms to accommodate this generation or qualified teachers to instruct them. *Parents* magazine estimated that the education of two million American children had been appreciably disrupted by severe overcrowding, with some districts going to half-day schedules and others annexing nearby office buildings and churches. Experts conservatively called for the construction of 130,000 more classrooms, not to mention adequate day care and pre-school facilities for the five million small children with working mothers. Problem was, as Kennedy lamented to an advisor, governors alone could not realistically squeeze any more from property taxes to get the job done. The nation's first comprehensive federal aid to elementary and secondary education would be necessary.[33]

One month to the day after his inauguration the president urged Congress to enact a broad $866 million, three-year program of federal grants to the states for public school construction and teachers' salaries. The ambitious bill moved through the Senate later that spring only to be soundly defeated in the House by the intractable conservative coalition that had dominated the legislature for a generation—Southern Democrats struggling to hold back integration and Republicans fearing the loss of local school control—together with, somewhat ironically, alienated Catholics who opposed Kennedy's principled exclusion of parochial schools. For the next two years, Kennedy labored mostly in vain to make any substantive legislative progress on federal aid to education. In this regard, the uphill and ultimately unsuccessful push for educational funding resembled the trajectory of the administration's other signature issue, the proposed Medicare program to provide medical insurance for the elderly under Social Security. Both decidedly liberal initiatives were strategically vital to fashioning the foundation of Kennedy's domestic record. Their passage would have conceivably counterbalanced a number of initial foreign policy setbacks while also shoring up the president's progressive credentials within the Democratic Party in the face of a perceived diffidence on civil rights. Their failures to get much congressional traction were perhaps the administration's most bitter disappointments.[34]

Pragmatism ultimately dictated a more measured approach, and Kennedy's 1963 budget acknowledged the pessimistic legislative forecast for education. Sweeping reform in this area was largely replaced with tax cuts as economic stimulus as the chief domestic policy priority during the remainder of the first term. Instead, the president focused on more scaled-down, targeted educational measures, either expanding existing programs or devising new avenues of specialized aid in order to allow districts the breathing room to maximize their precious funds on construction and salaries. The President's Council on Physical Fitness offers an excellent example of John Kennedy working where he could to educate the nation's children while tangibly making them stronger stakeholders in the New Frontier. While it began as an Eisenhower initiative to close a fitness gap between affluent—read "flabby"—American children and their more Spartan—read "strapping"—counterparts abroad, JFK made it unquestionably his own within weeks of taking office. On the heels of an essay he wrote for the December 26, 1960, issue of *Sports Illustrated* entitled "The Soft American"—which featured the president-elect and first lady boating on the cover under the headline "Sport on the New Frontier"—Kennedy reorganized the council under the leadership of the University of Oklahoma's legendary football coach Charles "Bud" Wilkinson. The president's more hands-on bureaucratic approach, plus consistent public identification with the council's mission to improve America's fitness, breathed life into this physical education effort while at the same time reinforcing his popular association with health and athleticism.[35]

Without the power to actually mandate a national exercise program, the President's Council instead created a well-rounded curriculum which supplemented existing physical education in schools and the usual sports activities of youth-oriented organizations like the YMCA. Beginning in the 1961–1962 academic year, the council launched an extensive national print, radio, and television publicity campaign promoting its fitness directives, which included a Marine-inspired, fifty-mile-hike-in-twenty-hour challenge along with a number of memorable popular culture tie-ins. Most notably, cartoonist Charles Schulz contributed a "Snoopy's Daily Dozen" manual with Charlie Brown and the rest of the Peanuts gang exercising, and *The Music Man* composer Meredith Willson contributed the ubiquitous children's workout

classic "Chicken Fat (The Youth Fitness Song)." "Chicken Fat"—sung by
The Music Man's Harold Hill himself, Robert Preston—echoed through thousands of gymnasiums via tinny public address systems to become the enduring soundtrack of grade school shuttle runs, soft ball tosses, jumping jacks,
and pull-ups. "Push up. Every morning. Ten times," Preston's infectious
Broadway-style cadence went in the six-and-a-half-minute school version.
"Push up. Starting low. Once more on the rise. Nuts to the flabby guys! Go,
you chicken fat, go away! Go, you chicken fat, go!"

The spontaneous enthusiasm broad buy-in generated by this concerted federal effort must also be understood within the greater dialectic surrounding
"ask what you can do for your country." For little citizens with limited means
to contribute to American greatness, their determined adherence to these
prescriptive measures were a sort of sweat equity. They grasped the national
scope of what was happening in their own gym classes, and they connected
those dots to the president's grander call to pay any price. "In school we are
doing many exercises," a fifth grader wrote Kennedy. "Our teacher says that
we are doing them for you."[36]

Young boys often related to JFK through their mutual love of sport, specifically football, and the Council on Physical Fitness inspired them to send
gridiron related memorabilia with anecdotal accounts of sandlot exploits as a
means of keeping him abreast of their fitness regimens and vigor ("vigah" in
the Kennedy brogue). Similarly, students proudly measured their ability to
bear any burden by how many miles they had walked or ran and their personal bests in various feats of athletic ability. "We want you to know about
our physical fitness program," eleven-year-old New Yorkers took it upon
themselves to report in October 1963. "The name of our group is the Jetsons.
There are 15 members in our group and they are from 9–13 years old. We are
part of Mobilization for Youth program [a social service agency operating on
the Lower East Side of New York City since 1961]. During the summer we
went on long hikes, swimming and other physical active [*sic*], for the winter
we are planning to hike, football, ice skating and have a special gym program
for physical fitness. We are having an indoor winter Olympic exercise on November 23, 1963 [a competition undoubtedly cancelled by the previous day's
assassination]."[37] Those too small to communicate effectively in written form
checked in with the White House through artwork.

As participation among schoolchildren nationwide grew exponentially
over the sixties with expanded programming and awards, general fitness em-
pirically improved as measured by a battery of speed, agility, and strength

tests. So too were the physical education programs and teachers in some of the most challenged school districts reinforced and strengthened. Clever parents even folded the strategies into their own "imperial" practices of childrearing, harnessing physical conditioning to pull the double duty of improving their children's health choices while also relieving the need to chauffeur them. "My mother and father have their own little idea about us keeping physically fit," a twelve-year-old from La Crosse, Wisconsin, noted. "Besides seeing that we get the proper amounts of rest and sleep and checking our food habits, they make it a policy never to drive us anywhere—rain or shine we *walk*."[38]

Children without the vocabulary to communicate the principles of Kennedy's qualitative liberalism lived it in the "native" practices of their own social environment. "I respect your physical fitness program and I went to one at the 'Y,'" a ten-year-old Girl Scout in Cleveland humbly explained. "I am fat but I want to be physically fit so that's why I went."[39] Getting the country moving again meant getting the children moving again.

As the President's Council on Physical Fitness advanced the cause of educational and health reform incrementally down the field, the most spectacular, and arguably most enduring, instance of Kennedy spending his limited political capital to change the world of children was the administration's orientation of attention and resources toward the mentally retarded and those with disabilities. In contrast to the signature fitness program, Kennedy inherited very little broad public appeal or federal initiative when it came to policies and funding aimed at these young Americans who were often hard to see and easy to overlook. Somewhere near two and a half million children were diagnosed as mentally retarded or otherwise suffering from some form of severe emotional and developmental disability, including significant speech and hearing difficulties. Each year of the boom brought 126,000 more. At that rate, only one in five would be enrolled in any type of special education course. Yet, despite new government monies in the 1950s for special education teacher training, counseling, and diagnostic services, mental retardation and the handicapped were not political priorities at the federal or state level. Even within the medical profession, few physicians pursued these research fields or were specifically trained to treat the disabled. In polite society, families usually shied away from openly discussing retarded children, and the traditional practices of isolation or institutionalization remained the norm.

These neglected inadequacies of American healthcare—what the president sarcastically deemed a "no care" system—were no mere abstractions to the Kennedys. Rosemary, JFK's younger sister by sixteen months, struggled with intellectual disabilities. Her confinement to a residential care facility as an adult inspired the family's lifelong commitment to changing social perceptions and improving the treatment of the mentally retarded through their Joseph P. Kennedy Jr. Foundation. It was another of the president's sisters, Eunice Kennedy Shriver, who later founded the Special Olympics in 1968, who was at the core of these endeavors as director of the foundation. Eunice served as the catalyst of her brother's determination to make their cause an administrative priority.[40]

Accordingly, a transition team laid the groundwork for the creation of the National Institute of Child Health and Human Development in 1961 to function within the government's broader National Institutes of Health network. The institute—renamed by Congress for Eunice Kennedy Shriver in 2007—coordinated an extensive research agenda on child development, especially targeting disabilities, but also maternal health issues and mass immunization programs in the fight against polio, whooping cough, and tetanus. Year two of the administration brought a more comprehensive and coordinated federal strategy based on an exhaustive report issued by the twenty-seven-member President's Panel on Mental Retardation. This collection of physicians, psychologists, social scientists, and teachers empaneled by Kennedy reviewed volumes of current research and conducted months of public hearings in several major cities, while comparing disability treatment in the United States with treatment in several European countries and the USSR. Their ambitious recommendations, delivered to the Oval Office on the third day of the Cuban missile crisis in October 1962, formed the blueprint for what would become the nation's first major legislation addressing intellectual disabilities.[41]

"Mental retardation ranks with mental health as a major health, social, and economic problem in this country," the president proclaimed in a special message to Congress urging passage of the legislative package in February 1963. "It strikes our most precious asset, our children." Within six months, under the floor leadership of Ways and Means Committee chairman Wilbur Mills in the House and HEW secretary Abraham Ribicoff in the Senate, Kennedy's Maternal and Child Health and Mental Retardation Planning Amendment to the Social Security Act became law on October 24. The measure called for $310 million in spending by 1970—incrementally doubling federal expenditures through Social Security from $25 million per year to $50 million—to help the states pursue new directions in addressing the needs of those then known as "crippled children." The majority of these projects were preventive in nature, reflecting the president's personal concern for the socioeconomic and environmental causes of retardation, which likewise informed the National Institute of Child Health and Human Development's work. Substantial grants went toward reducing premature births—identified as a primary culprit—by improving prenatal, maternity, and postnatal care in both private and public hospitals, with allied improvements in nursing curriculums. Other five-year grants to states and communities for early detection and diagnostic services were targeted toward children from low-income families. HEW funded new directions in special education teacher training and patient rehabilitation, including multiple initiatives for moving treatment away from state-run custodial institutions toward community-centered agencies. A companion bill signed by Kennedy a week later on Halloween subsidized the construction of these new local care centers and university-based facilities.[42]

This unprecedented federal movement, championed by John F. Kennedy with his own vested interest and eloquence, ignited a dynamic national conversation about children with disabilities. In anticipation of his Maternal and Child Health and Mental Retardation bill becoming law, that September Kennedy convened a much publicized White House Conference on Mental Retardation. These deliberations in Warrenton, Virginia, attended by leading healthcare and education professionals representing all fifty states, further shaped how the federal and state partnership inherent in the legislation would invigorate the field. Kennedy's own Massachusetts, for instance, drove discussions of prevention through early diagnosis with its mandatory blood testing to detect Phenylketonuria (PKU), the rare condition prohibiting infants from breaking down the amino acid phenylalanine. North Carolina helped set the timing and direction of treatment strategies by offering as examples its legislation for special education teacher preparation, counseling services for parents, and innovative life-skill and vocational training that afforded handicapped children the opportunity to become self-sufficient and self-supporting adults.[43]

Proactive community approaches like those pioneered in states as diverse as Louisiana, New Jersey, North Dakota, and Maine supplied structure and support for families, vital resources that were scarce in small town and rural America. The diagnosis of a child with mental disabilities traditionally left mothers, fathers, and siblings grappling in lonely isolation with personal demons of guilt and denial along with fatalistic visions of the future. But by mid-decade, local support groups, funded from above but headed and run by parents themselves, usually at the county level, existed to shepherd them through the seven stages of grief, providing educational materials to help them comprehend what their sons and daughters faced, along with a stable network of kindred spirits.

A Missourian born in 1956 described his mother's determination to seek out this type of local organization when his infant brother was diagnosed with Down's syndrome ten years later. Initially, the older brother's presence at monthly social gatherings in the city park, made mandatory by mom, were occasions for dread and resentment. He admitted hating that his parents "forced" him to spend all day in the public pavilion with his little brother. "I remember being so embarrassed that my peers might see me in the park with 'all the retarded kids,'" he wrote. "Obviously looking back, I can see that I too had problems accepting my brother's condition as well as suffering from peer pressure. I remember these gatherings were full of games, competitions, stories, rides, food, and lots of laughter. My first experience was to do nothing and not get involved. I chose just to sit there not engaged. I truly hated the experience."

However, certain activities required that the two boys be paired up, and through these simple interactions profound change occurred. "I slowly came out of myself (ignorance, fear, and pity)," he told me, "and began to 'see beyond' the handicap in these people. I soon realized that each one had an individual character. I also learned that most were more mentally challenged than my brother. This awareness seemed to give me a much needed perspective at the time." Watching peers, especially one very attractive girl, with younger siblings in the group likewise facilitated what was clearly the integration of Kolhberg's "interpersonal harmony" perspective into his moral thought. This developmental stage is often labeled the "nice girl/good boy" period due to the sense of self-respect derived from being seen as caring by family and friends. "Taking cues from her," he continued, "I began to see that it was 'ok' to spend a day with the [local group]. The more I engaged, the less of a stigma I felt, and the more I viewed myself as a helpful person. Regardless of the events at the gatherings, the day always ended with these kids giving me a genuine, happy, and meaningful hug. This totally caught me off guard and had an emotional impact on me. I would never forget the sincerity of these expressions."

Speaking directly to life course trajectories, this man, now a public school teacher, concluded that "in all cases, it was the efforts of local parents and residents of [his town] that played an active and critical role in [his brother's] progress and those of the other mentally challenged residents. This personal and local responsibility was unknowingly instilled in me by my parents who no doubt had an eye on me to be [his brother's] guardian long before I was appointed as such."[44] This personal journey from the heartland exemplifies the White House Conference on Mental Retardation's argument that the Kennedy way was more humane and much cheaper in the long run than culturally sanctioned, state administered banishment.

The conference's most consequential agenda item for the broadest segment of children was the mainstreaming of students with mental and physical disabilities into regular classrooms when possible. Districts had been trending away from segregating the disabled in special schools and classes for a while, but all parties involved were increasingly cognizant that physical integration did not automatically equate to social assimilation. Special-needs pupils, making up about 8 percent of the nation's total student population, often found themselves ostracized in regular classrooms, which may well have been worse than segregation. Experts tended to agree, leading many educators to discern a more thoughtful and nuanced mainstreaming paradigm by the time of the White House Conference. Teaching the handicapped in regular classrooms would be a learning laboratory for *all* students. The logic was that after an obligatory period of adjustment and related learning curve, well-trained teachers sensitive to the needs of all students should be able to facilitate an environment conducive to both disabled and abled students learning with, and maybe more importantly from, each other.[45]

With racial desegregation in American schools progressing unevenly and under challenge (when at all), exposure to mainstreamed contemporaries with disabilities offered sixties children some of their first notions of integration and, moreover, taught them their first fundamental lessons in diversity. Curriculums more closely approximating the realities and expectations of the "real" or "adult" world, emphasizing awareness of differences, were implemented across the country. Clear routines and boundaries taught handicapped students the life skills essential to managing themselves in environments not always within their control. For children achieving Piaget's more autonomous sense of morality, these structures were less important because they— not adults—were beginning to police their own moral behavior through the simple proposition of treating others the way they wanted to be treated. This invariably led to some tricky challenges for classmates and teachers who wrestled against instinct to overprotect special students. Most navigated an uncomfortable path between going overboard and withholding assistance, and only experience taught them that giving commonsense help when necessary offered the best course for co-existing.

To be sure, contact sometimes unfolded in unpleasant and hateful ways, with stereotypical teasing and name-calling. Yet, as schools diligently worked at the process through the decade, elementary students acclimated themselves to sharing the educational experience with the handicapped. Together they discovered preadolescent common ground in any number of places: amusement over a teacher's idiosyncrasies, a passion for extracurricular activities such as glee club, choir, and student council, or the determination to put chicken fat on the run in appropriately modified physical education classes. Fifth graders in Wisconsin watched in fascination as a blind classmate expressed their shared admiration for John Kennedy through her poems written in braille. One student took immense pride in the example of a ten-year-old mentally retarded boy inspired to learn to read and write because of his interest in a social studies unit on the presidents. Others still recognize their sense of importance and duty when paired in a "buddy system" with a challenged classmate as a milestone.[46]

The interpersonal relationships of differently-abled children fostered by President Kennedy's commitments are central mechanisms in the dramatic sea change in the 1960s in the lives of mentally retarded people and attitudes toward them. Compared to the previous decade, America experienced nothing short of a cultural enlightenment on these subjects, which fueled further dialogue and more federal action like Lyndon Johnson's President's Committee for People with Intellectual Disabilities. Increased public engagement and governmental investment led to even more holistic strategies as the emerging concept of disability rights joined a more inclusive national civil rights dialectic culminating in the Education for All Handicapped Children Act in 1975, which mandated equal access to public education for disabled children, and the anti-discriminatory Americans with Disabilities Act in 1990. Like the more high-profile struggle of African Americans, the disabilities movement, with its intrinsic issues of equality, worth, and respect, familiarized formative young minds with other decidedly humanist traits commonly associated with the adult sixties. In the recollections of the teacher from Missouri, one perceives the qualities of introspection and tolerance when he writes that despite his sibling's IQ of 81 and inability to speak more than three- to four-word sentences, he was coming to "understand my brother for who he was and what he was going to be." One last memory is equally revealing. "I also remember being able to laugh 'with' [my brother]," he explained. "This was important as these kids could really be funny to be with and I never felt comfortable laugh[ing] around them, because I was so scared someone would think that I was laugh[ing] 'at' them. This was the last and biggest barrier I had to get over. Once I could laugh with them, I felt so much more comfortable, and they seemed to be more comfortable and expressive to me."[47] These are unmistakably the early glimpses of the liberating process of defining for oneself which lives and lifestyles are "normal."

CHAPTER THREE

Space Rockets and Cuban Missiles

I don't think Russia has any feelings for her children and the US children.
Fifth grade student from Brooklyn, New York, to President Kennedy,
October 24, 1962

As it turned out, the fiscal and congressional realities that obliged President Kennedy to strategically postpone more extensive education and health care overhauls helped push the space program and national defense to the budgetary forefront. Developing geopolitics in Europe and the Third World factored into this reorientation of resources as well. Regardless of the specific motivations, shifts in Kennedy's spending priorities from domestic to foreign policy—of which outer space was always considered to be a part—meant a pivot from custodial practices targeted at children toward international and interplanetary phenomenon literally and figuratively aimed way above their heads. Space exploration and the omnipresent threat of nuclear war—coalescing around the Cuban missile crisis—bombarded the world of American children in dramatic, though very different emotional and psychological, fashion. An Athens, Georgia, man remembered, "Throughout this time, I was aware of the John Kennedy presidency. So for me, I will always link the unease of the dawning 'nuclear threat' age, the excitement of NASA space flights, and the 'Green Berets' and an early introduction to Vietnam with the Kennedy administration. This was the earliest sense of 'time and place' for me."[1]

For sheer preadolescent excitement, inspiration, and out-of-this-world romance, no other Kennedy endeavor remotely compares to his single-minded determination to beat the Russians to the moon. For the rocket-obsessed cohort reared in the high-stakes competition of the Space Race, Mercury

45

astronauts and Gemini capsules are still synonymous with the New Frontier. The Soviet launch of *Sputnik 1*, the first artificial earth-orbiting satellite, on October 4, 1957, heralded the start of that race for space, a contest in which the communists appeared to sprint out of the gate while the United States stumbled. Although the tiny *Sputnik* weighed less than two hundred pounds, it carried an enormous symbolic payload that not only called into question American technological superiority, but mistakenly caused broader concerns that "gaps" existed between the Russians and the United States in science, mathematics, and even imagination. The Eisenhower administration knew better and instead of being stampeded by public opinion chose to strengthen the nation's schools and create the civilian National Aeronautics and Space Administration (NASA) to coordinate a peaceful answer to *Sputnik*. That would be Project Mercury. With one ambitious program, NASA sought to surpass Soviet achievements by orbiting the planet with a manned spacecraft and returning both man and machine safely to earth. Seven daring astronauts—soon to be household names—were selected in 1959 for the series of missions: Scott Carpenter, Gordon Cooper, John Glenn, Gus Grissom, Wally Schirra, Alan Shepard Jr., and Deke Slayton.

Over the course of its five years, Mercury ultimately built critical expertise in orbital flight technology, how humans and apes perform in space, and vehicle recovery. But the project's awkward, mistake-prone beginnings were painted by candidate John F. Kennedy in 1960 with the same broad strokes of complacency he routinely associated with Eisenhower and Nixon. These criticisms, accompanied by a personal vow to beat the Soviets in space, fit within the campaign's narrative of contrast between national torpor and progress. However, in a deeper sense Kennedy was well ahead of the curve in understanding the propaganda implications of that "gap" mentality when it came to the stars. In the logic of the Cold War, perception mattered. If countries believed the Soviets to be world leaders in scientific achievement—whether accurate or not—it might lead to assumptions about their military, economic, and even cultural superiority across the board. Kennedy's running mate, Lyndon B. Johnson, put it this way: "In the eyes of the world, first in space means first, period. Second in space is second in everything."[2]

President Kennedy moved rapidly after the election to focus the space program by revitalizing the advisory National Space Council and appointing Vice President Johnson as chair. Even before Soviet cosmonaut Yuri Gagarin became the first man to orbit the Earth in April 1961 (yet another demoralizing blow), Kennedy had already privately conceded defeat in that critical milestone and had instead instructed the council to outline a list of potential space missions going forward. From these calculations, the president determined that within Mercury's present parameters of manned orbits, the United States would remain mired in second place for the foreseeable future. A real game-changer was only feasible in the report's longer-term goal: a lunar landing. Accordingly, on May 25—twenty days after Alan Shepard's suborbital flight gave the nation its long-awaited first man in space—Kennedy raised the ante considerably with the bold declaration before a joint session of Congress that "this nation should commit itself to achieving the goal, before the decade is out, of landing a man on the moon and returning him safely to the earth." In leaving the exact date deliberately vague, the administration hoped it would be the crowning glory of the second term.

Now the Space Race accelerated in earnest. At the beginning of World War II Franklin Roosevelt had derived tremendous psychological value from setting production quotas for weaponry breathtakingly beyond what experts thought realistic. Kennedy's moon challenge, and the additional billions for NASA that accompanied it, was of similar intent. The audacity of its scope purposefully injected a sense of national urgency into the space program. Innovative new facilities in Houston and Cape Canaveral were constructed, while NASA's expanded research and development agenda harnessed the talents of gifted professionals in the fields of process engineering, aviation, mechanics, and medicine. Mercury missions drew progressively more popular interest, and despite a number of aborted televised launches throughout 1961, in July Gus Grissom went up. Then on February 20, 1962, the Friendship 7 capsule put John Glenn into orbit, a seminal moment shared by millions. Friendship 7 circled the Earth three times at a maximum altitude of 162 miles before splashing down in the Caribbean off Bermuda. In a little over four hours in space, Glenn recaptured the momentum from the Russians and rallied the American spirit. As Kennedy kept reminding the country, it was not just NASA going to the moon, it was all of us.

The youngest Americans needed no such reminder. "That captivated little kids' minds like nothing I've ever seen in my life," a man born in 1956 observed. "We all went to school with our little NASA lunchbox . . . and you'd have these little toy rockets and it was like John Glenn this, and Alan Shepard that."[3] Children's hearts, and moreover their imaginations, were heavily invested, and once again television sparked the connection. As popular culture commentator Steven D. Stark noted, from Shepard's first fifteen minutes aloft to Glenn's orbits and Gemini's weightless walks, "the space program was

one long miniseries—an eight-year joy ride to the moon, hosted by Walter Cronkite, carefully scripted each year with increasingly better pictures."
As recently as the late fifties, however, television's seemingly natural role in
the space program was not a foregone conclusion. Traditional print media
mainstays such as *Life* magazine were the preferred vehicle for covering such
significant events, and, in fact, there were heated discussions at the highest
levels about the wisdom of televising risky launches. But the novelty of the
cool gadgetry just lent itself so well to a visual medium. Consider also that
in these formative years of television, network news divisions were angling
for ways to justify additional nightly news programming beyond the allotted
fifteen minutes. Thus, television and space ended up maturing together in a
mutually supportive relationship. First in black-and-white and later in color,
with simulated in-studio models giving way to live remote footage, television's imagery and genuine emotion—think of Walter Cronkite briefly losing
his composure to cheer, "Come on, baby! Come on, baby!" immediately after
Glenn's ignition—brought outer space into our intimate space in ways that
other media simply could not. In doing so, it gave children an almost capsule-
like window to the race.[4]

News coverage from live remotes in sunny coastal locales set the tone
over the course of the sixties. A man from Atlanta vividly remembered the
powerful message it sent when his teacher integrated Mercury into his sixth
grade science curriculum. "Television sets were wheeled into classrooms in
my school," just as they were for the inauguration the year before, "and we
watched it throughout the day. Later, of course, we watched and talked about
the other space mission which involved putting astronauts in orbit around
the earth and then recovering them at sea when the space capsule landed"
(although initially there was no live coverage of splashdowns because the
requisite satellites had not yet been launched).[5] Students like this instinctively
understood the value-added nature of material taught in their classroom reinforcing realities from the adult world, and vice versa. Put another way, distant, disconnected events in the wider world take on new immediacy when
teachers incorporate them into the familiar world of school, just as seemingly
irrelevant school lessons transcend the classroom the moment children hear
adults discussing them at the dinner table. That "aha" moment often came in
front of a television.

Of course, the vastness of space could never be contained within the puny
confines of network news, even those announcements important enough to
be prefaced with "We interrupt this broadcast for a special report." By 1962

space-themed entertainment programming increasingly competed with the traditionally popular action series and westerns for young prime time viewers. The *Walt Disney's Disneyland* show on ABC aired the first of these with the three-part series "Man in Space," "Man and the Moon," and "Mars and Beyond," aired between 1955 and 1957. Set in the theme park's Tomorrowland with live action narration and predictably cute animated sequences, the trilogy's success led to them being replayed in theaters with first-run Disney features as well as an accompanying book series for early readers. In September 1962, ABC introduced *The Jetsons* on Sunday evenings (running opposite the now renamed *Walt Disney's Wonderful World of Color,* which had jumped to NBC). An animated twenty-first-century version of Hanna-Barbera's beloved *Flintstones,* the equally iconic George, Jane, Judy, and Elroy Jetson (along with Astro the dog) lived out the standard situation comedy format in out-of-this-world scenarios. From their Skypad Apartments in Orbit City, George went off to work each day at Spacely Space Sprockets while Jane managed a fanciful household complete with food service computers, a robot maid, and an elaborate transportation system of pneumatic tubes. In prime time for only a year and then as part of the Saturday morning rotation until the early 1970s, this easily recognizable middle-class family helped domesticate the proposition of futuristic living among the stars. In addition to occasional episodes of Rod Serling's *The Twilight Zone* or *The Outer Limits,* family-style rocket adventures also appeared in CBS's *Lost in Space* beginning in 1965 on Wednesday nights. A live-action story of spaceship castaways—the Robinson family—*Lost in Space* brought robotics, extraterrestrial creatures, and weekly cliff-hangers to the genre for three seasons that roughly coincided with the duration of NASA's Project Gemini.[6]

Advertising brought space home too. Beyond numerous commercials for individual toys, television campaigns targeting children often utilized space travel to sell everything from Keds sneakers to breakfast food. With black-and-white footage of a Mercury-Redstone rocket launch opening the sequence, Cheerios cereal and V8 juice teamed up in one instance to encourage "junior spacemen" to try out this odd, but nutritious, combination each morning. To sweeten the pot, a free moon rocket game came with the appropriate number of box tops and labels. Post Count Off cereal offered another intriguing breakfast alternative. Made in the shape of numbers, individual puffs could be arranged in the bowl or spoon to simulate a countdown, and the back of each box featured the latest space news. General Foods also reminded children how every astronaut since Gemini IV drank orange-flavored Tang.

The influential series *Star Trek*, which ran in prime time from 1966 to 1969 on NBC, more appropriately belongs in a discussion of the years just prior to the Apollo moon landings. But it is instructive to note that creator Gene Rodenberry first pitched the idea for *Star Trek* in 1964. The exploratory five-year mission of the starship *Enterprise* and, more specifically, the multiethnic, interracial, and international flavor of the crew bear a striking resemblance to John F. Kennedy's emphasis on the idealistic and practical elements of the moon program, and his vision of worldwide cooperation in space. On a number of occasions, chief among them a September 1963 speech to the United Nations General Assembly, President Kennedy framed America's space program as a new field of international development, underscoring the global benefits of U.S. weather, navigation, and communication satellites and how coordination in tracking American spacecraft might encourage some countries to pursue complimentary space programs of their own. The proposed collaborations extended to the USSR, not only to preclude unnecessary duplication of precious research and construction funds, but also to devise joint operations between astronauts and cosmonauts that might one day incorporate human resources from all countries in the exploration of space.[7]

Reruns of *Star Trek* in syndication, beginning in 1969, may have helped dull the residual competitive edge of the Space Race after the United States won, but in Kennedy's day children would not have been ready to watch the Russian character of Pavel Chekov aboard the *Enterprise*. "I do not want to see a hammer and sickle on the moon," a third grader from New Mexico declared in admonishing his president to press on. The prospect of the Soviets getting to the moon first troubled many young minds. "Will they say they own it," a girl inquired of Kennedy, "or will they share it with us?" Some were vexed by the prospect that America's willingness to advertise the Mercury program was inadvertently giving the Soviets an unnecessary advantage. A twelve-year-old Connecticut girl gave voice to this concern in her letter beginning, "I would like to ask you a question, Mr. Kennedy, so would you please answer it in a way a sixth grader would understand it. Why do we publicize news about almost every rocket and how it runs, etc? The Russian leaders may be reading our magazines and getting ideas on making the same rocket a little different, calling it their own, get to the moon before us and get all the credit. I don't like our ideas in the hands of the communists. Who does?"[8]

For all the trepidation over what might go wrong, most children, however, remained faithful to Kennedy's inaugural spirit in pledging their modest money, scientific talent, and hard work to the challenge. From children in

New Jersey and New York came money—$1.00, $2.25, $5.00—for the "Moon Fund" (and/or a monument to John Glenn). Hundreds of rocket and capsule prototype drawings poured into the White House too, with elaborate schematics and handwritten notations on exactly how the various inventions operated. An eleven-year-old from West Virginia brashly wrote, "Now let's get down to business. I think I know how to get to the Moon or Pluto, last planet in the solar system. Or even farther into space. Space platforms + fuel at all (gas station in the air) space stations = (probably) success!" "P.S.," the young (and wary) inventor concluded, "I am sending you . . . a model of how I think the rocket should look. This is serious! Please don't print this in newspapers or anything. Some anti-American could look at this idea." In writing to Kennedy about her eleven-year-old son's newfound interest in science and current events thanks to the Space Race, a Dearborn, Michigan, mother shared a note the boy had left for her when she got home from work: "Mommy, Tonight I outlined a hole [sic] chapter in my Science book, finished a report for our team in Geog[raphy] & got my Geog[raphy] notebook in order for tomorrow. I'm not going to let Russia get ahead of me!!!!"[9]

Other children kept the faith with the Mercury Seven, because, in the opinion of a sixth grader in Illinois, in those capable hands there was, after all, little reason to worry. "I think we can beat Russia in space," the boy confidently explained—all we needed was a little bit of luck and John Glenn would take care of the rest.[10] It was not surprising that this twelve-year-old put so much faith in the Marine Corps lieutenant colonel. Thanks to television, and to a lesser extent transistor radio, all the Mercury astronauts, of which Glenn was the senior member in both rank and age, were shooting into the stratosphere, in terms of esteem, of the most admired adults by 1962. President Kennedy really liked John Glenn on a personal level, and children tended to follow suit. The beauty of these obviously fearless astronauts was that they were not fantasy spacemen like Buck Rogers or Flash Gordon from the generation before, but real-life flesh and blood whose nine-to-five occupation involved actually traveling in space. That had a profound resonance. "We used to be able to name all seven of the original astronauts. They were like superhuman beings in America," explained a Midwestern man who became a high school history teacher. "They were the best and the brightest and the most daring and adventurous. They were the pioneers; they were Lewis and Clark heading out into space. It just captivated your imagination and you'd sit there and watch it on television; the rocket blasting off and the splashdown. They were just absolute heroes." "How I idolized the Mercury, Gemini, and Apollo astronauts," another Midwesterner born in 1955 remembered. "If I ever had heroes . . . these were the ones." In reminiscing about the plastic spacecraft coin he received in a pack of Golden Flake potato chips, a rural Alabama man born in 1958 recalled how "the excitement of the 'space race' the President had called for" had already determined his career choice even before elementary school: "I wanted to be an astronaut!" In fact, for the remainder of the era, rock-n-roll musician remained a distant second to astronaut on the list of "what I want to be when I grow up," at least for boys.[11]

In classroom and bedroom desks across the nation, preadolescents labored to construct homemade scrapbooks chronicling the mission, often forwarding their creations to the White House in earnest homage. One seven-year-old boy from California obviously spent hours compiling an encyclopedia on space travel and the Space Race, highlighted by Glenn's orbit, for a science project. He lovingly emblazoned the cover with a color photograph of the president and astronaut peering into the capsule together. Hundreds of other handcrafted original works of art, newspaper clippings, and personal recollections of Glenn blasting off filled other construction paper pages. "As I was listening to the radio," a Delaware second grader's notation read, "I was excited when they started the countdown. It was all exciting but the countdown was the one I thought was the most exciting." Some admitted to being nervous. "I felt happy and a little bit sad," an ambivalent third grader acknowledged. "I couldn't know whether he would make it." Judging from material in the Kennedy Library, a few children speculated on whether Glenn had been scared, but the consensus in most classes was that such heresy was utterly preposterous. But children did ponder what John Glenn must have felt as the mighty Atlas rocket lifted his fragile body into the Florida sky.[12]

From a child's perspective, the allure of space travel—danger, flight, adventure, quest, exploration—involved familiar elements of fairy tales and science fiction literature and resounded with this last era of unsupervised play, climbing trees and probing muddy creek banks. "The space program, it just went off for young people," a Missouri man born in 1956 reminisced. "I think it astonished older people. It's like, 'Wow, I can't believe they did that.' But with us kids, when we would sit around . . . and talk about it, it . . . captivated our imaginations. We'd start projecting ourselves: 'Well, what would you do if you got to land on the moon? Can you imagine what it would be like sleeping [there]?'"[13]

Active young imaginations were further stirred when their toy and play culture were infused by the Space Race. If play is truly the work of children, and toys are their tools, then the Mercury astronauts not only had the right stuff, they *were* the stuff of toys for young astronauts- and rocketeers-in-training. The visual aesthetic of rocket ships and orbiting satellites was already well established across the spectrum of Cold War era material culture by this time, with atomic age motifs gracing everything from fabrics, dishes, and lamps to household appliances. Science fiction and space toys too—designed to stimulate autonomous fantasy play—had been around for over a decade. Homer Hickam's 1998 coming-of-age-in-the-Space-Race memoir *Rocket Boys*—which inspired the movie *October Sky*—speaks directly to just how central science and technology—chemistry sets, homemade radios, model planes—had become in Cold War boyhood culture. After *Sputnik*, scale model replicas of U.S. rocketry produced by the Kenner and Monogram companies proliferated, as did other futuristic toys marketed to boys. By the early sixties, Louis Marx and Company, a giant in the toy industry known for brightly colored and extravagant play sets, began offering multiple space-themed toys with the Project Mercury Cape Canaveral Playset. RCA's white plastic Astronaut Space Helmet (with pull-down tinted visor and three 45 rpm records) in 1960 likewise fostered hours of child-centered role playing, as did Ben Cooper, Inc.'s U.S. astronaut Halloween costume, complete with plastic mask and synthetic suit. Various toys with the Cape Canaveral theme (some with rocket launchers and others with missiles) entered the market as well as battery-operated metal and plastic space capsules. Often these toys were associated with science fiction comics, movies, and, more than ever, television. Akin to the opening of Tomorrowland as part of Disneyland in 1955, television drove the market for a host of "fantasy-fad" toys—including helmets, goggles, ray guns, spaceship pedal cars, and robots—based on, and often licensed by, popular space characters. Hanna-Barbara, for instance, licensed several Jetsons toys, including a Space Age board game in 1962 and lunch box the following year (perpetuating this cohort's lifelong anticipation of flying cars). By 1964, with the mounting importance of Saturday morning children's programming (brought to you by toy maker sponsorship), scaled, plastic-injection-molded toys increasingly allowed preadolescents to move beyond just chronicling space travel in scrapbooks and instead become a make-believe part of the real world they watched.[14]

Not all dreamers needed the store-bought variety. Programs like *Lost in Space* and *Star Trek* called to mind for many children of the sixties how space television sparked space play. "Younger kids just ate those [shows] up," one remembered. "The older folks hated them. 'Why are you turning that stuff on? Turn that stuff off. That's science fiction.' It's like, 'No it ain't, man, we're going to space!' So we'd go out and play space, play spaceman. We'd build little crafts and act like they were our Mission. It was just . . . very, very imaginative." A man who idolized the astronauts as a seven-year-old recalled devising just such an elaborate, but not especially well-thought out, plan with a cousin to live in their homemade cardboard box "capsule" for an entire week. The humble backyard mission was consistent with Mercury's wider objective of testing man's ability to function in space, but, probably to their parents' relief, "these plans fell through."[15]

The popularity of space toys diminished slightly by the mid-sixties, only to mount a serious comeback later in the decade led by Mattel's Major Matt Mason action figure and merchandise related to the approaching moon landing. Nevertheless, after Glenn's orbital flight, the rhythm of the Space Race quickened, steadily permeating childhood at a number of primary points. As any child would say, space was everywhere! And while the United States still lagged behind in manned flights, two months later NASA launched AT&T's Telstar I, a communications satellite that revolutionized the transmission of live television news feeds from anywhere around the globe. Television infrared observation satellites (TIROS) likewise dramatically improved weather prediction. In the months since Kennedy took office, roughly forty-five satellites had circled the planet; of those, some forty were American made. Further beyond the Earth, by the end of 1962 the deep range robotic probe Mariner 2 passed the planet Venus. Even the Soviets took notice and belatedly expressed at least tepid interest in Kennedy's earlier ideas on space cooperation.

For his part the president celebrated each of the Mercury astronauts in grand style, always cognizant of framing their quintessential New Frontier triumphs within the administration's broader public relations campaign to justify the time and money required by NASA. John Glenn's escape from the Earth's gravity had marked a turning point in the public's opinion of the race to the moon. But the spectacular glow of Apollo at decade's end has since obscured from popular memory how little consensus actually existed over space during the Kennedy years. Despite congressional willingness to substantially increase the space budget—total lunar expenditures would eventually run to $40 billion—initially only one-third of adults supported the enterprise, with almost twice that share believing it to be a particularly poor investment on a race the Soviets were likely to win anyway. How damaging to the national psyche would it be, cynics wondered, to commit so much prestige and treasure only to fail miserably? With delays between launches and postponements not only common but predictable (even Glenn's mission was put off ten times), skeptics openly questioned NASA's capability to accomplish such a Herculean mission by a seemingly impossible deadline. Maybe a more practical timetable and more modest budget would be the prudent course? From the partisan arena came harsh condemnations that Kennedy's colossal "moondoggle" was siphoning off finite funds for science fiction that might be better used fighting poverty and disease at home.[16]

It was precisely to these stubborn doubts and recriminations that John Kennedy spoke when delivering his most potent homily on space at Rice University in September 1962. The location, a Houston institution having since celebrated its fiftieth anniversary as an integral part of the allied research operations of NASA, helped set the address's overall tone. Even as the British musical group The Tornados' instrumental "Telstar" raced up the *Billboard* pop chart, Kennedy wisely positioned space exploration not as a fantastical outlier in American history, but rather as the logical next chapter in the grand story of the nation's progress. Without mentioning nineteenth-century scholars Alexis de Tocqueville or Frederick Jackson Turner directly, the president nevertheless clearly evoked their timeless observations regarding the restless drive for innovation and perennial "process of becoming" in the American character. The same wellspring of leadership—visionary thinking and refusal to remain fixed—that pushed westward expansion had also stirred our technological genius during the economic revolution and propelled our accession to global superpower. Now, standing behind a podium on the Rice football field, Kennedy argued that this heroic and hereditary energy demanded we stay the course on a New Frontier (or final frontier, as Captain James T. Kirk would say four years later).

"But why, some say, the moon? Why choose this as our goal?" the president questioned rhetorically that day in Texas. The answer, said longtime aide and confidant Ted Sorenson, reveals much about Kennedy's idealistic view on where space fit into politics and life. Kennedy continued: "We choose to go to the moon in this decade, and do the other things, not because they are easy but because they are hard, because that goal will serve to organize and measure the best of our energies and skills, because that challenge is one we are willing to accept, one we are unwilling to postpone, and one which we intend to win . . ." Always eager to balance the romance of the moon program with its practical scientific and foreign relations benefits, President Kennedy's equally memorable conclusion drove both points home: "Many years ago the great British explorer George Mallory, who was to die on Mount Everest, was asked why did he want to climb it, and he said, 'Because it is there.' Well, space is there, and the moon and the planets are there, and new hopes for knowledge and peace are there. And, therefore, as we set sail we ask God's blessing on the most hazardous and dangerous and greatest adventure on which man has ever embarked."[17]

The Rice speech functioned on almost the same plane as Kennedy's inaugural in terms of its inspirational impact in the minds of children. By May 1963, astronauts Scott Carpenter, Walter Schirra Jr., and L. Gordon Cooper had also orbited Earth. Each mission lasted longer than the one before and gathered more data. As the Space Race continued to intensify with each passing year, confidence in NASA's ability to be the first to reach the moon kept pace, leading third graders from New Mexico to brag to the president that "when the Russians get to the moon we'll ask them if they want cookies."[18] Kennedy's words and vision directly fueled watershed changes in what sociologist Glen Elder terms the "trajectories" of children's lives. An Arkansas woman born in 1957 today considers herself a political and social conservative because of the "moral downturn" she witnessed as a child. The only "positive impact" on her lifestyle choices from the era are centered on the exploration of space and her developing religious faith as she began to entertain specific ideas of intelligent design. "I saw the advances in space travel as awe-inspiring," she told me, "pointing to a Creator God who put the moon and the earth into orbit as well as the others [heavenly bodies] we saw as we put men into space. Today, I am still awed by the enormity and complexity of the universe. The men who flew in those spacecrafts were heroes to me, courageous and strong. Today, it's rare to find male role models who stand out like that anymore."[19] The space effort prompted many children to pursue adult careers as teachers, scientists, and, yes, even astronauts. Because the moon project represented only the most spectacular element of a more comprehensive push in scientific research and development, including greater emphasis on science education, elementary educators with a knack for math and science often facilitated these trajectories for preadolescent students who were already reading everything they could lay their hands on about NASA or building and flying model rockets. "The space program was incredibly fascinating and I remember staring at the TV with wonder," wrote a woman born outside of Los Angeles in 1960, "so much so that I'm currently a high school science teacher."[20]

Astronaut and physicist Linda Godwin considers herself fairly typical of the shuttle generation astronauts of the 1980s and 1990s who can trace their outer space journeys back to their fateful first steps during the years of Kennedy, Mercury, and Gemini. The connections are "pretty big," she believes, between the early space race and preadolescent determinations to make a career of manned spaceflight, but not always in an orderly, linear fashion. Just nine years old when John Glenn orbited the Earth, Godwin vividly recalls how her nascent interests in math and science—including science fiction—naturally merged with the excitement of Mercury in the competitive Space Race atmosphere of her elementary school classrooms. To her way of thinking, the president "sure seems" to have helped forge these connections, given that she grew up in a southeast Missouri household that "loved John Kennedy" and where his views, including those on space, were regularly discussed as a family. Godwin considers it "very likely that her parents listened to [Kennedy's Rice speech] and talked about it with her"; however, she admits that the 1962 address is now subsumed in her memory by the fact that Kennedy's stirring language became "so engrained in the culture of NASA." Like most, she says, "I grew up watching a lot of the early U.S. space programs" on television—inseparable in her mind from Walter Cronkite's narration—which, in turn, accentuated what she was discovering from her math and science teachers. Coincidentally, this was right about the same time that her love of reading led to the discovery of science fiction through Robert Heinlein's *Have Space Suit—Will Travel*, the adventurous 1958 tale of a juvenile hero exploring the universe through a colorful series of extraterrestrial encounters.

All these factors "kind of churned together in my head" during elementary school, she says, but the desire to work for NASA as an astronaut took years to germinate because at the time astronauts were usually military pilots and she had absolutely no interest in a military career. She also understood that the space program was closed to girls initially, and, in fact, NASA would not start to hire women for the astronaut corps until Godwin was in graduate school in the 1970s working toward her doctorate in physics. Still, Godwin credits John Kennedy with another unintended role in opening the doors to her shuttle missions on *Atlantis* and *Endeavour* and trips to the Russian space station Mir and the International Space Station. The assassination solidified the late president's call for reaching the moon by shielding the space program from critics who wanted it canceled. After November 1963, there was no chance the United States would not make it to the lunar surface, in her opinion; NASA's work "was going to be Kennedy's legacy."[21]

Other astronauts claim an even more direct lineage to the early sixties. Brian Duffy, the son of a Boston mailman, recalled for a NASA interviewer how at four or five years old he became interested in flying by lying on his back in the grass and watching jet vapor trails. "So I was interested in aviation and kind of amazed by it, and along the way," Duffy explained, "the space program started, when I was in third grade or so, '61, when Alan Shepard launched, and I remember watching that on television and it took my interest in aviation and my amazement to a whole new level, like, wow, they're actually leaving the planet, which was something that I thought was just the coolest." Duffy, the veteran of four flights totaling over forty days in space, pointed out, "Many children my age at the time wanted to be astronauts, because it was the coolest thing you could possibly do."[22]

When asked how he became interested in being an astronaut, William F. Readdy explained, "When I was in elementary school, there was no such thing as astronauts, of course. Starting out [with] John Glenn's flight—I was about nine—in the early '60s, all of a sudden there's the Space Age. Not just the Sputnik orbiting piece of metal up there, but people, and that got me very, very interested."[23] Then there is David Wolfe, born in Indianapolis in 1956, an astronaut who logged one hundred and sixty-eight days in space living out Kennedy's dream of U.S.-Russian collaboration. After completing cosmonaut training at the Gagarin Cosmonaut Training Center in Star City, Russia, Wolfe worked on a mission aboard Mir with Russian cosmonauts for nearly four months over 1997 and 1998, carrying out his duties and experiments entirely in the Russian language, including space walks utilizing both U.S. and Russian space suits. He decided to become an astronaut in 1965, when he was nine years old. "Before I wanted to be an astronaut, until that moment," Wolfe told NASA, "I wanted to be a garbage man, because Mr. Peacock, our garbage man, let me run the garbage truck—it was an old-time thing with big levers[and he]let me help him." His parents had already told him it was "okay if you want to be a garbage man, just so you're the best one," so when he announced his decision to change vocations, Wolfe remembers, they tempered their encouragement with a reminder: "Not many people get to do that, and don't be too disappointed if you can't."[24]

That same fall of 1962 in rural Missouri, yet another young space enthusiast came face-to-face with his intergalactic dreams, although of a decidedly different sort. "When I was riding the school bus," which went past an area military base, Steven Craig still keenly remembers, "I SAW A ROCKET SHIP!! I would have been 8 or 9 and since I was a nerdy, geeky sci-fi kid, no one wanted to believe me." Yet despite the boy-who-cried-wolf static from his incredulous family, friends, and neighbors, who had been told the base contained no rocketry, strictly speaking he was right. What he saw that afternoon rising from its underground silo may not have been a spaceship to the moon, but it was a missile, more correctly a Nike Hercules, part of the world's first successful, widely deployed, guided surface-to-air missile system. In this case, it was defending nearby Kansas City.[25] There was, after all, another parallel race against the Russians which played out across the sixties, a contest that also harnessed rockets and was intricately intertwined with the same technologies, prestige, and foreign relations issues, but this one was measured in warheads, not spacemen. Since the dawn of the atomic age in the 1940s, and particularly in the wake of the Korean conflict, the United States and Soviet Union had militarized the Cold War by recklessly matching the other's military strength in an escalating arms race. Fearing that increased military power by the other jeopardized not only national security but also upset the bipolar balance of power in the world, the two competing nations responded by building overwhelming quantities and qualities of conventional and progressively destructive thermonuclear weapons. The logic of this protracted competition for military superiority was relentless, as atomic bombs begat hydrogen bombs, which begat intercontinental ballistic missiles, which begat . . . seemingly ad infinitum. The United States had answered the first Soviet atomic tests in 1949 by detonating the much more destructive hydrogen bomb in 1952. After Russia exploded its own hydrogen weapon in 1953, America detonated the largest device ever tested by this country on the Pacific island of Bikini in 1956. That hydrogen bomb, which was dropped by a B-52 aircraft and decimated Bikini, contained fifteen megatons, the equivalent of 15 million tons of TNT or roughly 750 times more powerful than the "Little Boy" uranium weapon dropped on Hiroshima.

Under the fiscally conservative Dwight Eisenhower in the 1950s, the United States pursued a "New Look" military that de-emphasized conventional weapons and a large standing army in favor of nuclear armaments and increased airpower to give America "more bang for the buck." The nearly surreal doctrine of mutual assured destruction (MAD), as the name implies, in theory deterred the two Cold War belligerents from ever capitalizing on their first-strike capabilities. Still, with a huge nuclear arsenal, the former general and his secretary of state, John Foster Dulles, increasingly relied on the promise of "massive retaliation"—bringing to bear unalterable force—to contain aggression by the Soviets or their perceived communist client, the People's Republic of China. Dulles's practice of "brinkmanship"—not backing down in a crisis even if it meant going to the brink of nuclear war—gave the threat its teeth.

   The launch of *Sputnik* in 1957 startled America, as had the communists' first
intercontinental ballistic missile (ICBM) tests a few months before, but the
United States ultimately kept pace, and by the time of John F. Kennedy's election held strategic superiority in long-range bombers, submarine launched
ballistic missiles, and even ICBMs. These relative strengths gave President
Kennedy the room he needed after the disastrous Bay of Pigs adventure in
1961 to recalibrate American nuclear strategy based on his own inclinations
and understanding of the emergent Third World as the principal new battle-
ground between East and West. Though he could not arrest, nor even slow,
the arms race due to Nikita Khrushchev's hard-line posturing over the divided
city of Berlin and avowal to support wars of national liberation in tropical
locales, Kennedy moved steadily forward with ongoing nuclear test ban negotiations between the United States, British, and Soviets. Those thorny talks
in Geneva, Switzerland, and concomitant trilateral moratorium on all atmo-
spheric and subterranean nuclear testing were actually entering their third full
year when Kennedy was inaugurated. To eventually secure agreement on a
permanent treaty prohibiting nuclear tests, the president navigated a challenging high-wire course between the military industrial complex's intentions to
resume American testing and international endorsement of a test ban. At the
strategic level, Kennedy crafted a nuanced approach to containment, pursuing
a "flexible response" with heavier reliance on conventional forces (including
covert operations and counterinsurgency) to deal with communist expansion
based on calculating the relative degree of each particular threat.
   Nevertheless, with MAD still the bottom line and the Soviet space program
threatening to paint the heavens red, every new foreign crisis and moment
of Cold War friction in the early 1960s menaced the entire world with nuclear holocaust. As a cultural symbol, the ever-present specter of towering
mushroom clouds climbing above American hometowns in their awful purple, orange, and gray splendor haunted the nation, associated in the collective
mind's eye with nightmarish images of scorched main streets and millions
of casualties from the 7,200-degree Fahrenheit temperatures and radiation.
Two-thirds of Americans told pollsters that these prospects represented the
country's most urgent problem, leaving most of the population in a state of
what Cold War historian Paul Boyer characterized as a "nuclear numbing."
While deeply afraid, adults fatalistically resigned themselves to the eventuality
of nuclear war, skeptical of civil defense claims that surviving an attack would
be possible, or preferable.[26]

This was the grisly reality for all Americans of the early nuclear age, which reached a crescendo during thirteen climactic days in October 1962. The Cuban Missile Crisis, the most celebrated and perilous chapter of the Kennedy presidency, brought a frightened nation to the precipice of an unthinkable end. To fully understand its significance for children, it is again important to appreciate the broader developmental context. Most attentive elementary school children understood their country to be on some type of permanent wartime footing (U.S. defense spending under Kennedy reached the highest level yet in the postwar era) and themselves to be living in the shadow, if not the midst, of an actual war. Those younger than the fourth and fifth grades—not fully socialized politically—took the words Cold War literally. With few of the developmental resources necessary to tease out abstractions, the subtleties of the Cold War—where ideologies, propaganda, foreign aid, and sanctions could be harnessed as weapons—made no sense to children whatsoever. In their perception the United States and Soviet Union were locked in perpetual mortal combat. "Why does the Russians fight?" a second grade boy in Flushing, New York, asked President Kennedy in January 1962. "Why does Castro have to fight with us?" a female classmate wanted to know. "Why does everybody have to fight? Why can't everybody be happy?" A third grader from Pennsylvania admonished Kennedy with a letter concluding, "I hope you are ashamed of your self and Khrushlchev [sic] and all the Russians too. All of you are being very silly. Fighting like cats and dogs! What good is fighting going to do?"[27]

After the fourth grade—thinking at Piaget's formal operations stage—children knew the country to be technically at peace. They tended to approach geopolitics more logically and appreciated some of the complexities of a conflict often waged by competing alliances, covert operations, and regional combat by proxy. In every scenario, abrupt nuclear escalation and the ensuing fallout seemed quite plausible. By at least the age of four, the universal danger that prospect presented to their lives preoccupied a substantial number of children in the early 1960s. Contemporary evidence suggests that national apprehensions about the "life-and-death issues" of weapons proliferation and testing, shelters, and nuclear survival "had indeed reached the minds and hearts of many children" prior to October 1962 and were steadily rising. It seems that despite often being confused about the nature of the Cold War, most young people possessed a surprising grasp of nuclear war. Teachers believed their understanding to be considerably greater than most grownups credited them with, given the atomic language—fallout, radiation, H–bomb—commonly turning up in the vocabulary of preschoolers and the more pointed concerns older children expressed. "Do you think there will be World War III?" innumerable letters written to President Kennedy began in some variation. Usually the young writer's own grim assessment followed, as was the case in the correspondence from one concerned sixth grade class in Illinois in February 1962. "I think if there is another war that almost half of the world's people will die," a boy wrote, while his classmate figured "it would end the world." "I think that there will be another world war only a few years from now," a female student concluded. "It'll probably be a very awful and terrible war. Many people will die. It'll probably be the worst war that ever was to be heard of."[28]

Clearly, adults bore the primary responsibility. However inadvertently, virtually all the factual knowledge and resultant fear in the lives of children were being distilled through their parents, teachers, and, to a lesser degree, older siblings. Psychologists believed that a lack of honest communication between the generations presented a particularly salient issue in this troubling dynamic. For nursery schoolers between the ages of four and six, the prospect of a nuclear explosion—like all things very loud and sudden—was disorienting and extremely scary. Not in the irrational way a monster roaring from the closet might be, but rather rationally, as an act of violence well beyond their immediate control which threatened to disrupt the very fabric of the world as they knew it, their family. Anxiety over nuclear war in the youngest children followed proportionally their concern for how it conceivably might intrude upon life at home. In other words, as a concept, nuclear war seriously upset preschoolers only to the degree in which certain hypothetical questions were internalized: Does nuclear testing poison my snowman? How can I recognize a Russian bomber in the sky? When the nuclear war comes, will my parents be killed? If I am separated and lost in the battle, how will Mommy and Daddy find me? Will my dog or cat wander off? How will I learn to ride a bike if we live underground in a bomb shelter for a long time? What will the trees and birds be like when we emerge from underground? Will our neighbors, relatives, friends, stores, playgrounds still be there? The more they worried, the more terrifying the imagery. "I remember having a lot of separation anxiety as a young child," a Kentucky woman born in 1959 confided, "and found out later that my mother was always worried about us being away from her because of the situation with the Soviet Union . . . back when people were expecting nuclear war at any time."[29]

Developmentally, smaller children like this sought reassurance and security in the knowledge that adults had already thought things through and were prepared with simple answers, and, moreover, were ready to take charge. Yet, so complicated and unimaginable were children's queries and misperceptions that they defied concise explanations for even the most thoughtful of parents. Instead, adults frequently remained mute, either unwilling or unable to frankly address the nuclear concerns—especially during periods of heightened public alarm—which naturally intensified early preadolescent distress.

Take for instance the resumption of nuclear testing, in violation of the moratorium, and the near hysteria it touched off in children during the winter and spring of 1961 and 1962. Earlier that summer, simmering tensions over the divided city of Berlin began boiling again as the Soviet Union renewed its determination to absorb West Berlin into the East German fold and America resolved to protect the freedom of the former capital. Since World War II, Germany had been partitioned, first into four zones of occupation each administered by the respective allies: the United States, Britain, France, and the Soviet Union. In time, the first three zones solidified into the Federal Republic of Germany (West Germany) while the latter became the German Democratic Republic (East Germany). Berlin was similarly apportioned; however, the circumstances were considerably more complicated because while West Berlin remained aligned with democratic West Germany it was geographically located within the physical borders of communist East Germany. The inherent friction of this unsustainable division, and Soviet embarrassment over the steady stream of refugees from the east escaping communist repression by crossing into West Berlin, led Khrushchev to once again demand that the United States and its western allies terminate their access rights to West Berlin, effectively abandoning it behind the Iron Curtain.

The June 1961 summit between Kennedy and Khrushchev in Vienna brought no resolution and within weeks the crisis escalated, with the president flexing American military muscle in demonstration of his administration's commitment to the existence of West Berlin. During a nationally televised broadcast on July 25, Kennedy strongly reiterated his refusal to be bullied by Khrushchev. He would ask Congress for additional military spending—$3.25 billion—and significant troop increases—six new Army divisions and two Marine—with a tripling of draft calls and the activation of the reserves. Forty thousand troops were being deployed to Europe. In regard to nuclear preparedness, new funds would also be allocated for designating and stocking additional public fall-out shelters complimented by improved municipal air-raid warning capabilities and radiation detection systems. The Soviets responded in mid-August by building a barbed-wire barrier along the demarcation to physically cut off East Berlin from the western section of the German city. Mounting trouble at the checkpoints where citizens moved back and forth made the barricade volatile, and as pressure increased from within the Soviet Union to force America's hand, Khrushchev raised the stakes that September. In a performative show of force, Russia resumed atmospheric megaton testing for the first time since 1958 and, as in a choreographed waltz, Kennedy was obliged to follow suit with underground testing a few days later. American atmospheric testing recommenced the following spring. With the thirty-four-month moratorium brushed aside and test ban negotiations frozen, the superpowers now made up for lost time with more than 200 new thermonuclear detonations between them by the end of 1962.

As fall turned to winter, parents reported that a number of four- and five-year-olds were becoming agitated when commercial airplanes flew over their towns for fear that they were dropping bombs. Anxious children were also paying close attention to weather reports on local television and in the newspaper. When forecasts called for precipitation, outdoor play virtually ceased, with children sometimes flatly refusing to leave the house for any activities that might expose them to rain, even resisting the allure of puddle jumping. Reports from the Netherlands arousing worldwide concern were the underlying cause. Radioactive debris had been detected in the stratosphere over the polar regions, apparently from resumed Soviet testing. Specifically, lethal levels of strontium-90, a radioactive isotope of the chemical element strontium produced by nuclear fission, were present, which scientists guessed might contaminate parts of the world through rain and snow. Rumors began circulating across the country that both these forms of precipitation were "poisoned" or "bad." Umbrellas, raincoats, caps, and mittens offered no protection, so children chose to stay inside. Snow days ceased to be a cause for rejoicing in the child's calendar. Preadolescents feared letting the flakes touch them, so sledding hills remained empty, fewer snowmen peopled the wintry landscape, and eating snow was out of the question. Parents also noted disturbing trends in children's artwork, with vibrantly painted explosions and mushroom clouds, harshly drawn red crayon flames engulfing barely recognizable ruins, and frightened little stick children in the middle of it all.[30]

Stories about tainted precipitation that winter of 1961 and 1962 reflect how broken lines of communication were exacerbated by the fact that when children did hear adults talking candidly, they were usually only overhearing them. Typically upbeat parents might extol the virtues of NASA during dinnertime, only to be caught later around that same Formica topped chrome dinette worrying in hushed tones about strontium-90 finding its way into American milk, or somberly outlining the procedure for shutting off all home utilities in case of an attack. Similarly, eavesdropping children might surreptitiously hear moms and dads debating the dubious notion that whether the family lived through a surprise Soviet bombing depended on their having access to a well-equipped underground shelter (or at the very least a tornado cellar). The Atomic Energy Commission determined that in the first hours of a full-scale nuclear exchange, thirty-nine million Americans would be killed (roughly 20 percent of the population). By making calculations on a Nuclear Bomb Effects Computer or Radiation Dosage Calculator—both of which were hand-held, circular slide rules—moms and dads could forecast specific, localized damage. These grim conversations often hinged on predictions that if their town was located within the "A-damage ring" with 100 percent fatalities, all planning would be for naught. Yet, inside the "B-damage ring" only 50 percent would be dead and 35 percent injured, leaving 15 percent to face the unknown. Children's exposure to such conversations not meant for their ears reinforced the powerful impression that the world was an almost unbelievably perilous place, with danger lurking everywhere. Moreover, it confronted them with an unaccustomed and uncomfortable perspective on their parents as not all-powerful, reassuring and protective, but genuinely scared adults talking about . . . being genuinely scared.

"I remember at that time the adults seemed very concerned about 'nuclear fallout,'" a West Virginia woman born in 1954 wrote. "I had no idea what it was, but I knew it couldn't be good since the grownups were worried. On our farm was an old rock quarry where I played almost daily. One spot had a deep 'cave.' I made this my fallout shelter and sneaked a couple of cans of food to put in there, 'just in case.'"[31]

Sometimes the only "mature" dialogue available to smaller children was needlessly alarmist, coming as it did via elder brothers, sisters, or neighborhood adolescents who were either truthfully trying to warn children about toxic thunderstorms or deliberately scaring their pants off with tales of commie nukes decimating the city. Atomic teasing for a time became the favorite fodder for bullies who might convince their little victims to the point of tears that invisible radiation would make their fingers and toes fall off if they were not careful. Cues for domesticating social uncertainties normally drawn from popular culture were not much help either, as nuclear war was simply poor subject

matter for television, music, or toys. A few programs of the international in-
trigue genre broached the subject by mid-decade: *The Rocky and Bullwinkle
Show,* with the villainous Russian avatars Boris Badenov and Natasha Fatale,
NBC's *Get Smart,* and CBS's *Mission: Impossible.* Even *I Dream of Jeannie, Mister
Ed,* and *The Lucy Show* eventually offered spy-themed episodes. But atomic
missions usually remained ancillary for television spies, and the popularity of
these shows says a great deal more about heightened public concern over the
CIA's enhanced role as an instrument of foreign policy. Consequently, already
uneasy young minds tended to remain overwhelmed and anxious.[32]

Because children were largely kept in the dark, perhaps it was appropriate
that terror often manifested itself in their dreams. By the early 1960s parents
and psychologists noted with growing alarm how common nuclear-themed
nightmares were becoming in preadolescents of all ages. For example, an
eight-year-old in Chicago flailed in his sleep nightly, shouting out that nuclear bombs were targeting him. A sixth grader recalled a particularly trau-
matic experience when "I dreamed about a mechanical chicken. He was made
in Russia and everything he pecked blew up. It was an atomic chicken. He
pecked our next door neighbor's house—and it blew up. Then he pecked our
house and it blew up. Then I woke up on the floor." Doctors in the 1950s
would have diagnosed dreams like this in older baby boomers as simply developmental expressions of latent guilt, that the child had done something wrong
and needed to be punished. Now, however, experts theorized that a literal
interpretation might be more accurate. For some children, atomic dreams revealed actual panic over the threat of bombing, and, more ominously, these
fears "may be beyond tolerable psychological limits."[33]

The Berlin crisis concluded more or less satisfactorily in November 1961—
that is, the status quo was preserved without nuclear war—when the USSR
accepted the partition of the city by replacing the initial fence separating the
two halves with a permanent concrete wall, a structure considered to be the
symbol of the Cold War for the next quarter of a century. Although disaster
was averted, grave doubts about nuclear war continued unabated. More precisely, a countrywide argument intensified regarding the viability of American
defense systems and the dubious merits of fallout shelters as the cornerstone
of national preparedness. Preadolescents are generally not cognitively capable
of cynicism, but school-age children nevertheless recognized the inherent ab-
surdity of what the country, and *they,* were being trained to do in the name
of preparedness and picked up the distinct impression that at some level adults
knew it too.

Consider again that Nike Hercules rocket site in Missouri. At a time when American military planners believed the Soviet Union to be developing long-range nuclear-armed bomber aircraft capable of reaching targets in continental North America, the United States built a system of approximately 250 Nike sites (the first generation in the mid-1950s were called Ajax, which gave way in the 1960s to Hercules) to protect the country's urban areas. Hercules missiles could carry either a conventional or nuclear warhead and most cities of any size were ringed with these nuclear capable armaments; the number of sites around a particular metropolitan area depended on its size. Washington, D.C., New York (with almost twenty individual Nike sites), Philadelphia, Detroit, Seattle, San Francisco, and Los Angeles had the most, while secondary centers such as Kansas City, Dallas-Fort Worth, St. Louis, Cincinnati, and Minneapolis-Saint Paul had fewer. The military referred to Nike as the "linebacker" for the North American Air Defense Command because the system was considered a last line of defense to be used only if American aircraft were unsuccessful in destroying incoming Russian bombers. Imagine the illogic of shooting down entire formations of enemy planes—complete with nuclear payloads—using our own nuclear missiles and then having the subsequent wreckage and fallout raining all over Gotham below.[34]

Most children were socialized toward this pronounced ambivalence primarily at school, where teachers—every bit as well-intentioned as parents—facilitated most of the Federal Civil Defense Administration (FCDA) drills, literature, and programming directly geared toward children. Since 1950 the FCDA had mandated a national effort to prepare for, and survive, a nuclear attack through a federally coordinated series of family-, neighborhood-, and community-based civil defense initiatives. Usually predicated on a highly unlikely worst-case, sneak-attack scenario, civil defense in elementary schools attempted to reassure worried preadolescents by grounding nuclear preparation within the familiar context of existing emergency procedures, and empower them with the activities, skills, and resources they would need to participate in their own defense. Any self-respecting Vulcan could attest to the logic. Whereas preschoolers need to know grownups are in charge, developmentally those between six and twelve years old derive more confidence from knowing how to do things themselves and having the correct tools to do it. Although they still admire adults (and teenagers) who embody strengths they do not yet possess, this age group devises strategies to compensate for their shortcomings. Surveys completed immediately after the Berlin confrontation found that 70 percent of elementary school students were concerned, or had recently thought, about nuclear war and fallout shelters. Of these, the majority indicated that their concern took the form of learning specific procedures for protecting themselves and their families. As evidence of achieving Piaget's concrete operational cognitive stage and Kohlberg's conventional level of moral development, 35 percent also spoke of an obligation to protect people outside their immediate family.[35]

The prescriptive "forewarned is forearmed" curriculum—analogous to fire or tornado drills—satisfied the six- to twelve-year-old's need for advance preparation. Training with the latest in civil defense hardware helped them visualize nuclear events before they happened and formulate contingency plans accordingly. The first step involved adequate warning time—calculated by such factors as early detection, velocity of incoming missiles or aircraft, megatonnage involved, and the physical distance from ground zero—and toward that end, many schools employed warning devices and sirens together with daily drills. For almost a decade, CONELRAD (Control of Electromagnetic Radiation), the forerunner of our modern Emergency Broadcast System, had operated as the nation's civil-defense radio network. In case of emergency, AM disc jockeys and television announcers would advise their audiences that regularly scheduled programming had been temporarily suspended and listeners should tune into the CONELRAD wavelength—640 or 1240 kilocycles, depending on location—for information. Transistor radios frequently had a civil defense logo on them with this emergency information, and school principals routinely kept one in their offices perpetually dialed in to that station. By 1960 the short-lived National Emergency Alarm Repeater (NEAR) supplemented CONELRAD in some schools, homes, offices, and public buildings. The compact box plugged directly into a common electrical outlet, and its warning buzz could be activated by the FCDA center in Colorado Springs through alterations in the normal AC flow of electricity. Increasingly, however, schools opted for a version of the "Bell and Lights" Air Raid Warning System. Often located within easy sight of a school's central nervous system—the secretary—this device, designed by Bell Laboratories, looked and acted like a telephone. When a warning came via the telephone line, a bell rang and a color-coordinated light flashed corresponding to the threat level: white (all clear), blue (trouble expected soon), yellow (attack likely, so take cover quickly), and red (imminent attack, so take cover *now*).

Given that there would only be a finite period of time to act, schools routinely scheduled daily and weekly rehearsals—usually in the mornings around first recess—when the warning system would be tested and carefully scripted procedures practiced for maximum efficiency. Students were taught to recognize public buildings with "Fallout Shelter" signs—three upside-down yellow triangles in a black circle—as a place of safety, and not just where they were located, but also specifications concerning maximum occupancy and any requisite materials to bring along. Directions to the nearest designated fallout shelters were carefully memorized, based on where the child might be at any given time: school, home, park, supermarket. Teachers then walked their classes through the logistics of actually getting there during regularly scheduled evacuation drills. If the shelter happened to be the school gymnasium, orderly single-file lines streamed in, and if not, classes left the school grounds on foot or in volunteer car pools. Some in smaller schools took pupils all the way to their doorsteps while others arranged predetermined neighborhood rallying points for parental pick-up. A Memphis man born in 1957 told me that he has never forgotten the routine: "We definitely knew where the fallout shelters were . . . and how to get there. Basements, basically. Every Saturday at noon the air raid siren was tested citywide. You could set your watch by it."[36]

At some point all the serious planning ran headlong into the same dead end: nuclear war was just not survivable. Even the most self-confident children came to a realization that they probably lacked the physical and mental capabilities required. The enormity of the concepts involved and the complexity of survival procedures likewise overwhelmed them with feelings of inadequacy. How could such a small person's feeble attempts matter in the face of mankind's utter extinction? Civil Defense might not be outright deception on the part of adults, but brighter preadolescents judged the program's basic premise to be irrational, and were deeply confused by the irrationality of otherwise responsible adults. Shelters, specifically, raised another profound ethical conundrum. A survey conducted on student opinions of war and fallout shelters during the Berlin crisis by psychologist Milton Schwebel found that children commonly believed that shelters should be available to everyone. "With rare exceptions," he found, "the students have condemned the idea of excluding others from shelters and have been horrified at the suggestion to shoot neighbors who try to gain admittance." These cumulative cognitive disconnections further fueled the ambivalence.[37]

"I remember vividly," a man from Atlanta wrote, "being in the third grade . . . and participating in a drill that required all of us school kids to march outside and get into whatever car was available in a long line of cars, and then drive to a train station nearby. The drill was to prepare us for an evacuation in the event of a pending nuclear attack. Years later, I remember the duck and cover drills in the sixth and seventh grades, and I remember my family stocking the basement with canned goods and water to be used as a fallout shelter. I imagine most every kid my age has those memories. These memories are certainly not on the scale of British or German kids during WWII bombing campaigns, but nonetheless, they were sobering experiences."[38]

His recollection speaks to another routine which was among the first lines of defense through the 1970s. In "duck and cover," students regularly trained (led by the example of a timid cartoon turtle named Bert) to protect themselves from the initial blast through a simple two-step maneuver: 1) duck—upon seeing an intense flash of nuclear light, immediately stop what you are doing and get into a prone, face-down position on the ground; and 2) cover—preferably under something like a desk with your hands or coat covering the back of your head. After enduring the violent shock wave—flying glass, falling cement, twisted steel reinforcements—with only their bare hands and jackets, the class would then rise and proceed to an evacuation location in the same orderly and businesslike fashion of a fire drill. "When I was in the second grade and seven years old," one man remembers, "our teacher told us . . . that if the bell rings three times . . . it is a fire drill, but if it has one long ring . . . GET UNDER YOUR DESK . . . because the Russians are dropping an atomic bomb on us." Instead of this procedure instilling the desired sense of security, "we were scared to death. All we wanted to do was play kick-the-can and ride our bikes. We could not understand why someone would want to hurt us."[39]

Other perplexing measures were no less specious and just as chilling. During more extensive communitywide drills, children involved with the Boy and Girl Scouts and other youth organizations routinely canvassed neighborhoods distributing index cards with detailed air raid instructions. Junior citizens also sometimes served as "casualties," brought by ambulance to designated hospitals where they were "treated" by volunteer personnel. This usually involved registering them, dressing their mock wounds, and having them remain on cots for hours until the drill was complete.

Perhaps the most spectacular example of a civil defense device designed to promote security but that instead actually mortified children were the identification tags. Since the late 1950s, as more local Parent-Teacher Association (PTA) groups became involved with civil defense, identification tags were made available through the schools. Akin to military "dog tags," these FCDA authorized "Official Civil Defense Identification Tags"—first offered through displays in local grocery stores—were smooth metal on a non-tarnish chain (the original plastic cords were found to be flammable). Each was stamped with the child's name, plus the name and address of a person to notify in case of emergency, birth date, and religious preference. Obviously distributed to allay the common fear of being lost after an attack, their very existence seemed based on the certainty of mass death. "I don't remember the drills themselves," an Alabama woman born in 1956 revealed, but of the few artifacts that have survived from her childhood, "I still have a metal dog tag on a chain with my name and address on it so I could be identified in case of a nuclear attack."[40]

On the eve of the Cuban Missile Crisis, as the Central Intelligence Agency secretly monitored Soviet shipping in the Caribbean and a disturbing military buildup on the island, child psychologists tracing the casual manifestations of these nuclear tensions in the native practices of children were struck by how deeply atomic warfare had permeated their play culture, usually by subtle distortion and warping. For example, new wrinkles were added to playing school. One child assuming the role of principal would bring an alarm clock from home and at the proper time would make it ring, declaring "yellow alert, everyone evacuate." Then those playing teacher would line the pretend students up to be escorted to another yard.

A woman who grew up in Kentucky remembers playing near the railroad tracks as a little girl, counting the train cars that rolled through her valley, and being puzzled by the sudden appearance of very different looking ones as military preparedness ramped up one fall: flatcars carrying tanks and jet aircraft with folded wings. She and her sister also made a game of running outside to wave at cargo planes whenever they heard the hum of the engines overhead. The pilots, she fondly remembered, would roll their wings in salute. But the smaller, faster jets that started buzzing the town, so low the girls could see inside the cockpit, never acknowledged their little admirers because the pilots were focused so intently on their training. "Our area," she came to understand later, "was used a lot for dogfights because the terrain was like Russia, we were told."[41]

Besides official material from the FCDA, the Soviet threat also sometimes showed up in children's classroom literature. Parochial students recall the Catholic Guild's *Treasure Chest* comic book series, which usually featured inspiring stories about citizenship, morality, and patriotism. In 1961, *Treasure Chest* ran the serial "This Godless Communism" for several weeks, and one former student, who characterized the publication as "basically propaganda," spoke to its subtle intrusion into her reading routine. "Our Catholic elementary school had comic books in the back of the classroom," she reminisced. "We were allowed to read them if we finished an assignment fast or the weather was too nasty for recess. The comic books talked about how if the Russians took over the United States, they would take away all our liberties, maybe separate us from our parents, and force us to take our religion underground like the Christians in Rome. Needless to say, I was scared to death of communism."[42]

Reading about Russians at your desk often translated into drawing them—art teachers were among the faculty most likely to notice nuclear anxiety—and whoopin' them on the playground. Nuclear toys—an ephemeral phenomenon of the earlier Cold War years—were effectively a cultural dead end by the sixties. Few, if any, children still clamored for the intricate Gilbert U-238 Atomic Energy Lab, Uranium Rush by Gardner Games (complete with miniature Geiger counter), or Kix cereal's Atomic Bomb Ring that split atoms to smithereens right on your finger (for just fifteen cents and a box top). Irrational annihilation in the form of toys proved tough to market and, truth to tell, was not much fun to play with. That being said, educators noted how communists were replacing the Germans and Japanese as the preferred enemy in many traditional children's war games because, as one expert concluded, it was the Soviets who were now "endowed with all the powers of evil the children could imagine."[43]

Others wrestled with their fear of the Reds not in schoolyard battlefields with dirt clod grenades and stick machine guns, but through humor. A West Virginia man born in 1958 described using laughter to ward off the dread of knowing that "missiles could be flying through the air towards us at any moment," by joining in the rousing school bus choruses of "Khrushchev, the Bald Headed Russian" sung to the tune of "Rudolph, the Red Nosed Reindeer." For those with an edgier sense of humor—the gallows variety—that classic adult line of questioning "What are you going to be when you grow up?" became "What are you going to be when you *blow up*?"[44]

On Sunday morning, October 14, 1962, a U-2 aircraft overflew Cuban airspace to give John F. Kennedy the first vital reconnaissance necessary to deal with that particular communist problem as it brewed ninety miles off the Florida coast. Since 1959 the United States had labored in vain to destabilize or overthrow the Cuban dictator Fidel Castro, a revolutionary who had publicly declared himself a Marxist-Leninist in late 1961. Besides formally implementing a trade embargo and cutting off diplomatic relations with Cuba under Eisenhower, the Kennedy administration had also authorized the ill-fated Bay of Pigs invasion that same year. While not toppling Castro's communist regime, each U.S. action may well have pushed Cuba deeper into the Soviet sphere. So much so, that as Cuba intensified its military buildup in preparation for another anticipated American attack, Castro and Khrushchev struck a deal to deploy Soviet tactical nuclear weapons on the island for defensive purposes along with strategic missiles to be aimed at population centers along the American East Coast.

The CIA's aerial photography taken on Sunday, October 14, revealed one of the six Soviet medium range ballistic missile (MRBM) sites under construction near the San Cristóbal area west of Havana, which in their haste the Russians had not properly concealed. The president learned of this intelligence while reading the morning paper on Tuesday and swiftly convened the Executive Committee of the National Security Council, or ExComm, for the first of what would become nearly around-the-clock, top-secret meetings over the next week and a half to formulate America's response. Kennedy and his advisors had anticipated the Soviet deployment of defensive weapons in Cuba (the president pronounced it "Cuber") based on Khrushchev's previous public and private statements, but the clandestine existence of offensive weapons was both duplicitous and a serious challenge to national security. Secretary of Defense Robert McNamara and others agreed with the president that while the weapons did little to alter the military balance of power in the world—missiles on Soviet soil and aboard submarines already menaced the continental U.S.—the administration's handling of the predicament would be carefully scrutinized at home and abroad. Resolve and strength were the currency of the Cold War, to be spent wisely and never needlessly squandered, whether in partisan politics or foreign relations. The missiles simply must be removed.

On that much ExComm unanimously agreed. However, the means of removal was hotly debated, and these deliberations were further complicated by the fluid and incomplete nature of the intelligence. Kennedy considered this a personal test from Khrushchev and, in a combative temper, leaned toward the hawkish position of taking out the missiles by force with some combination of airstrikes and invasion. While some in this school of thought, former Secretary of State Dean Acheson among them, argued for a sudden surgical airstrike targeting only the missile sites, Joint Chiefs of Staff Chair Gen. Maxwell Taylor recommended a much broader air assault against a number of Cuban military targets. Bobby Kennedy saw the wisdom of an invasion, even speculating on how a manufactured incident at Guantanamo might provide the international justification for such provocative, and potentially unpopular, action. Director of Central Intelligence John McCone held a more dovish perspective on air strikes, maintaining that 100 percent accuracy could never be guaranteed and even the best aimed bombing may well force the communists to retaliate. McNamara favored a naval blockade of Cuba. United Nations Ambassador Adlai Stevenson and Soviet expert Charles "Chip" Bolen, the new ambassador to France, stressed the need for quiet, private diplomacy to broker a deal with the Soviets, perhaps swapping America's obsolete Jupiter missiles in Turkey for those in Cuba.

Day five of the crisis saw ExComm narrowing these options to a blockade or airstrike with the understanding that the latter be followed by an invasion. But new information on the 20th that at least eight MRBMs were already operational significantly dampened enthusiasm for leading with the military option. The president's outrage had also cooled somewhat by this time and increasingly his preference for more measured action finally helped broker a compromise: a naval blockade coupled with diplomacy (both public confrontations and back-channel negotiations)—and failing that, escalation. With a clearer strategy now in hand, the administration requested television airtime on all three channels for October 22 at 7:00 p.m. to alert the American people to the Cuban missile crisis and make public Kennedy's gambit.[45]

Although critical negotiations would take place behind the scenes in the United Nations with acting Secretary-General U Thant and between Bobby Kennedy and Soviet Ambassador to the U.S. Anatoly Dobrynin, the president's speech on live television rebuked Khrushchev for his "clandestine, reckless and provocative threat to world peace" while presenting the communists with a stern ultimatum in front of a worldwide audience (via Telstar satellite). Kennedy's calm delivery that evening belied the severity of the single most frightening address given during the Cold War, as he laid out the recent discovery of "the urgent transformation of Cuba into an important strategic base" from which the Soviets now unequivocally possessed an offensive "nuclear strike capability against the Western Hemisphere." In response, the commander in chief explained that he had "directed that the following *initial* (his voice clearly emphasizing the word) steps be taken immediately. First: To halt this offensive buildup, a strict quarantine on all offensive military equipment under shipment to Cuba is being initiated. All ships of any kind bound for Cuba from whatever nation or port will, if found to contain cargoes of offensive weapons, be turned back." The "quarantine" (the term chosen because blockade is legally an act of war) would be lifted only after United Nations observers supervised "the prompt dismantling and withdrawal of all offensive weapons in Cuba." Until that time, Kennedy was instructing "the Armed Forces to prepare for any eventualities."[46]

Kennedy used the word "nuclear" eleven times, but never to more unnerving effect than when articulating the doctrine of mutual assured destruction: "It shall be the policy of this nation to regard any nuclear missile launched from Cuba against any nation in the Western Hemisphere as an attack by the Soviet Union on the United States, requiring a full retaliatory response upon the Soviet Union." In more muted terms, President Kennedy concluded his grim address by casting the crisis in the spirit of his inaugural and the Rice University speech delivered just one month earlier: "My fellow citizens, let no one doubt that this is a difficult and dangerous effort on which we have set out. No one can see precisely what course it will take or what costs or casualties will be incurred. Many months of sacrifice and self-discipline lie ahead—months in which our patience and our will will be tested—months in which many threats and denunciations will keep us aware of our dangers. But the greatest danger of all would be to do nothing."

These resolute words commenced six more anguished days during which mankind braced for nuclear war. And in so doing, they left the first of two indelible "flashbulb memories" of John F. Kennedy's presidency in the consciousness of children, recollections of an extraordinary event so intense and vibrant that they have remained imprinted on their minds like film. When asked what he remembered of the sixties as a child, a man who was twelve years old on the night of October 22, 1962, began, "Well, I can tell you I was watching the TV at home alone when JFK made the announcement on the Cuban Missile Crisis, standing at attention with my hand on my heart all the way through."[47] Indeed, in slightly less than eighteen minutes, the speech dramatically sharpened prevailing childhood anxieties about nuclear holocaust into very real terms, with specific names and places. Even more resoundingly, this marked the first time many youngsters had heard a respected adult speak to them forthrightly and fearlessly about the prospects for nuclear war, and not just any adult either, but President Kennedy. Literally overnight the address served as a catalyst, finally fueling meaningful family conversations at home—both parents and children facing down fears on the common grounds of faith and patriotism—and spontaneous dialogues in classrooms nationwide (to compliment increased civil defense drilling).

Teachers at all elementary grade levels, especially along the East coast, were surprised by the serious manner in which their students carefully followed the details of the crisis and were moved by their earnest efforts to work through its pressures. While the most sensitive cried in class and some boys made jokes, students' preoccupation with understanding the Cuban Missile

Crisis dominated instruction time as the routine curriculum stood still. They talked about what they heard from their parents and read aloud newspapers brought from home, trying to figure out what everything meant. "I have been following you in newspapers, on television, and on radio," a fourth grade girl in Brooklyn wrote to the president. "I am aware of most of the important happenings that concerns the United States. On October 22, 1962, I watched you on television and agree with every word you said about Cuba. My class has and still is studying about you and what is happening."[48]

These concrete operational thinkers often tried to imagine the perspective of their counterparts on the conflict's other side. "Did you ever think what the children in Russia and Cuba feel like?" a fifth grade girl wondered. "Maybe they feel just like us? How do we know?" Sometimes, these older students questioned specific strategic calculations, such as whether the president should have acted sooner. But thousands of letters from preadolescents at the Kennedy Library about what they called "the Cuban situation" offer simple sentiments of support. "I hope that your great speeches will scare Castro away," a sixth grade boy in Miami wrote. "You have great braveness and you have great honesty. I heard your great speech Tuesday and I thought it was great. And I hope that you handle this matter carefully." A sixth grade girl in Pennsylvania agreed, writing, "I am happy about your decision about blockading Cuba. I and many others would do the same. I liked the speech you made on Oct. 22, 1962 very much. I think you are doing everything that can be done about this problem." Perhaps because the correspondence from a third grader in Ohio was done as part of his first cursive writing assignment, he kept the message more succinct: "Today is colder—48 degrees. Cuba seems to be a hot spot. We are hoping you are making the right choice—Mr. Kennedy."[49]

Amid nearly constant television coverage, the three belligerents—the United States, the Soviet Union, and Cuba—worked through various combinations of military contingencies, posturing for each other's benefit, but struggling at each step to keep the rapidly intensifying situation from spinning out of their control, always cognizant that war might be coming within a matter of hours. Khrushchev immediately denounced the quarantine and instead of acquiescing, hurried construction schedules at the missile sites ahead of the blockade, which went into effect on Wednesday, October 24, at 10:00 a.m. Eastern time. In the Atlantic, Soviet destroyers and submarines joined the cargo ships already approaching the blockade line with additional military hardware to escort them the rest of the way. The Pentagon ordered the United States to DEFCON 3, the defense readiness condition halfway between peacetime and all-out war, as interceptor aircraft armed with nuclear weapons for the first time were scrambled. The Strategic Air Command (SAC) issued its highest alert level, which kept one in every eight strategic bombers in the air around the clock.

On the island, Castro's soldiers dug in and waited for an estimated invasion force of 300,000 American troops.

The world held its breath when the first Russian transports carrying more missiles were met by American warships at the blockade line and naval commanders prepared to board and search. America and the Soviet Union were standing eye to eye. No one could recall having seen grocery store shelves so barren or houses of worship so overcrowded as panicked citizens stocked home bomb shelters and church congregations swelled to standing room only. A nine-year-old living in New Jersey still distinctly remembers that day "riding in our coral and charcoal Dodge with my dad glued to the radio listening to reports of the Cuban Missile Crisis."[50] Then the communists appeared to blink. Twenty ships under the hammer-and-sickle flag stopped dead in the water and turned back. Yet the collective sigh of relief proved short-lived, as Soviet surface-to-air missiles brought down a high-altitude U-2 on Saturday the 27th after Cuban antiaircraft batteries had begun firing on low-altitude American reconnaissance flights days before. ExComm's directive called for immediate retaliatory airstrikes, and for the first and only confirmed time in the nation's history, the Strategic Air Command moved to DEFCON 2.

No other incident of John Kennedy's presidency generated nearly the volume of letters from children (correspondence about the assassination was sent to Lyndon Johnson) and the vast majority of these were mailed to the White House in bulk by classroom teachers during this week. Teachers often referenced the fact that it was actually the students who spontaneously came up with the idea to write the president as a therapeutic means of coping with their distress and had done so together as a group activity. "I know the trouble our country is in," wrote a Michigan girl, "and I wish we weren't in it. I won't lie to you but, I'm scared!" "When I heard about the crisis in Cuba I became very upset and terribly frightened," a New York fourth grader confessed in a delicately penned missive, imagining that the leader of the free world "must have been just as afraid as I was." "The night the Cuban Crisis started do you think I slept?" her classmate asked rhetorically. "Not very much I was so scared, I imagined I heard missiles over my house."[51]

This tendency to intimately confide in the president was consistent with children's understanding of Kennedy as a father figure, as even the six- to twelve-year-olds took a great deal of personal comfort in reaching out to the man they watched staring down the Russians. "I think what you did was right," a fourth grader in Pennsylvania explained, indirectly expressing a sense of confidence in the president's wisdom with her admission "Our teacher explained it to us. But somehow I can't explain it to you. I know that I don't have to." Others felt fortunate that patience and good judgment guided the republic in these critical hours. "We acknowledge your speech with great pride knowing that their [sic] is a great man in the White House to lead us to full freedom that the United States has known for the past centuries," a patriotic spokesman for a New York sixth grade class explained. "We all know that you shall carry us through this crisis. Remember our country depends on you." From Brooklyn came another illustrative fifth-grade perspective: "I am in panic just like almost everyone is. But there really isn't nothing to be nervous about, because you are such a great president that I feel like a baby in a mother's arm."[52]

Egocentric children making these fictive, personal connections also often ascribed to Khrushchev and Castro qualities they recognized from their limited experience, formulating solutions through the simple application of elementary school values. Nikita Khrushchev was a terrifically scary villain to children, and although the name lent itself well to sardonic epithets like "Nutty Nikita," younger children associated the Soviet leader, and his toady Castro, with all the evils of communism incarnate: deviousness, sneakiness, cruelty, ruthlessness. To their mind, the missile crisis might be, as an eight-year-old in Iowa guessed, Khrushchev's long-awaited "surprise war on us," warning the president to "watch out for him and Castro, too, because they are tricky and mean." The communists were bullies pure and simple, trying to boss America around. And as everyone knows, "We cannot back down from a bully. We have to stand up and face him." "Can they mind their own business," a California third grader—who started her letter by exclaiming "I hate Russia"—asked Kennedy. "Why don't they shut up, behave and shut up?"[53]

When these types of issues arose on the playground, teachers and principals usually stepped in with corrective reminders about the virtues inherent in friendship, respect, and cooperation. Could this crisis be solved, younger students wondered, if Kennedy, Khrushchev, and Castro lived out these fundamental lessons being taught in elementary school? If the three primary actors learned to be friends, then tensions between the countries would ease and, in the words of one 11-year-old, "there will be no more fighting and we would not have to live underground." Older students reasoning on Kohlberg's conventional level of moral development may not have been quite so naive, but they still applied the same basic notions of fairness and justice grounded in mutual respect. For example, more insightful students sometimes suggested ending the standoff by trading Cuba to the Russians in exchange for West Berlin. The stakes of the missile crisis were infinitely higher, but from a student's perspective the confrontation could be understood as a schoolyard squabble, which left them frustrated by the adults' refusal to simply practice what they preached. "If two large countries cannot get along," a girl in Chicago wanted to know, "how can two small children?"[54]

By October 28, desperate for a way out diplomatically, Kennedy and Khrushchev did, in fact, culminate a tense week of secretive talks with a deal to resolve the crisis peacefully: Soviet missiles would be withdrawn and never reintroduced, in exchange for an American pledge to not invade Cuba (along with a hush-hush assurance that America's warheads in Turkey would similarly be removed). Although no equally dramatic televised presidential address announced the resolution of the Cuban missile crisis, its end thawed international relations at the nuclear level. Within ten months, the United States, the Soviet Union, and Great Britain, leaning back from the precipice, signed the long-awaited Limited Test Ban Treaty prohibiting open-air and underwater nuclear testing (a momentous occasion that did warrant a hopeful presidential statement on national television). A new "hotline" installed between the Pentagon and the Kremlin offered better communication between the superpowers to preclude future misunderstandings. The conclusion also quickly tempered the most extreme public anxieties in the United States. It was as if "almost overnight," historian Paul Boyer observed, "the nuclear fear that had been building since the mid-1950s seemed to dissipate."[55]

Contemporary child psychologists, educators, and clergy, however, were more worried than ever about how the prevailing culture of fear, now galvanized by the missile crisis, was already triggering potentially troublesome developmental problems for this cohort. "Any preparations for war have a harmful effect on the population, especially children," began the essay "Nuclear Threat Harms Children" by renowned juvenile author and psychoanalytic researcher Judith Viorst in the winter of 1962. She and other psychologists were specifically concerned about how the ambivalence engendered by civil defense initiatives was becoming a disruptive force in childhood. "America's fallout shelter program may be damaging the mental health of our children," Viorst maintained, especially during the crisis, when many schools staged emergency shelter drills, because it unnecessarily heightened levels of conflict and anxiety in their lives.[56]

Consider, for example, that at 8:42 a.m. on October 30—just prior to a routine civil defense drill that morning—the "Bell and Lights" system at Miraleste Elementary School in Los Angeles County malfunctioned, flashing the yellow-alert alarm signal which meant that a nuclear attack was coming within the hour. For twelve full minutes, three hundred and seventy-five students plus faculty and staff believed that the Cuban confrontation had been reignited and proceeded through their practiced steps. With megaphone in hand, the principal guided teachers, who in turn calmly told their classes—although some were visibly shaking—that this was the real thing, not a drill. As they moved to predetermined assembly areas, teachers sought to reassure each other, the oldest students comforted the youngest, and in some cases children encouraged teachers. Only after everyone was safely off school grounds—the final step in the evacuation process, never actually taken before in drills— did the telephone company trace an equipment failure in the line to the false alarm. While petrified students were left emotionally drained by the ordeal, many parents optimistically commented to reporters that it felt like their families had miraculously been given a second chance . . . to prepare for the next time, when it would be for real.[57]

Left unchecked, preadolescent conflicts with authority over civil defense could account, experts posited, for increased instances of rebellion, delinquency, and, perhaps more disturbingly, erosion of confidence in both themselves and adults. "When the Cuban crisis happened, we were the ones who jumped under school desks and protected our heads from falling roofs that were sure to come," a Tennessee woman wrote. "We were the ones who had slumber parties in the neighbor's fallout shelter. We were the ones who came to the realization that there might not be room for us in that shelter. I think that realization molded" a general skepticism and mistrust which carried over into other phases of children's relationships with the adult world, she said.[58]

Psychologist Sibylle Escalona explored these cognitive matters further, beyond just the impact of civil defense, to include other developmental consequences of nuclear anxiety, the Cuban Missile Crisis, and the worst adult behaviors these times brought out. What she noticed, based on surveys of school-age children conducted around the beginning of 1963, was that the atomic realities of the 1960s were conceivably weakening and impeding the critical developmental processes involving identification and the formation of personal identity in preadolescents. Considering that patterns of adaptation distinguish each stage in child development, for most elementary schoolchildren the chief adaptive processes involve the synthesis and integration of all previous examples of identity into a cohesive sense of self and their proper place in the grander scheme of things. Put another way, children developing normally draw from past internal notions about who they think they are and an external reservoir of role models to formulate their individuality.

In the wake of the Cuban Missile Crisis, nuclear dangers may have made this developmental progress more difficult by polluting children's healthy sense of usefulness with feelings of inadequacy, while also denying them affirmative adult role models. Children not only witnessed their parents' and teachers' fear, despair, and resignation, they were also constantly exposed to adults in print and broadcast media demonstrating a lack of trust and hatred for the communist enemy, reflexively scapegoating the Reds' "worldwide plot to destroy us" for every international incident that did not break America's way. Taken together, these were particularly poor adult behaviors from which to model and integrate.[59]

Escalona's studies raised similar concerns regarding moral development, which she thought could only properly progress when the promise of fulfillment in adulthood is deemed possible. When asked how they imagined the future of the 1970s being different from the present, children offered Great Society-meets-*The Jetsons* visions of less poverty and discrimination against blacks, and better education, healthcare, and housing, together with interplanetary space travel, space stations, domestic automation, flying cars, and household robots. All of these outcomes (fantastical and otherwise), it seemed, were contingent, however, on the future not being ruined by nuclear war or fallout. Seventy percent of respondents revealed that the likelihood of nuclear destruction colored their conceptions of the future, worrying, as a ten-year-old girl from Connecticut did in a letter she sent to Khrushchev, about never getting the opportunity as an adult to experience "a world that is not black with ashes and red with blood." Back in the fall of 1961, when renewed testing was arousing such concern, Escalona had asked fourth and fifth graders in New York City to write one question they had about themselves, their school, or the world. Ninety-eight percent mentioned that there might not be any world waiting for them because of nuclear weapons.[60]

"I am eleven years old and every night I worry," a little boy told John Kennedy. "I worry about what will happen tomorrow, not so much as tomorrow, but as the future. What will be left of this wonderful world in ten years if someone presses the button? What will be left of you and your family? All I'm asking is please think before you press the button, please." A fourth grader at a California Catholic grade school confessed his own disquieting

vision of tomorrow to the president on October 24, 1962. "In my spare time
I will hope and pray for world peace," he solemnly revealed. "For such power
unleashed could cause world destruction. Such destruction would mean war
and there would be little left on this world. . . . [I]t would be a chill to think
of all the people killed in one such explosion of the hydrogen bomb. Here on
my shivering knees I pray there will be no Third World War. No side would
win such victory of a nuclear war. Here I stand one individual." That same
dreadful day, a girl in Texas also wanted her president to understand how,
although only a child, "I find myself in a world of constant fear. A fear of the
Communists, the destruction of the only thing we live for—freedom, but most
important fear of myself. The terrible happenings of today are worse than
those during World War I and II—not materially but spiritually and morally
in all of us. What kind of ideals can young people today have with such things
as segregation and being afraid of our own man-made bombs?"[61]

It should come as no surprise that Benjamin Spock weighed in as well, cau-
tioning parents that so much emotional and cognitive weight heaped on their
children's narrow shoulders would "increasingly distort our children's outlook
on life and impair their ability to cope with it." Referencing other recent studies in his regular column for *Redbook* magazine after the test ban treaty, Spock
decried the disservice done to the nation's children by adults raising them in a
climate of "unwholesome, passive fear." Historically, the baby and child care
guru argued, American children had been socialized by our culture and their
parents to take a "constructive point of view about solutions of the world's
problems," but the current anxieties betrayed this heritage, replacing it with
a worldview built on fatalism, frustration, and blind hatred. Consequently,
this generation of preadolescents "will end up with distinctly impaired personalities compared to Americans of the past. Instead of thinking positively
about what they and other Americans should be doing, they will be worrying
passively about what may be done to us."[62]

It was precisely this atomic alienation which has figured so prominently in our understating of what sparked social activism in the sixties. But in
the younger cohort, born too late to engage in purposeful anti-nuclear work
with organizations such as the National Committee for a Sane Nuclear Policy,
how deeply did the grim prognoses burrow into the immature personalities of
those prone toward helplessness or nihilism? "I'll never forget how I felt when
the Cuban Missile Crisis took place—the feeling of dread, that we were all
going to die and there was nowhere to hide," recalled a woman from Pennsylvania. "It's an unforgettable feeling that sears the mind; I've told my children

that I hope they never have to go through that. When the crisis was resolved, it only made us love JFK even more . . . he confirmed what we already knew—that he was a great leader."[63]

Yet, although this faith in the leadership of John F. Kennedy may have temporarily helped sustain many children through the Cuban Missile Crisis (though it might not have if it had been known how much of Kennedy's management had been at the mercy of chance), his successful handling of the situation does not appear to have reversed fearful trends long-term. As Spock warned in 1964, a cohort preconditioned out of fear to need an evil adversary (if not Communists, then some other group) are particularly susceptible to future presidential calls to arms, and inclined toward more intense McCarthyist hysteria.[64]

CHAPTER FOUR

The Assassination

Kennedy was the first president I remember. I remember
little of his life but lots about his death.
Arkansas woman

A RAINY MORNING IN Dallas on Friday, November 22, 1963, gave way to a
beautiful sunny sky by noon, sixty-seven degrees with a slight wind, absolutely
picture perfect weather for those fortunate enough to be watching the much
publicized presidential motorcade then moving steadily through the downtown
streets from the Love Field airport toward the Trade Mart. A dozen city mo-
torcycle police were escorting the festive caravan of sixteen cars and three buses
featuring the midnight blue, convertible limousine carrying John and Jacqueline Kennedy with Governor John and Nellie Connally, followed by details of
Secret Service and local law enforcement, Vice President Lyndon and Lady Bird
Johnson, administrative staffs, and various other notables of Texas politics. The
enthusiastic lunchtime crowds lining the route down Main Street—quite gratifying given administration concerns over right-wing, John Birch hostility in the
state—stood several deep on the sidewalks and leaned out from office windows
to cheer the passing President and First Lady, he looking tanned in a blue-gray
suit and she positively smashing in a watermelon-pink ensemble with matching
pillbox hat. As the procession slowly turned south onto Elm Street along the
western edge of downtown Dallas around 12:30, the dignitaries—like the two
small American flags on the front bumpers of the presidential limousine—gently
waved at the adoring spectators gathered on the green lawn of Dealey Plaza
park beside the Texas School Book Depository building.

Within a horrific matter of seconds, a sequence of high-powered rounds
from an assassin's Italian bolt-action rifle struck the young president, the sharp

crack of its discharge reverberating off the tall business district walls through American history. The assassination of John F. Kennedy is the second—albeit obviously the most pronounced—of what psychologists refer to as a "flashbulb memory" in the lives of sixties era preadolescents. So exceptionally emotional was the reaction to the president's death that the event was mentally captured with freeze-frame-like clarity and a half-century later can still be summoned with remarkable detail. Those who were adolescents and adults on November 22, 1963, can usually tell you exactly where they were at the time, as can many who were children. For the youngest, these recollections are especially complex, because as one of their earliest memories, if not the first, the death of Kennedy also often brought the first real taste of grief, a consuming emotion that stretched a child's developmental capacities.

When Americans talk about remembering the Kennedy assassination, what most really mean is how they first heard that the president had been shot from a friend, coworker, teacher, or news broadcast, and then how they experienced the memorial ceremonies on television. Although the grainy 8mm images of bystander Abraham Zapruder's color home movie have since provided the nation's choppy mental visualization of the awful series of events—the final bullet's violent impact, a blood-splattered Jacqueline scrambling across the back seat, Secret Service agent Clint Hill leaping onto the trunk of the limousine speeding toward Parkland Hospital—no Americans outside of the grassy area where Main, Elm, and Commerce streets converge under a railroad overpass in Dallas actually witnessed the assassination. There was no footage available in real time, and even if there had been, only housewives and preschool children (and students home from school sick) would have been near a television to see it. Yet, by the time Air Force One carrying President Johnson and Kennedy's coffin arrived back in Washington, D.C., 92 percent of the population had heard, as news traveled across the country, *Newsweek* magazine said, like a "shock wave."[1]

ABC's Don Gardiner in New York broke the story on radio within minutes of the shooting, followed shortly thereafter by Walter Cronkite's interruption of *As the World Turns* on CBS television. Only local stations were covering Kennedy's Texas trip—arranged to shore up state Democratic Party divisions in preparation for the 1964 re-election campaign—which meant that the three networks initially pieced together scattered details from the wire services and network affiliates already on the ground in Dallas. An emotional Cronkite—on his way to becoming "the most trusted man in America" after the *CBS Evening News* expanded its nightly programming to a half-hour in

September—reported that shots had been fired at the motorcade, leaving the president seriously wounded. Over the next hour, speculation over Kennedy's condition, exact whereabouts, and the questions surrounding this attempt on his life filled television and radio air time, leaving the nation increasingly frantic, until at 1:35 p.m. the CBS anchorman somberly confirmed that in the emergency room at Parkland Hospital the president had indeed died. Shock, disbelief, and sorrow were now undeniably binding the nation together, as were anger and conspiracy theories. Even before news of the president's death reached the stunned country, reports came in that Dallas patrolman J. D. Tippit had also been killed. By the time most families were sitting down to dinner around the TV, Lee Harvey Oswald was being charged with the murder of Tippit and Kennedy.[2]

"I remember that day so clearly, even though I was only five," a woman in the rural Midwest said, without a doubt speaking for millions. A San Diego woman who was four that day told me, "I remember being at the Safeway on University Boulevard when President Kennedy was shot. One of the cashiers began to cry. My mother was stunned and speechless, like just about everyone else in the store. I felt like the world had stopped and only I was able to move. When we got home, my mom turned on the TV and spent the rest of the day crying and listening to Walter Cronkite." Across the country in Connecticut, a university professor wrote, "I was born January 2, 1960, the day John F. Kennedy announced his presidential run. As the child of an Irish Catholic family on my mother's side, I was named after him. I wasn't quite four years old when he was assassinated, but I remember it vividly. I was playing with a neighbor in an adjacent yard when my mother called me into the house. The world stopped for several days. I didn't understand it all, but I knew it was a huge deal."[3]

Those old enough to be in school found out there, dumbfounded by the strange sight of shell-shocked teachers pouring out of the classrooms to talk about it and by principals offering prayers over the intercom. A man who was then nine years old remembered, "On the day of JFK's assassination I was a student at St. Mary's School in Dumont, New Jersey. An announcement came over the school loudspeaker that JFK had been shot. That was all we knew. School was dismissed and we were told to pray for the president as we walked home. I did."[4] Speaking to the flashbulb nature of the memory, a Missouri man offered these "absolutely vivid" recollections of being the first grade door monitor at his Catholic elementary school: "You didn't interrupt during teaching time, [but] that afternoon we had just come in from recess, or lunch, I think it was . . . probably about quarter until one, ten until one, in the afternoon on that Friday. And the sister came to the door, knocked on the door, and I jumped up and it was the head teacher there, the principal. She was very gruff and hard, and kind of a Vulcan-like nun, very difficult nun to be with, and she was crying. And when I opened that door and saw Sister Xavier crying, I knew something was wrong. That was very out of character. So I motioned to Sister Paul, my teacher, and she went over and talked to Sister Xavier . . . Sister Paul shut the door, and turned to us kids, and said, 'Kids, I've got some bad news to tell you . . . Today, in Dallas, while the president was going through the parade, a bad man . . . ' Now, she used the words 'bad man,' because we're seven-year-old kids. 'Bad man.' And she motioned pulling a gun out of a holster, and said, 'While the president was in Dallas, a bad man pulled a gun and shot the president.'" Overcome with sorrow, the teacher requested the class take out their rosaries. "We knelt on the floor for probably about an hour and a half, until the buses came at three, to pray the rosary over the intercom. So we prayed the rosary for an hour and a half, kneeling down on wood floors. So we knew it was serious."[5]

In terms of national mourning, the deaths of Abraham Lincoln and Franklin Roosevelt are most comparable, although in the fall of 1963 the overwhelming magnitude of the tragedy reminded many of Pearl Harbor. The Kennedy assassination and particularly its aftermath, however, are unlike anything in the American experience, primarily because television gathered the country together—as if in one vast living room—to bear the sorrow collectively. For four days, from the shooting Friday afternoon to the funeral Monday, the three networks took the unprecedented step of canceling all regularly scheduled programming and advertising to broadcast the ceremonial period of bereavement with no commercial interruptions. The A.C. Nielsen Company reported that an audience of 166 million Americans in 51 million homes—almost nine out of every ten people—tuned in at some point, with millions more viewing around the world via satellite. The average viewer in the United States watched almost thirty-two hours of television coverage, or roughly eight hours a day.[6]

In the hills of West Virginia, a man remembered, "I was not yet in school on this day in 1963, but I can surely remember it. That sunny afternoon (for some reason I can distinctly recall the sun shining on the living room paneling), our normal television programming was taken over by news of the shooting of President Kennedy. Although I may not have understood all the implications, I remember being scared by the apparent gravity of the situation. I also recall a series of phone calls as people reached out to each other about this stunning event." And from the farmlands of Illinois: "I remember watching television and the sudden and constant interruptions and eventually the constant commentary of Walter Cronkite. I kept asking my parents what was happening to the television shows that I always watched. I was five years old at the time and didn't quite understand until they sat with me and informed me of the major events that were happening."[7]

These were also the four days, historians of television point out, when "Uncle Walter" helped transform the culture of American television, the extensive coverage not only legitimizing television in the public mind as the authoritative source for news, but also demonstrating its unparalleled power to alter the stories it covered through the infusion of news *reporting* into the world of news *making*, a trend soon to gather speed in Vietnam. Over a soundtrack of funeral music, recorded Kennedy speeches and videotaped appearances ran along with live interviews from Dallas and Washington, D.C. The networks switched back and forth between images from Andrews Air Force Base, where the casket was lowered down from Air Force One on a hydraulic lift and Jacqueline Kennedy—still in her bloodstained pink dress—accompanied it away in a Navy ambulance, and reports from Dallas, where police were releasing information on Oswald, before returning to political commentators providing the details surrounding Lyndon Johnson's oath of office. On Saturday, as Kennedy lay in state in the White House East Room, cameras showed hundreds of mourners keeping vigil in the drizzling rain outside the executive mansion and in Lafayette Park. Correspondents followed the visitation of public figures such as Harry Truman and Dwight Eisenhower paying their respects as well as pointing out the world leaders representing ninety-two nations, including Khrushchev's first deputy Anastas Mikoyan, who were beginning to arrive in the wet city.

Sunday, November 24, brought the solemn procession of the president's flag-draped casket from the White House to the Capitol and the first "live" televised murder. With nearly 300,000 crowded along Pennsylvania Avenue, the caisson drawn by six grey horses moved almost without sound, only the haunting, muffled drum cadence and clicking hooves, including those of the lone riderless black horse with polished boots reversed in the stirrups. ABC and CBS stayed with the procession, but NBC switched its coverage to the basement garage of the Dallas Police Department, where Lee Harvey Oswald was being transferred to the county jail. There, at 11:21 a.m., viewers witnessed nightclub owner Jack Ruby step from the crowd to gun the suspect down at point-blank range.[8]

Back in the Capitol Rotunda, the national drama continued to unfold Sunday afternoon around the casket, which had been placed reverently upon on the same catafalque used when Lincoln lay in state there in 1865. Jacqueline, Caroline, and John Jr.—the mother in black and the children in matching baby blue—drew near, Mrs. Kennedy and her little girl approaching together hand in hand after her son became a bit fidgety. Describing the poignant and pivotal scene, broadcasting historian Erik Barnouw observed: "The mother showed perfect self-control; the daughter looked to her for cues. The mother knelt and so did Caroline. The mother leaned over to kiss the flag. The child slipped her gloved hand under it and did the same. For millions it was the most unbearable moment of the four days, the most unforgettable."[9]

Before this, news rarely pre-empted prime-time programming, but NBC cameras stayed throughout the night Sunday to continue chronicling the seemingly endless queue of hundreds of thousands who followed the family at the casket, filing past in silence during the public viewing. Ceremonially resting the flag-draped coffin on the Lincoln catafalque in the Rotunda was a deliberate part of the widowed First Lady's directive that all funerary details carefully follow those of America's other martyred president. And the next day, Monday, November 25, the day of the funeral, the symbolism worked to great effect. An audience of essentially every living American watched Jacqueline, her face obscured by a black veil, and the president's brothers, Attorney General Robert Kennedy and Senator Ted Kennedy, elegant in their grey pinstriped pants and dark morning coats, lead the presidential caisson procession back to the White House and then eight blocks away to mass at St. Matthew's Cathedral. At times the networks pooled their camera resources to maintain comprehensive coverage and although on-air commentary remained minimal, the funerary music and bagpiping spoke clearly. A woman recalled, "The only actual thing I remember from November 1963 was the drumbeat in his funeral on TV. Bum-bum-bum, brrrrr ump-bum-ba-bump. Over and over."[10]

Then, on the sidewalk outside St. Matthew's as the military honor guard bore his father's casket back to the caisson for the final procession across the Potomac to Arlington National Cemetery, John F. Kennedy, Jr.—on the occasion of his third birthday—gave Americans another of the most iconic images of our civil religion, lifting his tiny right hand in a farewell salute.[11]

To understand how the assassination of John Kennedy provoked meaningful change in the lives of children, it is necessary to look at the nation's extraordinary immersion in television coverage through the familial relationships of those glued to the set. Much of how preadolescents made meaning of the tragedy, and what their flashbulb memories have meant to them since, stems directly from the dynamic of the intimately interlocked experiences of parent and child in the aftermath. As developmental psychologists point out, "change in the lives of parents is one major route by which broad historical changes alter the lives of children. Conversely, children's life changes . . . have powerful effects on the experience of parents."[12]

A man born in 1959 in a small town in northeastern Pennsylvania highlights these domestic connections: "While at home in the newly built ranch house, Mom tells me Kennedy just got shot. She was fixing her hair in front of my sister's large mirror in the pink bathroom Dad had built especially for them. Tile walls with tile floors with a splash of gray . . . very sixties. I then went to the television to check out the news regarding Kennedy. This was my first initiation into politics and understanding who the president was. It was probably Cronkite who blurted out the bad news. The turquoise rotary phone rings. It was Aunt Andrea informing Mom to check out the news."[13]

"One of my first vivid memories is watching the funeral of President Kennedy on TV," a West Virginia woman told me. "I was only six years old, but I remember the sadness that filled our home. My grandmother, who lived with us, was Catholic and President Kennedy was nearly a saint in her eyes. We were one of those households that had a portrait of him on our wall. Our home was so sad but I didn't know why because at that age, I don't think I was aware of anything that occurred outside my home."[14]

West of the Mississippi River, a high school coach remembers what happened upon dismissal from school that Friday afternoon: "I'm walking across the crosswalk to get into my mom's car, there was a police officer there every day after school, helping us little kids across the street, and he had a badge and a hat and a gun, and to us seven-year-olds he was like, you know, God, and he was crying. So as a young kid, I know this is the first time I ever saw adults cry, maybe outside of a funeral, out in public, just falling out. Losing it. And I thought, 'holy mac' . . . I get into the car, and it's on the radio, and there's my mom, and she's upset. So we picked up all the other siblings from the various schools in the community, and went home. Dad came home from work later, and he was very quiet. Just like everybody else, we just stayed inside, and watched it on the television for the next two or three or four days."[15]

There was initially a striking symmetry between parents and their children, both speaking a common language of progressive shock, disbelief, heartache, and sympathy. This can be accounted for in the way adults helped

preadolescents organize their thoughts by explaining the sequence of events—
"I heard a lot about things I didn't really understand and learned a lot of names
of people," remembers one woman—in addition to unconsciously modeling
emotionally distraught behaviors.[16] One notable exception, though, is crying.
While parents sometimes noticed comparable physical disruptions—loss of appetite, headaches, sleeping difficulties—in their smaller children, the propen-
sity for tears remained a glaring difference in how the generations mourned.
Adults were uninhibited about openly weeping, but from about five years old
to adolescence, the cultural embarrassment associated with this stigmatizing
conduct strictly bounded children's willingness to express their feelings in this
manner. Girls seemed generally more tearful than boys, but both sexes self-
consciously struggled to keep their composure around adults, and in school
often waited for a classmate to break down first in order to help overcome the
shame.[17]

In the greater developmental scheme, the observable reactions of preadolescents may be less meaningful than the ways in which children were challenged by seeing their mothers and fathers, normally efficient and composed,
now reduced to powerlessness, depression, and tears. More than any other
aspect of that day, an Arkansas woman remembers being "traumatized as a
kindergarten student when my parents reacted so intensely to the shooting
of President Kennedy." This was analogous in some respects to the culture
of nuclear numbing, but the immediacy and, moreover, the finality were far
more acute; there was a sense that things were radically out of control. Children simply were not prepared to see their parents, police, and teachers in
such a blatant state of despair. These grownup breakdowns caused bewildering emotional dissonance, which manifested itself in varying degrees and
durations depending on the child's developmental age. For their part, parents
likewise were puzzled, consistently underestimating how upset their sons and
daughters were because of the different nature of childhood grieving. When
there were inconsistences between how children responded and how parents
thought they *should* respond, tensions within the family developed which still
color how both generations experienced the assassination.[18]

For the youngest preschoolers, the level of parental dependency was the
determining variable. When faced with inattentive caregivers who were im-
mobilized hour after hour in front of the television, they tended toward egocentric feelings of resentment toward parents who were unresponsive to their
needs. (Imagine the disappointment of having a birthday fall on one of those
days.) For others in Piaget's preoperational stage, Kennedy's death intensified

and sharpened the common, age-related disorder of separation anxiety. These children had made the Kennedys "real" by imaginatively constructing bonds of affection with the First Family, so they felt the assassination at a more emotional level, as a personal violation of this fictive relationship, and as the death of a father figure. "I first realized" a week after the assassination, a boy told psychologists, "that he wouldn't make another speech like he made in West Berlin or wouldn't be back to his family in Ireland every ten years as he promised nor would he address us in a television speech as Dear Fellow Americans."[19]

In fact, in some of the first research conducted after the assassination, 79 percent of adults similarly described feeling as though someone personally close, perhaps a member of their family, had been killed. A rural Midwestern woman recognized that intimacy in calling to mind how at five years old she had been loaded with three brothers into "the old blue four-door Ford" and driven by their mother to a grandparent's house right after hearing the news. "They were both shocked that something like this happened. My mom and grandma acted like they knew Kennedy personally, and Grandma had tears in her eyes." She continued, "Since his daughter Caroline was my age I felt a connection to the family too," evoking early feelings of empathy and sibling concern. "I wondered how she felt knowing her dad was dead [and] couldn't help but wonder why his mother, Jackie, [let] John-John wear shorts at the funeral when it was so cold in November."[20]

Born in 1958, a woman from small-town Tennessee underscored how close to home the loss hit: "What I remember vividly, even after all these years, was that we had a black-and-white TV in the den and it was on all the time . . . And the part that got my heart for some reason was seeing that horse with the empty soldier boots riding backwards. That was a picture that said to me, well, he's gone forever . . . I don't think I cried, [but] my favorite daddy was no more." Like others between the ages of three and seven, she understood that the father of *real* children had died, leaving his wife a widow and his daughter and son orphans, which invariably started preadolescents thinking about their own families. John and Jacqueline were, after all, roughly the same age as their parents, Caroline and John Jr. their contemporaries. What if something equally bad happened to Dad or Mom? Children grew quite anxious about any parental health problems, especially those requiring a visit to the hospital. A six-year-old girl whose father traveled for a living became so concerned for his safety after the assassination that she tearfully pleaded with him to not get on planes. Many were distressed by thoughts that someone would shoot their father at his workplace and were reluctant to let him out of their sight.[21]

Together with the dread of losing parents, preadolescents shared adult worries about the nation moving forward from November 22. Although there were, of course, vast cognitive differences in how the generations assessed the political and international consequences of the assassination, children were more anxious and felt more vulnerable, just about different things. Race seems to have played an additional role. Scholars found that African Americans demonstrated more grief than any other population group, with black children often more upset, hostile toward Oswald, and worried for the future than whites. African American girls were the most nervous and deeply affected emotionally of all, clearly related to feelings of vulnerability, leaving experts to conclude that "obviously in the minds of Negro children Kennedy was intimately associated with the fate of the Negro."[22]

Preschoolers, already feeling most helpless during the age where sleep and appetite disruptions appear, were developmentally only crossing the threshold of political socialization, and to their way of idealized thinking the existence of the United States depended on President Kennedy. Now robbed of their Rosetta Stone for understanding government, these youngest children in Piaget's preoperational stage struggled with the uncertainty of whether America would now collapse. Although general concern over the future of the country was a constant at every age level after the assassination, apprehension about political continuity decreased sharply with age as older elementary students in the formal operational stage of cognitive development reasoned with increasingly realistic appreciation for the mechanisms of presidential succession. Television coverage proved essential in buttressing their confidence in this process, with images of Lyndon B. Johnson standing next to Jacqueline Kennedy and taking the oath of office alleviating lingering doubts about the stability of American democracy (precisely as the new president reasoned it would).[23]

Indeed, President Johnson's adroit handling of the ship of state during this critical transition period was heralded by the contemporary public and subsequent scholars alike. Just five days after the assassination, he stood before a joint session of Congress and the country quoting from the now prophetic lines of Kennedy's inaugural speech that although the nation's work would "not be finished in the first thousand days, nor in the life of this administration, nor even perhaps in our lifetime on this planet . . . let us begin." Binding himself to that legacy, Johnson pledged: "Today, in this moment of new resolve, I would say to all my fellow Americans, let us continue. This is our challenge—not to hesitate, not to pause, not to turn about and linger over this evil moment, but to continue on our course so that we may fulfill the destiny that history has set for us."[24]

For junior citizens this steady leadership was of particular import since the sanctity of the presidency figured so prominently in their understanding of the national road ahead, and that, in turn, depended in large measure on the smooth continuation of their highly imaginative, fanciful relationship with the officeholder. Thus for many frightened children the assassination of Kennedy was inextricably linked with their being introduced for the first time to the tall Texan and the paternalistic role he would play over the middle years of the sixties. The fluidity of political socialization allowed children to rather quickly transfer their affections to LBJ, "adopted," one might say, by a new political daddy (although black children were suspicious of this Southerner's record on civil rights).

In the weeks and months after November 1963, children set pencil (either the thicker Husky or thinner No. 2) to paper, getting acquainted with their new president. Those letters, at the Lyndon B. Johnson Presidential Library, chronicle preadolescents' perspective on this historic transfer of power and their evolving feelings toward LBJ. True to their predisposition to construct a personalized narrative with the president, all but the oldest elementary school students were likely to imagine Kennedy and Johnson as having been involved in a close partnership—either political or business—and an equally close friendship, both notions fairly wide of the mark. In offering their allegiance and support for Johnson's vow to carry on his fallen friend's efforts, many confidently predicted that Johnson would be ranked alongside Kennedy as "the best presidents ever." "You did a very very good job of taking over the world after President Kennedy died," a ten-year-old girl from New Jersey applauded. In one of the clearest expressions of how political and social change permeate a child's world, a sixth grader in Alaska explained the most difficult presidential succession in American history in the simple language of play: "I have a Kennedy toy when he was rocking in his chair [from an Aurora plastic model kit]. My father is going to make me a toy of you. I will paint it. Then I will make a house, my Barbie as your wife . . . "[25]

Children wanted to get to know the still unfamiliar Johnson and were curious about the personal details of his life, especially as they pertained to his hallowed relationship with Kennedy: what had the two men talked about together, was Kennedy as interesting to be around as he appeared on television, and what did they do for fun? There was a cathartic quality to some of the letters, eager to engage President Johnson in a conversation about Kennedy's greatness, including one from the future presidential historian and Kennedy and Johnson biographer Michael Beschloss, born in 1955. Time and again children asked Johnson to convey their condolences and thoughts to the former occupants of the White House. "If you ever see Mrs. Kennedy tell her that I, and the family are really proud" of her composure and strength, wrote a twelve-year-old Massachusetts girl. Her seven-year-old sister had recently received *The Caroline Kennedy First Lady Dress-Up Book*—with colorful illustrations of Caroline playing dress-up in the clothes of her mother and other first ladies through history—and wanted to let the Kennedy family know how much she loved it.[26]

Still, not all hearts were quieted by thoughts of Lyndon Johnson in the Oval Office. With America, "at a point of uncertainty and vulnerability," as a Pennsylvania woman born in 1960 recalls, fears of other oncoming calamities, occasionally natural disasters, but more often violence and nuclear war, insistently troubled children (and adults as well).[27] Given recent history, some of these fears centered on which one of Kennedy's arch enemies—Nikita Khrushchev or Fidel Castro—was behind the murder. Once Lee Harvey Oswald was apprehended, however, children, unlike adults, almost universally discounted the notion of a Soviet conspiracy. Even while grownups continued to explore the potential connections between Oswald and communism, preadolescent concern with communist involvement was limited to whether the Soviet Union would interpret the assassination as a window of opportunity for aggression and whether Khrushchev might be plotting to test President Johnson in the same manner he repeatedly tested Kennedy. "I remember being in the second or third grade when JFK was shot [and] I will never forget it," a West Coast man wrote, mainly because it happened on his ninth birthday but also for the teacher making the class immediately "get under our desks because they thought we might get bombed."[28]

Given the persistent popular interest in conspiracy theories—involving communists, domestic extremists, organized crime, the military–industrial complex, the CIA, what have you—it is worth noting that in 1963 comparatively few preadolescent children thought anyone other than Oswald killed the president. This adherence to the lone gunman theory is consistent with the Warren Commission's official findings released in September 1964, but was out of step with adult opinion. According to Gallup, the majority of Americans have always supposed that Oswald did not act alone. At the time, 52 percent, counting adolescents, believed "some group or element" to be behind the assassination. These include Bobby Kennedy, who drew connections to Castro's Cuba and the mob, and Johnson, who had assumptions about blowback from CIA plots in the Caribbean. By 1967, as faith in government and Johnson was eroding rapidly in the face of Vietnam, 64 percent of Americans bought into a conspiracy, which is only about three points higher than the number today.[29]

Preadolescents remained hopelessly puzzled by Oswald's motives, though, so the best explanation for this discrepancy is probably developmental. Despite what they heard from parents and other adults to the contrary, children are just not conspiratorially minded by nature. Similar to their incapacity for cynicism, even the most concrete operational thinkers generally still lack the cognitive resources to consistently follow such intellectual shadings. Then there is the case of Jack Ruby. Adults wanted Oswald brought to trial so that the legal system could investigate the plot and bring to light all its nefarious details. To grownups, the assassin's murder was a miscarriage of justice that only deepened the mystery. Preadolescents had fewer qualms. Though Ruby's actions were clearly wrong, in the moral reasoning of those around Kohlberg's level of preconventional ethics, where obedience is predicated on the threat of punishment, Oswald got exactly what he deserved. Children expressed virtually universal hatred and hostility toward Oswald, accepting Ruby's vigilante brand of justice on November 24 as righteous closure to his sinister deed.[30]

Whatever anxiety children may have experienced about whether Lee Harvey Oswald acted by himself paled in comparison to their fear of a lone gunman coming to get them. In the forty-eight hours between that Friday and Sunday, many remembered, they were terrified that Oswald would escape from jail—or be found innocent—only to harm their families. An Ohio man born in 1957 says his most lasting memory of Kennedy being shot involves that restless Friday evening. "I stayed awake that night thinking LHO was still at large and was going to break in our house," he wrote. "Every time the furnace would come on, the air would blow the curtains and I was sure it was him coming in my window. My mom came in during the night and I was still awake. She told me they caught him and I went right to sleep." The fear of a stalking assassin—especially pronounced in seven- to ten-year-old boys, who psychoanalytic researchers recognize as being in Freud's latency period, when sexual energy is directed into other areas—compelled some children to carry baseball bats and other weaponry around in anticipation of having to protect themselves and their loved ones. An eight-year-old in Washington said that upon being told of the assassination at school, the first instinct for he and his classmates was to arm themselves and "immediately set out to the woods to find the killer." Even after Oswald's death at the hands of Ruby, the fear lingered well into 1964, transformed into that of a prowling, anonymous assassin.[31]

While these phobias might last for months, the duration of the mourning period, which was directly correlated to developmental age, remained comparatively short, often abbreviated to the point where children were cast into moral conflict with parents and their peers. Preadolescents, particularly preschoolers, simply cannot sustain grief for as long as adolescents and adults. As the nation observed a weekend-long bereavement, children desperately sought a return to normalcy, getting back into familiar leisure and amusement routines much more quickly than their older siblings and parents. For these young people, everything in the world had just stopped for almost one hundred hours. To manage this distressful intrusion—to maintain some proportion that made sense to them—they engaged with the resource at their disposal: play. By going outside to toss around some Fireball XL5 Magnetic Darts or holing up in a bedroom to assemble a Mr. Machine robot, children were not necessarily isolating themselves from the collective experience as a sign of disrespect. Rather, they were integrating these strange events into their real life (admittedly with varying degrees of success). After all, even the Kennedy children were deemed too young to continue on with the funeral procession from St. Matthew's to Arlington. But as the weekend wore on, parents complained of detached sons and daughters not properly observing the seriousness and solemnity of the occasion, even when that meant something as innocuous as styling Barbie's hair in front of the television. On occasion, punishments were meted out.[32]

In recounting her own dutiful sense of joining in the televised wake as an adult, cultural critic Marya Mannes reflected many other adults' expectations for their children. "This is not viewing. This was total involvement," Mannes wrote. "I stayed before the set, knowing—as millions knew—that I must give myself over entirely to an appalling tragedy, and that to evade it was a treason of the spirit."[33] For older elementary school students just beginning the difficult chore of basing their ethical decisions not on "what's in it for me" but rather on higher ideals of loyalty and family expectations (Kohlberg's conventional ethics), being considered unfaithful to the president really stung. Yet, many still begrudged Kennedy for this unwelcome interruption of their personal lives. "I remember the whole funeral went on for days with them carting the body down the street before finally being buried with this big ceremony where they lit the eternal flame," one man wrote. "Mostly I remember how I just wished that they'd bury his ass and get it over with."[34]

All the highlights of a child's autumn social calendar were wiped out: school plays—postponed; dance and music recitals—canceled, extracurricular activities—forget about them. Preemption of regularly scheduled programming may have been the most disturbing development of all. Saturday mornings were just different without *Captain Kangaroo* and *The Adventures of Rin Tin Tin* to start the day on CBS or *The Magic Land of Allakazam* over on ABC. And while no primetime on Friday and Saturday nights was not so bad, Sunday was a whole other story, with children deprived of CBS's *Lassie* and *My Favorite Martian* leading up to *Ed Sullivan*, or *Disney* a couple of clicks down the dial. "Most people my age remember what they were doing or where they were the exact moment of President Kennedy's death," a Florida woman born in 1957 says. "I only remember that his funeral was on every channel that we had on our TV, preventing me from watching anything more uplifting for a child."[35]

So intimately attached to Kennedy—the affection and admiration already beginning to deepen with his passing—but so resentful of him and their parents' disapproval, children experienced ambivalence in the truest sense: simultaneous and contradictory attitudes or feelings toward an object, person, or action. Some acted out inappropriately, either as a defense mechanism or in defiance. An overweight twelve-year-old joked at school that he wished Oswald would have saved him all the trouble by doing this before Kennedy had created the President's Council on Physical Fitness. There was a noticeable decline in shooting games among boys; however, a few adopted Kennedy themes and targets. Always out of adult earshot, other jokes in distinctly poor taste made their way through the playground and lunchroom circuit: "What did Caroline get for her birthday? A Jack-in-the-box."[36]

Strictly speaking, the interment of President John F. Kennedy brought to a close these harrowing days of national observance. States declared Monday, November, 25, 1963, a legal holiday, closing many banks, schools, and offices across the land. In the elementary schools that were still open, teachers hauled the black-and-white televisions back into the same classrooms where their students had watched the inauguration not three years before. At noon church bells chimed and the nation's flags were officially lowered to half-mast, although most had been in that position since Friday. On Tuesday, when businesses reopened, regularly scheduled television programming resumed, students returned to class, and Americans carried on. Some things were postponed or discontinued out of propriety and respect. President Johnson postponed lighting the national Christmas tree until December 22. Kennedy

Halloween costumes never reappeared in stores—the Ben Cooper Company destroyed all remaining stock—and the best-selling *First Family* record album, a comedic parody, was removed from the market, and many copies already purchased as Christmas presents were never opened. A DC *Superman* comic book story titled "Superman's Mission for President Kennedy," featuring the Man of Steel helping children meet the goals of the President's Council on Physical Fitness, was postponed until July 1964 (issue #170) as a tribute. The story was fitting, given that a typical six-year-old boy later described how he pretended to be Superman so that he could catch Oswald's bullets before they reached Kennedy.[37]

As a woman in Pennsylvania remembers, "everyday events continued and before you knew it life's daily tasks took over the sadness. Life moved on . . . Our country and its business would be handled by people who knew what needed to be done and they would take care of it. Children needed to be raised, and my father who worked as a laborer in the steel mill in Bethlehem had a family to take care of." The mood and mind of the nation certainly wandered in the weeks thereafter—the seven episodes of *The Beverly Hillbillies* airing immediately after the assassination are among the fifty most watched programs of all time—but would not really be uplifted until seventy-three million people (the largest non-news audience to date) tuned in to Ed Sullivan on February 9, 1964, to see the Beatles. In the eyes of the young, the exuberance of those four Englishmen—and the five catchy songs they played that Sunday night: "All My Loving," "Till There Was You," "She Loves You," "I Saw Her Standing There," and "I Want to Hold Your Hand"—finally made it all right to smile again in America.[38]

What were the developmental results, or at least the implications, in the lives of preadolescents from this period, possibly the most intensely painful of the last half-century? Psychiatric researchers Martha Wolfenstein and Gilbert Kliman predicted in 1965 that for the youngest children, "to the extent that their personal experience survives," the death of Kennedy "will evoke something strange, something that intruded into the usual round of life and could not be quite assimilated."[39] This undoubtedly has held true, although the emotional disorganization Wolfenstein and Kliman spoke of has served as something of a catalyst in the pursuit of cognitive equilibrium. Put more simply: children learned important lessons from Kennedy's death which have informed their behaviors since. The notion of equilibrium is central to Piaget's theory of how children understand new social experiences. When preadolescents make sense of their world using the mental "schemes" currently at their disposal, they are said to be cognitively in a state of equilibrium. If something of a peculiar nature disrupts this comprehension—disequilibrium—children naturally modify their schemes to account for these new realities and reestablish comprehension. In this recovery of equilibrium, a child's thinking advances; development has taken place. Some ages—five to seven years old and again between nine and eleven—are more inclined toward this ongoing dialectical process because greater engagement with the wider world exposes children to more confusion. In general when children craft new states of equilibrium, broader worldviews are changed and personal histories are revised. Accordingly, all new environmental stimuli encountered along the way to maturity will be processed in relation to this new reality, with the learner moving, as historian William Tuttle explains, vertically upward through development.[40]

For many children, Kennedy's assassination was their first real experience with grief, their first true sense of loss intruding upon their childhood. In the hundreds of stories that were shared with me, vivid language about how this "profoundly significant event" is still "embedded in my mind" often evokes Piaget's theory of adaption or adjustment of schemes in working through anguish toward equilibrium. The most immediate example of this process is how the assassination experience enabled children to later cope with the loss of *real* loved ones.[41]

In their 1964 yearbooks, elementary school students displayed these approaches publicly by eulogizing Kennedy and designing "In Memoriam" tributes, while the more emotionally invested frequently expressed themselves privately through poetry. A New York City girl of twelve—"a democrat even though I'm not old enough"—struggled to sort out her complex feelings of mortality and transition in just such a poem, entitled *John F. Kennedy (Present) and (Past)*, that she shared with Pierre Salinger (who stayed on as Johnson's press secretary until March 1964) in hopes that he might find time to critique it.

One Minute the President steps of[f] the plane and straightens his suit a bit
His smile is reassuring and content on his face
He takes hold of Jackie[']s hand and helps her to be seated in the car
Then he gets in and settels [*sic*] himself in his seat
He reaches in his coat pocket
He pulls out some notes and studies them
He looks up What does he see?
He sees smiling faces, waving hands, All are waiting to be recognized
Once more he looks up more hands waving more enthusiastically

He waves back because he is thrilled and very happy he has a feeling that he
likes Dallas
People smiling, waving, and cheering
Suddenly and horrified there is the ringing of a shot that roared through the
crowds of Dallas
Another shot and still one more
He slumps in Jackie[']s lap
Is he still thrilled and very happy?
It is not a different man that boards the plane but a different body
He steps of[f] the plane and clears his throat hurriedly He grasps Jackie[']s
arm, but is unsure of himself
She is seated in the waiting car and followed by Mr. Kennedy uncomfortably
he settels [*sic*] down in the back seat
He [Johnson] takes out a worn paper and goes over the events of the past few
hours of tragedy
he falters
In time to come he will learn balance (poise).

The inspiration for exploring her depths of emotion in verse came from
Mrs. Kennedy's boldness and poise, the girl wrote. In thinking of the very
recent death of her own grandmother, she confided that initially "I don't think
I could have done so well" because "I loved her more than anyone in the entire
world." But on further reflection on the president's death she had come to the
realization that "on second thought nobody can live forever."[42]
    A San Diego woman born in 1959 remembers a similar accommodation. "I
think it was my first recollection of feeling deeply sad," she reveals. "Several
years later, when my own father died, I thought a lot about John-John and
Carolyn. Knowing that they had experienced losing their dad helped me and
made me feel less different."[43] A boy from the heartland, born in 1956, remembered drawing on the assassination to adjust his perspective on the thousands of soldiers sacrificing their lives in Vietnam. From his small, hometown
vantage point, the war in Southeast Asia was a remote, far-off abstraction,
with little relevance save for the disconnected images of combat and perplexing casualty numbers on the evening news. He admittedly never "got"
the significance of the Vietnam War, or thought much about it, even when
a young serviceman from his community was killed. Only when confronted with the flag-draped coffin at the funeral home did the war become real
for him. Instantaneously his mind seized on November 1963—"this is like

Kennedy, this is like Kennedy's funeral"—and he solemnly understood the occasion, and, more broadly, the war in Vietnam, for what it was becoming for America: bitter, anguished, and bewildering. After that day, he remembered, he followed events in Southeast Asia with grave concern.[44]

These developmental processes also involve reconciling uncomfortable feelings of shame and guilt. Probably the most striking difference between what preadolescents took away from the assassination compared to adults and adolescents is their guilt-ridden recollection of not being sufficiently sorrowful. The most extreme, and isolated, examples come from the South-Texas, in particular—where students, often seated in segregated elementary school classrooms, actually cheered or otherwise celebrated the news of Kennedy's assassination. Even those who only witnessed reactions so foreign to the normative experience still shudder at the memory of these disgraceful displays.[45]

Often, children who felt ashamed for being selfish have taken steps over their life course to atone. A West Virginia man born in 1958 told me: "I will say that your memory of the Watergate hearings is similar to my pre-school memory of the JFK assassination. It seemed the news coverage and funeral went on for days, and deprived us little kids of our cartoons . . . As I grew older, I realized my reaction was a bit 'childish' and perhaps became more appreciative of JFK to make up for my lack of concern about his death," he continued. "I regret that the feeling I most remember from those dark days in November was resentment. As a preschooler, I didn't like it that my cartoons were being pre-empted for this wall-to-wall news coverage on all three channels. All-news, all-the-time formats may seem normal to today's cable news channel generation, but it hardly ever happened in the old days."

The Kennedy influence extended over this man's life course, including his moderate politics. He "became somewhat embarrassed by this main memory of being more upset over missing my cartoons than by the assassination of a good president. It made me more interested in JFK as a way to make up to him for the disrespect I displayed." He completed a law degree and worked for NASA in Washington, D.C., as a program analyst in the mid-1980s. "One item I treasured [while still an undergraduate] in the Student Government office at UC [University of Charleston, West Virginia] was the framed JFK picture. During my first stint in Washington, I purchased a similar JFK poster from the gift shop at the Kennedy Center, which followed me through grad school, law school, and beyond (I'm guessing my ex-wife finally talked me into getting rid of it)." Today, while teaching constitutional law and American government in the evenings at a West Virginia university, those imprints are still never far from his mind. "I have a recording of his inauguration speech that I have played for many of my classes," he wrote, "so that they can hear his immortal words—'Ask not what your country can do for you, ask what you can do for your country'—in their original context. I'm still captivated by the events of November 22, 1963, and hope that in the long-term future, this date is not looked back upon as the high-water mark of the American empire." Although well into his fifties, he recently joined the Peace Corps and served in the West Indies alongside a new generation of volunteers.[46]

By grounding his account of his own trajectory within broader judgments regarding America in the early 1960s, this man reveals how some preadolescents approached equilibrium by beginning to think historically. More so even than Kennedy's inauguration, his death compelled children to contemplate for the first time the context of history, and, moreover, their place in it, using exactly the types of higher-level thinking skills their teachers so arduously promoted. They were not just remembering where they were on November 22, but purposefully weaving their own personal threads into the tapestry of our national narrative, in what historians Roy Rosenzweig and David Thelen term "popular history making." In tracing a personal trajectory that led back to the classroom, a man born in 1956 described the role of the assassination in these mental operations: "I think that was the point that I knew that I, too, could live in history like the history I was reading in the books. And I was already reading history at six, seven, eight years old. I read every Daniel Boone book I could get my hands on . . . It triggered real quick that this is historic . . . that's where I got a sense of the political world," he wrote. "And as a history teacher now, I look back and think 'what motivated me to get into history?' and I would say two things: My grandmother lived with us, she was born in the 1890s, and she would tell me stories, and that kind of inspired my thinking about what it must've been like. And then, I think, the JFK assassination . . . knowing that the Lincoln assassination was a big topic, I realized that this too would be a topic in a book, and I was alive during it. That placed me in history, and placed history on me."[47]

Of course, relatively few can map out such a neatly unfettered path in making sense of their lives. For most, the developmental results of the Kennedy assassination are far more ambiguous. In fashioning their own popular histories, many who were ten to twelve years old at the time share the baby boom sense of incompleteness and nostalgia for what might have been were Kennedy's vision not cut short. With the Cuban Missile Crisis behind them, a nuclear test ban treaty, and tax cuts and civil rights bills in Congress, they were getting so close—much was still forthcoming. British journalist Henry Fairlie referred to this promise as the "politics of expectation," and indeed, the older baby boom children of the 1950s heard in Kennedy's death a clarion call to activism. Born in Atlanta in 1950, one man explained that when he says "JFK's assassination was burned forever into my consciousness," what he means is that "the assassination was a dividing point for me. I remember 'Before Kennedy' and 'After Kennedy.'" Socially conscious adolescents of the 1960s devoured Paul Goodman's *Growing Up Absurd* and strained to decipher *The Freewheelin' Bob Dylan* album so that they might write the idealistic position papers and form the organizations that would provoke America to fulfill its unrealized potential; they mobilized the sixties.[48]

But for preadolescents, the meaning of the assassination was quite different. They got all the agony, but none of the ecstasy. Way too immature for Ginsberg or Kerouac, or, later, even Barry McGuire's "Eve of Destruction," they were still too young to participate in any way with the movement forming around them. They were Kennedy's children, all right, but just not far enough along in their political socialization or intellectual and physical maturity to leave the nest quite yet when he died. Which leads to the first appearance of a theme that runs through this book: this cohort's frustration at being left out of the era's sound and fury, at having *missed* the sixties. In their fascination with the Kennedy aura and the romance of the space program, these children got close enough to almost touch what they now consider to be the hallmarks of that decade, but by the time they were old enough to engage meaningfully, the battles had already been fought, the joy diminished, the historical moment passed.

People comment time and again that the death of Kennedy hurt them more profoundly, more deeply, than did the deaths of their own parents. What they are trying to say is that when a parent—or someone close—dies, part of your past is laid to rest with them. When Kennedy died, there was a sense of losing the future. Many children felt doubly cheated, out of their relationship with a beloved president an, by virtue of their age, out of their chance to carry on his crusades of commitment and sacrifice. Several correspondents told me about hearing that the nation lost its innocence when Kennedy was assassinated. While they believe they were too young to know what that meant at the time, it makes sense to some now that their bitterness over being left out is linked to the innocence that was lost.

Consequently, this cohort's idealization of Kennedy and the idealism his New Frontier engendered can become frozen in place, in much the same way mental pictures of JFK and RFK remain forever young, pristine, and immune to the ravages of aging. A few days after Kennedy's funeral, Jacqueline Kennedy gave an interview to journalist and historian Theodore White, published in *Life* on December 6, 1963, in which she solidified her husband's martyrdom for progress and equality by likening it to the end of Camelot. Those emotionally involved with Kennedy—especially those identifying themselves as Democrats—tell of how they remain "occupied" with his "fairy-tail [*sic*] Camelot" and what it stood for in their minds so long ago. As Mrs. Kennedy—now buried next to her husband near the Eternal Flame she lit on the day of his funeral—had hoped, some still liken him to the only other president from their civics class they remember being assassinated, Abraham Lincoln. And while older baby boomers may have grown cynical and skeptical of Kennedy's dispassionate "corporate liberalism" during the exhausting conflicts of the 1960s, younger boomers find it more difficult to surrender—like those last layers of an onion—their unquestioning adulation. This helps explain why, despite scholars generally placing John Kennedy somewhere between thirteenth and eighteenth (squarely in the above-average category) in their rankings of American presidents, the public still consistently grades him closer to Lincoln and Roosevelt. Just think of how differently the American story would have proceeded, they ponder, had Kennedy spared us from Vietnam and Watergate.[49]

It appears those who are unfulfilled still search for Kennedy in some capacity. Lincoln's secretary of war Edwin Stanton is reported to have said upon the president's death, "Now he belongs to the ages," but many children of the sixties still want their time with JFK. They imagine they catch glimpses of him periodically, in the lowest places—legend has it that the marina flag in the opening sequence of *Gilligan's Island* is at half-mast for Kennedy—and in the highest. In one of the first presidential elections in which they could vote, the charisma and dynamism of Republican Ronald Reagan struck those chords. And in 2004 millions rushed to embrace the Kennedy analogies with the Democrat Barack Obama, reliving in that campaign, they thought, the exhilaration as an adult of what they could only remember from a child's perspective in 1960. In both cases, the attraction may have been unrequited. Yet, they remain vigilant. As a woman in Pennsylvania explained, "When President Kennedy was assassinated we all cried and the awful feelings permeated our lives . . . I didn't think anyone could ever take his place. Until this day, I'm still looking for another JFK."[50]

CHAPTER FIVE

LBJ and the Great Society

You may not be as popular as Abe Lincoln but you will be in a few years.
Illinois schoolboy to President Johnson

"THE CHALLENGE OF the next half century," Lyndon B. Johnson told University of Michigan graduates on May 22, 1964, "is whether we have the wisdom to use [America's] wealth to enrich and elevate our national life, and to advance the quality of our American civilization . . . For in your time we have the opportunity to move not only toward the rich society and the powerful society, but upward to the Great Society." With these commencement remarks—exactly six months to the day since taking office—President Johnson introduced Ann Arbor and the nation to what would become the defining vision of his administration, and in so doing began assuming the presidency in his own right. "The Great Society rests on abundance and liberty for all," he explained that afternoon with an inspirational tone the country certainly recognized, even if the cadence and Southern accent still rang a bit oddly. "It demands an end to poverty and racial injustice, to which we are totally committed in our time." But these structural reforms to American life would be "just the beginning," the president said. Qualitative changes must shape the political agenda ahead in order to ensure the realization of his vision: "The Great Society is a place where every child can find knowledge to enrich his mind and to enlarge his talents. It is a place where leisure is a welcome chance to build and reflect, not a feared cause of boredom and restlessness. It is a place where the city of man serves not only the needs of the body and the demands of commerce but the desire for beauty and the hunger for community."[1]

In the broad context of modern American political history, Johnson's ambitious Great Society can be understood as the third (and final) major era of reform in the twentieth century, building on the Progressives' regulatory state while expanding the New Deal's welfare safety net through the pursuit of social justice for all. The cherished notion of equality of opportunity lay at its core. LBJ believed that what had left so many mired in poverty and prohibited countless others from achieving the American Dream, even in the midst of unprecedented national affluence, was a debilitating combination of scant education, inadequate health care and nutrition, substandard housing, insufficient job training, and outright racism. Johnson aimed to eliminate these barriers and level the playing field so that his fellow Americans could master their own fate. "I know that government cannot resolve all problems," he conceded. "It cannot make men happy or bring them spiritual fulfillment." But he steadfastly believed that "it can attempt to remedy the public failures at the root of so many human ills."[2]

And so, this political force of nature from the Texas Hill Country, arguably without peer in the annals of American government for his negotiating instincts, knowledge of congressional procedure, and mastery of legislative tactics, harnessed those tremendous talents—along with Democratic majorities of 68 to 32 in the Senate and 295 to 140 in the House during the 89th Congress—to enact hundreds of laws and public policies which for a stretch between 1964 and 1966 outpaced the legislative yield of even his mentor, Franklin D. Roosevelt. In its sheer breadth, there was seemingly something for everyone in the Great Society, and friend and foe alike detected more than a hint of paternalism in Johnson's approach to governing. A "Big Daddy from the Pedernales [River]," in the words of historian Paul Conkin, Johnson provided for the nation's manifold needs with the common parental expectation of gratitude and compliance. His three civil rights laws—the Civil Rights Act of 1964, the Voting Rights Act of 1965, and the Fair Housing Act of 1968—remain the centerpiece of a series of landmark legislation highlighted by the Economic Opportunity Act (1964), the Elementary and Secondary Education Act (1965), the Higher Education Act (1965), the Medicare and Medicaid amendments to the Social Security Act in 1965, and the Model Cities Act of 1966. Beyond these major bills, the Great Society covered a diverse spectrum, from consumer protection in the form of a truth-in-packaging act to highway beautification and urban mass transportation, and from the creation of the National Endowment for the Arts and National Endowment for the Humanities to conservation measures aimed at clean air, water quality, and solid waste disposal.

Despite the often contentious and complicated legacy of the Johnson presidency, due primarily to his handling of the Vietnam War and the nation's rightward political orientation since, any understanding of the 1960s must take account of LBJ, one of the era's most towering figures. The Johnson years are of particular significance in examining how the rapidly changing political landscape of the sixties produced consequences for children, given that a substantial number of his initiatives either focused on or disproportionally benefited youth, especially those growing up in poverty. Every president since Theodore Roosevelt has articulated in some fashion how vital it is to our health as a nation to keep the road toward the American Dream open to all children, and modern child welfare policy in the United States is predicated on the federal and state role in safeguarding equality of opportunity for the youngest of its citizens. Many scholars characterize the Great Society as a watershed in this progressive expansion of the federal government's responsibility for children's well-being over the course of the twentieth century.[3] Historians point out that there is a shared framework between Kennedy's unfinished New Frontier and Johnson's Great Society. Indeed, several pieces of legislation most pertinent to children—ending racial segregation, funding education, housing reforms and urban renewal programs, a national health care program—were first introduced into Congress prior to the assassination and only brought to fruition by LBJ. To take one example, the food stamp program was a food assistance voucher through the Department of Agriculture piloted by Kennedy in 1961 that Johnson expanded and made permanent.

Yet the imprints of these two presidencies on the lives of preadolescents are distinctively different. John F. Kennedy's hold on children's hearts and imaginations was broad and deep; theirs was primarily an emotional bond. Lyndon B. Johnson's presidency, despite its messianic spirit, was less emotive and was mostly tangible through its laws and public policies. Johnson himself inspired less passion and romance. There was no sense of triumph or tragedy, nor were there memorable performances of presidential eloquence and charm. If LBJ was giving a speech on television, you were out of luck—it was going to be a long night. I found far fewer enduring recollections of Johnson and no flashbulb memories of exactly where one was when he declared war on poverty or signed the Elementary and Secondary Education Act. Lyndon Johnson's effective absence from children's material culture reveals as much. Supply and demand had made Kennedy's likeness a routine part of playtime, with any number of now very collectible costumes, scale plastic models, books, puzzles, and games, such as The Exciting New Game of the Kennedys, introduced by the Harrison & Winter company in 1962. This campy game, with Kennedy family faces featured on a Mount Rushmore-like illustration on the box, afforded young players the fun of managing important Kennedy family matters—"Personal Image" and "Social Standing" among them—using play money illustrated with the image of patriarch Joseph Kennedy. Although Johnson's personal fortune was intriguing to the public as well, aside from a coloring book and an LBJ cowboy costume in the Sears Christmas catalog, only Remco marketed LBJ toys. One was a sixteen-inch doll with fitted fabric clothing and plastic Stetson hat, and the other a bobblehead doll for the 1964 election (there was a Barry Goldwater version too).[4]

This is not to say that the normal course of childhood political socialization failed to produce the same warm feelings of adulation and idealization that were expressed to John Kennedy. To the contrary: "As far as I'm concerned," a fifth grade boy wrote to Johnson, "you are the best president I have heard of," adding, "And I think I have heard of most of them." A ten-year-old in Kansas launched a personal campaign to have LBJ pictured on the largest denomination of currency the United States Treasury printed, although he was unsure exactly what amount that might be. And in many cases, affections were transferred from Kennedy to Johnson in the healing process. "In my bedroom over my bed I have a picture of The Late President John Fitzgerald Kennedy," a twelve-year-old New York girl explained, and now "a picture of you The New Present President Lyndon Baines Johnson." "You are good to us," an eight-year-old Maryland boy expressed. "We need a president to take Mr. Kenn[e]dys place." A letter from a Texas girl spoke to the transfer of benevolent parental qualities to this new father figure. "I am eleven years old and in all my life I think I never thought anyone could do as much as you and Mr. Kennedy did," she wrote in May 1964. "You two, and my dad, are the finest men in the world." She continued, "Father's Day is coming soon, and the way I figure, you and Dad will get a Father's Day gift from me. I would like to know what you want. You see, you're kind of like a 2nd father to me. You're sort of the father of our country."[5]

Just as Lyndon Johnson's landslide victory over his Republican challenger Sen. Barry Goldwater in November 1964 legitimized his presidency and the Great Society, the election delighted his preadolescent backers, whose support in the My Weekly Reader poll and classroom ballot boxes far outdistanced the 61 percent of the popular vote the president received. "Johnson, Johnson, he's our man, Goldwater lives in a garbage can!"[6] The imaginative relationships constructed by egocentric young children to help them grasp the concept of the presidency in their first steps toward political socialization can be seen here too. A six-year-old from Brooklyn wrote that he was inviting himself to the White House to eat spare ribs with his friend Lyndon Johnson, and a group of Ohio boys invited the president to be an honorary member of their club, enclosing a membership card and ten dollar invoice for his share of the clubhouse building fund. Children with the same initials as the president were eager to let him know what they had in common and how much they loved the rhyming slogan "All the way with LBJ!" In their gifts of artwork, children took pains to incorporate symbolism the president would recognize: horses, the state of Texas, a Texas flag, and cowboy hats. They posed jokes along the lines of "What is the national Bird? Mrs. Johnson" and often portrayed Lady Bird with actual feathers. Whereas some boys had related to Kennedy through sport, both girls and boys often connected with Johnson though their mutual love of animals, usually dogs. The presidential beagles—named Him and Her—were particular favorites; aside from Snoopy, the two were the most famous beagles in America, and *Life* even put them on the cover in June 1964. Although children voiced concern earlier that year when Johnson lifted Him up by the ears for reporters—"If you think that picking up dogs by the ears is funny. Have someone do it to you!!"—they sent him elaborate, and sometimes long-winded, stories about their own pets. When Him died in the summer of 1966, the White House received an outpouring of sympathy from American children for the loss of Johnson's "happy friend," some sharing stories of grieving over their own pets killed by a car (as Him was) and others poignantly expressing—a few in poetry—how it felt like their own beloved family dog had been taken from them.[7]

In the children's correspondence at the respective presidential libraries, there is an intriguing variation in the way children looked at Johnson as compared to Kennedy. Preadolescents appear to have innately grasped the paternalistic nature of the Great Society, and they asked Johnson for things far more frequently than they did JFK. Whereas children sometimes *sent* money to the Kennedy White House for the space program, *requests* for money were more common in the mid-1960s, usually modest amounts ranging from five to forty dollars on behalf of themselves or their parents. Sometimes they wanted material objects—bicycles, typically—that their hardworking moms and dads could not afford. A few of the more creative children appealed to Johnson with ideas for Great Society programs that might remedy the public failures at the root of so many children's ills.

"I am writing a letter of protest," a crusading New Yorker wrote, "in defense of all students in the United States besides myself . . . I'm twelve and in sixth grade. In our school, it starts at 9:00 and ends at 3:00. Isn't school officially over at 3:00? I don't mind homework, but wait till I get older. I think school should not be 'extended' with homework. It is a law, as far as I know that there is only 5 hours of school, not more." On the related matter of cheating, she beseeched the president, "Can you make a teeny (for me) law against this copy-cat business?"[8]

A fourth grade student in Indiana grounded her appeal to Johnson in their mutual concern for pet safety. "I'm worried about all the dogs that are being dognapped for experiments," she explained. "Try to get the Congress to pass a bill to pervent [sic] this. We would hate to have our Cocker Spaniel dog 'dognapped.' We love her very much. I know you would hate this to happen to 'Him' or anyone else's pet dog. Please talk to the Supreme Court too. Maybe they could do something. P.S. My dog's name is Taffy."[9]

Others went right over their parents' heads, seeking federal arbitration to settle any number of family quarrels. A number of letters involved the generational tension over the cultural phenomenon of Beatlemania surging through the country during that group's first American tour in 1964. Girls loved John, Paul, George, and Ringo, and when parents did not share this fondness with equal enthusiasm—or even banned the *Meet the Beatles!* album or prohibited concert attendance—preadolescents (and adolescents) took their case to LBJ, whose own young daughters, Luci and Lynda, probably understood what it meant to be a fan. A group in California invited the president to become an honorary member of their Beatles fan club, pointing out that it made good politics considering Paul McCartney had told reporters in Chicago that he supported Johnson over Goldwater. Many just sought validation from the White House that their affections were not as misplaced as their parents said. Others wanted an official statement in support of the Beatles that could be taken back to mom and dad. "My friend and I are having trouble with her daddy," one Mississippi child wrote. "We want to go see the Beatles, and we could go if we had an older person to go with us, accept [sic] we can't find one. We were wondering if you would write me back a letter telling us whether we should go or not, and I'm hoping that you think we should, because there comes only one chance in a girl's lifetime to see the Beatles in person." They apparently did not know that Johnson was already on record refusing sixteen-year-old Luci's request that the Beatles play at the White House during their February stop in Washington, D.C., two days after their first *Ed Sullivan* appearance, because, the president thought, a chorus of "Yeah, yeah, yeah!" echoing through the Executive Mansion would be improper so soon after the assassination.[10]

A ten-year-old fifth grader in Arizona succinctly captured these preadolescent sentiments toward the decade's second political father figure with her ode to LBJ entitled "Our President."

> President Johnson is a good president indeed
> If I had a political problem
> I'd go to him in need
> He makes a lot of speeches
> He gives a lot of talks
> And back at the White House
> He takes his beagle for walks
> I know he comes from Texas
> Where the long horned cattle grow
> And if he wanted relaxation
> I think that's where he'd go
> I like President Johnson alot [sic]
> I am sure
> If I went to the White House
> I'd want him to give me the tour
> He has a wife and two daughters you know
> And of course all four of them
> Are always on the go
> They all have the initials L.B.J.
> That is most unusual
> Wouldn't you say?
> So if someone asked me
> Who's the best president I know
> I'd say L.B.J. is the best
> From head to toe[11]

Nevertheless, the truest measure of Lyndon B. Johnson on the lives of children in the 1960s remains the means by which his Great Society affected their material circumstances, resulting in empirical improvements in child welfare and a number of qualitative developmental outcomes as well. Like the New Deal that inspired it, the Great Society never followed a coherent blueprint—Johnson's grasp of the actual policy details seems to have been as questionable as Roosevelt's—and it instead comprised various imaginative plans crafted by an administration working to address societal problems as they saw them at mid-decade. This has led many Americans to see Johnson's Great Society and his War on Poverty as synonymous. In terms of children, this confusion is academic, considering that both made federal investments in the future of youth that were carried out at the local level by child welfare agencies, public health services, school boards, and community organizations. Liberal advocates envisioned the two entities being mutually supportive, with antipoverty strategies such as job training picking up the slack for shortcomings in other areas, such as inadequate entitlements from Aid to Families with Dependent Children (AFDC). Believing that federal money can substantively impact the life of a child, Johnson recommended and Congress enacted legislation investing $7.3 billion in American youth in 1965, up from $3.5 billion in 1960. In fiscal 1968, those federal expenditures rose to over $11.5 billion, or more than three times the amount spent the year Kennedy was elected. As investments, some initiatives paid off with immediate dividends while others did not reach fruition until the 1970s or beyond.[12]

In proclaiming that "this administration, here and now, declares unconditional war on poverty" in his first State of the Union address on January 8, 1964, President Johnson was advancing another programmatic idea from John F. Kennedy. The basic concept of the War on Poverty—channeling federal monies into neighborhood organizations developed and facilitated with the "maximum feasible participation" of the poor—took root with the Kennedy brothers just weeks before the assassination. John had been increasingly interested in Michael Harrington's observations on the limitations of the liberal welfare state in his influential 1962 book *The Other America* as well as Martin Luther King's economic critique of race relations. Robert had been similarly impressed by the 1961 Juvenile Delinquency and Youth Act's experimental emphasis on empowering the poor to help reduce urban crime. At President Kennedy's urging that fall, Walter Heller, the chair of the Council of Economic Advisers, began a wide-ranging conversation with the White House over poverty and possible federal action, a dialogue that continued in earnest with Johnson. For the new president, the War on Poverty presented a golden opportunity to reconcile his empathy toward the disadvantaged with immediate political realities. Smoldering suspicion of his liberal credentials by the left wing of his own party (which had almost torpedoed his selection as Kennedy's running mate in 1960) needed to be headed off at the pass prior to the 1964 election, and a campaign to eradicate poverty (along with meaningful civil rights legislation) was not only in sync with the Great Society, it could also elevate this Southerner in the eyes of progressive Northern Democrats.

Thus, Lyndon Johnson enthusiastically embraced Heller's recommendations, pushing through Congress an Economic Opportunity Act that in turn created the Office of Economic Opportunity (OEO), the central headquarters for waging this war, and wooing a Kennedy brother-in-law, Sargent Shriver, away from his post as director of the Peace Corps to be its general. Over the remainder of the 1960s, until it was dismantled by Richard Nixon, OEO's Community Action Program—with grants eventually reaching $1.7 billion by 1969—led the charge against poverty. It was supported by numerous complementary programs oriented toward manpower training: Job Corps, which offered vocational education for adolescents in electronics, cooking, woodworking, welding, drafting, and the industrial arts; a domestic Peace Corps known as Volunteers in Service to America; housing subsidies; and legal counseling.[13]

Given the heightened sensitivity to race in the mid-sixties, the Johnson administration was careful not to encourage the perception that the War on Poverty had anything to do with the civil rights movement then about to crest with Martin Luther King's fifty-four-mile march from Selma to Montgomery, Alabama. But of course there were connections, especially in regard to social policies aimed at poor African American children. One of the closest links came from Assistant Secretary of Labor Daniel Patrick Moynihan's controversial 1965 report blaming a "tangle of pathology" for elevated rates of unemployment, dropouts, crime, and welfare dependency in the black community relative to whites. Moynihan posited that three hundred years of first slavery and then systemic discrimination had eroded the institution of family in the black community through illegitimacy, divorce, and separation, leaving almost a quarter of families headed by a single, female parent. The matriarchal nature of contemporary black families obliged young African American males to overcompensate when asserting their masculinity, which in turn not only led to delinquent behavior but also made it difficult for them to take advantage of new opportunities afforded under Johnson's civil rights laws. Moynihan called for the mobilization of War on Poverty resources to stabilize the black family so that the Great Society's assurance of equal rights might extend to true racial equality. His ideas accounted for the administration's focus on job training and affirmative action and, for minority children, improved medical and nutrition programs combined with preschool educational opportunities stressing learner readiness.[14]

One way in which the Great Society aimed at helping children was to make changes in welfare policy. In 1962 the Social Security Act—the central pillar of modern child welfare policy—was amended under the Department of Health, Education, and Welfare (HEW) in ways that greatly expanded the federal government's definition of, and responsibility for, child welfare. Beyond providing public social services for poor, abused, and abandoned children—the traditional role of agencies like the Children's Bureau and other federal initiatives—the new law mandated that the government make a host of protective services—that supplemented, or substituted for, parental care and supervision—available to all children in need, regardless of family income.

This broadened scope coincided with other important changes in Aid to Dependent Children, a program created by the original 1935 Social Security Act, which, as its name implies, provided an income maintenance safety net to children who were deprived of a wage-earning parent due to death, incapacity, or continued absence from the home. Also administered through HEW, the program's name was changed in 1962 to Aid to Families with Dependent Children (AFDC), reflecting a substantial increase in the availability of financial assistance and the amounts provided to recipients. States still had wide latitude in determining eligibility and disbursements, but the rules were liberalized throughout the mid-1960s, first by allowing AFDC payments to families with an unemployed father (in which twenty-five states eventually participated) and later with alterations in HEW administrative guidelines to prohibit unannounced home visits by social workers to check eligibility. The Supreme Court likewise invalidated what was known as the man-in-the-house rule, deciding in the 1968 case *King v. Smith* that AFDC payments could not be withheld due to a single mother's boyfriend making frequent visitations to the household. As a result, AFDC caseloads increased 24 percent between 1960 and 1965 and then again by 125 percent between 1965 and 1970. The size of benefits increased as well. In real dollars, the value of AFDC assistance accelerated in the first five years of the 1960s almost as much as it had over the previous decade. Between 1965 and 1970, the average payment jumped by 24 percent. It jumped more in some states than in others, as a family of four on AFDC in New York could receive $2,700 per year (the highest payment) while in Mississippi payments were closer to $380 (the lowest). Couple this with other new Great Society programs such as food stamps, Medicaid, and public housing or rent subsidies, and, experts calculated, real benefits increased nearly 50 percent, much of the increase coming after 1964. In addition, Congress raised Social Security survivor benefits for dependents of a breadwinner who had died, become disabled, or retired, by 7 percent in 1965 and 13 percent in 1967.[15]

All in all, the Johnson administration oversaw the postwar era's most substantial and costly enlargement of the federal safety net supporting impoverished children. By 1967, 3.2 million children were receiving AFDC assistance, and about another 3 million were covered by at least some Social Security benefits. In a pattern that would come to characterize Johnson's public role, however, the president found himself in the increasingly difficult position of championing further expansion while at the same time deflecting mounting criticism. In his February 1967 Special Message to Congress on Children and Youth, Johnson pointed out that inequities in administering AFDC allowed thirty-three states to pay out well under the "poverty line," which then stood at $3,100 a year for an urban family of four and $1,860 a year for a comparable rural family. AFDC reached only one in four Americans below that subsistence level, with millions of poor people receiving nothing because they did not apply or did not know they were eligible. Yet in the last years of Johnson's administration, AFDC—what most Americans referred to as "welfare"—served as a lightning rod for conservatives denouncing the Great Society's liberal permissiveness and its perceived role in the country's growing unrest. Public alarm over seemingly bloated welfare rolls and a "welfare culture" in which ineligible people—assumed to be African-American—abused the system fueled a more punitive national mood toward entitlements. A few months after Johnson delivered his special message on children, urban violence in Detroit and Newark emboldened welfare opponents, and as American cities burned through four long, hot summers of rioting, this theater in the War on Poverty became a bruising uphill battle.[16]

It is important to note that even though many children's letters appealing to President Johnson's paternalism were clearly informed by Lawrence Kohlberg's pre-conventional market-exchange level of moral development, based as they were on judgments of self-interest and "what's in it for me," a significant sampling were motivated by the more conventional-level morality of concern for others. Political scientists David Easton and Jack Dennis found in the 1960s that students at every elementary grade level overwhelmingly approved of a compassionate government assuming a direct role in aiding the less fortunate—as AFDC was intended to do—and the Great Society would have appealed to maturing children at various levels of decentered thought. It is conceivable that for some children, Lyndon and Lady Bird Johnsons' highly publicized crusade to focus the nation's attention on poverty helped facilitate these developments. Catalyst or not, it certainly gave preadolescents food for thought as well as specific instances—most notably the Johnsons' evangelism for destitute families in Appalachia—to integrate into a new approach to moral decision making.

In the spring of 1964, during a tour with the First Lady of depressed areas in Kentucky, West Virginia, North Carolina, and Tennessee, the president characterized the plight of poor Appalachians as a national obligation whose solution should remain nonpartisan. Many children responded to those sentiments—eventually resulting in the Appalachian Regional Development Act of 1965—and were moved by the stark images of the First Couple greeting the family of an unemployed sawmill worker on the front porch of their hard-scrabble, tarpaper shack in the mountains of eastern Kentucky. One eleven-year-old boy who wanted to be president someday likened these efforts to Johnson physically "pick[ing] the whole United States off the ground." Two New Jersey boys, eight and nine, told the White House that they had been inspired to start "earning money by working in the neighborhood doing yard work and cleaning garages and basements. We did this," they explained, "to earn money for the people in appalachia mountains [sic]. We want you, if you can, see that this money gets to them. Please!" The letter was accompanied by a personal check from the eight-year-old's mother made out to the U.S. Government for $4.40, along with a picture the boys drew.[17]

That these attitudes, so much in harmony with the Great Society, were expressed in letters disproportionately written by girls might be an illustration of what psychologist Carol Gilligan identifies as a developing feminine "ethic of care." Gilligan, a close colleague of Kohlberg, pioneered this more gendered perspective on the stages of moral reasoning, which suggests that while boys mature ethically by progressively incorporating notions of rules and justice, girls tend to approach issues of morality by thinking in terms of caring and relationships. The acquisition of an attitude of care in girls (although certainly not exclusive to females) usually coincides with Kohlberg's pre-conventional ethics (around ten years of age) and may explain why so many not only felt empathy for people's suffering as underscored by the Great Society, but more importantly wanted to help their president do something about it. "I am 10 years old and I am at the stage where I start to listen to the news and read the newspapers and read and hear alot [sic] about you," a Long Island girl wrote the president, "but there are some things I don't understand." In seeking clarification to her questions, she, like many others her age, was recognizing in Lyndon Johnson an ethic of care and reaching out and sought to engage him in a meaningful conversation framed by a perceived mutual sense of a responsibility to others.[18]

A ten-year-old in Minnesota included a poignant "drawing of a [sic] unfortunate child that lives in the Appalachian region. As you can see," the fifth grader added, referring to the child's gaunt face, "she needs the help of what you are trying to do." Child-development scholars believe that caring about, and for, others is a vital starting point for integrating a healthy appreciation of social justice into our ethics. The moral dilemma of a twelve-year-old girl from Henderson, Kentucky, who corresponded with LBJ in 1967 reflects that developmental process. She had become very interested in government and specifically the War on Poverty, and the more she found out the more she wrestled with how a wealthy nation could allow its people to be hungry and homeless. "Everyday [sic] I read about different people in this country who are starving and who live in run down homes and can't go to school because they do not have the right clothes," she wrote to Johnson. "I started a drive last year to send food to the Salvation Army to try and help. I know it want' [sic] much but it was all I could do. I pray every night that God will help you Mr. President to help all these poor children and to help me understand why they can not get more help." Other letters indicate that this ethic of care contributed at a fundamental level to political awareness, such as a twelve-year-old girl's pledge of allegiance to Johnson and the Democratic Party—"even if I can't vote"—based on her assumption that "the Democrats do more for the people."[19]

In recalling her religious upbringing in Tennessee, a woman born in 1958 told me she still strongly associates the preadolescent development of her sense of ethics with President Johnson. "I was churched at the First Christian Church, also known as Disciples of Christ, which was very liberal," she wrote. "And there are plenty of folks today in the South who believe if you are not a Baptist, just don't bother." Yet, "Lyndon Johnson was a member of Disciples of Christ" and this helped galvanize her basic outlook. "I guess as a kid, my main thing was being fair. Social injustice [is] bad."[20]

In their imaginative rapport with the president, preadolescents frequently extended this ethic of care to Lyndon Johnson's health. After the well-managed illusion of Kennedy's vigor, Johnson, with his well publicized surgeries and hospital stays, appeared sicklier to children. Their "get well soon" cards came by the score after his successful gall bladder surgery in October 1965—lifting up his shirt to show the scar played really well among boys—and letters regularly referenced his other bouts of illness. Similarly, children were clearly cognizant

of how overburdened and faded Johnson began to look on television, expressing their worry over his obvious weariness as being president of a country
riven by violence and the war in Vietnam took its toll. Mostly unaware of
how these conflicts were eroding his Great Society and popularity, children
remained upbeat—"You may not be as popular as Abe Lincoln but you will
be in a few years"—and by mid-decade their polite and chatty sympathy cards
expressed confidence that his labors, as they saw it, to make peace in Vietnam
and put an end to the "civil rights riots" would prove successful. "I watched
you on T.V. last Sunday night," a ten-year-old Wisconsin girl wrote. "My dad
made the remark that you looked tired. So I told him he would be tired too if
he had your job." Her solution was to invite LBJ to her home for some rest and
"a nice home cooked meal with homemade bread and pie." She concluded her
invitation: "I am a girl scout and earning my cooking badge . . . if I knew you
were coming I would cook something myself for you."[21]

Such concern as this indicates a certain symmetry with the Great Society's
record on health care. Lyndon Johnson was looking out for the health of
American children too, even though most in this cohort might not have appreciated it while nervously thumbing through the pages of *Highlights* magazine in a doctor's office, waiting for their turn to be vaccinated with the
dreaded hypodermic needle. Besides the monumental Medicare and Medicaid (pronounced by Johnson as Medeecare and Medeecaid), the administration passed some forty healthcare measures as federal expenditures on health
programs more than tripled during the 1960s from $4 billion to $14 billion.
In the lives of preadolescents, the foremost of these was Medicaid. When it
became law in 1965, this "means-tested" form of health insurance coverage
for low-income youth, pregnant women, and the disabled effectively shifted the burden of healthcare for poor children in this country to the federal
government.[22]

The story of how Lyndon Johnson managed to extend healthcare to the
many millions subsequently served by Medicare and Medicaid is a textbook
example of how government functioned in the years of the Great Society.
Since Franklin Roosevelt's Economic Bill of Rights in 1944, Democrats—John
Kennedy among them—had pushed for some type of national health insurance without success. Prospects looked equally poor in 1965 until Johnson and
powerful House Ways and Means chairman Wilbur Mills, a fiscally conservative Democrat from Arkansas, pulled off a masterstroke of political horse trading by deftly stitching together three competing Democratic and Republican
versions of the bill at the last moment to create one, three-layered bipartisan

package. Medicare Part A was the administration's moderate proposal to expand Social Security in order to pay hospital costs for senior citizens. Medicare Part B was the Republican and American Medical Association's conservative counterplan (largely to block the former) that paid doctor's costs for the elderly. And Medicaid was the more liberal House Democrats' version to insure the poor through a joint federal-state program. When the president finally signed the Social Security Amendments that created Medicare and Medicaid in July, his approval ratings with adults reached 79 percent, which for the last time in his administration approached the numbers he always enjoyed with children.

As with most far-reaching pieces of legislation with numerous moving parts, in order to manage the costs—there was no Congressional Budget Office at the time to project the price tag of Medicare and Medicaid out over the years—the Johnson administration left additional improvements (pharmaceutical benefits and catastrophic insurance) and expansion to other eligible groups for future lawmakers to add. By the time Johnson told television audiences in March 1968 that he would not run for reelection, over half the states had joined Medicaid, and with increased funding the program had begun to pay hospital costs and doctor's bills for more than 3.5 million preschool and school-age children a year. In addition, hundreds of thousands of poor mothers and infants in urban and rural areas were being examined and treated, many for the first time, through local public health agencies. Studies show that since its enactment in 1965 almost half of Medicaid's nearly 50 million beneficiaries have been children.[23]

Many of the Great Society health care initiatives geared toward the young today comprise the complex, clumsy, and mostly decentralized health care system that Americans inherited from the sixties. Medicaid and Aid for Families with Dependent Children joined the Food Stamp Program as what one historian termed "the holy trinity of federal welfare policy."[24] Johnson made Kennedy's trial food assistance program—now the Supplemental Nutrition Assistance Program—law in August 1964 as part of a much larger agricultural price support package. In its original incarnation, the Food Stamp Program helped needy families purchase foodstuffs using federal vouchers, with participation rising from 424,000 in 1965 to 2.2 million people served by 1969, disproportionally children. Other Kennedy efforts were similarly augmented. A National Summer Youth Sports Program was added to the President's Council on Physical Fitness, and federally funded measles vaccines were included with the polio, diphtheria, whooping cough, and tetanus inoculations already available under the Vaccination Assistance Act of 1962. Efforts on behalf of disabled children intensified with greater emphasis on early detection and prevention, including regular eye examinations for low-income preadolescents.

Improved access to dental care followed as a part of Johnson's Child Health Act of 1967. Provisions within the act authorized HEW grants to state and local health departments to support additional maternity and pediatric clinics—the president later recommended additional money to train more pediatricians and obstetricians—and facilities serving the handicapped. Since almost two out of every three poor children between the ages of five and fourteen had never set foot in a dentist's office, the government funded 75 percent of projects providing comprehensive dental care for poor children, with monies also going toward training dental assistants to work in schools and other community agencies.[25]

A Child Protection Act and truth-in-packaging law strengthened the Food and Drug Administration's (FDA) ability to safeguard childhood nutrition and safety. The sale of hazardous toys and harmful household articles was banned, and in 1967 Congress amended the Flammable Fabrics Act of 1953 to outlaw combustible materials used in children's clothing and furniture. That same year, President Johnson used the bully pulpit to chastise conservative congressmen who had sidetracked his Rat Extermination and Control Act—sardonically labeling it as just another "Civil Rats Act"—that sought to eradicate the threat of these rodents for inner city children. As public polices proliferated, at Johnson's urging OEO piloted innovative Parent and Child Centers (PCCs) through its Community Action Program in 1968 to systematize and streamline accessibility to the new health and welfare services. These clearinghouses, strategically located in areas of acute poverty, made available the vast range of Great Society services in one centralized location. Nutritious meals for preschoolers and day care for toddlers were offered in conjunction with nurse and dentist checkups—via nearby public health facilities—while classes and counseling for parents covered topics ranging from home management and accident prevention to nutrition. For maximum efficiency, PCC facilities often affiliated with nearby OEO manpower training centers to help prepare young adults to work in day care centers and preschools, or with universities to provide undergraduate training practicums for teachers, counselors, social workers, librarians, and nurses.[26]

Adding breakfast to an augmented school lunch program was another instance of better health care serving as an adjunct to better education. The Child Nutrition Act, which the president signed in October 1966, recognized "the demonstrated relationship between food and good nutrition and the capacity of children to develop and learn," a connection that Johnson—a former teacher in hard-pressed Cotulla, Texas—understood personally. Washington had been helping state departments of education serve lunches to students since the National School Lunch Program began in 1946. Under its auspices, on any given day of the school year, three in every four elementary students purchased a red or green lunch ticket for somewhere around twenty-seven cents. That price covered about half the cost of the meal, state and local government put in most of the other half, and the Department of Agriculture kicked in the remaining few cents with cash and donated food. A tickets entitled the bearer to what was known as the "standard Type A" meal, which included meat or some other protein-rich food, fruits and vegetables, bread and butter, and a half-pint carton of milk. The actual combination of selections depended on local budgets and food supplies along with the culinary vision of school cafeteria managers planning the menus, but students agreed that the best items were hamburgers, fried chicken, spaghetti, hot dogs, oversized sandwiches, and anything with peanut butter. Yet, for all the delicious entrees served on innumerable hard plastic trays, there existed wide gaps in accessibility, and closing them were the reasons behind the Child Nutrition Act. In poor districts without the resources to afford basic food service equipment, federal funds updated kitchen facilities, and most schools constructed after 1967 featured modern cafeterias. Increased funding also kept free and reduced-price lunches available to qualified students, while other initiatives offered meals to very young children enrolled in preschool activities not previously covered by the law, along with summer food service to day-care centers. But the law's signature provision was the free and reduced-price school breakfast program—serving the poor and those traveling greater distances in the mornings—which has since fed over one hundred million hungry schoolchildren. Johnson's efforts notably expanded and strengthened the government's responsibility in meeting the nutritional needs of children, but to children, they were arguably not the biggest lunchroom news in the fall of 1966. That honor would have probably gone to the brand new Batman and Robin lunch box from Aladdin Industries, a piece of merchandising surrounding *Batman: The Movie,* which had come to theaters that summer after the first season of the dynamic duo's television series.[27]

Considering Great Society educational policy more broadly—sixty separate bills in all—its emphasis on young learners' nutrition is consistent with the more holistic paradigm informing the field of American pedagogy in the years after *Sputnik*. As America's educational system struggled to keep pace with the ever increasing demands of the baby boom, the progressive teaching theories and practices of philosopher John Dewey again guided our schools' efforts to nurture "the whole child." The developmental needs of each individual learner were recognized—curriculum and instruction adjusted accordingly—to better teach reading, writing, and arithmetic (with a strong Cold War emphasis on science and technology), but equally to cultivate a child's personality, social skills, emotional growth, and creativity. By the early 1960s, educators were focusing on how to reach children at a younger age and provide early childhood intervention programs in order to accommodate the reality of more working mothers and to shield culturally disadvantaged children from the potentially damaging effects of their environment. The Kennedy administration had made education a priority, leading the way in addressing the special requirements of handicapped children, but ultimately confronted a political truism of federal aid to education which Lyndon Johnson often voiced in the Southern vernacular: "Kids is where the money ain't." Johnson nonetheless overcame this traditional legislative parsimony and in doing so helped institutionalize educational progressivism. His Elementary and Secondary Education Act and resultant Project Head Start spearheaded a decade-long period of public and private investment in experimental and special educational programming for underprivileged preschool and elementary school students which still helps shape the federal role in education.[28]

The Elementary and Secondary Education Act (ESEA) was signed into law on April 11, 1965, in front of the president's former school, the one-room Junction Elementary near tiny Stonewall, Texas. "As the son of a tenant farmer," Johnson proclaimed, with his first teacher, Mrs. Kathryn Deadrich Loney—"Miss Kate"—seated next to him, "I know that education is the only valid passport from poverty." To assure that every child had the chance to capitalize on that promise, this sweeping legislation worked to largely federalize the funding of public education. Like Medicaid, which Johnson signed three months later, the ESEA enlarged the role of the federal government: it shifted the burden of educating children, especially those living in poverty, to Washington, D.C., from which an unprecedented stream of revenue—$1.3 billion in the initial implementation period between 1965 and 1969—began to flow. Whereas Kennedy had tried, and failed, to direct federal grants to the states for the general purposes of constructing new facilities and paying teacher's salaries, Johnson avoided the previous administration's missteps by pursuing the explicit goal of raising student achievement, while also equalizing the quality of education between low-income urban or rural systems and their middle-class suburban counterparts via a wide range of targeted, categorical assistance. This aid was dispersed to the states—so local control might be preserved—which then allocated the funds to their respective districts based on a selective formula factoring in a given area's concentration of poor students and with the standing directive that each district use the money exclusively to improve services that met the special developmental needs and learning styles of Dewey's "whole child." Such reasoning similarly diffused the thorny issue of public aid to parochial schools. Architects of the legislation applied the "child benefit" doctrine handed down by the Supreme Court's *Everson v. Board of Education* (1947) ruling, which held that instances of state financing which principally benefited the student, and not the religious school—funding secular textbooks or transportation, for instance—were permissible under the First Amendment. As Johnson noted in his remarks with Miss Kate, by its very design ESEA facilitated his War on Poverty. And while targeting improved educational outcomes in the poorest ghettos and small towns, by decade's end ESEA monies were being distributed to 90 percent of American school districts in 95 percent of the nation's counties.[29]

The various titles of the ESEA determined the parameters for how this money was spent. Districts applied for funds based on these provisions—not to simply pay bills—and carried out projects accordingly to address local needs. Title I, with the largest portion of funds, went to improve schools and student performance through new staff, facilities, equipment, and services. Specialists in psychology, speech and hearing, and social work were hired and more teaching positions created to reduce class sizes. Title II strengthened school libraries and paid for innovative instructional and resource materials, covering everything from more film-strip projectors, tape recorders, and typewriters to the application of new audio-visual technologies in the classroom like radio and television media centers. Titles III and IV promoted Projects to Advance Creativity in Education (PACE), which encouraged teachers to create groundbreaking curriculums and funded supplemental teacher development programs that likewise advanced pedagogy. And Title V helped state departments of education modernize their administration. One of the considerations in awarding these types of ESEA grants was whether the proposed initiatives could serve as models for other schools, and thus some of the most imaginative initiatives proliferated across the land: counseling services, health and nutrition programs, math and reading enrichment, foreign language laboratories, ecology and geology curriculums including field trips, student concerts, art exhibits, and theater, and after-school activities in both the arts and sciences.

These were the first forms of such diverse federal assistance, and within a few years other Great Society measures and amendments to the ESEA deepened the law's penetration into the world of preadolescent students. The Education Professions Development Act of 1967 opened new opportunities for teacher training, helping to perpetuate progressive education among elementary school teachers in the bargain, as did Teacher Corps, created by Johnson's Higher Education Act, that sent over a thousand intern and veteran volunteer teachers into underserved areas throughout Appalachia, the Ozarks, Native-American reservations, and inner-city slums. The Bilingual Education Act of 1968, an amended Title VII to the ESEA, mandated bilingual education in public schools for the first time—although programs already existed in states with sizable Hispanic populations—and subsidized school districts that were adding bilingual teachers to their staff and starting to offer instruction to students whose first language was something other than English. So too were the first federal dollars made available to school districts serving young people with physical or mental disabilities by Title VI of the ESEA, the Elementary and Secondary Amendments of 1966. This law, which also created the Bureau of Education for the Handicapped and National Advisory Council (today's National Council on Disability) continued to solidify the notion of a legal right to free, public special education.[30]

The ESEA was originally authorized through 1970 and has thereafter required reauthorization and amendment at regular intervals, most conspicuously in 2002 when President George W. Bush renamed it No Child Left Behind. Prior to the initial 1970 reauthorization, Johnson had already tripled federal expenditures on education, and over the forty-plus years since, Title I grants have amounted to nearly $15 billion or almost half of all Washington spending on K–12 education. A detailed evaluation of what that money has actually purchased, like definitively assessing the War on Poverty and Great Society overall, remains problematic, however. Contemporary observers found the results of ESEA to be underwhelming and, as with the War on Poverty, blamed chronic fiscal malnourishment for its limited effectiveness. By the 1980s, as it became more fashionable to dismiss ESEA along with the rest of the Great Society, conservative critics argued that the federal government had hampered schools by disincentivizing some districts from securing their own funding through local taxes, and questioned the basic premise of taxpayer money closing the achievement gap between rich and poor students. Libertarian political scientist Charles Murray went so far as to speculate that 1960s liberalism gave the poor incentives to make bad choices in education, employment, and crime, which accounts for steadily declining standards of living among the disadvantaged during times when their socioeconomic status should have been improving.

As with Aid to Families with Dependent Children, historians tend to agree with Paul Conkin's conclusion that "insofar as money can buy better education, the act boosted the quality of education for most American children."[31] Yet, measuring education as an investment in youth—to improve the standard of living of those living in poverty and, moreover, help children climb out of impoverished conditions—must at some point tie back into the wider debate on the merits or failures of Johnson's domestic public policies. For better or worse, this comes down to statistics—chiefly, how far was the needle moved on poverty in America? By most measures, poverty rates declined over the course of the sixties, but those who contend the United States lost the War on Poverty can point to numbers showing relatively little decrease, from 19 percent of Americans below the poverty line to 15 percent. Those claiming victory focus on studies which reveal much steeper drops since the mid-1960s, from as much as 23 percent to 12 percent today. A recent study by economists at Columbia University recalculated formulas for measuring historical rates of poverty and argues persuasively for these more dramatic latter estimates, crediting various Great Society anti-poverty programs for playing a larger role than previously thought. Two demographics benefiting above all, these scholars maintain—conclusions well established by other examinations—are the elderly and children. According to their research, the child poverty rate, which stood near 30 percent in 1967, has plunged by nearly a third to 18 percent in 2012.[32]

To add some perspective to these statistical achievements, there remain two elements of Johnson's Great Society with an ESEA lineage which must be accounted for: Project Head Start and its beloved cousin, the Children's Television Workshop. Head Start began with a $150 million ESEA allocation in 1965 to deliver preschool programming for culturally and economically deprived children, who, studies increasingly found, were arriving in kindergarten already lagging developmentally behind their more affluent classmates. What professional educators recognized was that after about eighteen months old, preadolescents living in poverty were no longer keeping pace with middle-class children in either language development or general intelligence, and those deficits widened to the point of being painfully obvious by the age of three or four. The culprits, experts maintained, were primarily socioeconomic. Middle-class students, parents, and teachers in public schools often took for granted how their normative lifestyle prepared young children for learning, but poor children experienced a fundamentally different reality by comparison which frequently eroded their trust in authority figures and conditioned them to an alternative system of cues and rewards with quite different developmental results. For instance, no bedtime stories or parental reading stalled an appreciation for books and magazines, which were generally pretty scarce commodities around the house anyway. Without many toys—those pieces of material culture in the preadolescent sphere that best exemplify adult values and expectations—children were also left wanting for this important insight into the grownup world, just as an absence of crayons, paints, and paper retarded artistic expression. Many inner-city preschoolers were at a loss to identify basic zoo animals in photographs, let alone draw them. Staying out of trouble usually meant keeping quiet, which discouraged verbal expression, and exhibiting a healthy curiosity for one's environment was another surefire way to run afoul of household rules. Overburdened parents might not offer much more in the way of interpersonal communication than terse commands and rebukes, further hindering the cultivation of language skills and creative thought. Frequently, loud music on the AM radio or television afforded not entertainment (and certainly not education) so much as the only opportunity to tune out the world.[33]

In the spirit of the War on Poverty, Head Start facilitated a nationwide organization of community- and neighborhood-based nursery schools with holistic curriculums designed on a compensatory model to help these low-income children make up for lost time in school readiness. The very first projects were modest six- or eight-week summer courses for students about to enter kindergarten. While local sensibilities and available talents dictated the scope and sequence of curriculums, the general blueprint remained pretty much the same. For each successful proposal, the government agreed to fund about 80 percent of the project, with locals responsible for the balance through cash and in-kind donations of classroom space, playgrounds, or administrative staff. Many projects began with just a single paid teacher, maybe an aide or cook, and multiple volunteers. The better programs drew these volunteers from all socioeconomic levels—finding that teenagers made enthusiastic helpers—and partnered with nearby institutions of higher education for basic teacher training.

One of the most challenging aspects often proved to be identifying potential students, and toward this end organizers had to get creative. Beyond neighborhood word of mouth they consulted family services caseworkers,

Children's Bureau representatives, Salvation Army centers, and church groups, and scoured public school lists of those receiving free lunch in the hope of finding younger siblings. Early home visitations with potential enrollees were also critical in the organizational phase, not only for recruitment, but to best tailor curriculums and lessons to pupils' distinct needs, while fostering the necessary parental buy-in and involvement. Head Start always stressed the agency of parents in the overall educational process by encouraging them to participate in activities that might strengthen parenting skills.

The key to Head Start was to address the child's total environment, offering teachable moments in preschoolers' limited world that might make them feel more at home in the wider world. This meant following a basic hierarchy of needs: before classes could begin to meet students' social, psychological, and cognitive requirements, organizers had to look out for their physical well-being, with attention given to nutrition and health. The earliest projects reported acute dietary deficiencies with as many as 1.5 million preschoolers simply not getting enough to eat before they showed up at school. Serving nutritious meals at Head Start put food in their tummies and also introduced parents to the FDA's most recent (since 1956) foundational diet approach using the four basic food groups: fruits and vegetables, milk, meat, cereals and bread. Likewise, and again through volunteers from the medical professions and partnerships with local hospitals, Head Start operated what were essentially well-child clinics, scheduling pediatric checkups for early detection—including vision and hearing tests—so those identified with problems could be serviced by the appropriate agencies.

Nurturing emotional and social development—a mission Johnson characterized as helping "launch poor children on the path toward self-discovery"—was always prioritized over intellectual skills, so the majority of instructional time usually focused on socialization exercises and learning through play. Many Head Start projects exposed preschoolers to the basic concepts and skills needed for kindergarten by organizing the summer around weekly themes—You, Animals, Homes, Plants, Water, Going Places—with a premium placed on variety and new experiences. In classrooms arranged to promote maximum freedom of movement, children were taught to work and play well independently—and with confidence—away from home, but also to trust grownups, accepting their help and direction when needed. They dressed up in donated adult clothes and role-played scenarios emphasizing a variety of personal skill sets ranging from common household procedures (properly answering a phone call) to making good choices. To promote those interpersonal skills needed to effectively work and play well with others, activities focusing on verbal communication often reinforced how to value one's own experiences equally with classmates. Volunteers regularly engaged children in conversations that required sustained verbalization, and in some programs periods for just chatting with one another got built right into the day's lesson plans. Local public libraries lent books for volunteer led story periods so children could hear the written word spoken aloud. Many programs set aside time for show-and-tell as well, or in the absence of anything to show, just telling the class about something interesting that had happened at home.

Mealtime presented multifaceted opportunities to learn and organizers purposefully served foods in containers requiring preschoolers to practice asking for, passing, and serving food to oneself. So too did menus usually feature unfamiliar foods, especially fruits, requiring new vocabulary. Moreover, Head Start curriculums highlighted those types of exercises that boosted a child's intangible sense of competence and self-worth, of being a valued member in a community. Birthday boys and girls always received the royal treatment, their special day recognized by a class full of well-wishers with a party filled with decorations, games, and, of course, a cake. And arts and crafts encouraged preschoolers to see themselves in the unfamiliar role of creator, just as planting and growing small vegetation cast them in the part of caregiver.[34]

What started as pilot programs in the summers of 1965 and 1966 with approximately 500,000 disadvantaged preschoolers grew appreciably through trial and error over the remainder of the sixties. By 1967 2,400 communities—representing three-fourths of American counties with high poverty concentrations in all fifty states—were operating a Head Start program. Most of the over 1.3 million enrollees aged four to six attended summer sessions, but the strongest Head Starts extended their programming out to year-round. At the local level this expansion often meant adjusted curriculum with added enrichment activities, better facilities, or the enrollment of more students, even the addition of another paid full-time or part-time staff member. Critics still groused that Head Start was failing to make poor children any more ready for school because it offered only remedial academic lessons when what these students, who were so far behind intellectually, really needed was instruction in cognitive skills like reading readiness and math. Others, most notably the Westinghouse Learning Corporation in its 1969 study, maintained that due to poor local planning and haphazard implementation participants in the summer programs were not significantly any better off in kindergarten than nonparticipants and that whatever gains in language or cognition derived from the full-year programs were ephemeral, largely "fading out" by the third grade. But supporters countered, saying these criticisms did not fully account for Head Start's positive impact on underprivileged children's health and diet, or the even less tangible, although equally significant, enhancement of self-esteem and positive predisposition toward school in young students and their families. Two women from the rural Midwest who contacted me for this study specifically mentioned those facets of the Head Start experience—plenty of food, mastering crafts, learning to write your name, the sweetness of teachers—among their only enduring recollections of the 1960s. Many of these gains were more pronounced among African Africans and other preadolescents enrolled in the nation's inner cities and across the Southeast. Here, observers argued, where civic relations may be the most fragile or strained, by reinforcing the family, Head Start's comprehensive methodology likewise helped strengthen the community's social fabric. With an increasingly polarizing political climate disillusioning entire segments of the adult population, Head Start was also offering preadolescents beginning to navigate the stages of moral and cognitive development a positive model of governmental investment in racial and social justice.[35]

Sufficiently encouraged that such achievement validated plans for further growth, in the late 1960s the Johnson administration pushed Congress and the OEO for more all-year programs and the broadening of eligibility to youngsters as young as three and as old as ten. Making sure that Head Start was not relegated to being just a random one-and-done crash course for the poor— ESEA already underwrote remedial summer school and day camps for over two million children and the OEO offered recreational programs to a million more through its Operation Champ—the president likewise launched Project Follow Through. With numerous intervention strategies to effectively continue Head Start-style services to young learners beyond preschool, Follow Through efforts were designed by educators to mitigate that "fade out" phenomenon in the early elementary grades.

All this federal attention on early education in turn reflected and reinforced the growing school of thought in the field that public schooling should begin at three years old, a trend which motivated many school districts to utilize ESEA Title I grants to develop their own preschools along the Head Start model and hastened the day of compulsory kindergarten in a number of states. Although the majority of states began providing some funding for it by 1973, kindergarten only became mandatory in nine states, but of those, Connecticut, Illinois, Maryland, Massachusetts, Rhode Island, and Texas passed legislation making it so during Lyndon Johnson's second term. After Johnson left office in 1969, this growing momentum behind the general concept of early childhood learning carried Head Start through the presidency of Richard Nixon and beyond the Vietnam era. Despite numerous critiques and conservative condemnation, Nixon did not scuttle Head Start as many thought he might during his major reorganization of Johnson's OEO; instead he perpetuated it by transferring operations to a newly created Office of Child Development in the Department of Health, Education, and Welfare. To date, the program has served nearly thirty million preschoolers, and while subsequent studies still parse empirical student learner outcomes, its longevity—one of the last remaining vestiges of the Great Society—speaks to the soundness of this experiment in early education. And like all great American ideas, someone ultimately made a television show about it . . . which is how we get to *Sesame Street*.[36]

One of the most widely acclaimed series of all time, *Sesame Street* pioneered the concept of television "edutainment," imaginatively harnessing early learning to that medium's nearly magical capacity to entertain. Since its debut in November 1969, the televised teaching of *Sesame Street*—the longest running children's program in American history—has enhanced the childhood of untold millions worldwide through the amusing development of good cognitive habits, and, with its delightful Muppet characters, occupies a very special, pervasive place in American popular culture (Kermit the Frog and company reside in the Smithsonian!). For all its innovation and commercial success, however, the educational focus and rationale behind *Sesame Street* was firmly rooted in those same sociopolitical realities and educational priorities that had produced Head Start, and actually their early years were closely related. Both the Children's Television Workshop (CTW), the creator of *Sesame Street*, and Head Start owed much of their creative energies to the idealistic spirit then coursing through the Great Society and civil rights movement. Indeed, it can be argued that the zeitgeist of the sixties may have been most purely distilled down to children through the prevailing emphasis on early education which informed both of these enterprises. Joan Ganz Cooney, the center of the workshop's visionary core and its first director, specifically credited this shared inheritance in tracing the origins of *Sesame Street*. "We only knew that we wanted to make a difference on the lives of children and families. And in the late 1960s in which we were first working," Cooney explained of being present at the creation, "this seemed immanently possible, a time when many of us believed we had both the responsibility and the power to try to make the world a better place." And again like Head Start, Cooney's CTW pursued early learning strategies as the favored means toward this end, always guided by a mutual understanding of how cognitive progress during the preschool years offers a fairly accurate prediction of later adolescent and adult intellectual growth.[37]

Yet, even as the pedagogical trend for some form of public schooling beginning at age three continued to gain traction among educators—endorsed by the National Education Association—such plans would have meant somewhere near five million additional little students in the nation's already crowded elementary schools at the unworkable cost of around $2.75 billion, a political nonstarter. This is where Head Start entered the conversation, to, by design, pick up at least some of the slack. But once more even the most enthusiastic advocates admitted that the fledgling program was spending $127 million to reach only about 10 percent of those five million potential new preschoolers (middle-class and poor). Consequently, a few innovators started looking into more economical "alternative modes" of instruction outside the traditional classroom setting, including, almost counterintuitively for most in the profession, the use of the notoriously mindless television. Although commercial television programming had been derided as a "vast wasteland," by none other than Kennedy's Federal Communications Commission chair Newton Minow, its role as a primary socialization agent in the lives of children was becoming increasingly hard to discount in some educational circles. Having never known a time without it, preadolescents already had a familiarity—if not a natural enthusiasm—with the medium, and their viewing habits were statistically staggering. Preschoolers up to six years old spent on average nearly fifty-four hours per week in front of the set—the heaviest watchers of any American demographic—and had already logged four thousand hours of television time before entering the first grade. Any morning episode of the popular *Captain Kangaroo* regularly drew an audience of four million, or eight times Head Start's preliminary annual enrollments at a production cost of pennies on the dollar compared to federal outlays for education.

The proven salesmanship of television commercials was also unprecedented, even before toy companies discovered the profitability of sponsoring animated Saturday morning shows. No one doubted television's power as an entertainment diversion and selling machine, but it was the Children's Television Workshop—as conceived by Cooney, a documentary producer, and the Carnegie Foundation's Lloyd Morrisett—that dared to gamble on fundamentally reorienting that power as a primary educational agent as well. So, with the founding of the nonprofit organization in 1966, the workshop sought to answer an emerging question, in the words of a *New York Times Magazine* headline: "Since the Kiddies Are Hooked—Why Not Use TV for a Head Start Program?"[38]

Working initially under the aegis of the philanthropic Carnegie Foundation, Cooney orchestrated the unique collaboration of educators, psychologists, child development specialists (including Head Start leadership), and television production professionals who gravitated toward the CTW's experiment in quality educational programming for preschoolers. In those first years, funding came through an equally inventive partnership of private and public sources, with the CTW's original $8 million budget covered primarily by both the Carnegie and Ford foundations and the Great Society. The administration's Department of Health, Education, and Welfare underwrote the bulk of that spending, channeling federal money from the Office of Education and National Institute of Child Health and Human Development as well as the OEO and newly formed National Endowment for the Humanities and Corporation for Public Broadcasting. Since the educational mission was always foremost, such generous support bought an almost unheard of—at least by broadcast television standards—period of research and planning. For a full two years before the program *Sesame Street* aired (or even had a name), Gerald Lesser, a Harvard professor of education and another of the workshop's chief architects, guided the research and development of a narrowly focused curriculum for children between the ages of three to five—emphasizing four-year olds—built on a solid foundation of "behavioral objectives" which could be both rigorously and continuously assessed. These instructional goals that came to define the series were painstakingly hammered out over a number of curricular seminars with expert consultants during the summer of 1968 with Lesser and the CTW eventually breaking from the Head Start model by deliberately favoring cognitive over emotional development, and, despite common misperceptions, eschewing the compensatory approach. *Sesame Street*'s daily hour-long "classes" were less about closing any perceived educational deficits between poor and middle-class students, and more about giving all preschoolers what they needed to be successful in the first grade—as Cooney later said, teaching "young children how to think, not what to think."[39]

CTW distinguished four broad instructional areas—symbolic representation, cognitive processes, physical environment, and social environment—with respective seasons of the series highlighting one of the four as their curricular focus. In support of each, student learner objectives, or what a child should be able to accomplish after instruction, were written out in much the same way classroom teachers organize lesson plans. Beginning with symbolic representation, young viewers would be taught to recognize letters, numbers, and geometric forms and accomplish simple operations using these symbols. As the foundation of reading readiness, letters were prioritized, with vowels and the most useful consonants repetitively reinforced, often through visual and verbal exercises requiring preschoolers to identify words beginning with a certain letter. The entire alphabet was presented together only for the purposes of reciting. Sequencing mattered more with numbers, so children needed to be capable of verbally counting up to twenty, defining subsets (picking out three items from a group of ten), and identifying objects by their ordinal position (finding the fourth item in a series of six). So too should preschoolers distinguish between circles, squares, rectangles, and triangles and know how to draw these geometric forms when given their verbal label. Mastering the cognitive processes required the proper application of higher-level reasoning to order, classify, and understand relational patterns with new objects and events. Viewers were taught to match similar items presented in varied contexts and understand the relationships between given things based on variables of size, amount, distance, and temporal position. Moreover, with guided practice over basic concepts of inference and causality, the televised instruction offered space to continually refine problem-solving skills. To know their physical environment, children must grasp general information about the built and natural world and, in the case of the latter, its diverse flora and fauna, seasons and weather, natural processes and life cycles. And understanding their social environment meant also knowing not only the form and function of institutions, but how to successfully navigate society's often confusing road map based on an awareness of their and others' role-defining characteristics. Lessons drawn from this category often promoted moral development by presenting situations where preschoolers might better appreciate multiple points of view or the necessity for various societal rules, especially ones supporting justice and fairness.[40]

The overall comprehensiveness of the curriculum certainly ranked among the nation's most ambitious endeavors in preschool education, but the real genius of the CTW rested in its methodological marriage of sound pedagogy to some of television's most effective production techniques. The CTW producers—several of whom cut their children's programming teeth, so to speak, on *Captain Kangaroo*—masterfully brought the educators' instructional material to life with an imaginative sense of enchantment and adventure from which the series finally (at the eleventh hour) derived its name, Ali Baba from the *Arabian Nights* tale commanding "Open Sesame" to a vibrant new world of learning right in the middle of a typical American street. Again, extensive research and testing into precisely how television captured and held the attention of preadolescents guided every production choice on *Sesame Street*. Young children, explicitly those from inner-city and poorer backgrounds, would probably not willingly tune in to a show characterized as "educational programming," so the primary trick was to reach their heads through their emotions, and in that regard television commercials were the preferred model. Familiar advertising devices—catchy music, busy graphics, and repetition—captivated children in so many ways that regular programs did not, and in fact, imaginative prime-time shows like *Rowan & Martin's Laugh-In*, which debuted on NBC in 1968, and ABC's *Batman* were already incorporating commercial sensibilities into their production. Without much prompting, almost any child could hum the *Batman* theme or sing verbatim the "Oh, I wish I were an Oscar Mayer wiener" ditty. The CTW believed learning symbolic representation and cognitive processes could be "sold" in similar fashion.[41]

Therefore *Sesame Street* operated from what the industry termed a "magazine format," each show consisting of diverse and repetitive assortments of longer and shorter segments, with constantly changing styles, pace, and characters. And since children would conceivably watch irregularly, there was no serial sequencing of installments. Viewers were free to leave off and pick up whenever they chose without significantly weakening the educational message being conveyed. For maximum appeal to city audiences, the setting and cast were intentionally urban and multiethnic, featuring human characters metropolitan children might readily identify with—Gordon and Susan, a black husband and wife, along with Mr. Hooper the candy-store owner—and, because preschoolers enjoyed watching children who looked like them, racially integrated young guests played prominent roles. Theme music was already a staple of the television programs children loved best—cartoons, game shows, and situation comedies—and so the opening verse of "Sunny day, sweepin' the clouds away . . ." set the tone just as other tunes throughout the episodes functioned as a wide range of auditory cues for magical phenomena, danger, sneaking around, or thinking. Infectious jingles buried the content deep into the subconscious. *Sesame Street*'s colorful action came at a fast pace (sometimes even slowed down or backward), moving just about equally between live and animated segments and at times the device of pixilation blurred those lines by inserting actors in the most cartoonish of places.

Related special effects also made a given episode's designated letters and numbers magically appear out of nowhere or subsets of animals grow to extravagant proportions. The clever incorporation of surprise and incongruity in the storyline often helped suggest how there might be multiple solutions to the same problem. Humor, the more physical and slapstick the better, was always the common denominator. Some gags aided memorization with catch phrases and nonsensical sounding words, just as trickery allowed underdogs to achieve justice. Scenes gently poking fun at adult idiosyncrasies and grownup characters comically blundering through obviously simple tasks likewise permitted neophytes to successfully apply new learning with feelings of pride in their competence.

More often than not, the grownups' foils were exaggerated personalities crafted from foam rubber and cloth, the irrepressible Muppets. Jim Henson, a veteran television puppeteer, joined the CTW early in its planning stages with his core group of Muppet creations, to drive content home using the puppets' unique brand of charm and vitality. The reliably eccentric roommates Ernie and Bert were joined in the original cast by Oscar the Grouch, purposefully a contrarian for use as a negative example, the gluttonous Cookie Monster, and a huge yellow canary named Big Bird who remained forever optimistic despite perpetually falling victim to easily identifiable gaffes. Kermit the Frog—a green, sort of straight-man emcee—soon became the most renowned of Henson's Muppet characters, but during the first season mainly delivered brief lectures while working as a news reporter interviewing nursery rhyme and fairy tale characters.

Early test showings of *Sesame Street* in the Philadelphia market during the summer of 1969 (the initial episode conflicted with live coverage of the Apollo 11 moon landing) drew rather lackluster reviews except for those segments containing Bert and Ernie, so producers significantly enlarged the Muppets' role while Henson expanded the troupe with new characters such as Sherlock Hemlock, the skinny blue Grover, and Count von Count. In eventually becoming the stars of *Sesame Street*, almost inseparable from the show in the public's imagination, the Muppets functioned brilliantly in both directly teaching basic intellectual skills—with small children using their fingers to imitate the counting vampire—and indirectly modeling desired social attitudes. Without condescendingly talking down to preschoolers or trivializing their worldview, this observational learning subtly, yet powerfully, shaped essential interpersonal skill sets by encouraging young people to treat one another with kindness and courtesy and work through conflicts cooperatively toward fair solutions. The integrated cast equally prompted respect and tolerance for racial differences, just as the commonsensical portrayal of black children succeeding—"hey, that kid looks like me and he knows the answer"—stirred the fundamental racial pride some adults increasingly referred to as Black Power. Perhaps above all, the Muppets were endearing characters showing off an exuberant enjoyment of learning (excepting Oscar, of course).[42]

Sesame Street aired in color on public television stations across most of the country on Monday morning, November 10, 1969 (although NBC, a potential competitor, had taken the extraordinary step of broadcasting a special sneak preview during prime time the previous Saturday). Twenty-six days later at the Altamont Speedway in northern California, the implosion of the decade's countercultural vibe during a Rolling Stones concert-turned-violent-melee conveniently, and oversimplistically, marked the end of the "good" or idealistic sixties. Not four weeks apart, these two seemingly unrelated cultural milestones reflect at once the waning influence of the sixties generation, that older cohort of the baby boom, and the waxing of the younger Sesame Street generation. Despite its experimental nature, Sesame Street was an immediate sensation with viewers. Over the first season, which concluded in May 1970, the series drew an astonishing audience of fully half of the nation's twelve million preschoolers ages two through five, impressive numbers made even more so given that America's 190 public television stations (the sole channels carrying Sesame Street) only reached 72 percent of U.S. homes and almost half of those were within reception range of weak UHF signals. Surely some fans initially tuned in for love of the show while others watched because their parents decided it was good for them. Yet by the end of 1972 Nielsen estimated that the numbers regularly watching had swiftly grown to almost nine million as Sesame Street consistently began topping the list of children's favorite television shows.

All those dials set to heretofore obscure channels proved that the CTW's formula for producing quality educational children's programming could be commercially viable, and Sesame Street put public broadcasting on the cultural map. It can be said that the Public Broadcasting Service (PBS) as well as National Public Radio (NPR), in effect, grew up with the Sesame Street generation. President Johnson had reinvigorated the concept of educational television with his Public Broadcasting Act of 1967, creating, among other things, the Corporation for Public Broadcasting (CPB) to federally support educational, cultural, and local programming on public television and radio stations. Before that, only a loose handful of educational channels—designated as National Educational Television in 1963—operated in the United States, and those mostly labored in vain to compete with commercial stations, caught as they were in public broadcasting's inherently self-perpetuating cycle of low-budget programming, which virtually guaranteed poor viewership, thus diminishing sponsorship further and squeezing budgets ever tighter. Johnson's Public Broadcasting Act aimed to change this self-defeating calculus by mandating public programming through the law's new PBS and NPR networks while supporting them, and other local stations, through the CPB. Distributing federal money as grants, the CPB allowed public stations to purchase or produce more expensive programming which might better compete in the open market with commercial stations. The application of this funding recipe, along with the start of PBS—the country's first nationwide public television network—coincided quite advantageously with *Sesame Street*'s debut in 1969. Financial support from the CPB made *Sesame Street* possible, and in turn the series' popularity helped launch PBS by giving the untested network its first viable television hit and marketable Muppet stars. Over the long term, *Sesame Street*, as well as PBS's other iconic children's series *Mister Rogers' Neighborhood* and the CTW's 1971 version of Project Follow Through, *The Electric Company*, also seems to have acclimated this cohort to the expectation of excellent programming from public television and radio sources.[43]

Empirical evidence from numerous studies conducted over the years attests to the substantive and consistent effects of *Sesame Street* as an educational tool for preschoolers in the sixties. The CTW deliberately built into its developmental agenda close working relationships with the academic research community, most notably the well-respected Educational Testing Service (ETS), an independent nonprofit assessment institute that conducted extensive summative surveys after each season of *Sesame Street* to measure educational outcomes without CTW bias. This association would make the series one of the most researched shows to ever appear on American television and provided the CTW with an invaluable yearly report card which clearly demonstrated statistically significant gains among viewers in all four instructional areas of the curriculum after the first seasons. Heavy viewers learned more than light viewers, and this held true for boys as well as girls, blacks and whites, poor and middle-class, urban and rural viewers. Those objectives that were stressed with proportionally more air time were likewise better retained. This continual data stream guided producers as instruction was tweaked when needed, and subsequent seasons introduced carefully chosen new objectives.

The second-season curriculum, for instance, was expanded to include new mathematical skills like addition and subtraction and a twenty-word reading vocabulary. (Kermit, however, was written out, only to return more prominently in season three.) In time, more social and emotional subjects, ranging from an exploration of Latino culture to eventually even death and grieving, were featured as well.

Supplemental studies of parents and educators buttressed the early ETS cognitive findings. Mothers of *Sesame Street* enthusiasts told the CTW of noticeable—and gratifying—improvements in their children's social interactions with peers, heightened confidence when tackling unfamiliar tasks, and, moreover, improved outlooks about learning in general. Other adults observed more positive attitudes toward children from other races in regular *Sesame Street* viewers. Elementary school teachers reported that their students who were veteran watchers "ranked higher than children who had watched less, especially for general readiness for school, quantitative readiness, positive attitudes toward school, and relationships with peers." Contrary to cynical predictions that a "boring" old traditional classroom would necessarily pale in comparison to the more "lively" *Sesame Street*, thus leaving unrealistic students restless and prone to mischief once they arrived in the first grade, research revealed that *Sesame Street* was actually making the adjustment to elementary school smoother and that, in fact, watching the series discouraged misbehavior because children arrived more self-assured in their ability to master the new learning environment. Inner city parents certainly believed this to be the case, with 90 percent telling researchers *Sesame Street* definitely was helping their children succeed in school.[44]

A few conservative critics detected a subversive communist plot afoot on *Sesame Street* with all the warmly received appearances by folksinger Pete Seeger, not-so-subtle promotion of "women's lib"-type working mothers, and racial integration (the series was briefly banned in Mississippi and elsewhere in the South) surely threatening to undermine the American way of life for generations to come. But the CTW always projected a far more sanguine developmental picture beyond the early 1970s. Its in-house experts figured it eminently "logical and plausible" that if a life course consisted of a continual progression of steps and choices beginning in the formative years and extending out toward horizon, preschool children faltering at the onset of their journey may well continue to stumble down the road while a surer footing in the beginning of the sequence boded a much better outcome.

Sesame Street producers anticipated that students commencing their academic career with a better attitude, coupled with a deeper cognitive toolbox, would grab the attention of teachers in the earliest grades. Having identified a pupil as bright and well-behaved, these teachers would then set in motion a self-fulfilling succession of higher expectations, more meaningful feedback, and supplemental educational opportunities, a trend which would place the student on a "trajectory of long-term achievement" throughout elementary and high school. One of the few later longitudinal measurements in this regard—the Recontact Study tracing adolescents identifying themselves as frequent viewers of *Sesame Street* as preschoolers in the early 1980s—seemed to confirm as much. The *Sesame Street* students maintained better grades all through high school, read more books for pleasure, were motivated to pursue higher levels of achievement, and exhibited less aggression compared to teenagers who had not been regular watchers.[45]

Taken together, was this nurturing of the whole child not precisely Lyndon Baines Johnson's dream of a Great Society, building a "place where every child can find knowledge to enrich his mind and to enlarge his talents . . . a place where leisure is a welcome chance to build and reflect, not a feared cause of boredom and restlessness [and] a place where the city of man serves not only the needs of the body and the demands of commerce but the desire for beauty and the hunger for community"? Indeed it was. From the White House, President Johnson set the tone for the decade's national dialogue concerning the proper role of government in remedying the many public failures still dragging on American advancement, while moreover fabricating the requisite legislative apparatus to translate vision into program. Across the sixties, activists took advantage of the administration's organizational platforms and newly available federal resources, working in their own local communities to realize the Great Society's promise of equality of opportunity. And, in turn, it was the Big Daddy from the Pedernales's associated investments in educational progressivism, greatly expanding the public's commitment to teach those early learners who were not hearing bedtime stories or lacked a record player to sing along with, that unmistakably drove this central facet of his overall child welfare policies into the daily lives of children. Which means that even if preschoolers did not know it at the time, *Sesame Street*, such an integral experience in their young lives, was brought to them, at least in part, by the Great Society, and the letters L. B. and J.[46]

CHAPTER SIX

The Southern Struggle for Civil Rights

Freedom to me meant being treated equal. I mean,
not just because I'm a black boy, but treating me right. That's all.
Larry Martin, eleven years old during Freedom Summer

In COMBATING THOSE debasing conditions identified as natural enemies of the American Dream—poverty, disease, and ignorance—Lyndon Johnson's Great Society inevitably converged near mid-decade with the most dramatic social movement in the nation's history: the struggle for African American civil rights. "The effort of American Negroes to secure for themselves the full blessings of American life . . . must be our cause too," the president had told Congress about the necessity of black voting rights in March 1965, a few days after bloodshed in Selma, Alabama, and eight months since passing his seminal Civil Rights Act of 1964. "Because it's not just Negroes, but really it's all of us, who must overcome the crippling legacy of bigotry and injustice. And," to further underscore his administration's alignment with the movement, in language borrowed from civil rights activists' own freedom songs, Johnson resolutely vowed, "we shall overcome."[1]

As a Southerner speaking directly to the South, the president understood well how race still kept the former Confederacy and some border states woefully mired in the nineteenth century culturally, politically, and economically. How stubborn adherence to a hateful caste system which kept poor, rural blacks just one step removed from slavery also acted as a regional drag on postwar affluence, beggaring both races. How televised coverage of racism's ugly face embarrassed America's moral leadership around the Cold War world. Nearly a century after the Civil War, the South's Jim Crow segregation—known legally as *de jure* in that this separation of the races was based in state law—mandated second-class citizenship for all African Americans in residential patterns, public accommodations, and social relations.

Just as "White Only" and "Colored Only" signs explicitly demarcated the separate facilities—which by their nature were never intended to be equal—various associated customs drew equally powerful, if less visible, lines: white customers were always served first, no eye contact between the races, blacks staying to the outside of sidewalks and walking out in the street if approached by whites. Systematically marginalized black schools, the first feature of Jim Crow to gain much national attention, were routinely no more than dilapidated houses lacking gymnasiums, lunchrooms, and sometimes running water or indoor restrooms. Starved of financial support, their bare-bones curriculums offered little in the way of physical education, art, music, home economics, or extracurricular activities, just as shabby textbooks and maps came second-hand from white schools. When civic texts were published for black students, the chapters on democracy and voting might be missing altogether. School boards thought such omissions a mere educational expediency considering that three-fourths of the old Confederate states had effectively disenfranchised their black citizens generations ago through clever constitutional subterfuge involving poll taxes and literacy tests. Estimate the number of bubbles in a bar of Ivory soap, a county clerk might ask of blacks seeking to register. Denied the vote and its political power, Southern blacks toiled in an economic system controlled by whites. Drawing scarcely subsistence paychecks as menial laborers and domestics from white employers, or by design accumulating insurmountable debt sharecropping, African Americans faced few options to spend that money other than patronizing local white-owned businesses.

And, lest any blacks appear too "uppity" or forgetful of their place, the vigilante Ku Klux Klan, cross-pollinated as they could be with local law enforcement, stood watch over the Jim Crow way of life, zealously guarding its parameters through intimidation and violence.

From such sweltering oppression Southern blacks in the late 1950s transformed their ongoing fight for integration and voting rights from what had been primarily legalistic courtroom battles into a multidimensional, and interracial, mass movement of the people. With each passing year after the storied 1956 Montgomery bus boycott, this crusade for civil rights gathered momentum, inspiring thousands to participate in creative direct action protests by courageously putting their bodies on the line in nonviolent defiance of Jim Crow. Indeed, of the nineteen million African Americans in the United States at the time—nearly 60 percent of whom resided in the South—it is estimated that somewhere near seven hundred thousand—roughly 4 percent—joined the fray.

Nearly every day during the most tumultuous years, from 1960 to 1965, local activists carried out some form of peaceful demonstration in one Dixie community or another: boycotts of downtown businesses, sit-ins at segregated spaces, songful marches, or freedom rides. As a tactic, these collective acts of nonviolent, civil disobedience—embodied in Martin Luther King's leadership—confronted racism across the South by simply refusing to comply with *de jure* discrimination and oppression any longer. Protesters faithfully believed that the sights and sounds of their undeserved suffering at the hands of reactionary segregationists, in retaliation for this refusal, would move Northern public opinion through moral suasion and ultimately compel federal intervention on their behalf. Activists spoke often of Gandhian spiritual awakenings forged in shared struggle and the ways in which participation engendered fresh perspectives on personal liberation and political empowerment. By exposing idealistic youth and students of both races to the liberating promise of an alternative, interracial America—what they called a "beloved community"—the civil rights movement, in due course, catalyzed the much wider movement of social activism in the 1960s, shaping its timing, direction, and vocabulary.[2]

While it is tempting to focus on this "Southern" phase of the civil rights movement here, concentrating on those rare preadolescents who became viable actors—foot soldiers—on the shifting front lines, perhaps the most critical entry points into black childhood are the less obvious or heralded ways in which historic social change transformed how children identified and understood themselves based on the color of their skin during the formative years of life—in other words, what it meant to grow up black in America. In those years before the movement—in both the Jim Crow South and Northern ghettos—the daily lived experience of most African American children resembled in most aspects a common Cold War era childhood, with one distinctly inherent difference: there existed a duality in the lives of these children. On one hand recognizably American, yet unlike their white contemporaries, blacks learned out of necessity the convoluted constructions of racial self-identification which involved a constant awareness of where society prohibited them from physically going and what, over their future life course, they most likely would, or could not, be.

Through diligent parenting, these core lessons were fairly mastered between the ages of three and seven, but such an education on race was truly

ongoing and cumulative. The civil rights movement altered the scope and sequence of this often tortured socialization for incalculable numbers of young
people. The same energy radiating from each of the unfolding steps toward
social and political equality in the adult world was reflected in childhood as a
series of psychological milestones at key developmental points which progressively improved black children's agency to redefine relative worth, theirs and
whites'. Consequently, life moved quickly for African Americans growing up
in the civil rights era. Year to year, the very meanings of black childhood became more fluid in the sixties, influenced by news footage from the March on
Washington, local elementary school desegregation, the removal of "White
Only" signs, and pop cultural manifestations of Black Power. By the early
1970s, a black child's fundamental frame of reference and perspective on life,
and what trajectories existed for moving successfully through it, looked radically different from the way they looked in 1960.[3]

As that added developmental dimension of black childhood, color-
consciousness began in infancy with parents already cognizant of the degrees
to which shades of skin color affected social standing within the African American community itself. By the age of three, as black preschoolers explored normal developmental ideas about their own appearance, a fuller understanding
of self was predicated on how their own color compared to that of other black
children. With increased playful interaction came greater awareness of how
they looked, and within a couple of years children too were capable of making
those value judgments about where they fit in a racialized African American
culture that valued lighter skin (and straight hair) while denigrating blackness.
In this perplexing world where some adults obsessively purchased commercial products for straightening hair and whitening skin, the term "black" was
actually pejorative, a slur usually taken to mean you were too dark and thus,
by definition, ugly.

Jordana Shakoor, born in Mississippi in 1956, remembered that before
moving North to Ohio eight years later she had never heard the words "black"
or "Afro-American" in a positive light. In fact, during the summer, black children were frequently admonished by adults to come in from the sun, lest they
get "too black." Similarly, to be considered "African" in any capacity, Shakoor
wrote of her Southern childhood, was unkind, "an offensive and demeaning
charge, an insinuation that you were less than human—ignorant, uncultured,
dark-skinned, and ape-like. It meant that your features, such as big lips or a
wide nose, were too African-looking and were less than beautiful, even if
you were light-skinned. Some black person referring to you as an African

American when I was a kid was trying to hurt your feelings." Even the proper, middle-ground terminology of "Negro" and "colored" raised a host of thought-provoking questions. "What really confused me as a little girl," Shakoor noted, "was what my own people wanted us to call ourselves . . . What did being 'colored' mean? Did it mean that we were supposed to be white but had been colored, like crayons? Or did it mean that we had been dipped in various shades from white to deep blue-black and were therefore 'colored'? Did that mean that we were supposed to have been white and by some quirk or accident we had changed color? I had no idea what being 'colored' meant or why this term was preferred by some over 'Negro.'"[4]

It certainly did not help when the same adults might use the two terms interchangeably depending on present company. But then again, parents' role in the socialization of their children to race was exasperatingly difficult, and often emotionally painful. Comparatively speaking, helping their children make connections between skin color and social constructions among other African Americans proved to be easier than teaching them what blackness signified in the dominant white society. Invariably, when childhood curiosity turned to the mysterious subject of white boys and girls, black parents—in conjunction with extended family and fictive kin—walked a long and tenuous tightrope discussing the realities of race, somehow purposefully inspiring a confident self-image while instilling a healthy fear of all whites.

To mitigate the corrosive feelings of inferiority and worthlessness intrinsic to Jim Crow—which ascribed even to black adults the childlike qualities of folly, wantonness, and arrested development—mothers and fathers had to devise a battery of explanations to queries about discrimination and why African Americans were not as good as whites. Often their unfulfilling answers rested on the logic that it was not so much that whites were better, they were just more privileged or wealthy, and that black children should never confuse being poor with being inferior. In his *Notes of a Native Son* (1955), James Baldwin cast this dismal obligation of black parenting as a basic question of "how to prepare the child for the day when the child would be despised and how to create in the child . . . a stronger antidote to this poison than one had found for oneself."[5]

The real challenge lay in trying to reconcile the nurturing of self-respect with the irreconcilable realities of segregation. Black parents dreaded the age at which preadolescents started asking about what made white swimming pools and white-only snack bars so much better. Where in the definitions of second-class citizenship are satisfactory explanations of what exactly

constitutes an "uppity look" and how whites determined whether or not you
were giving them one? Best to err on the side of extreme caution, and in so
doing many African American parents conditioned their children to accept
Jim Crow unequivocally.

Since black children who did not know their "place" were left vulnerable
each time they ventured from home, it was incumbent on family to instruct
them early and often about discretion in what they said, alertness to where
they went, and readiness to run fast. Out of fear that their children would not
take the menace of white racism seriously enough—as everyone knew Emmett
Till had not—Southern mothers and fathers were by necessity and coercion, in
the words of child psychiatrist Robert Coles, "firm and abiding segregationists," effectively sanctioning through child-rearing the South's caste system in
order to keep their kids safe. In his landmark studies of the psychological implications of segregation, desegregation, and civil rights participation on children of both races in the 1960s, Coles found that virtually all learning relating
to local segregation laws and conduct came during the preschool years from
the family. As one grandmother explained to him, "It'll be with her for life
. . . we tell our children that, so by the time they have children, they'll know
how to prepare them . . . It takes a lot of preparing before you can let a child
loose in a white world." "The first thing a colored mother has to do when
her kids get old enough to leave the house and play in the street," another
woman spelled out, "is teach them about the white man and what he expects."
This meant facilitating the development of their own unique styles for dealing with white people, some of which Coles conceded were stereotyped in
folklore: "subservience, calculated humiliation, sly ingratiation, self-mockery;
or, changing the tone somewhat, aloof indifference, suspicion, withdrawal,
sullen passivity or grim, reluctant compliance." By school age—though ma-
neuvers and postures varied by developmental age, region, and class—most all
African American preadolescents knew how to utilize one, or a combination,
of these ploys when around whites. What is more, parents actually considered
the South's absolute parenting style preferable to that of the North, where *de
facto* segregation—based more on economic fact than on law—was less cut-
and-dried. On this sentiment children tended to agree. "In the North I'd have
learned the same thing," an elementary school student revealed to Coles, "only
it's worse, because there a mother can't just lay it on the line. It takes time for
the boy to get the full pitch, and realize it's really the same show, just a little
dressed up; and until he makes that discovery, he's liable to be confused. The
thing we're not down here is confused."[6]

Negative reinforcement customarily instilled such clarity on how the rules of the game applied to blacks, with Coles determining that when a black child transgressed, any resultant "spanking and threats [came] not from [her] city or its police or judges, but from [her] mother, and especially from [her] father." In equal measure, black preadolescents were strictly taught to assiduously govern any feelings of resentment or hatred toward whites. "I guess we don't like white people too much deep inside. You could hardly expect us to," a Southern mother told Coles, "[but] we have to live with one another, black and white I mean. I keep on telling that to the children, and if they don't seem to learn it, like everything else I have to punish them to make sure they do."[7]

Even something as seemingly innocuous as joking about whites in the privacy of the home was expressly forbidden, in case youngsters might accidently slip up—uttering what they really thought about whites—later in public. "Just the other day my Laura started getting sassy about white children on the television," a mother confided in 1961. "My husband told her to hold her tongue and do it fast. It's like with cars and knives, you have to teach your children to know what's dangerous and how to stay away from it; or else they sure won't live long. White people are a real danger to us until we learn how to live with them. So if you want your kids to live long, they have to grow up scared of whites; and the way they get scared is through us; and that's why I don't let my kids get fresh about the white man even in their own house."[8]

No matter the amount of parental preparation in the abstract, children's eventual encounters with the harsh reality and ubiquity of segregation—especially their initial experiences—were extremely jarring, and unforgettable. Indeed, so resonant are these racist experiences from childhood that it is not uncommon for black adults to pinpoint their introduction to Jim Crow as their most humiliating memory. For all the ambiguities in racial socialization, "there was nothing confusing about the 'white only' and 'colored only' signs on public facilities, however," Jordana Shakoor concluded. "'White only' meant just that, and was not intended to include any shade of black whatsoever. 'Colored only' signs referred to all black people, Negro, colored, whatever you called yourself; that was where you went." Aside from schools, stores and recreational facilities were customarily the settings in which black children were collectively introduced to Jim Crow. Most of these experiences involved subtle torments, like hearing oneself conspicuously referred to as "nigra" in public, learning that the local public library did not allow children's books featuring black and white rabbits together, or not being able to shop without a salesclerk handling the merchandise for you.

An Alabama woman distinctly recalled just such a shock, when she was ten or eleven years old and a white saleslady snapped at her for looking through a drawer of clothing by herself. "That stayed with me a long time," she remembered, as did her first instance of not getting the same quality of goods as white shoppers from a local five-and-dime store. When she asked to purchase a cookie on display behind a glass counter, the salesperson produced a cookie, but a different one, from someplace below the shelving. "I found out they were the old cookies they had taken out and replaced with fresh ones. She was giving me these old ones from a box underneath." Likewise, a Southern man spoke of his early revelation over the peculiar notion of separate drinking fountains when he was around twelve years old. "I used to think, what's the difference between colored water and white water? What does white water taste like? I couldn't wait to catch the drop on somebody to find out." Only when he and a friend surreptitiously drank white water from a department store fountain did he learn that "it tasted no different. Water was water. The only thing different, was with the black one you practically had to put your mouth on the thing to drink out of it. On the white side, they barely had to bend over. Their water came up so free. This was mystifying." The South's more blatant rejections—such as being refused service in a restaurant outright—were every bit as infuriating, but it was their cumulative weight which children of the civil rights era still consider to be the most psychologically damaging, tearing away at their dignity piece by piece. "When it happened," another Alabama man reflected, "it dawned on me that the lady didn't know if I was a good child, or a bad child, or a loving son, or an angel. Just because I was brown and had black hair, I could not eat there."[9]

The sense of unfairness, that these unnatural distinctions between people were based capriciously on race, not only wounded the individual but also stirred up important developmental discord for children whose moral reasoning and behaviors were just beginning to be governed by a sense of mutual respect. The spatial and psychological boundaries erected between black and white children distorted social interactions for both races. African Americans ordinarily grew up almost exclusively in the company of black relatives and peers, having only minimal and random association with white children, who lived outside their part of town. "I wasn't supposed to be around them," Shakoor understood early in childhood, "and they weren't supposed to be around me." And even when black and white kids crossed paths naturally, parental socialization to segregation strictly guided the nature of all interracial relationships. Young Southern whites, as a product of their upbringing, felt a higher comfort level—almost an innocent friendliness—around blacks of all ages, which often had to be tempered by adults. Coles related a relevant instance from the early sixties where an eight-year-old white girl accidently bumped into a black woman, and instinctively as a matter of etiquette, said, "Excuse me, ma'am." The girl's mother publicly corrected her, explaining that while it was acceptable for a well-mannered young lady to say "excuse me" to a black adult, it was not at all proper to call a black woman "ma'am." This rebuke struck the girl as a contrived adult construction analogous to grown-ups making you dress up for some places and not for others.[10]

Conversely, Coles pointed out that just as white children learned to forgo courtesy titles for blacks, children of color—automatically wary and feeling none of this natural easiness—learned that formality was expected from all whites. "Up until the time I was about ten years old, I always played with those white kids," a Mississippi man remembered. "But once I became ten, their parents came straight out and told me they didn't want me playing with their kids no more. Their mama told them they were better than I was, and told me I couldn't associate with her son, and I had to call him 'Mister.' And the kids themselves adopted that attitude."[11]

"Aside from the women being maids . . . gosh, it was like they were invisible," a white woman born in 1958 told me of growing up in small town Tennessee. "Only later did I begin to wonder, where the hell were they? They weren't at the drive-in, or the restaurants, or in church, or the grocery store. Where did the men work? Where did they get groceries? Did they have cars, and if they did, where did they go? They sure didn't go down our main street. They lived in Colored Town and that's all I knew."[12]

Lack of familiarity borne of segregation bred not only curiosity and jealousy but sometimes contempt among blacks as well. "I didn't know anything about the white kids who lived on the other side of town," Shakoor underscored of her Mississippi childhood. "I had never seen a white boy or girl up close, at least not that I could recall." She, like so many of her cohort, speculated often on whether white voices sounded like those of her African American friends, about their mannerisms, habits, the games they played. In particular, she sought a way to see their skin and hair close up. Nearly all black children thought they knew something about Caucasian facial features based on ample media evidence from television, movies, magazines, calendars, and play with white dolls—which some intuitively kept segregated from the black ones, imagining their occupations to be employer and employee. Yet, mindful that media caricatures of blacks were often exaggerated, African American youngsters wondered if perhaps white children looked different in real life. To make sure, one had to steal furtive glances whenever possible—"I catches a look sometimes, real fast like"—or take advantage of that rare occasion to study them carefully. "The first time I saw a white boy up close enough to tell if white people really had blue eyes was in 1964," Shakoor continued, surprised by how, in fact, his distinctly non-Negro features turned out to be as advertised: fine, yellow crew-cut hair, snubbed nose, small lips. So too were those forbidden "white-only" areas the subjects of much conjecture—and coveting—for children whose tiny homes were weathered and whose asphalt playgrounds slowly rusted out. Could all white neighborhoods be as comfortable as those on television, with their trimmed lawns, flower beds, and freshly painted homes? What adventures waited behind a city park's chain-link fences and thick hedges—so high as to make only the tops of the monkey bars, slides, and swings visible from the street—with its unknown acres of green grass for hiding-and-seeking and huge trees for climbing?[13]

Robert Coles' study of preadolescents "coming of age" in regard to these issues of race and racism during the civil rights era—to borrow from the title of Anne Moody's classic autobiography on the subject—concentrates on the developmental consequences of that aforementioned duality in black childhood. Coles determined that since most of the "usual" difficulties and issues of growing up in postwar America were inseparable from this additional racial dimension, black preadolescents learning at their corresponding developmental ages to either accept or hate themselves, the differences between themselves and others, and what was forbidden about the world and their own bodies, did so based principally on skin color. The very meanings of their color conveyed feelings of worthlessness and foreboding, with only the narrow prospect of poverty and relentless persecution to look forward to—a society perpetually saying no to them about everything—and they invariably came to judge their value as individuals and citizens accordingly. These were effectively the same social science findings used by the National Association for the Advancement of Colored People (NAACP) to argue against school segregation a decade earlier in *Brown v. Board of Education of Topeka*. The remarkable feature of Coles's work, however, was that in interviewing five- to seven-year-olds— the age when, in his professional opinion, African Americans' socialization to their "place" was freshest—he encouraged his subjects to express themselves through drawings. More remarkable still, in these fascinating artworks Coles captured some of the first available evidence of how the civil rights movement was imprinting black children's developing sense of race, which was informing their immediate lived experience in the 1960s but also affording potential insight into their future as adults.[14]

In their storytelling-through-art, Coles recognized—only "faintly disguised"—a childhood in which white children, like adults, were big and strong, their power directly correlated to a black person's defenselessness. African American preadolescents consistently drew their white counterparts larger, more intact, and more lifelike than themselves or their black friends. Not only were blacks drawn smaller and less defined, the figures usually lacked some features, as if incomplete. Coles' most famous subject, Ruby Bridges, the first grader who gained national attention by desegregating an all-white New Orleans elementary school in 1960, drew white children very carefully: limbs systematically proportioned, the correct number of fingers and toes, full, wide mouths with lips and teeth. Yet her drawings of blacks often had no mouth—Ruby said it had been "forgotten"—their ears were exaggerated, and their half-finished feet were either bare or had tattered shoes. In self-portraits she, too, might lack fingers and toes, her arms obviously shorter, truncated, or at times simply absent.

Interestingly, in regard to color, most African American children Coles worked with avoided black and brown crayons to shade in their black people, routinely saving these colors to designate dirt or the ground. Some even deliberately depicted themselves as white. By their own admission this was nothing more than harmless, wishful thinking, but it was nonetheless consistent with the groundbreaking, pre-war "doll test" which had shown black children demonstrating a significant preference for white dolls over "colored" dolls. Ruby made use of black and brown only sparingly, with just enough of those colors to indicate the subject's race. "It was as if," Coles speculated, she "started drawing all people as white, then turned some of them into Negroes by depriving them of a limb or coloring a small section of their skin (she preferred the shoulder or the stomach) brown." When questioned, Ruby explained by saying, "When I draw a white girl, I know she'll be okay, but with the colored it's not okay . . ." The only exception was her grandfather, a Mississippi Delta farmer working land Ruby proudly described as "his and no one else's." "With enthusiasm and determination," Coles wrote, Ruby drew him as a huge brown man—taking up an entire sheet of paper—his eyes large, mouth normal with defined yellow teeth, proportionate ears, long arms, oversized hands, the correct number of fingers, and black boots.[15]

By the time she was ten years old in 1964, Ruby Bridges drew all black people with this much accuracy, telling Coles of the transformation, "Maybe

because of all the trouble going to school in the beginning I learned more
about my people. Maybe I would have anyway; because when you get older
you see yourself and the white kids; and you find out the difference. You
try to forget it, and say there is none; or if there is you won't say what it be.
Then you say it's my own people, and so I can be proud of them instead of
ashamed."[16]

Drawings by black children involving both races commonly reflected
asymmetrical relationships wherein African Americans were performing some
task for white children, either by request or of their own volition. One example from a seven-year-old North Carolina boy showed Freddie, a fragile-
looking black child at the bottom of a mountain landscape, and Billy, a larger
white boy near the top. "Freddie wishes he were up top, like Billy," the artist
narrated, "but he isn't because there's not room for both of them up there, at
least not now there isn't. They're not talking, they're just there. Freddie would
be afraid to be on top. He wouldn't know what to do. He's used to where
he is, just like Billy is. Billy is a big eater, and he has to have food with him
everywhere he goes. So Freddie is getting some food for him from the farms
and maybe he'll carry it up. But he'll come right down. He might get dizzy,
and Billy would not like for him to stay too long, because he might slip and
get killed if the two of them were there when there's only room for one."[17]

By comparison, the drawings of white preadolescents stood as an intriguing
counterpoint. Throughout the South, white children routinely learned the
adult practice of compartmentalizing all decent traits in whites while projecting undesirable qualities and social ills onto black figures. In their drawings,
black children likewise appeared smaller, less intact, and with disproportion-
al features, their actions exemplifying disobedience, impoliteness, rambunc-
tiousness, and poor hygiene—essentially, all the things white parents taught
their children not to be. As a white elementary student highlighted for Coles,
what made blacks different ran much deeper than darker skin. After all, he
could always get a tan. Pictures of houses and neighborhoods were similarly situated. White neighborhoods featured uniformly drawn houses—large,
sturdy, and well-furnished—decorated with vibrant crayons, on plush lawns
below the sun shining overhead. On the other hand, black neighborhoods
looked hurriedly drawn, the irregular houses—makeshift and flimsy—piled in
a jumble almost on top of one another, in muted brown and purple hues, without a sun. A prominently placed traffic light—colored bright red—separated
the white and black neighborhoods in one of these drawings to warn cars to
stop, but also, as the white artist clarified, to caution blacks that they were not

supposed to cross the street. Of course, a black child "knows about the light," he concluded, "he's so close to it that he can't very well forget it, can he?"[18]

Nevertheless, even in those white children identified as coming from militant segregationist homes, Coles observed a noticeable thawing by the mid-1960s, though he doubted if they realized how their racial views were slowly changing. With more frequency, he reviewed white children's drawings, which seemed to acknowledge—with a hint of shame—that black children in fact lived less hopeful and more vulnerable lives than theirs. Some started sketching blacks, in Coles's words, "with care and courtesy, with the same respect for his legs or arms that they lavish on the white people they portray." Like thousands of tolerant white adults across what journalists still called "the silent South"—those who respected black civil liberties and sought to navigate a moderate path toward integration without mayhem—these childhood illustrations began revealing a tacit acceptance—if not outright embrace—of the inevitable. Hence, in picturing a lone rabbit hopping through a schoolyard, a small white boy expressed a growing awareness that "The bunny wants to get in the school and have lunch, but we don't want her . . . Maybe she will, though." Or, as a white elementary schoolgirl captioned her drawing of a shy black girl hiding behind a tree in the schoolyard, apprehensively peering at the school, "The little colored girl wants to stay with us and I think she will."[19]

Throughout late spring and summer in 1961, a series of Freedom Rides concentrated national and international attention on a group of interracial activists traveling across the South aboard Trailways and Greyhound buses to protest segregated waiting rooms in stations along interstate highways. Fueled by the same spirit of nonviolent civil disobedience which had launched the Southern sit-in movement the previous year—with its still escalating shop-ins, swim-ins, kneel-ins, and dance-ins—these Freedom Riders—beaten nearly to death in Alabama before being jailed in Mississippi—ultimately succeeded in integrating bus terminals nationwide, and in the bloody process helped recruit hundreds of thousands of younger blacks to the struggle. Of those new volunteers considered to be "youth" within the movement, the majority were actually teenagers or college-age people in their twenties. This is the well-documented post-Emmett Till cohort of African Americans, those baby boomers whom scholars would later call "the integration generation." Students, like clergy, made for good protestors, having comparatively little to lose, being less beholden to whites economically, and already relatively organized on campuses. Their idealistic passion and preference for more confrontational activism, coupled with their sheer numbers, propelled

organizations such as the Congress of Racial Equality (CORE)—which initiated the Freedom Rides—and the Student Nonviolent Coordinating Committee (SNCC)—which completed the trips—toward the movement's vanguard
during the early sixties.[20]

Despite the NAACP's tradition of successful youth programming, most established civil rights leadership, including Martin Luther King and his Southern Christian Leadership Conference (SCLC), initially remained disinclined
to incorporate younger children, expressly elementary-school-age, as active
participants in mass demonstrations, which conceivably put them in harm's
way. Nevertheless, there were powerful historical and developmental forces at
work that were more compelling than the threats of beatings and arrest—or
parental rebuke—which motivated hundreds, maybe thousands, of preadolescents to eagerly join in when the movement spread to their hometowns and
neighborhoods.

There is no real modern precedent for children physically involving themselves in challenges to the adult political and social system, and developmentally it stands to reason. To Piaget, childhood learning is an upward, dialectical
process involving the perpetual quest for equilibrium. And here, in the civil
rights era South, the blatant discrepancy between the way it was and the way
it ought to be required precisely this type of advance in black preadolescents'
reasoning and morality. The comfort zone of equilibrium generally occurs from
two to four years old, seven to nine years old, and then again after eleven. In
most families, adults' accommodationist approach to Jim Crow formed the unfortunate basis of these periods of childhood equilibrium. Where mothers and
fathers appeared hopelessly compromised by their generation's submissiveness,
and even the American Dream they preached—an ethic of hard work equating
to success—was always relative to whites, expectations that things would change
in a lifetime were modest. Almost by default, parents teaching fear based on
the past offered little encouragement to imagine alternatives. With increased
age, however, came new experience accompanied by advancements in logical
and abstract thinking, which sooner or later tested what children thought they
already knew, and in turn produced those vulnerable periods of cognitive disequilibrium. Whereas the older generations measured progress in terms of how
far blacks had come since World War II, the civil rights struggle perpetually
challenged children to measure the distance left to go. Parental socialization
and personal submission to segregation were simply inadequate to explain the
new realities of the sixties, so black children were consequently adjusting their
schemes, synthesizing new learning in order to restore their equilibrium.[21]

Along these developmental journeys, preadolescents achieving a broader worldview were naturally more open to change—as evidenced by the shifting mindsets Coles identified in their drawings—and, when opportunities arose, more willing to act. There certainly were plenty of disruptive new influences sparking such intellectual adjustments. Not all parents fully acquiesced to Jim Crow's negativity, and in some politicized families—often correlating with higher education levels and middle-class status—fathers and mothers passed on their rising expectations, instilling hopeful lessons in black history and the reciprocal nature of justice. In many homes, children also learned, almost through osmosis, inspirational stories of the movement's heroes, battlegrounds, and martyrs: the Little Rock Nine, Freedom Summer, or the four little girls killed in Birmingham's Sixteenth Street Baptist Church bombing. Oral traditions in the black family fostered a common cultural awareness of the movement's history among children, and while preadolescents lacked personal recollections of the *Brown* decision or the Montgomery bus boycott, they embraced as role models Freedom Rider John Lewis and the four North Carolina Agricultural & Technical State University freshmen—Ezell Blair, Jr., Franklin McCain, Joseph McNeil, and David Richmond—who ignited the sit-ins by ordering coffee at a Woolworth lunch counter. Engaged teachers told a lot of stories as well, not only poignant accounts of murdered activists James Chaney, Andrew Goodman, and Mickey Schwerner, but broader Cold War messages celebrating America as the global champion of democratic principles, liberty, freedom, and human rights. These were worthy ideals— epitomized in the Pledge of Allegiance—but ones ringing increasingly hollow when juxtaposed with nightly newscasts covering the sit-ins, the first extensively televised movement events. In elementary school libraries, even the beloved Dr. Seuss, as historian Rebecca de Schweinitz points out, "consistently albeit humorously urged young readers to recognize societal constraints and to imagine new ways of ordering the world through his characters . . . "[22]

Mass meetings, more often than not held at churches, functioned as a parallel educational experience outside of school. Ministers opening their congregations to activism preached a particularly positive message to young blacks, as Martin Luther King himself did, about self-image and worth, while also exposing children, some for the first time, to the reality "that somebody else agreed this was not right. And it wasn't just one other person." In the church, children heard movement news, learned the language of freedom songs— *Oh, deep in my heart, I do believe, we shall overcome some day*—and were recruited into organized actions. As activist-turned-scholar Vincent Harding characterized the progression, "From those praying sessions in the kitchens in the mornings with aunts, uncles, deacons and many 'mommas,' to every step of the hard-fought yardage to the school door, to all the questions and all the tears and anger that children brought back home, the black family and its community were fully engaged. Parents had to answer a thousand questions from their children about the white gauntlets they had run, and the savagery and fear which they had seen. Preachers had to say something about the threats, the bombs, the state troopers. Someone had to explain to the children (and to themselves) why all this was going on in America the Beautiful. And in the course of this process of acting and reflecting a new political conscious began to develop, starting with the children."[23]

Sometimes this consciousness was manifested in simple, spontaneous deeds. An Alabama boy remembered that in elementary school he became "poisoned" by the Pledge of Allegiance and refused to hold his hand over his heart when reciting it. Others, like Jordana Shakoor in Mississippi, sang. "When we learned to sing the freedom song *We Shall Overcome*," she reflected, "Daddy taught us how to cross our arms with extended hands so that we could lock hands with one another in a straight line. As we sang the lyrics, we would sway back and forth from side to side. We giggled a lot when we tried to synchronize our swaying, though we were somewhat aware of the seriousness of the song." An Alabama girl recalled an incident at nine years old when, after purchasing a three-cent cone-shaped paper cup of water from the soda fountain, the clerk matter-of-factly told her she could not drink it at the counter. "So I poured my cup of water on the counter," she said, "instructing my brother and cousin to do likewise. The people in the store were absolutely shocked. That was our first protest and boycott."[24]

Still, even though the eyes of the nation had been upon the trailblazing young people desegregating Southern schools for nearly a decade, civil rights leaders only belatedly began incorporating children as viable activists in organized demonstrations during 1963. With the movement's momentum peaking, the use of children was a calculated matter of political strategy to rally national support and marshal fundraising in order to leverage the federal power required to topple the state laws underpinning Jim Crow. This realist approach, balanced—uneasily—with Martin Luther King's optimism, helped humanize civil rights in the court of public opinion by connecting the polarizing struggle to popular, family-oriented conceptions of childhood. Whereas adults standing up against the humiliation of segregation stirred the national conscience, the contrast of racism set against a sentimentalized idea of childhood innocence and its perceived tendency toward color-blindness had much greater persuasive power with the white middle class.

"One day right there in Alabama," King said, picturing the beloved community of which he dreamed, "little black boys and black girls will be able to join hands with little white boys and white girls as sisters and brothers." Segregation's affront to the American Dream could, likewise, be presented as dangerous to national security, considering childhood's centrality in the realization of the notion of an "American Century." Given the high Cold War stakes, the reckless waste of precious human resources—as exemplified by a black boy's sign reading "I want to grow up to be an airline pilot" at a CORE demonstration—imperiled the future: his, democracy's, and the republic's.[25]

Just as most Americans were less tolerant of segregation when it directly handicapped children, they also expressed disgust when segregationists brutalized child activists who were practicing nonviolent civil disobedience. In this capacity, the mass media was happy to oblige with appropriately provocative publicity. Print and television reporters, requiring easily identifiable storylines in order to narrate these extraordinary times for living room audiences, routinely framed movement activism as a passion play involving a moral struggle between unambiguously righteous heroes and racist villains. Stories and footage of white mistreatment of vulnerable black children did just that, casting preadolescents in the sympathetic lead role, with segregationists as one-dimensional, obnoxious bullies. So effective was the media in utilizing childhood to frame the victimization of blacks that journalists even characterized a twenty-seven-year-old activist like Bob Moses as a "kid," and many historical accounts still refer to his older baby boom cohort of activists as "youth." White and black critics—Malcolm X among them—accused parents of having "brought out" black children to protests as a crass publicity stunt, and Martin Luther King criticized them for cynically using young people as bait. The enlistment of more white children into the opposing segregationist protest and picket lines grew in direct proportion to increases in youthful black activism. These young white demonstrators were utilized as a counterbalance, their parents showcasing their childhood innocence—even dressing them in little robes at KKK rallies—to symbolize America's obligation to uphold traditional white values.[26]

The preadolescents who committed themselves as scripted actors in direct action protests, picket lines, and marches were developmentally drawn to activism, which aimed at integrating the local facilities most familiar and exciting in their lives. These were commonly educational and recreational:

schools, five-and-dimes, theaters, restaurants, swimming pools, skating rinks, zoos, and playgrounds. Whatever the target, their childhood involvement became intimately intertwined with their psychological development, just as the abuse they endured had parallel implications for supporters, opponents, and onlookers alike. Norman Rockwell's decidedly unRockwell-like painting, *The Problem We All Live With*, captured this reality in its uncomfortable depiction of a dignified African American elementary school girl being escorted by four towering federal marshals past a wall splattered with thrown tomatoes over the letters "KKK" and the word "Nigger" scrawled in graffiti. Although the artwork appeared as *Look* magazine's centerfold in January 1964, Rockwell's solitary little protagonist was commemorating the fact that many black children were already seasoned civil rights veterans, still walking point—to use military terminology from the Vietnam War—in the unending fight to integrate schools. When the 1954 *Brown vs. Board of Education* decision overturned the "separate but equal" justification for public segregation, declaring instead that separate schools were "inherently unequal" and mandating that the nation's schools must desegregate "with all deliberate speed," the Supreme Court effectively guaranteed schoolchildren's leadership role in the movement.[27]

This meant that in towns throughout Kentucky, Tennessee, Delaware, West Virginia, Virginia, South Carolina, and Arkansas, students were the first to experiment with legal racial integration, ten years before the Civil Rights Act of 1964 finally prohibited segregation in the adult world. School integration proceeded cautiously, and each Southern community was different. Policy changes, and reactions to them, occurred unevenly, with advances in some locales unfolding simultaneously with setbacks in other towns. Within five years of *Brown*, over seven hundred districts had desegregated relatively peacefully. Under court order to comply, besieged school boards would agree to desegregate through some freedom-of-choice plan—wherein students were supposed to be able to choose the school they attended—announce the decision publicly, and then set a conservative timeline for implementation. Far more school boards equivocated, employing legal and extralegal means to only minimally accommodate the law. Usually these districts took advantage of the ruling's "all deliberate speed" loophole, drafting a desegregation plan but only using a handful of black students to carry it out, or incrementally phasing in K-12 integration one grade per year over twelve years. In a few of the most publicized cases, school boards resisted on a massive scale. Single schools and entire districts closed their doors altogether—in Prince Edward County,

Virginia, from 1959 to 1964—while elsewhere protests and riots broke out over busing, and private schools—"segregation academies"—flourished. In all these local variations, classrooms and playgrounds emerged early on as the center stage where integrationists and segregationists tested—in precisely the dramas favored by the mass media—core arguments about sociology, federalism, and foreign relations. Both sides loudly held up for public and legal scrutiny their respective interpretations on what interracial childhood socialization would do for, or to, America and the American Dream.[28]

School integration was, accordingly, a parental decision carried out by children. Civil rights leaders offered encouragement and advice, sharing with interested families Dewey's theories about black and white students being the vehicle for a future post-racial America if only grownups would stop indoctrinating them with racist ideas and simply allow them to share classrooms as natural friends. But mothers and fathers made the fateful call. Many instinctively said no, fearful of the hardships their children would face, and unwilling to risk losing jobs or other retaliatory strikes against the household. Those who might guardedly look into the application process often were dissuaded by obtuse districts or outright Klan intimidation. For all the strain and soul-searching involved, though, in the end the courageous parents who either inspired their children's participation or relented to it weighed the dangers against the optimistic desire to see them transcend the inferior education which handicapped previous generations. They concluded that seizing the opportunity now for a good education positioned their children for a better life and might spare their generation from the worst of Jim Crow. Said one Kentucky father whose son had requested to be one of those to integrate the local school, "If you've got the guts to go, I got the guts to take you."[29]

Robert Coles was never able to identify a standard criteria that Southern school boards followed in selecting black students for integration. In the cases he researched, age and place of residence were sometimes the only variables considered, rather than academic aptitude or personality. Neither could he determine a typical profile for the young integrators themselves. "Many of these pioneer children," Coles noted, "have not been hand-picked or particularly able and bright—not natural leaders, chosen for that reason to lead their race into white schools. Whatever has enabled them to get along as well as they have is no mysterious and rare gift of intellect or 'personality development.'" The adolescent students chosen by school boards generally had a good understanding of the "punishment" awaiting them for seeking a better education: the relentless bombardment of psychological and physical cruelty from white students and teachers, vulgar insults, eggs smashed into books, ink smeared on clothes, tacks on chairs, weapons brandished, and death threats. They used the restrooms only when unoccupied or not at all. They made sure to be always quiet, respectful, and sincere, never argumentative or inflammatory. All the while at home, their parents agonized every minute of every school day, for the entirety of the academic year, a purgatory exacerbated by media coverage.

Preadolescents integrating elementary schools came much less equipped cognitively and emotionally, even if the punishment tended to take different forms. They too exhibited more courage than most adults when walking through screaming crowds, but they were also more surprised at the depth of white hostility just because they wanted to take advantage of newer textbooks and better swing sets. Once inside, younger integrationists missed the comforting—and safer—routines and companionships they had left behind at their old black school. And whereas teenage blacks faced harassment, in elementary schools the problem more often centered around being ignored and lonely: a whole year without anyone talking to you except the teacher, no one to compliment your pretty new plaid dress, not a soul to borrow a pencil from or a playmate to teeter-totter with, and not a single birthday party invitation.[30]

As a case study of these "tender warriors," Ruby Bridges—Rockwell's inspiration for *The Problem We All Live With*—offers some of the best documented evidence of school desegregation's developmental imprint on preadolescents. Just six years old when she became the first African American to enroll at New Orleans' all-white William Frantz Elementary in 1960, and therefore one of the Deep South's earliest precollege integrators, Ruby attended much of the first grade as the only black student in a school which normally enrolled almost six hundred students.

Owing to predictable legal delays at the onset of the school year, the district had pushed back its initial hesitant step toward integration, which was to admit four black first graders at two elementary schools—Ruby in one and three other girls at another—until November. This postponement gave segregationists ample time to organize a boycott and public confrontations. Nearly all white parents held their children out of William Frantz—their defiance encouraged by the state legislature—and amid citywide racial unrest, a mob of one hundred or so, mostly jeering housewives and teenagers, surrounded the school to discourage Ruby and any remaining white students from entering. In a daily ritual, police maintained order along the sidewalks with barricades, while deputy federal marshals escorted Ruby, accompanied at the outset by her mother, through the onslaught of Confederate flags, handmade signs, and taunting chants: "Two, four, six, eight, we don't want to integrate; eight, six, four, two, we don't want a chigeroo," and, sung to the tune of "The Battle Hymn of the Republic," "Glory, glory, segregation, the South will rise again." Ruby was too short to see the protesters' faces, but she likened these before-school spectacles to Mardi Gras, except for the rocks being hurled at her and the black doll lying in effigy inside a little coffin.[31]

Although several white children eventually managed to cross the picket lines, they were brought through a rear entrance and were so well hidden from Ruby that she assumed she was effectively alone in Frantz Elementary. Isolated all day in a vacated classroom, Ruby learned one-on-one with her white teacher, but ate lunch silently at her desk as marshals stood guard outside in the hall. The teacher-student bond grew progressively closer, with Ruby emulating her teacher's Boston accent by year's end. But despite innocently incorporating the crowd's ugly "Two, four, six, eight, we don't want to integrate" into a jump rope rhyme, the constant exposure to such unadulterated animosity, and the loneliness of being socially ostracized, exhausted the frightened first grader. She struggled to make meaning of what was happening to her, suffering from regular nightmares and longing for some type of escape or refuge. "They don't seem to be getting tired, the way we thought," she told Robert Coles of the mob's persistence. "Maybe it'll have to be a race, and I hope we win. Some people sometimes think we won't, and maybe I believe them, but not for too long." At some point that school year, Ruby stopped eating. Coles figured her loss of appetite stemmed from a protester telling her every day that she was going to poison her food. He also believed that while Ruby stoically ignored the threats when entering school, she nevertheless internalized their underlying message. "Is it *only* my skin?" she asked Coles and her parents repeatedly, leading the psychiatrist to understand that while Ruby came to comprehend the resistance to her presence, she had trouble sorting out the nature of the hatred behind it.[32]

Eventually, by spring 1961, as the crowds diminished and white students gradually returned to the school, other first graders joined Ruby's classroom for portions of the day. One boy, Jimmie, the son of committed segregationists, also spent time with Robert Coles, and what the two children witnessed and experienced together inside Frantz offers unique insight into the perspective from the other side of the barricade, as well as the remarkable resiliency of these preadolescents. Nothing in American history provided a model from which to accurately gauge white reactions to school integration. How white mothers and fathers approached the matter was comparable to the way black parents did, in that these were protective adult choices played out in childhood, a world where preadolescents tended to imitate their parents. Only a visible minority of reactionaries—confident that *their* schools belonged to whites exclusively—militantly opposed school integration. Moderates, and those who took part in the boycott, adhered to "respectable" arguments against integration—that white students' progress would be held back by academically inferior and poorly behaved blacks, or that liberal social experimentation was making guinea pigs of American youth. Most parents—that "silent South"—fell in line at some point. Granted, few Southerners actively promoted school integration, but while whites may have been opposed in principle, respect for rule of law kept them from shutting down schools. Moreover, an unwillingness to derail their children's future by denying them vital months of schooling encouraged compliance. At the end of the day, white parents' choices boiled down to no school, the unaccredited make-shift kind, an expensive private one, or one that was marginally desegregated.[33]

Jimmie's parents sent him back into the boycotted school for fear of his missing the entire first grade, but also because, as his mother told Coles, "I decided that Frantz School was as much mine as that nigger's . . . besides, Jimmie wanted to go back real bad." By the time he encountered Ruby, Jimmie already, Coles observed, "knew his racial distinctions as well as his letters and numbers." This was a typical "conforming prejudice," directly imitated from his mother and father and which, mixed with a six-year-old's ignorance of blacks, helped to organize the boy's worldview around racial stereotypes. The bitter climate of resistance no doubt intensified the teaching of bigotry, just as it also must have introduced hate to those white children who, like Ruby, had never spent time pondering that feeling before. Besides parental racism, adult mockery of public education and the law also influenced impressionable schoolchildren like Jimmie, potentially compromising their developing moral behaviors, which are based on mutual respect and obedience to the law.

Having been taught not to play with "niggers" because they were dirty, Jimmie thought all blacks to be unsuitable playmates and never considered Ruby a permanent member of the school. Someday, he hoped, she would give up and Frantz Elementary would get back to normal. So when Coles asked Jimmie to draw Ruby, the boy claimed he could not "because I don't know what she looks like. I don't look at her close if I can help it." When pressed, he finally drew Ruby in grotesque miniature, with wild black hair and exaggerated teeth—not unlike a vampire—and always drew her cordoned her off from the school in a waiting room or jail. One of his biggest worries, he told Coles, was that if Ruby stayed, Frantz might soon be "flooded with them [and] it's when a lot of them come that we'll get dirty with all them around . . . They do bad, and make us sick."[34]

Whether or not a child developmentally advances beyond such racist attitudes and prejudiced reasoning depends in large measure on positive adult influences, and, in Jimmie's case, increased socialization. By the second grade—when comparative normalcy again prevailed and Ruby's class numbered over twenty students, including other African Americans—Jimmie's attitudes toward her were changing, albeit unevenly. "Jimmie plays with me okay," Ruby reported to Coles, "but then he remembers that I'm colored, so he gets bad." He would play nice for a while and then run away to say bad things about her, probably using racial issues, like many white children, to gain attention. It was as if, Ruby speculated, "he forgets, and then he remembers again."

In his drawings, Ruby grew proportionally larger, appeared more human—Jimmie even privately admitted she had pretty clothes—and was located within the school. Conversely, the demonstrators, previously drawn with prominent mouths and arms, got smaller and more abstract. Now, even in the most racially liberal homes, parental tolerance of integration rarely extended to interracial social fraternization among children, including casual conversation. For Coles, the most fascinating aspects of Jimmie's evolving association with Ruby were the subtle alterations in his family dynamic. Throughout the boycott, Jimmie's parents forbade any mention of Ruby at home, a strict prohibition which continued after he went back to school. Then, in the following year, they became increasingly curious about Ruby, stopped calling her "nigger," and instead questioned Jimmie nightly about how the "nigra" was doing in school or the "nigra's" behavior. Jimmie at first recounted the day's classroom stories by mimicking a black dialect when narrating Ruby's role—to his parents' delight—but eventually dropped these impersonations in favor of using his own voice for hers. Although never exactly welcoming Ruby, Jimmie's development through this shared crisis was nonetheless significant so early in his life, and, according to Coles, he was not an outlier. "Other children in their school, their city, all over the South," Coles concluded, "have been similarly aroused and affected."[35]

The shifting gears set in motion by school integration ground on, further raising levels of engagement for children of both races and focusing young African American eyes on the prize more intently. Which brings us to that 1963 watershed in organized preadolescent activism, the so-called Children's Crusade in Birmingham, Alabama. Civil rights leaders deliberately chose the notorious city of Birmingham for massive nonviolent demonstrations during the first week in May in order to refocus national attention on a specific grievance: segregation of public accommodations. The multidimensional strategy called for various sit-ins, an economic boycott of downtown businesses, and disruptive mass marches carried out by local activists and invited outside supporters. The logic was that with thousands of peaceful protesters in the streets, in direct violation of the city's court injunction again such demonstrations, Birmingham's jails would inevitably overflow. Chanting the mantra "Jail, no bail," those arrested would be locked up intentionally, at the heavy-handed direction of Birmingham's menacing police commissioner, Eugene "Bull" Connor. Their cheerful suffering for a principle—from the example of Mahatma Gandhi—would, as a result, shame the city with negative publicity while showcasing the hypocrisy of the segregation laws. Over the course of several days, two thousand, including Martin Luther King, were, in fact, summarily arrested, jailed at a rate of ten every minute during one intense two-hour stretch. This attrition rapidly depleted the adult ranks, however, and the determination was finally made to use high school, junior high, and some elementary school children as marchers in order to sustain the demonstrations. Proponents of using the children argued that since children were already playing a visible role in the movement, the time had come to stop sheltering them and allow their fuller participation. Or, as the SCLC Director of Direct Action Rev. James Bevel explained to King, if children as young as five could freely choose Jesus Christ, then they were not too young to act on that faith.[36]

Thus waves of adolescent and preadolescent volunteers took part in a series of Birmingham marches, leaving from designated staging areas in churches, especially the Sixteenth Street Baptist Church across the street from Kelly Ingram Park, to, in the minds of many, "take their turn." Audrey Faye Hendricks, nine years old in May 1963, recalled that she had been exposed to civil rights activism for nearly two years by then through her church: "there was no way for me not to know about the movement." "I remember it being warm the morning I marched," she continued. "The night before at a meeting, they told us we'd be arrested. I went home and told my mother that I wanted to go. She just said, 'Okay.' I was in third grade. My teacher knew that I was going, and she cried. She thought, I guess, it was admirable that I would go. Teachers had the threat of losing their jobs. I did not go to school the day I went on the march. I wasn't nervous or scared."

Children like Audrey joyfully sang to stay confident and calm—*And before I'd be a slave I'll be buried in my grave, And go home to my Lord and be free*—with most later recalling an exhilarating feeling of satisfaction when walking through the black community, where clapping supporters lined the streets. "You always had a focus on why you were marching," Hendricks said. "It meant to me a change." Side by side, the children were also struck by another unexpected change: how activism brought blacks from different socioeconomic levels together in common cause. Some experienced for the first time, as Hendricks did, mature feelings of self-esteem and community that only came with gaining a measure of respect from adults. To be sure, not all were successful at keeping fear at bay for long, with its stomach butterflies and heightened senses. After all, they had heard, and many had seen, the previous days' marches turn ugly in a hurry. Hendricks's first memories of the Birmingham protests are of watching a defenseless black man attacked by German Shepherds, and being shocked that law enforcement would *sic* dogs on an old man. What would happen to them if events escalated and the crowds turned into mobs? Where would they run to? Yet, for all the worry, perhaps the heavier psychological burden was—and maybe continues to be—regret among those children who chose not to walk.[37]

The marches did, of course, turn violent. White onlookers rained obscenities, rocks, and cans down on the children throughout their first day of protest on May 2, and hundreds were arrested and hauled away in paddy wagons and school buses. As one of the youngest taken into custody, Hendricks was kept in a juvenile facility—twelve to a room—where men interrogated the nine-year-old concerning the mass meetings and, she suspected, possible ties between movement leaders and communism. Although denied contact with their parents throughout a seven-day jail stay—during which time they started calling themselves "Freedom Fighters" and "Freedom Riders"—these first youth put behind bars would be overshadowed by the subsequent police overreactions that have come to epitomize the Children's Crusade. In one of the defining moments of the civil rights struggle—galvanizing public opinion worldwide—on Saturday, May 4, Birmingham police began wading into the crowd of youthful marchers, deploying tear gas, high-pressure fire hoses, and dogs. Rousing the protective instincts of adult African American spectators—who, unlike the young activists, had not been trained in nonviolent tactics—the police force's brutality triggered retaliation. Bricks flew at officers, as the previously peaceful demonstration degenerated in the midst of adult determination to escalate the direct action protests with knives and guns. In Birmingham's wake, new rounds of white-on-black and black-on-white violence erupted across the country.[38]

Yet it was the national outrage over the injuries to defenseless black children, fed by notions of childhood innocence, which finally broke the nation's racial impasse and forced leadership at all levels to the bargaining table. Within a week, agreements were reached between the city and activists ending the protests in exchange for a desegregation plan covering Birmingham businesses. In due course, police freed those jailed during the marches, and the courts eventually overturned a board of education decision to expel all crusading children. In June, President Kennedy—moved by the footage of battered African American youth and the resultant crisis of black militancy—introduced a sweeping civil rights bill banning racial discrimination in public places once and for all. "We are confronted primarily with a moral issue," Kennedy solemnly told his television audience. "It is as old as the scriptures and is as clear as the American Constitution . . . The events in Birmingham and elsewhere have so increased the cries for equality that no city or state or legislative body can prudently choose to ignore them." Even as activists shifted their attention toward the March on Washington later that summer to support Kennedy's legislation, terrorism back in Alabama guaranteed that children would continue to be a central theme in the civil rights conversation, which was reaching its most critical days.[39]

On Sunday morning, September 15, 1963, dynamite destroyed the basement of Birmingham's Sixteenth Street Baptist Church while the congregation prepared for its Youth Day celebration. Nearly twenty were injured. Four girls changing into their choir robes after Sunday school died: eleven-year-old Denise McNair and three fourteen-year-olds, Addie Mae Collins, Carole Robertson, and Cynthia Wesley. The city was instantaneously under siege again, and as blacks faced off against whites in weeks of street corner rock-throwing fights, police shot sixteen-year-old Johnny Robinson in the back, and thirteen-year-old Virgil Ware was shot to death, while riding his bike, by a white sixteen-year-old. Black Birmingham embraced these children as if they were their own family. Some called for retribution, but committed civil rights workers doubled down on nonviolent activism as the surest vindication for, and permanent protection of, all black children.

"They are the martyred heroines of a holy crusade for freedom and human dignity," said King in eulogizing the four girls. "And so this afternoon in a real sense they have something to say to each of us in their death . . . They have something to say to every Negro who has passively accepted the evil system of segregation and who has stood on the sidelines in a mighty struggle for justice. They say to each of us, black and white alike, that we must substitute courage for caution. They say to us that we must be concerned not merely about who murdered them, but about the system, the way of life, the philosophy which produced the murderers . . . The innocent blood of these little girls may well serve as a redemptive force that will bring new light to this dark city."[40]

In Washington, President Kennedy likened the girls' deaths to civilian casualties in wartime, telling the Rev. Fred Shuttlesworth that "as tragic as it is, in every war, some people have to die." Indeed, with victory for the civil rights bill far from certain, Coretta Scott King reflected on the Sixteenth Street Baptist Church bombing as the point at which "you realized how intense the opposition was, and that it would take a lot more than what was being done to change the situation."[41]

To that end, the Council of Federated Organizations (COFO)—a partnership between SNCC, CORE, SCLC, and the NAACP to coordinate activities in Mississippi—organized Freedom Summer for 1964. After months of planning, the program placed some five hundred volunteers—mainly white, Northern university students—throughout the state to build on the existing COFO political organization with increased voter registration, and to operate parallel institutions for segregated blacks. Many of the Freedom Summer projects—community centers, health care and legal services, and schools—were specifically geared toward youth. The innovative Freedom Schools, in particular, stood out as something new in the civil rights movement, a do-it-yourself educational experiment where white volunteers taught black children using a student-centered curriculum outside the control of Mississippi's public education system. In whatever church, empty lot, or house happened to be available, any makeshift place where the hosts were willing to accept the risk, Freedom Schools tutored several thousand high school and elementary students that summer in English, arithmetic, and writing, while introducing them to new worlds in black literature, art, and success stories beyond George Washington Carver's peanut products and Harriet Tubman's underground railroad.

Such book learning was frequently punctuated with sing-alongs, guest lectures, live theater performances, and, just as significantly, social interactions which exposed students to the foreign concept that not all whites in America were like Southern whites. In the Freedom Schools, historian Howard Zinn observed, "nine-year-old negro children sounded out French words whose English equivalents they had not yet discovered . . . wrote letters to the local editor about segregation, and discussed the meaning of civil disobedience.

Some wrote short stories about their lives, and others wrote poems." Beyond enhanced self-esteem and broadened horizons, one of the Freedom Schools' most gratifying accomplishments was that mere attendance was a form of protest. It took real courage to openly defy local standards and practices—some schools were burned or otherwise attacked—and such audacity proved contagious, rubbing off on adult organizers. Classrooms were, in this way, civil rights incubators, generating interest in other community campaigns while motivating all ages to take up the fight. As Ben Chaney, the brother of murdered activist James Chaney, reflected, "There was always something happening there. You never got bored. We would sit around on the floor in a group and everybody would sing. There was always a discussion going on. Mostly adults would talk about voter registration, and what was happening. They talked about the latest attack, who got whupped recently by the racists. And we were listening."[42]

The eleven-year-old Ben Chaney and Larry Martin became the self-described "ringleaders of the young guys" who hung out at the COFO office in Meridian, Mississippi. The younger Chaney was following in the footsteps of his brother James, a twenty-one-year-old veteran Freedom Rider when he died. "By him talking to me and my family," Ben later explained, "[t]hat's when I got an idea what the movement was about . . . Whatever my brother wanted to do or did, I wanted to do." Larry lived across the street and received a friendly invitation to play in the COFO "Freedom Center" from Michael "Mickey" Schwerner, a white, New York CORE activist sent to run the summer programs with his wife, Rita. The two boys, and a number of other curious and bored children, soon were coming early and staying well into the night every day, drawn by the ping-pong table and the largest collection of books any had ever seen. Mickey mesmerized his young audience with magic tricks, and Rita taught them freedom songs: *Paul and Silas bound in jail, had no money for to go their bail. Keep your eyes on the prize, hold on.* No one ever told them to go home.[43]

John Steele from nearby Longdale recalled that before meeting Mickey Schwerner and James Chaney during Freedom Summer, he "thought maybe this place, Neshoba County, might be the only place that was like this." As an avid ten-year-old fan of the Lone Ranger, Superman, and Batman—heroes "that stood for right and justice"—he "couldn't understand why they couldn't come here and do the same things. Straighten up Neshoba County." Schwerner and Chaney showed the preadolescents how that was up to them. "I wanted to be in the demonstrations," Larry Martin stressed when describing his initiation into the civil rights movement. "I wanted to be part of it."[44]

At a lunch counter sit-in with Ben and several older workers—"me and Ben Chaney were the youngest in most everything we did," said Martin—the waitress brought out the apple pie they ordered, but salted it. The protesters ate it stoically. Other restaurant sit-ins were followed by picketing businesses which refused to hire blacks, lining around the block when there were sufficient numbers, and only around the entrance when the ranks grew thinner. "They let us go where other kids couldn't go, or didn't want to go, 'cause we weren't scared of anything," Martin stressed. "At eleven and twelve years old, we weren't afraid." On one occasion, a white adult snatched the sign from Ben's hands, throwing the boy to ground and warning him to never return. Although scared and bloodied, he retrieved another sign from the COFO office and rejoined the picket line.

"I remember Mickey saying if we could get the vote, we can make a change," Martin wrote, and "that sounded about right to me." So he started canvassing for voter registration meetings, often walking many miles a day distributing pamphlets to get people registered. "We weren't out there shooting basketball or playing marbles," he underscored. "A lot of times I didn't even go swimming. I'd rather pass out leaflets, sit-in, or something. I enjoyed doing what I was doing. I felt it was right." Martin's mother told him she never worried because the boys were in good hands with Mickey Schwerner, but they got arrested nonetheless. "They kept me and Ben, and then let us go," Martin said of one incarceration. "They'd take us to scare us, talk to us real mean, tell us to go on. But the older men, they kept them." Ben Chaney proudly acknowledged being "arrested more than twenty-one times before I was twelve years old," typically for demonstrating without a permit. Often, the adults retrieving him from jail were his brother James or Schwerner. "That's where the action was at in the sixties," he concluded. "That was it."[45]

John Steele remembered feeling dumbstruck by Schwerner's declaration during a rally that "We have come here to die if necessary." "I looked at him and said this man is talking about dying, and I'm just getting to know him, and I like him too," Steele recalled, and he later questioned Schwerner about his meaning. "One day, young Mr. Steele, you might find something worth dying for," the activist replied. "Freedom is worth dying for, fighting for other people's freedom."[46]

In late June, Schwerner, James Chaney, and another white activist, Andrew Goodman, did, in fact, die in the service of civil rights, murdered near

Philadelphia, Mississippi, while investigating the burning of a church which had agreed to house a Freedom School. Folks knew that the outreach activities of the Meridian office where the boys read, talked, and played had gotten the attention of the local KKK. Larry Martin had even seen white men carrying sheets from a laundry down the street from the COFO office at night, long after business hours. Larry and Ben had planned on accompanying Goodman, Chaney, and Schwerner to Neshoba County. "On Saturday Mickey had promised us that we could go with them," Martin maintained, "but later Saturday night he said, 'No, you guys can't go. Something might happen. It just might not work.' So Ben and I got mad. Oh, we were angry."

In the forty-four anxious days after their disappearance, before federal authorities found their bodies in an earthen dam—the weeks depicted in the fictionalized 1988 movie *Mississippi Burning*—Larry and Ben redirected that anger as they waited with others in resignation at the once busy COFO office. Everyone "knew," said Roy DeBerry, a teenager at the time, "that when you disappear in Mississippi, you're dead." "I thought they were dead, killed," Martin told an interviewer. "I believed they were dead 'cause I knew Philadelphia was mean, mean people there, very hateful and prejudiced people. In 1964 they didn't want to see no blacks riding together with no whites. They'd rather see anything but that. That's why Mickey told us we couldn't go." Stories swirled in the black community about three magnificent strikes of lightning in the sky during a thunderstorm. "I will never forget that as long as I live," added Martin. "I thought it meant they were dead and buried."[47]

The losses crippled the COFO office in Meridian, and as Freedom Summer passed into fall, workers tearfully packed up and left. "Like the heart of it was gone," Martin remembered. "Those guys were the backbone." He and Ben stayed involved in the movement, wishing in vain that local adult leadership would emerge to keep the office open. "Somebody," Martin lamented, "could have carried the torch on after all they'd been through." At his brother's memorial service, Ben wrestled, as many, more mature activists were doing by 1964, to reconcile deep feelings of rage and a desire for vengeance with the abstract philosophy and tactics of nonviolence. "I kept wondering why didn't people do something?" he told an interviewer. "Why didn't my father, my grandfather, my great-grandfather? Why wasn't things made different? Why wasn't change taking place then, so that this event wouldn't be taking place now?"

His closing words at James's funeral spoke to his anger and a developing assertiveness that would soon be understood as Black Power. "And I want us all to stand up here together and say just one thing," the eleven-year-old proclaimed. "I want the sheriff to hear this good. We ain't scared no more of Sheriff Rainey [the leading Neshoba County law enforcement officer implicated in the murders]!" "I didn't have any idea this would be history," Ben Chaney later admitted. "Having a sense of black people being put in an American history book was unrealistic. That's the way it was." But he has remained committed to the relevance of peaceful change as the founder and president of the James Earl Chaney Foundation, a nonprofit advocacy organization carrying the torch for human rights and social justice. "It made you feel good," Larry Martin reminisced about his work during Freedom Summer. "Like you were doing something that really meant something . . . I believe if it weren't for Mickey and them now, I don't know what kind of guy I would have been. That's right. They really made a difference when I was growing up . . . I loved the work they were doing. I'd really like to be a part of it again."[48]

There was a natural kinship—cross-pollination, really—between the Mississippi Freedom Schools and the Great Society's Project Head Start. In many locales, Head Start can be understood as a more codified extension of the grassroots Freedom Summer classrooms. The two initiatives certainly shared the same pedagogical principles for educating and serving poor children, and, likewise, a temporal continuity. Freedom Schools looking for students were struggling to compete with regular public school schedules and the cotton picking season in the fall of 1964, and Head Start launched in the summer of 1965. Head Start fostered an activist synergy between its young students and adult organizers comparable to that of the Freedom Schools. These federal projects were almost exclusively African American enterprises in the South, because whites refused to participate. And it did not take long for socially conscious adult reformers to harness Head Start's organizational platform and access to federal resources as a practical vehicle for advancing the movement in their own local communities.

The Child Development Group of Mississippi (CDGM) was one of the nation's most notable Head Start success stories early on. The brainchild of a New York veteran of Freedom Summer, the CDGM received $1.5 million in OEO money—the largest Head Start grant in that initial summer of 1965—to operate a network of eighty-four early childhood education centers across the state, serving some six thousand students. Like Head Start projects nationwide, including a number of others also getting under way in Mississippi, the CDGM offered a compensatory curriculum to inspire creativity while providing needed medical exams and food. Preschoolers prepared storybooks about their lives using show-and-tell materials brought from home, and to learn about African culture they made tie-dyed shirts and macaroni necklaces to replicate the fashion of their ancestors. But where the CDGM really stood out was in its activist leadership, whose unrepentant association with SNCC, COFO, and the renegade Mississippi Freedom Democratic Party often informed their approaches to community organizing.[49]

One CDGM program in Glen Allan, a tiny plantation town, is particularly representative of the potential for intergenerational empowerment that could be unlocked by the War on Poverty's "maximum feasible participation" philosophy. Jake Ayers was a civic-minded Glen Allan resident known for his willingness to take advantage of any initiatives for the betterment of local African Americans, and in 1965 he secured one of the original CDGM centers for his rural community. Ayers and other blacks then took the extraordinary step of forming their own school board to manage the Glen Allan Head Start. Their first order of business was to petition the white school district for permission to occupy a currently unused building over the summer, and in circulating the paperwork they got every black in Glen Allan to sign it—an unparalleled demonstration of unity. But the petition was rejected, and the Head Start had to open in a church, overenrolled by 50 percent.

Ayers's Head Start board hired underemployed Glen Allan adults as teachers and paraprofessionals, and at unheard-of wages approaching eighty-two dollars a week, compared to the three dollars a day commonly paid to plantation laborers. This meant that a federal program operated by, and for, local blacks brought jobs and money into Glen Allan which for the first time were outside white control. As this money rippled through the town, the positive multiplier effect allowed blacks more purchasing power while also driving up the salaries whites paid for other menial work. A *Life* magazine reporter covering the CDGM also recognized a broader transformation. "There was a by-product for the community," he wrote, "a new pride. The people had accomplished something independently and, indeed, against the wishes of the whites. They had brought in money. They had the beginnings of organization and thus of strength."[50]

When bureaucratic troubles at the OEO and mounting political resistance in Congress threatened CDGM funding, statewide leadership brought buses carrying forty-eight black preadolescents and their teachers to Washington in February 1966 in order to show what Head Start was accomplishing in Mississippi. This politicized "romper lobby" briefly turned the House Education and Labor Committee's hearing room into a spirited preschool classroom, with crayons and scissors scattered about the floor and songs and games echoing down the halls. For all the commotion, the group did manage to keep the controversial CDGM alive for at least another year. Eventually, white reprisals against what Glen Allan townspeople correctly saw as the civil rights movement being funded by Head Start galvanized the African Americans' sense of solidarity, and, in another demonstration of power, blacks boycotted local white stores. By late 1966, as Glen Allan blacks began registering to vote for the first time, their children were enrolled en masse in the previously all-white school, a move which prompted the busing of all white students out of town. Parents who had witnessed an awakening in their children from this one modest Head Start program strove for improvement in themselves. Throughout Glen Allan—and to varying degrees across Mississippi—houses received fresh paint, gardens were tended more judiciously, clothes appeared clean and mended, and other evidence of community abounded. It was as if, the *Life* journalist noted, "the success that began with the children came to give hope and dignity to the adults."[51]

Preadolescent black children were also there alongside adults on the Edmund Pettus Bridge outside Selma, Alabama, in March 1965 during the three marches that are considered the culminating nonviolent events in the Southern phase of the civil rights movement. As in Birmingham two years earlier, the strategic objective in Selma was to compel federal action on a specific grievance: voting rights. For weeks, protesters carried out demonstrations and voter registration drives in and around Selma—with teachers and older students figuring prominently—before organizing a march from the city to the state capital in Montgomery, fifty-four miles away along U.S. Route 80.

Eight-year-old Sheyann Webb, perhaps the youngest marcher, lived across from the Brown Chapel AME Church, where the planning took place, and found herself drawn in by the novelty of seeing blacks and whites gathering together socially for mass meetings, along with a curiosity over Martin Luther King. "I didn't know anything about any of these things," she remembered of sneaking into the back pew to investigate the goings on inside Brown Chapel instead of going to school one morning, "but it was something that seemed exciting. It was like something was about to happen." The fact that neither teachers nor parents punished her for being late that day, instead nervously questioning Sheyann about what she had overheard, further convinced the little girl that she was on to a major happening in Selma: "They were fearing something . . . [and] this made it even more interesting to me." She continued: "I wanted to know about voting. I didn't know what that was about. And then I wanted to know who was this man Dr. Martin Luther King." The congregation's enthusiasm over King's impending arrival in Selma underscored in her mind "that he had to be somebody great . . . My parents knew of his name, but it was like I shouldn't know him or want to know him. This made me even more inquisitive. I was told to stay away from around there. I had no business being there."[52]

Yet, in the days leading up to the marches, Sheyann and a friend kept returning to the Brown Chapel mass meetings against her parents' wishes. "I became a very disobedient child. That's how deep I got into it." And the more she attended, the more she learned, her education unfolding largely through song. *Ain't gonna let nobody turn me 'round. I'm gonna keep on a-walkin', keep on a-talkin', walkin' into freedom land.* "That song itself," Sheyann Webb stressed, "told me a lot about what freedom was. It naturally meant there was going to be a struggle for rights that were owed to the black race . . . The words equality and justice were mentioned so much. I put all the pieces together just with those words. I may not have understood it well, but I understood enough."

The congregation soon came to embrace her as something of a novelty and Sheyann was often invited to lead the singing, at times getting to sit on King's lap. Even her parents' constant admonishments about what happened to the little girls at Birmingham's Sixteenth Street Baptist Church helped shape the eight-year-old's burgeoning activism. "Why children? Why us?" she recalled thinking. "It made me realize that it didn't matter who you were. If you were black and you were in an area they didn't like or where the cause for freedom was being fought, you were at risk. It didn't matter—children, boy, girl, or whatever." Thus, when the time came to make a decision on whether to join the ranks of civil rights marchers on March 7, Sheyann had already made up her mind, explaining to her mother, "I want you and Daddy to be free. I want you to be able to vote just like the white folks."[53]

Sheyann Webb's memories of that first march remain sharp and vivid. Together with nearly six hundred others, she followed SNCC's John Lewis east out of Selma toward the Edmund Pettus Bridge over the Alabama River on their way to Montgomery. As the marchers neared the bridge, Alabama state troopers and local police blocked their approach. "The closer we got to the bridge, the more I began to get frightened," she recalled of the first time she really felt afraid, " . . . and as we got to the top of the bridge, I could see hundreds of policemen, state troopers, billy clubs, dogs, and horses, and I began to just cry. I remember the ministers who were at the front of the line saying, kneel down and pray. And I knelt down and I said to myself, Lord, help me."

Thinking back to her training in nonviolent techniques, the probability of violence sank in. She wanted to go home. "Out of all the times my parents had talked to me about what could happen, this is when it really came to me." Then, after protesters refused an order to turn around, the police attacked. "Once we had gotten up all I could remember was outbursts of tear gas," Webb told historians, "and I saw people being beaten and I began to just try to run as fast as I could. And as I began to run home, I saw horses behind me, and I will never forget a freedom fighter picked me up, Hosea Williams, and I told him to put me down, he wasn't running fast enough. And I ran and I ran. It was like I was running for my life." Television networks interrupted local programming with footage showing dozens of black and white marchers beaten senseless, nearly fifty needing hospitalization, and as the coverage went on into the evening, the tragedy was already becoming known worldwide as Bloody Sunday.[54]

After making her way safely home, Sheyann "was still determined to go back to Brown Chapel Church, but my parents wouldn't let me. I was shut up in my room. I remember taking a pencil and writing down how I felt about what I saw. Then I wrote down my funeral arrangements because even with what I saw, I still wanted to go out and fight. And I said if I did that, I would probably die. So I wrote down my funeral arrangements . . . I realized on that day everything about what Dr. Martin Luther King was trying to say. It was wrong to be beaten for something that you was trying to fight for that was right. I realized it more on that day than any other day. It all came together."[55]

She did not participate in a second abbreviated march on March 9—known as Turnaround Tuesday—but did rejoin the rank-and-file for the triumphant final journey on March 21. Triumphant because 25,000 people protected by U.S. soldiers and federal law enforcement officers completed the three-day walk to Montgomery in an overwhelming show of support for African American voting rights. And triumphant also because a week earlier, on March 15, Lyndon Johnson had introduced his Voting Rights Act before a joint session of Congress and national television audience with the words "we shall overcome."

"I felt real good at the last march," Webb concluded. "It was like we *had* overcome. We had all reached the point we were fighting for, for a long time . . . I asked my mother and father for my [ninth] birthday present to become registered voters. They took me to the polls with them to vote. I would never forget it. I was very excited and, you know, what even made it so unique to me was the fact, just something being so simple, just a check on a ballot at that particular time, they didn't have machines . . . And it was just a matter of walking over to a building and making that check. It was very exciting. And it was exciting for them to have that right as well as for me to see them do it."[56]

The Voting Rights Act, signed into law by Johnson on August 6, 1965, banned literacy tests, and, in conjunction with the newly ratified Twenty-fourth Amendment's prohibition on poll taxes, removed Jim Crow's racially prejudiced requirements for casting a ballot. The previous year, the Civil Rights Act of 1964 had outlawed both segregation in public accommodations and discrimination in employment. Together, these federal measures marked the culmination of the struggle's nonviolent years, effectively accomplishing the movement's objective to end *de jure* racism in the South. In the lived experience of most Southern black children, the civil rights movement up until this time manifested itself primarily in their developing mindset, inspiring improved racial and self-esteem. As one middle-class black boy in a large Southern city far removed from the activism commented to his mother while watching Birmingham on television, "Gee, I really hope that people will understand everything better . . . soon, because I don't want to have to 'protest' before I can become an astronaut."[57]

For the remainder of the Vietnam era, however, social changes brought on by this activism—primarily physical desegregation and greater, more honest representation of blacks in American culture—were the chief entry points into childhood, family life, and parental socialization for both races. The dogged pace of such change remained slow and uneven from an adult's critical perspective. As hard-core resistance cracked and most Southern whites resigned themselves to integration, the enforcement of the Civil Rights Act brought white-only signs down sooner or later, and the Voting Rights Act was fully enforced by 1966. The Civil Rights Act also nudged along school desegregation by empowering the U.S. Attorney General to file suits against noncompliant districts, and the percentage of black students in the former confederacy attending integrated schools rose from 6 percent in 1965 to 12 percent in 1966. Yet, in the world of childhood and family life, change seemed to come much more rapidly. The South after 1965 was largely desegregated rather than integrated, but preadolescents took the lead in many families in navigating the uncharted course between these distinctions. As with school desegregation, children were usually the first group to encounter their peers on the post-Jim Crow landscape—on playgrounds and in other after-school activities—and, due to their adaptability, these interactions could lead to innocent invitations home and sometimes form the basis of an interracial friendship. In this way, the historical transition of bringing preadolescents together in closer proximity led them to make personal transitions by starting to think of their new playmates, and relating to them, as equals.[58]

Child psychologists believed that by nine or ten years old, children should be able to sort out these concerns for themselves, but mothers and fathers of both races still faced uncertainty over parenting strategies in this new reality. African American parents, especially, worried about whether to promote integrated experiences, for instance sending a six-year-old to a white birthday party she had been invited to, which might expose her to the humiliation of someone not wanting to hold their hand during a game or sit by them to eat cake. Should they forewarn their children about the undercurrents of racism and bigotry that persisted in small towns and suburbia, preparing them in advance for subtle awkwardness at recess, suspicious stares on neighborhood streets, or outright rejection from social circles? Most eventually opted for allowing their children to discern where the racial lines were being redrawn and react accordingly, resentful that blacks were still expected to address these considerations instead of the white parents and children who often perpetuated the problems.

For their part, even the most well-meaning white parents, including those educated, middle-class suburbanites who never considered themselves prejudiced, were ill-prepared to adapt based on their own life experiences. Commonly they experienced surprise and shame at how uncomfortable they felt when their children were around African Americans, and grappled with whether to encourage racial interaction. Should they urge their children to make black friends out of a sense of moral principle or social responsibility? And how should their children respond to the resultant criticism and teasing from white peers who were unwilling to be so accommodating? Those with open minds and confidence allowed childhood friendships to develop naturally, as opposed to forced and artificially, while parents unable to cope frequently joined the mass migration known as white flight.[59]

By the mid to late sixties, the civil rights and Black Power movements were entering the lived experience of many more American preadolescents—black and white, Southern and Northern—through popular culture, primarily in television programming and commercials, the sports page, and music, as well as children's literature. Even those children who followed the struggle closely were often more interested in the increasingly pronounced media representations of the black experience. On television, where African American children had always noticed the lack of black characters—sometimes even cheering when they saw the rare black actor—NBC's espionage adventure series *I Spy* brought the first African American in a lead dramatic role to prime time—comedian Bill Cosby as secret agent Alexander Scott—for three seasons starting in 1965.

When that program ended in 1968, NBC debuted *Julia*, starring Diahann Carroll as a nurse and single mother (her husband died in Vietnam) in one of the first sitcoms to portray a black woman as nothing less than a mainstream American. (Mattel introduced a *Julia*-inspired Barbie doll in 1969, a year after Talking Christie became the first bona fide black doll in Mattel's Barbie line, if one does not count the short-lived black-face version of its Francie doll in 1967.) Actor Lloyd Haynes began playing the beloved and well-respected American history teacher Pete Dixon on ABC's integrated high school drama *Room 222* in 1969. While Mr. Dixon addressed the major social issues of the sixties, including prejudice, on Wednesday nights, ABC featured the urban character Lincoln "Linc" Hayes on Tuesdays as one-third of a hip detective unit on *The Mod Squad* tackling America's rising crime rate. By the mid-1970s, African American actors were being cast as police—an occupation whose uniform signified respect and authority to many inner city black children—more than in any other kind of role on television. *The Flip Wilson Show*, a weekly variety series hosted by the African American comedian, aired on NBC in 1970, the year after children had been introduced to the multicultural cityscape of PBS's *Sesame Street*.

But perhaps television's most groundbreaking and important character to African American children was actress Nichelle Nichols's Lieutenant Uhura, the USS *Enterprise*'s communications officer on *Star Trek*. Not only did Uhura represent a competent and confident black role model to little girls—she agreed to stay with the show at Martin Luther King's request for that very reason—but her onscreen kiss with William Shatner's Captain Kirk in 1968 is also widely considered to be the first interracial kiss seen on American television.[60]

Mass media similarly brought greater numbers of African American athletes into living rooms as easily recognizable celebrities in increasingly integrated college and professional sports leagues. The undisputed hero was heavyweight boxing champion Muhammad Ali, whose 1971 fight with Joe Frazier came to define the growing divisions between integration and Black Power within the civil rights mindset. Besides Olympic sprinters Tommie Smith and John Carlos—expelled from the 1968 Summer Games for raising a black-gloved fist salute on the medal stand—sports fans followed the St. Louis Cardinals' pitching ace Bob Gibson while the National Football League had stars such as Chicago Bears running back Gale Sayers and defensive lineman "Deacon" Jones of the Los Angeles Rams. When the rival American Football League commenced play in 1960, eventually merging with the NFL in 1970, its teams, unlike the older, established NFL teams, routinely signed players from smaller and primarily black colleges, like the Denver Broncos' Marlin "The Magician" Briscoe, the AFL's first starting black quarterback. In basketball, another renegade league, the American Basketball Association, competed for fan allegiance with the National Basketball Association and the likes of Wilt Chamberlain of the Philadelphia 76ers and the Boston Celtics' Bill Russell, who as player-coach in 1966–1967 had become the NBA's first black coach. When the inaugural ABA season began in 1967, the upshot league quickly built a reputation, wowing young fans with a freewheeling, offensive brand of basketball, flashy red-white-and-blue balls, three-point shots, and the Afro hairstyles favored by scoring machine Connie "The Hawk" Hawkins of the Pittsburgh and then Minnesota Pipers, Roger Brown of the Indiana Pacers, and Roland "Fatty" Taylor of the Washington Caps.

Musically, record producer Berry Gordy's Motown label is remembered by many African Americans growing up in the 1960s for providing the radio soundtrack of the movement with AM anthems like Aretha Franklin's "Respect." Few white children, for whom Motown had major crossover appeal, seem to have made this connection. Given that Motown was a high-profile African American-owned record company, and its music's role as the official "sound of young America," it is easy to understand why the songs of Stevie Wonder, Marvin Gaye, and the rest were closely associated with the civil rights era in the minds of black children. It is not exactly accidental that whites never noticed. Although the growth of Motown's popularity coincided with the struggle, Gordy consciously steered his stable of performers away from overt racial polemics—and talk of Vietnam—to protect the brand's noncontroversial image. By stage-managing virtually every facet of its musicians' careers—from music and choreography to etiquette and manners—Motown produced a standardized, recognizable look and sound—The Jackson 5, The Temptations, The Supremes—that was also marketable to whites. So, whether white children appreciated it or not, those catchy, continuously looped melodies played a civil rights role after all by integrating Top 40 radio.[61]

At the same time, a "new realism" was taking shape in children's literature, a trend toward inclusiveness and more thoughtful depictions of minorities which followed similar sixties-era developments in adult literature. Since the 1950s, civil rights leaders had been concerned about the negative consequences of teaching millions of black and white students to read, and understand America, using books that were unrealistically populated exclusively with white characters living tidy lives in a bucolic setting. In all but a handful of children's books published in the postwar years, blacks were either completely omitted or barely mentioned. *We Live in the City*, a book about Chicago, for instance, showed no black citizens at all. On those rare pages where blacks did show up as anything other than random faces in the crowd, most characters were either of African or Caribbean origins, or historical trapped around the time of slavery. The market for the older, disturbingly stereotyped *Little Black Sambo* or its newer cousin *The Lazy Little Zulu* remained robust.

The civil rights struggle generated a pronounced demand for more honest storytelling in order to both provide positive role models for blacks and develop more open-minded racial attitudes among their white classmates. This, in turn, revolutionized—in quantity and quality—how blacks were portrayed in elementary school libraries, classrooms, story hours, and bookstores. By the late 1960s, as part of this proliferation, a number of publishers issued books that depicted multiracial stories including black characters. Many were simply "color-me-black" books, with characters who previously would have been middle-class, white children now darkly shaded, with some slang thrown in. But others were less forced and unnatural, presenting black characters dealing with relatively universal issues common to growing up. William H. Armstrong's 1969 young adult novel *Sounder*—about the son of a poor black sharecropping family and his dog—was, along with the 1972 movie adaptation, perhaps the most decorated example, although one written by a white author.

Charles Schulz introduced a black character, Franklin, into his *Peanuts* comic strip after the death of King in the summer of 1968. Franklin, whose father was a soldier in Vietnam, eventually joined the rest of the gang at the dinner table (albeit, as some noted, sitting alone on one side of the table) for their holiday feast in CBS's 1973 special *A Charlie Brown Thanksgiving*. In the world of comic books, Marvel introduced the earliest popular black superheroes with Stan Lee's Black Panther character—an African king with superpowers derived from a meteoric mineral—appearing sporadically in the *Fantastic Four* series after 1966 and the Falcon, who started flying through issues of *Captain America* in 1969. DC Comics' Black Racer followed in 1971. Marvel also gave young readers the first black superheroes to star in their own featured title with the superhuman *Luke Cage, Hero for Hire* in 1972 and the Black Panther's own series in the *Jungle Action* comic books. *Little Black Sambo*, with its embarrassing reminder of Jim Crow racial caricatures, quickly fell out of favor before virtually disappearing.

The most meaningful books written for black children came from black, civil rights–influenced authors who embraced racial differences, not similarities, and thereby created a new generation of African American literary characters doing African American things and speaking in the cadence and language of African Americans. These books ranged from the serious—Kristin Elaine Hunter's 1968 coming-of-age story *The Soul Brothers and Sister Lou* about an inner-city girl discovering self-worth and racial identity through singing—to the whimsical, as in Walter Myers's *The Dragon Takes a Wife* in 1972 chronicling life's uphill battles for Harry, the lonely dragon. Myers began writing after his son saw a black character in a picture book and exclaimed, "That one's me!" In between these two books came *Black Fairy Tales*, *Lillie of Watts,* and nonfiction works like *African Heroes*, *Black Champions of the Gridiron*, and *Black Is Beautiful*, all published in 1969.

School librarians found it difficult to keep anything by writer and illustrator John Steptoe on their shelves. A product of the Bedford-Stuyvesant neighborhood in Brooklyn, Steptoe went on to write multiple award-winning books, most notably *Mufaro's Beautiful Daughters* (1988), but his early work—completed when he was still a teenager—characterized this author's new sensibility. Steptoe's first offering, *Stevie*, in 1969, following the tribulations of a black boy stuck babysitting a smaller neighbor, was unapologetically drawn from inner city black culture and vernacular speech. "The little boy's name was Steven but his mother kept calling him Stevie," the protagonist says of his new burden. "My name is Robert but my momma don't call me Robertie. And so Steve moved in, with his old crybaby self." Within two years Steptoe also published *Uptown*, about two friends pondering what they wanted to be when they grew up based on available male role models from the streets—junkies, cops, and brothers—and *Train Ride,* in which children navigated New York's public transportation system. "The story, the language, is not directed at white children," Steptoe explained of his intentional lack of racial balance. "I wanted it to be something black children could read without translating the language, something real which would relate to what a black child would know."[62]

Outside the South, the civil rights movement was seen by white children as a disjointed sequence of television news programming showing innocent demonstrators getting hurt, occasional politicized speeches, and newspaper headlines. After all, slightly less than half of all African Americans lived in the North during the sixties, with the majority of these residing in the city, which meant that white suburban children had even less familiarity with black people than Southern children did. "I'd never even known any African Americans before," many from this cohort told me. Consistent with Piaget's observation that preadolescents grasp local circumstances before identifying with national life, the civil rights struggle was detached from their all-white neighborhoods and towns almost as if it was taking place in another country.[63]

This appears to have changed, at least in popular memory, with Martin Luther King's assassination on April 4, 1968, in Memphis. Many whites consider his tragic death as the first time the civil rights movement penetrated their world and the first time the principles King fought for made any sense to them. For African Americans, King's murder robbed the movement of its most recognizable voice and, of course, struck more viscerally. Sheyann Webb remembers the mournful outcry, how she could "hear people responding in the community. You could hear it through the walls." Surveys showed parallels between the impact of King's death on black children—referred to by many as the "President of Negroes"—and the reactions of all children when John Kennedy died five years before. Almost unanimously blacks despaired, as if they had lost someone very close personally, and were anxious about what might happen to the country, except that most also professed anger, with three-quarters admitting they were ashamed of America. Northern whites, however, tended to credit the death of King with reawakening Kennedy's language of idealism in their preadolescence, inspiring less egocentric moral thinking about racism and issues of social justice. As one woman recalled of being ten years old in Michigan in 1968, "I was watching *The Flying Nun*, with Sally Field, when the news bulletin came on that Dr. King had been shot. Following that we watched at least one news special at school on TV regarding Dr. King's assassination (and watching TV at school was not the norm). Within the year we were singing "We Shall Overcome" and "Blowin' in the Wind" in class, and having long discussions on race and prejudice and discrimination."[64]

Urban rioting triggered by the death of King erupted in thirty-seven Northern cities during April 1968. These latest rebellions of collective violence were an early start to the fourth in a series of long, hot summers in American cities, which had begun in the Watts neighborhood of Los Angeles, somewhat ironically, just five days after the Voting Rights Act was signed. The riots of the mid1960s, totaling over three hundred eventually, marked a conceptual shift in civil rights activism away from a coordinated, nonviolent struggle against the South's *de jure* discrimination toward the more radical and confrontational assaults on the intractable *de facto* segregation that came to characterize the militant "Northern" phase of the movement. Racism in the nation's ghettos was comparatively more subtle, grounded in economic realities and social pathos instead of law. The lives of inner city blacks differed in degree, but not in kind, from city to city; there was a tragic sameness in issues such as unemployment, involuntary residential segregation, deteriorating schools, and police misconduct which did not really lend themselves to interracial cooperation or legislative solutions. Gains for African Americans in the South were not readily felt by these urbanized populations, but the civil rights movement raised their expectations nevertheless, and, faced with the prospect of permanent subordination, a significant minority of disillusioned Northern blacks used rioting—performative violence—as a viable, direct action strategy for continued change. Although the civil disorders varied from city to city, all displayed a similar pattern of looting, arson, and assault, often in the form of restrained, selective, and carefully articulated protests against the most immediate black grievances.

There is still a tremendous amount of work to be done for historians seeking to understand how this "Northern" phase manifested itself in urban preadolescent lives. The riots, in particular, disrupted family and school routines for ghetto children who for their personal safety amid swirling smoke, burning buildings, and armed soldiers patrolling streets, while feeling helpless in the knowledge that the adult world had spun out of control.

"I thought the world was coming to an end," a Washington, DC., elementary school student wrote of that city's post-King riot. "I felt like a man in a house of fire . . . Right now, I want to be saved from the riot and live in another city . . . I would like to forget Black Power, 'soul' and all the burning of stores . . . I want to be in another country." White suburban children remember seeing news reports showing the inner cities in flames and under martial law, fearing that all blacks were angry at them personally, and feeling anxious about total civil war. On the other hand, some inner city black children were fascinated by the carnivalesque atmosphere in their neighborhoods, recognizing with pride a reversal of order in which mothers appropriated all the food and clothing they could carry, young people took their fill of candy and cookies, and armies of black men controlled the streets for once.[65]

We also need to more fully consider the developmental impacts of the dynamic urban culture which created in cities a climate conducive to rebellion, a depressing world where sickly children suffered from bad teeth and vitamin deficiencies, out-of-work fathers fell too quickly into liquor, drugs, and crime, and mothers passed down their contempt for landlords, police, and social workers. Moreover, we must take into account the Black Power phenomenon, an essentially cultural revolution that sought to inspire a political revolution by celebrating color consciousness and promoting black self-reliance independent of the white power structure. Black children seem to have understood this as "soul," meaning racial pride without fear of whites. Further exploration will necessarily shed light on preadolescents raised in households headed by members of black nationalist groups competing to articulate the Black Power agenda, namely various Black Muslims and the Black Panther Party. The Black Panthers, known for their outreach "survival programs" including free breakfast for schoolchildren, offer insight into the influence of a revolutionary strategy for black liberation on childhood education and political socialization. The Panthers' chauvinism, in which the drive to recapture black manhood was defined by aggression and violence in defense of family, reshaped constructions of masculinity and femininity, which in turn informed notions of fatherhood. And fresh studies will add texture to the 1970s story of busing black elementary students into white schools as a federally mandated desegregation tool in places like Philadelphia, St. Louis, Baltimore, and Boston.

Ultimately, these studies will supply some needed perspective on the unfolding racial dialectics over this cohort's life course, helping to explain why there is a timeless quality in one African American mother's account of the fierce white opposition to her son's busing in 1967. "Sometimes," she told Robert Coles, "I'd like to go out there and let them know that we're not trying to force our way into their backyards. We just want the best for our children, the best that you've got and we haven't got . . . We get discouraged, yes. But I tell my children it's a luxury to get discouraged. We've made big gains since I was their age and a day don't go by that I don't remind my kids what's happened—and I have to remind myself, too."[66]

CHAPTER SEVEN

The Vietnam War

We were also always aware of the Vietnam War in our home. It was on the news every day so we saw firsthand how horrible war was. Because the horrible news was followed by such innocence, it made it all the more poignant to me growing up.
Minnesota woman born in 1964

WITH HIS AVUNCULAR air of detachment, Walter Cronkite concluded an all-too-ordinary *CBS Evening News* broadcast in the summer when American troop levels in the Vietnam War first exceeded 300,000 as all network newscasters of the era reliably did, by tallying the most recent numbers in television's seemingly endless arithmetic of war. The "latest casualty figures put American battle deaths last week at 91, the South Vietnamese lost 216 killed," the anchorman reported succinctly on this given night, "and enemy dead number 1,827, the second highest weekly figure this year."

And that's the way it is, August 25, 1966.

For children raised exclusively in wartime—that is, a Cold War to contain monolithic communism turned hot in the jungles of Southeast Asia—and the first to grow up with televised combat, Vietnam was predominantly a mediated experience; Cronkite's was the voice of the conflict and those grim, nightly statistics its most recognizable feature. It is said that without Vietnam, the civil rights movement would have been what we think of as "the sixties," but instead, as Lyndon B. Johnson "Americanized" the war in the spring of 1965, the escalating military commitment became the nation's most pervasive, and devastating, collective undertaking. As U.S. involvement grew, Vietnam effected numerous changes in child life, comparable to the childhood impact of previous conflicts—chiefly the Civil War and World War II—whose intensity and duration likewise dominated American culture.

The effects of wartime experience followed closely the development of abstract thought—preadolescents grasp local circumstances before identifying with national life—as the impact of Vietnam, similar to civil rights activism, was directly proportional to the conflict's penetration of the child's proximal world. In this protracted struggle which took on the look of permanence from a child's perspective, adult lives were increasingly militarized, leaving few preadolescents totally insulated. Over the years 1965 to 1973, the vast majority of American children integrated at least some elements of the war into their own reality, most often through television imagery, war play, and, to a lesser extent, music. Parents, in turn, shaped their children's socialization to Vietnam, while the more politicized mothers and fathers exposed them to the bitter polarization the war engendered. The fighting only became truly real to children insomuch as service in Vietnam called away older community members—neighborhood teenagers, lifeguards, church members, a teacher's son, a babysitter's boyfriend—or was driven home literally when families shared the hardship of separation from cousins, brothers, and fathers. All of these circumstances involved frightening absences culminating in provocative reunions and anxious days of readjustment. Such intensified Cold War anxiety during formative childhood stages and the perplexing nature of the Vietnam experience tended to shape political socialization and moral development largely independently of factual knowledge. Hence the opinions formed during this time remain stubbornly resistant to later revision based on new learning over the life course.[1]

Although the political turmoil and conflict in Southeast Asia was grounded in the seething Vietnamese rebellion against French colonialism typical of the post-World War II era, American interests were more narrowly framed by the Cold War policy of containing the global spread of Soviet communism. A nationalist victory by the Marxist Ho Chi Minh and his army of Viet Minh revolutionaries—operating under the direction of Moscow, the United States assumed—threatened to hand the Kremlin another communist triumph in Asia and further destabilize the other countries in the region like a row of wobbly dominoes. Thus President Harry S. Truman had sought to contain Ho's revolution by underwriting the French war effort, a multibillion-dollar commitment Dwight D. Eisenhower continued even after France's humiliating defeat at the hands of the Viet Minh in 1954. Without that European surrogate to contain communism, and with Vietnam now partitioned Korea-style into two separate states by international accords, the Eisenhower administration embarked on a problematic strategy of building a stable,

Western-style democracy in the newly conceived country of South Vietnam as a bulwark against communist North Vietnam. With millions of dollars of economic aid and guidance in the 1950s, the United States fashioned a brittle government around an unpopular authoritarian, Ngo Dinh Diem, sending military advisors to train an army which might protect the regime from an indigenous insurgency, the Viet Cong, that rose up against American interference and Diem's misguided rule. By John Kennedy's inaugural, America was thoroughly invested in an intractable three-way civil war, defending the South from the North (backed substantially by the Soviet Union and People's Republic of China), which, with its Viet Cong allies operating below the 17th parallel, were hell-bent on unifying the temporarily divided land as one communist country of Vietnam.

In the absence of significant numbers of U.S. troops and causalities, relatively few in the generally apathetic public—certainly not children—paid close attention to the trajectory of foreign policy in such a remote locale, even as Kennedy deployed counter-insurgency Green Berets to pacify the Viet Cong and authorized the coup which replaced Diem. It was not until the 1964 presidential campaign, almost two decades into U.S. involvement, that the Vietnam War began consistently capturing widespread adult attention and triggering social changes in the family lives of preadolescent Americans. Lyndon Johnson could no longer sustain South Vietnam without bringing substantially more American military power to bear, and in August the president maneuvered the Gulf of Tonkin Resolution through Congress for that very purpose. By vaguely authorizing Johnson to "take all necessary measures to repel any armed attack against the forces of the United States and to prevent further aggression . . . including the use of armed force" Congress sanctioned the president's prosecution of this conflict directly from the Oval Office without the requisite declaration of war. Beginning in 1965, these measures evolved into a strategy of gradual escalation, keeping the actions limited to Vietnam (so as not to provoke World War III with the Soviets and Chinese) through a calibrated ratcheting up of military pressure in the unjustified confidence that at some future point mounting U.S. strength would break the resolve of the North Vietnamese and Viet Cong by denying them victory in the field.[2]

The scale of such a military buildup required substantial increases in draft calls, which jumped from 112,386 in 1964 to 230,991 in 1965, peaking in 1966 at 382,010. Consequently, for the nearly twenty-seven million baby boomer men who came of draft age between 1964 and 1973, the unrelenting prospect of military service in Vietnam became the generation's preeminent consideration, informing personal decisions about the timing and direction of career, marriage, and fatherhood. Because the nature of selective service left men eligible between the ages of 18 and 25, their life choices were subject to tremendous uncertainty for the duration of an eight-year draft window. Around one-third of the armed forces in the Vietnam era—1,857,304— were indeed draftees, and for untold numbers of them, conscription meant delaying the choice of whether to become husbands or fathers until later in their twenties. Early in the decade, twenty-three was the average age of an inductee, but as the war dragged on, the inductees got younger, with the average age falling to 21.6 by 1964 and 20.6 in 1966. Those with small children may well have allowed anxiety over the impending letter from Selective Service to influence their parenting style. Since most draftees went to the Army for two years—one spent in training and, for 648,500 soldiers, another year's tour in Vietnam—their families also experienced a disruptive absence. The remaining two-thirds of the military were enlistees, men who joined as a vocational choice or out of a sense of patriotic duty, but frequently as a conscious alternative to being drafted. Increased enlistments corresponded favorably to rising calls for induction as draft-eligible young men—usually with higher levels of education—preferred to enlist in order to enter the military under more favorable circumstances.[3]

The preponderance of draft-eligible men avoided the military, though, by a number of convoluted legal and extralegal means inherent to the Selective Service System. Local draft boards classified all eighteen-year-old registrants as either available for service (1-A), exempted, or deferred. Those designated as 1-A received pre-induction physical and psychiatric examinations, and upon passing were required to report for service when the board determined who would be called in order to meet the Defense Department's monthly draft requests. Failure on any of the test's physical, mental, psychiatric, or moral components brought exemptions to slightly over five million young men. Most commonly, potential draftees pursued a series of deferments to either postpone or permanently avoid conscription, principally on the grounds of education, occupation, hardship, marriage, or fatherhood. Prior to Vietnam, these various deferments operated as the Selective Service's Cold War method of allocating human resources, by utilizing the draft to channel manpower into the civilian and military occupations deemed most important to the national interest. For instance, male college students making progress toward their degree at a four-year institution of higher education were deferred from service until they turned twenty-four. Even during the Kennedy years, when draft calls remained relatively low, the huge number of baby boomers easily outpaced the military's demand, and channeling the liberal deferments continued to be quite manageable.[4]

Vietnam strained the system, however, quickly producing draft shortfalls that necessitated adjustments to tighten up the channels, which produced several unintended consequences for family formation patterns and the timing of births. Marriage had briefly been a sufficient condition for deferment starting in 1963, but in the summer of 1965 Johnson signed an executive order eliminating those deferments for men who were married after August 26. What had been a noticeable trend in hastily arranged weddings accelerated, as young sweethearts quickened their pace down the aisle ahead of the deadline. Nonetheless, Selective Service removed marriage deferments entirely two months later, announcing instead that all *childless* married men of draft age (regardless of when the nuptials took place) were subject to the draft; only husbands with dependent children now qualified for deferment. Together, these two mid-decade measures, coming unexpectedly and widely publicized, incentivized marriage and the conception of children for men willing to manipulate the system. Statistics suggest that similar to educational deferments—college attendance rates for men increased relative to women by almost 7 percent in the late 1960s—marriage and paternity deferments positively impacted the decision to start families. Marriage rates for twenty- and twenty-one-year-olds rose by 10 percent between 1963 and 1965. What is more, while the overall birth rate for American women was already decreasing rapidly, the number of firstborn deliveries to women in their early twenties jumped by 7 percent in the summer of 1966, roughly nine months after the policy changes. This was also the year in which hardship, fatherhood, and marital deferments were outnumbering student deferments almost two-to-one. As yearly draft calls began steadily declining in 1967, and family deferments were finally replaced by Richard Nixon's "lottery" overhaul of Selective Service in 1970, the draft's relationship to the number of children families had, and subsequent birth spacing, became more ambiguous, just one of several cultural variables driving birth rates further downward by the early 1970s. Still, any effects the draft had on the fertility behavior of women and their draft-eligible spouses also had important consequences in the lives of their children, including effects on maternal education, mother and child health, and maternal participation in the job market.[5]

Just over 3.4 million men and women eventually served in Southeast Asia, which in a country with a population approaching 200 million meant that for the overwhelming majority of Americans the Vietnam experience was anchored nearly entirely in television. Typically, whole families congregating during or after dinner around one of three network evening newscasts witnessed together their society's first extensively televised war in prerecorded three-minute segments and enumerated body counts. Here, in far greater measure than was the case with the threat of nuclear war and the Cuban Missile Crisis, television and parents were the two most important, and mutually supportive, agents of socializing preadolescent children to military affairs. The war was at once seemingly far away, yet somehow also the background context to virtually everything in the news. Kentucky woman born in 1963 remembered it as "a sort of nebulous sad thing happening forever and ever." The yearly *Bob Hope Vietnam Christmas Show* specials became a holiday tradition in some homes for the duration of the war, although NBC did not run the programs until January. Mothers and fathers watched the nightly news broadcasts with somber faces, discussing the war among themselves, but unlike the lack of communication surrounding nuclear war, their tones were often less muted around young ears, and in many households Vietnam was a lively topic of intergenerational conversation. When the televised pictures were deemed too shocking or otherwise upsetting for the smallest viewers, parents rose abruptly to turn the television off.[6]

The proliferation of network news coverage followed closely the pace and intensity of U.S. involvement in the first several years of the war. Garrick Utley of NBC was the first television journalist to be stationed in Saigon, in mid-1964. Within weeks other correspondents and cameramen arrived, reporting on the massive scale of American troops and supplies entering South Vietnam, or presenting "bang-bang" stories extolling the advantages our forces held in terms of technology, air mobility, and raw firepower. Initially, prior to 1968, network newscasts managed to maintain objectivity, echoing the Johnson administration's official line, though coverage was often too brief or condensed to convey a consistent point of view. At NBC, Chet Huntley and David Brinkley read the news and body counts without betraying any sense of approval or disapproval of the war. Over at CBS, when Cronkite spoke of Vietnam, his deliberately even inflections conveyed equal significance to all war news, landing him on a 1966 cover of *Time* as "the single most convincing and authoritative figure on TV news." With the exception of Morley Safer's dramatic *CBS Evening News* report of a Marine "Zippo raid"—burning the thatched huts of Cam Ne villagers on an August 1965 search-and destroy mission—television newsmen lagged well behind print journalists in their critical analysis of the government's intentions or the military's prosecution of the war.

Contrary to many popular recollections, television did not commonly focus on actual combat. Correspondents moved relatively freely among the troops without direct censorship, but cameramen were not allowed on bombing sorties in the sustained air campaign against North Vietnam and were only rarely permitted on search-and-destroy operations. Even as American soldiers launched the first offensive against the Viet Cong just north of Saigon in June 1965 and fought the North Vietnamese Army in the largest battle to date that fall in the Ia Drang Valley, most of the fighting erupted suddenly in small skirmishes at night or in remote locations away from the camera. Nevertheless, by 1966, as U.S. troop strength rose from 184,000 to 385,000 and the conflict emerged as the foremost world event, it was as if every news story had to do with Vietnam. From half a world away, graphic videotape—beginning with Buddhists immolating themselves in fiery protest of South Vietnamese religious repression—and unsettling depictions of the war's difficulties, hardships, suffering, and horror took over the medium, intruding into American family rooms. The transition to color amplified the war's presence; as television historian Erik Barnouw pointed out, "mud and blood were indistinguishable in black and white; in color, blood was blood. In color, misty Vietnamese landscapes hung with indescribable beauty behind gory actions."[7]

While television's role in bringing the visible face of Vietnam home to the United States is clear, exactly how it helped mold American perceptions of the conflict remains complicated, particularly before the Tet Offensive. These were the middle years of the decade in which the majority of Americans supported the war, with Gallup finding in November 1965 a high-water mark of 75 percent of adults under thirty years old and 68 percent of those between thirty and forty-nine believing the United States was right to be in Vietnam. The real differences were between those favoring escalation, negotiations, or other nonwithdrawal options to achieve American objectives. There is a certain symmetry to the public opinion findings in that preadolescents up to third grade—Piaget's preoperational and concrete operational stages—were likewise supportive of American involvement. Strictly speaking, the common adult pro- and anti-war labels—"hawk" and "dove"—were not applicable to younger sixties children. Very few preadolescents would have considered themselves *for* war, and almost unanimously they condemned warfare as something extremely bad. Until at least sixth grade, children almost universally demonstrated a basic ignorance, or severe misconceptions, about even the most widely known factual information. Another woman from Kentucky recalled hearing on the news that American soldiers were battling armed *gorillas* and laboring under that misperception for some time before seeking parental clarification. A San Diego woman remembers visiting her father at a Veteran's Administration hospital and scouting around the facility to find the arms and legs of patients she was told had "lost" them in the war. Several studies indicate that boys were better informed in regard to facts and military terminology, but even with a rudimentary knowledge of Vietnam, pre- and early elementary school children were not equipped to conceptualize the complexity of issues required to make value judgments about the war. By piecing together scraps of information from television and parents, the smallest preadolescents formed an appropriately simple picture of Vietnam. The United States was still at war with communism, but it was not being fought here. "Our boys" were being sent "over there" to fight for "our country." And some of them would die. Victory and defeat were likewise subject to a simplified structuring of reality into the more manageable scale of a child's mind. As a Missouri woman born in 1959 remembered, "every night they would give a count of how many people were killed, how many American soldiers were killed that day and how many Vietnam soldiers were killed. I remember thinking as a little kid, 'well, we won today' or 'we lost today' by the number of soldiers that were killed."[8]

This preoccupation with Defense Secretary Robert McNamara's statistics, in conjunction with television's dramatic inclination toward "shooting bloody" footage, left children tremendously fearful of Vietnam, and eager to see the killing stop. "I know that I had bad dreams from hearing about the Vietnam War on the news," a woman born in 1957 said, recalling how Vietnam honed a finer edge to her Cold War apprehension, "and dreamt of being under the cafeteria tables at school and having big cannonball-looking bombs landing on the tables." "They still haunt me today," a Tennessee woman born in 1961 said of how the causalities being divvied up on-screen helped her overcome her egocentrism. "It struck me as very strange and scary. I remember thinking: those are dead people." Youngsters motivated to write to President Johnson poignantly expressed their hopes that, as a nine-year-old from Alaska put it, "we can find a way to stop the war without the atomic bomb. I also hope that most of the people can be saved." A Virginia grade school boy concluded a letter to Johnson with, "I hope the war in Vietnam will end soon, to [*sic*] many of our boys are dieing [*sic*] on the battlefields. May God be with them."[9]

Yet, the youngest children should not be understood as pacifists. Already instinctively capable of grasping war and progressively socialized to Cold War conflict, those reasoning at Piaget's preoperational and beginning concrete operational stages—with limited abstract thinking—appear to have in varying degrees accepted, or at least tolerated, Vietnam. That is, as long as the outcome was swiftly scoring a decisive victory over the hostile communist enemy. "I know why we have to win the war," a New York boy advised the president in 1966, "because if we don't Britain, Russia, and Red China would say that we cannot defend ourselves and attack us." This patriotic wish to see America prevail over evil—a basic developmental inability to see beyond one-dimensional anti-communism—dominated most young children's thinking about Vietnam. But it also opened many up to the worrisome possibility that on any given night the numbers would no longer add up in America's favor. "Too many people are loosing [sic] there [sic] friends, and families," an uneasy Illinois fourth grader figured, and "we will soon run out of men to send. Then without men, Viet Nam will really get us."[10]

Whereas the Tet Offensive in early 1968 marked the war's turning point both militarily and in terms of American public opinion, the upper elementary school grades saw an analogous watershed for children's views and beliefs. Political scientist Howard Tolley surveyed thousands of New York, New Jersey, and Maryland children in early 1971 on what they knew, and how they felt, about Vietnam. His attitudinal research found that of all the salient variables impacting children's socialization to Vietnam—parents, gender, race, income, and school—age was clearly the most important. Between third and eighth grade, preadolescents' overall knowledge of the conflict progressed sharply, with nearly all of the new factual learning coming from continued exposure to television. By sixth grade, students possessed a strikingly improved understanding of the war. Together with the accompanying concrete operational stage of Piaget's cognitive development—as logically based thought becomes more complex—fairly definite viewpoints on Vietnam steadily crystalized in the child's mind. While one in five third graders did not hold much of an opinion, almost all fifth graders expressed coherent sentiments. Among those with strong ideas, third and fourth graders—nine- and ten-year-olds—demonstrated the most support for the war effort of any childhood age group. That support waned incrementally in each succeeding grade toward adolescence. Indeed, fifth and sixth graders—eleven- and twelve-year-olds—showed the most opposition toward Vietnam, or at least the lowest tolerance, when compared to younger preadolescents and even older children, including adolescents. So, within just a year or two of strongly backing U.S. efforts, the majority of fifth graders surveyed came to believe instead that the United

States had made a mistake in getting involved with Vietnam. Fully half advocated withdrawal of American forces, even if it meant defeat. These results led Tolley to conclude that children developed, and then subsequently lost, the deepest feelings against the Vietnam War around ages ten and eleven.[11]

From the Piagetian developmentalist perspective, Tolley's observations are consistent with the quest for cognitive equilibrium between the concrete operational stage and the onset of formal operations around eleven years old. Nine- and ten-year-olds are the oldest children still thinking at the concrete operational level, and it stands to reason that with better, though still incomplete, comprehension of this war against communism, they would be the most confident in their simplistic acceptance. That is, until deeper perceptual understanding of Vietnam opened the door to doubt. As formal operational thought increasingly permitted a more sophisticated abstract and hypothetical reexamination of their perspectives on issues like U.S. foreign policy, the president, and the definition of victory, eleven- and twelve-year-olds found themselves developmentally vulnerable, in a state of disequilibrium. The pronounced opposition to the war in Vietnam expressed by fifth and sixth graders probably reflects various reservations and negative opinions which developed during their drive toward reestablishing equilibrium. In this ongoing process through which intellectual development occurs, all new experiences and stimuli related to the war would have been assimilated using their advances in critical thinking skills—including the ability to contemplate "what if?" questions of history—to create new schemes and broader worldviews.[12] Available evidence in regard to political socialization toward the presidency appears to bear this out.

It is doubtful children would have been influenced by the two notable 1964 Johnson campaign television advertisements which ran only once yet still managed to frame adult perceptions of Johnson as the thoughtful peace candidate in contrast to the recklessness of Barry Goldwater. The most memorable of these groundbreaking political "spots" showed a little girl picking petals off a daisy, which leads to the countdown to a nuclear explosion, followed by Johnson's voice-over: "These are the stakes. To make a world in which all God's children can live, or go into the dark." Nonetheless, the youngest children, whose imaginative personal relationship with Lyndon Johnson still colored their formative political learning during equilibrium, kept faith with the notion of the president as peacemaker. Even when adult antiwar venom and derision toward Johnson reached its ugliest—*Hey, hey, LBJ, how many kids did you kill today?*—preadolescents unequivocally understood the president's role to be dovish, making peace, not war, in Vietnam.

By 1966 considerable numbers of children were writing the White House to express their personal sadness about the war continuing, but also their confidence—offering encouragement and compliments—that the president would end the fighting and bring the boys home. Collectively their correspondence reveals growing recognition that war is a regrettably regular hazard in international relations, dovetailing with a deeper appreciation for the president's diplomatic role in making peace (stopping this war) and keeping the peace (preventing future war). Many who expressed concern for Johnson's beleaguered and melancholy appearance attributed this to how heavy the burden must be for the only man on the planet capable of negotiating peace with Vietnam, the Soviet Union, and China. "I know that you are doing what you think is best for our country and for the benefit of the world," an eleven-year-old girl wrote. An eight-year-old New Jersey boy reassured the president, "I want you to know that I think you have a very hard job. Please keep your chin up and try not to let some people make you feel bad. I think you are a great President. I will keep praying for you every night. And I will pray for peace for all the people in the world." A nine-year-old supporter in Maryland spoke for many with his belief that "I think you are doing the best you can to stop the war in Vietnam. I am sorry we have to go on living with wars. I hope this will be our last war. Please accept my best wishes in your very important job."[13] Any doubts in Lyndon Johnson—the so-called "credibility gap" between policy and military reality—appeared almost exclusively in letters written by older preadolescents struggling through disequilibrium, and in the last years of Vietnam when confidence in the president did begin to falter.

Childhood conceptions of death, in the context of an apparently perpetual war, were developmental features that were likely involved as well. By kindergarten, as children's maturing awareness of death allows for emotional bereavement, they begin tracing causal connections that show death as the probable outcome of violence. For several years thereafter, interest in this linkage grows, leading some, especially boys, toward a fixation on warfare as a means of voicing aggressive and hostile tendencies. As in the years of World War II, preadolescents working through such thoughts were confronted with violent deaths in the media—"hearing about death on the evening news became part of normal life"—and their curiosity was excited by the war. "Night after night, I suppose I developed a morbid fascination with watching it," a Southern woman born in 1958 recalled. "I saw our soldiers getting shot, sometimes their buddies dragging them off. I saw naked screaming children running. I saw Viet Cong get shot . . . I was a kid, and those nightly broadcasts became part of my psyche." But around the age of ten, the tipping point in children's attitudes, when they start grappling with the concept of their own mortality, a fear of death cast the Vietnam War in an ever more threatening light. The conflict's length—"Viet Nam is lasting so long," a fifth grader lamented to Johnson—and the prospect of it sparking World War III, made boys worried they were going to grow up and die in it. "I wish there wasn't a war," a California sixth grader wrote the president in 1968, because "in a few years I will be going to Viet Nam." A man born in Alabama in 1958 remembered, "I felt I would probably have to go there, and I did NOT want to!" A rural Missouri man who turned ten years old near the end of the ordeal remembered no longer wanting to go to elementary school because he came to suspect that "when you graduated you went to Vietnam."[14]

After the sixth grade, when older preadolescents consistently reasoned in formal operational equilibrium, parents increasingly became the most influential socializing factor. Though children acquired mental images and familiarity with the facts about Vietnam from television, among the oldest grade schoolers, Howard Tolley detected "a strong, predictable, positive relationship between children's views of American policy in Vietnam and the perceived opinions of their parents." This high level of agreement was confirmed in hundreds of recollections I received. As more adults began questioning the war effort and expressing dissent after 1968, their elder children settled into a pattern of shared criticism.[15]

Television's role in these public opinion shifts remains highly debatable. Many who thought coverage of Vietnam was slanted or prejudicial have cited this ever since as a primary reason for U.S. failure. But the Tet Offensive did provoke a new period of subjectivity in televised newscasts. This coordinated attack by the North Vietnamese and Viet Cong on virtually every military base and city in the South during the Chinese Tet New Year starkly demonstrated that despite inflicting astronomical casualties on the enemy, U.S. forces and the South Vietnamese regime they defended remained dangerously vulnerable. Tet provided an inconvenient answer for an increasingly polarized nation demanding to know how much longer our troops would be mired in this bloody quagmire; perhaps Vietnam might go on indefinitely. After Cronkite traveled to Vietnam in Tet's immediate aftermath, his on-air expression of personal doubt—that the United States might have to accept a stalemate—made CBS's February 27, 1968, commentary a defining moment in broadcasting history, reverberating all the way to the Oval Office. "To say that we are closer to victory today," the most trusted man in America editorialized, "is to believe, in the face of the evidence, the optimists who have been wrong in the past . . . But it is increasingly clear to this reporter that the only rational way out then will be to negotiate, not as victors, but as an honorable people who lived up to our pledge to defend democracy, and did the best they could." Other television correspondents followed suit by suggesting what most of them already personally believed to be true, that the war was a colossal waste of blood and treasure. These included NBC's Frank McGee, who first stated on-air that the United States was losing, while scrutinizing the specious logic of destroying Vietnam in order to save it.[16]

Even if children paid little attention to television commentary of this nature, they tuned in to what their parents had to say about it. "I definitely had an awareness of the war on TV, if only the scattered snapshot images and understanding that it was a topic covered a lot by the news," a Kansas man born in 1967 recalled. "[A]dults took it seriously, so I understood it to be a topic without humor." In those homes where educated, or otherwise informed, parents assumed a definite position on Vietnam, mothers and fathers actively engaged their children on the subject through the promotion of certain viewing, reading, and listening habits, while deliberately cultivating opinions and perspectives in harmony with their own. A significant number of sixties children told me that they distinctly remembered thinking as a preadolescent that they could not recall a time in their childhood without the family talking endlessly about, and debating, the Vietnam War. "My first real awareness of Vietnam was the words 'Tet Offensive,' so I was ten or eleven before that war penetrated my consciousness," a Tennessee man explained of these unending family exchanges. Practically their whole lives were unfolding simultaneously with, as a Kansas City woman born in 1957 put it, "the frenzied dialogue concerning Vietnam." Tolley concluded that disapproval of a war which was growing increasingly unpopular—the defining attitude of the divisiveness of the late 1960s—appeared "with equal clarity in children." In tracking the nation's declining support, Gallup showed the number of Americans believing the United States was right to be in Vietnam dropped consistently after Tet. In August 1968, 45 percent of adults under thirty years old, and 39 percent of those between thirty and forty-nine, still agreed with that statement, but those numbers fell to 36 and 37 percent, respectively, in September 1969, and finally to 34 and 30 percent in May 1971. These statistics are virtually identical to those in Tolley's survey of older preadolescents. "I knew 1968 was a year lost in time," a Connecticut man said, "even at eight."[17]

If parents, commonly young mothers and fathers who were baby boomers themselves, adamantly opposed the war, their children could identify with some semblance of the various arguments articulated in the adult world: Vietnam was peripheral to America's vital interests, funding of the war skewed domestic economic priorities (especially affecting poverty programs benefiting African Americans), the draft was rife with inequality. Honest disagreement might rest on morality, as well, grounded in pacifism or religious opposition. As the slogan went, war is not healthy for children and other living things. "My parents fought vigorously FOR civil rights and AGAINST the Viet Nam war," a Michigan woman told me, "and they were pretty candid about anything I dared to ask." Two Berkeley, California, boys were probably echoing their parents' anti-war judgments in a letter to Lyndon Johnson in 1967. "We feel very strongly against the 'illegal' war," they wrote. "You said while you were campaigning that you would try preventing further war in Vietnam, but now you're sending in troops and bombers. The war has not been declared war by Congress. You're spending money on 'illegal' wars that should be spent on the War on Poverty. You're spending money on sending in troops when most of the people in the troops get killed. You're actually 'double killing'—you spend money on our troops, they get killed and more people are starving to death, so just think about it!" Reflecting the broader opposition to Vietnam among poor urban and middle-class African American adults compared to lower- and middle-class whites—due in some measure to mounting resentment over racism and the rise of Black Power—black children viewed Vietnam with more skepticism than their white counterparts. In constructing his statistical profiles, Tolley found that the child most likely to be an outspoken advocate for military involvement in Vietnam would be a middle-class white boy in the third grade whose parents supported the war, while the most outspoken opponent of Vietnam would be an upper-class black girl in the eighth grade.[18]

Although only a small fraction of children actually participated in physical demonstrations—handing out leaflets during neighborhood canvasses, accompanying mom on petition drives, or riding on dad's shoulders during a march—considerably more remember a desire to be older so that they could join the protests. Often those aspirations are still closely, and maybe disproportionately, associated in their memories with parental tastes for folk music. It is a common misperception that protest songs were popular, or for that matter commercially viable, in the 1960s. Quite the contrary. Bob Dylan, for instance, the most recognizable populist troubadour of the cultural rebellion, had only four Top

Forty hits, and his "Blowin' in the Wind" was the only one of his protest songs to make it on the *Billboard* charts, when Peter, Paul and Mary's version went to number two in 1963. Still, these fervent anthems of peace were an integral facet of many children's socialization to Vietnam. "My parents apparently didn't hide much from us as far as politics, music, and current events go," a Georgia woman born in 1960 remembered. "Having young parents [both nineteen at her birth] was definitely an advantage at that time . . . I was exposed to a lot of the great music of the time. But the most memorable was the Peter, Paul and Mary album with "Where Have All the Flowers Gone?" and "500 Miles" [the 1962 album *Peter, Paul and Mary*]." Above all, she said, "watching the war protesters with them on TV just made my 9-year-old self want so badly to be 19 in 1969 so I could be old enough to get out there out protesting the war!" "Being younger than the college kids who were in the protest marches," said a woman born in Vermont in 1958, "I studied what was going on from afar. I heard many adult grumblings about long hair and hippies, but I was impressed that people were willing to say that war was wrong and segregation was despicable. During the nightly Vietnam body counts on the national news, I secretly cheered for those who wanted the insanity to end. I loved the music of Joan Baez and Pete Seeger and memorized their words." Like others who only dreamed of being the "peace loving hippies" as seen on television, her antiwar activism remained confined to "throwing up an occasional peace sign" at school and "probably drawing a few here and there too."[19]

"Too young to participate in peace demonstrations," an Oregonian born in 1957 wrote, "I was in awe of students who took over administration buildings on college campuses. My one (pathetic) act of rebellion was to embroider a peace sign on a white T-shirt, and wear it defiantly in front of my dad. He was, and still is, a supportive parent, but he was not pleased that I was taking this stand and said several times that he was glad I wasn't older because he knew I would be 'one of those kids causing all the trouble.'"[20]

Some of the more musically inclined children were inspired enough to channel their folkie influences and try their hand at writing protest songs themselves. Early in the war, an eleven-year-old South Carolina girl sent Lyndon Johnson such an original piece, "The Brave Soldiers in Vietnam." The lyrics were her own, with the handwritten music written in collaboration with her mom. She meant the song as a requiem for those who "gave their life for there [*sic*] nation and neighbor," because, as she put it, "I feel like I am part of each one of the soldier [*sic*] that die on the battlefield." A twelve-year-old girl from Michigan composed a song (set to the tune of "'Twas the Night before Christmas") for the school talent exhibit, which won a blue ribbon that became a keepsake. The lyrics describe how all through the base camp the men were "waiting for the next day, which I assumed they would dread. When all of a sudden, with a boom and a flash . . . they arrived at their windows, just in time to see a crash" of a rocket attack which "gave a luster of death to the men below . . . I could see them all struggling, trying to rescue in vain." The song continued:

And then I saw one man, running about,
his buddy was killed, as least that's what he'd shout.
I tell you, this war was getting them down.
You'd never see a smile, you'd just see a frown.

Then one happy day, a letter came in.
It said, 'Hallelujah' to all of the men.
The war was over, no worry, no fuss.
Don't you wish that could happen to us?[21]

When parents, in particular those from the Great Depression and World War II generation, supported the war or at least remained noncommittal, children generally approximated their Cold War orthodoxy concerning America's role in the world. These attitudes and opinions, as it happened, adhered closely to those satirized in folksinger Tom Paxton's 1962 song "What Did You Learn in School Today?" The student in the song is taught that the United States must stand up to aggression anywhere, anytime, never rewarding a bully, to avoid the mistakes which allowed Hitler to run amok in Europe. He is taught, as Paxton sang, that politicians do not lie, just as soldiers rarely die. Presidents are inherently honorable, and the government is "right and never wrong," meaning that fighting in Vietnam had to be a just and noble cause. Serving one's country is a patriotic duty, as well as a distinct and sacred honor. After all, "war is not so bad" when we think back to the good ones we have had in places like Germany and France. And, as the student concludes from his lessons, "someday I might get my chance."[22]

In these homes, the war in Vietnam was mostly a black-and-white issue. Dissent was the confusing part. Protesters and hippies were scary, almost inexplicably so, and children accepted their parents' condemnation of these familiar folk villains. "I didn't understand why people were protesting the war," said a Florida woman born in 1960. "I understood at a young age, the servicemen were just trying to do their job and serve their country. I suppose my parents must have enlightened me about this." The escalation of activism only aggravated these children's sense of alienation and confusion. Mass demonstrations gave way to resistance—civil disobedience at induction centers and military installations—eventually culminating in virtual rebellion after 1968 with the Columbia University strike and Weathermen's Days of Rage and the radical wing of the anti-war movement igniting campuses and streets across the country. "As a child," a woman born in 1957 Kansas City said, "this contradictory nature of people using violence to protest the violence of the war created a lot of cognitive dissonance for me."[23]

The sources of such "cognitive dissonance" and doubt were by no means limited to radical and militant protest. Even in the most supportive households, with the most hawkish fathers and mothers, there were shades of gray to befuddle children in their socialization to war. Vietnam altered traditional perceptions of military service, which in turn could affect how parents communicated ideas about soldiering and service. Staff Sergeant Barry Sadler's 1966 crossover hit "The Ballad of the Green Berets," and the military virtues the record celebrated, resonated with a far broader audience than did any protest music. Quickly selling over one million copies, and staying at number one on *Billboard*'s Hot 100 chart for five weeks during the spring of that year, the song's fallen hero makes a heartfelt last request for his son to uphold the family's commitment to military service. "Put silver wings on my son's chest," he implores his young widow. "Make him one of America's best / He'll be a man they'll test one day / Have him win the Green Beret."[24]

But numerous children recognized a troublesome disconnect between a parent's sense of duty in the abstract and reluctance to see their own son serve in Vietnam. "The old WWII rules did not seem to apply—serve your country, no matter what," a Midwestern man born in 1957 said. "The reality at home was this: most middle- to upper-class white parents, however philosophically they felt about the war, did not want their children to go and fight it." For one Missouri man born in 1956, dissension of this sort left the indelible memory of a heated quarrel between his parents heard from the backseat of the family car in 1968. "Dad's a staunch Republican," he said,

and I can remember distinctly him and my mother having an argument about us boys getting called up to the war. Dad served in World War II. He didn't think this war was a war. He thought it was a political war. He hated the war, and he thought it was a bunch of bologna, and it's not a real war, and it's just the politicians. And he said he did not want his boys in Vietnam. He made the statement that he would rather see us boys go up to Canada than fight in an unjust war. Now I'm, like, 12, and I'm listening to this, and that's shocking coming from my staunch, World War II veteran, Republican dad, because that sounds real liberal. And my mother, who always seemed to me to be the more liberal of the two, had a brother who died in World War II. And she was gung-ho. She said, 'These boys will serve if they're called. It's their duty. It's the right thing to do.' And having lost a brother, you can see where she would be committed to the cause more than Dad, who didn't. But then, Dad served, and maybe he knew the real stuff about war anyway, and didn't want his boys to be exposed to it. Who knows. But they split on that.[25]

"As a kid, this complicated what it meant to be 'patriotic,'" the earlier man explained, and perhaps nowhere was this more consistently evident than in the contested culture of war play. More precisely, these very misunderstandings surrounded the fickle relationship between consumers and early incarnations of the iconic, twelve-inch action figure named G.I. Joe. Early in the sixties, when imaginative war games required considerable role-playing—complemented by costuming and tree branch guns, nail "antennas" hammered into wood for a walkie-talkie, and forested encampments where tents fabricated with blankets hung over chairs—make-believe combat and military toys still oriented children toward parental conceptions of how previous wars had been fought (and won). Then a veritable martial toy craze swept the country, beginning in earnest during the 1963 Christmas season, the first major gift-giving holiday after the Cuban Missile Crisis. As the sale of accurate looking military models, miniaturized helicopters, and other related plastic weaponry surged—Louis Marx and Company offered a cool Gung Ho Commando Outfit with belt-fed .50 caliber machine gun on a tripod, .45 caliber pistol, knapsack, and dog tags—this genre, including other violent playthings like Daisy BB guns, ranked among the toy industry's hottest commodities for a period. This was particularly true in the male demographic between the ages of five and twelve. And although a robust market for combat toys was in place already—enhanced, as many now were, with machine gun, jet plane, or exploding sound effects—an intense television advertising campaign helped drive the retailing bonanza. Indeed, those commercials saturating Saturday mornings led more than a few Americans to wonder if a nefarious conspiracy orchestrated by manufacturers and broadcasters was aiming to militarize childhood on the eve of war.[26]

The military toy boom peaked in 1964 with the introduction of G.I. Joe, a costumed soldier marketed by Hasbro as "America's Moveable Fighting Man." Akin to Mattel's fashion doll Barbie, five years his senior and one-half inch shorter, G.I. Joe gave preadolescent boys the plastic musculature of a flawless adult male body, and soon lifelike hair, with a seemingly inexhaustible arsenal of realistic accessories. Upwards of thirty different uniform variations from all four branches of service could be purchased separately along with a plethora of weapons, supplies, and vehicles to be stored in a handsome foot-locker with blank spaces for each new owner's name, rank, and serial number. G.I. Joe's lineage can be traced back centuries in the toy world through cast-metal and later plastic miniature soldier play sets. But Joe's real genius, and what immediately distinguished him as a watershed in childhood war gaming, was the shift in perspective downward from the child-as-general reenacting a battle by arranging little soldiers and armaments, as if they were so many chess pieces, toward living the battlefield experiences of a singular soldier you dressed and posed, pretending to be an ordinary G.I. Joe. To facilitate such play, the early G.I. Joes came with basic training manuals on the proper poses for firing weapons, maneuvering hostile terrain, and throwing grenades. An official G.I. Joe Club (with certificate suitable for framing) encouraged its many thousands of members to act out the daily adventures described in the club's comic book. This dynamic worked so well with five- to twelve-year-olds because, at least initially, the action figure represented a generic "every-soldier" character from World War II or Korea. In a sense, G.I. Joe promoted intergenerational identification between boys and their fathers' or male relatives' wartime post-war military service. Hasbro offered no line of enemies for the G.I. Joes to fight. Pretend battlefields usually just pitted Joe against Joe, in predominantly American recreations. After all, the G.I. Joe experience was less about conquering a specified enemy than it was an affirmation of the values surrounding adult male military action and valor.[27]

Well on his way to becoming a "perennial fad" like Barbie, G.I. Joe was by 1968 the best-selling toy for preadolescent boys. That is, until the increasingly confused nature of the Vietnam War and the country's growing antimilita-rism drove the popularity of all war toys sharply downward and this particular warrior fell out of favor for the duration of the war. Television, the reservoir from which young minds drew the raw resources for their imaginative play, became polluted with uncomfortable distortions of the good guy/bad guy sto-rylines from the "good war," World War II. Vietnam never inspired prime-time television programming in the way the Second World War did with radio, and although military programs proliferated in the 1960s, the heroic or amusing martial life portrayed was nearly exclusively from bygone eras: *Combat, Rat Patrol, Twelve O'Clock High, Jericho, McHale's Navy, Hogan's Heroes, Mister Roberts, F Troop,* and old John Wayne movies.[28]

The ready frame of reference for war play these shows provided—ranging from soldiers' basic appearance and demeanor to their actions—contrasted harshly with the portrayal of Vietnam era troops on the evening news. A woman wrote me, "I remember really being shocked at how different this war seemed compared to what we had seen of the history of WWII. The soldiers looked so much more beaten down." Morley Safer, who had so shocked American sensibilities with his depiction of the Cam Ne incursion, spoke to these incongruities most clearly and directly: "I think," the broadcaster said, that viewers "saw American troops acting in a way people had never seen American troops act before, and couldn't imagine. Those people were raised on World War II, in which virtually everything we saw was heroic. And so much of it, indeed, was. And there was plenty in Vietnam, too, that was heroic. But this conjured up not America, but some brutal power—Germany, even, in World War II. To see young G.I.s, big guys in flak jackets, lighting up thatched roofs, and women holding babies running away, wailing—this was a new sight to everyone." Definitely one that did to lend itself as well to emulation through play.[29]

So too did that element of intergenerational bonding around military service break down under the strain of Vietnam. For World War II and Korean War veteran fathers, purchasing G.I. Joes for their children might have been a way to memorialize their own youthful military service. But unfortunately this sometimes prompted comparative criticisms of the U.S. soldiers currently in Vietnam. A Missourian born in 1958 recalled such conversations about his father's distaste for "how Vietnam was being handled," because, in his father's opinion, which had been formed during WWII, "we weren't trying as hard. Dad always said they never had enough men fighting and soldiers weren't trained right. I remember he would sometimes call them spoiled little babies and then go on about what he had to do when he was in Europe." Trying to socialize children with military toys was another matter entirely. The fundamental difficulty for Vietnam era adults who attempted to pass down traditional American values by gifting action figures like G.I. Joe or Stony "Stonewall" Smith was that this war offered far fewer World War II or even Cold War certainties on which to ground their teachings. Given the fluid nature of the government's rationale and the absence of conventional warfare,

in the adult world the very concepts of patriotism and duty were being vigorously disputed. Were U.S. troops fighting to contain communism or make
the nation's power credible? Was South Vietnam a remote domino to be kept
from falling or an invaluable ally requesting that its freedom be protected?
With few exceptions, there was no territory gained or lost, no dramatic campaigns, and no epic battles with the fate of armies and nations hanging in the
balance. Who could say what winning would even look like;—the protracted
occupation of a wholly dependent client state? G.I. Joe's socializing role could
be even trickier for young fathers reaching manhood during the Vietnam
War. Whether they actually fought in Vietnam or opposed the war, most men
simply sought to distance their families from the conflict, not introduce their
sons to a toy whose make-believe jungle battles constantly brought to mind
this very real, and humiliating, military misadventure.[30]

As G.I. Joe's footing deteriorated on the home front, a relatively small, yet
inspired "anti-war toy movement" was hard at work denouncing all violent
playthings. This network of predominantly concerned mothers, bolstered by
the views of Dr. Benjamin Spock and other child-rearing experts, sounded the alarm on how the popularity of convincing military toys and guns,
set against the backdrop of unrelenting televised warfare, was warping and
magnifying conventional war play. The activists worried that children as
young as four were being integrated into the pretend world of bedroom
search-and-destroy missions, dangerously below the ages of seven and eight,
when war gaming normally enters into play culture. They also alleged that
in wartime—where real human beings could be seen suffering and dying
every day—martial toys advertised on that same TV screen were unhealthy
teaching tools perpetuating a militarized culture of violence. By glorifying
war in the informal environment of home, were military toys desensitizing
boys to violence in the bargain? Would pretend reenactments make war appear to be an inevitable part of American life? And through their complicity
in purchasing such toy weapons and uniforms, and condoning combat play,
were parents modeling for children a tacit approval of war? These were legitimate questions for any mother who found her son's ragged G.I. Joes strewn
across the backyard, killed in action by bottle rocket, fire cracker, and BB
gun attacks.[31]

As one Utah youngster advised President Johnson in 1967, "I think you
should send 9 thur [through] 14 year old boys to War," basing his case on the
premise that he and his third grade friends required "no wisky, Play Boy eta.
[etc.]," because "We no [sic] how to play war" already.[32]

Although a nervous apprehension over military play existed within the
Cold War era peace movement prior to Vietnam, it gained more urgency
in the late 1960s out of fears that the drawn-out conflict would further encourage American children to truly make a game out of war. In this way, an
anti-war toy crusade developed as but one distinct facet of the broader antiwar
movement. While the decade's public protests against Vietnam were, again,
rarely a factor for many children, the loose coalition of local organizations
agitating for the "disarmament" of play was one of the very few ways antiwar
activism was manifested in the lives of preadolescents.

The *Peace Education Bulletin*, published in 1966 and 1967 by Women Strike
for Peace, functioned as a primary organ for disseminating the opinions and
undertakings of those concerned individuals and groups—principally in the
fields of child development and teacher education—who advocated constructive and creative play alternatives to war and kill toys. Another movement
publication, *The Toy*, put out sporadically between 1965 and 1967 by the
group No War Toys and its founder, Los Angeles author Richard Register,
an early supporter of a worldwide organization against war toys, featured the
writings, songs, and works of like-minded artists and intellectuals including
Shel Silverstein, Margaret Mead, and Joan Baez. In Minnesota, a branch of the
established Women's International League for Peace and Freedom distributed
the booklet "Let's Train Them for Peace" as a resource for people involved
in childhood education, while a group known as the California Committee
conducted parent and teacher workshops promoting peaceful play. Democrat
John L. Burton introduced legislation in the California State Assembly requiring labeling for toy weapons and military toys. Despite the bill finding little
traction, none other than Captain Kangaroo himself, Bob Keeshan, bucked
the commercialism of his network by steadfastly prohibiting advertising for
warlike toys and guns on his show. As a result, major department stores carrying war toys in many cities were convinced by activists to stop advertising
those lines, including Sears, which removed toy guns from its catalogs but not
shelves. One toy manufacturer, Lionel, challenged convention as well, forgoing its military lines in favor of trains, racetracks, and science and space toys,
which reinforced the company's principled theme "Sane Toys for Healthy
Kids."

Others opted for more direct action. A group of students and faculty from
the Princeton Theological Seminary peacefully picketed the 1968 Armed
Forces Day ceremonies at Fort Dix, New Jersey, where local children had been
invited to join in such soldierly activities as throwing grenades (deactivated),

practicing bayonetting with broomsticks, and the simulated bombing of a Vietnamese village. In perhaps the lone instance in this context of the humor-as-protest guerrilla theatrics made (in)famous by Yippie showman-activist Abbie Hoffman, The Committee, a San Francisco improvisational comedy troupe active in the anti-war movement, collected used war toys to drop on the Pentagon by parachute. Their absurdist "bombing" campaign in February 1966—publicized with a full-page ad in the *San Francisco Chronicle*—merged counterculture aesthetics with political activism by employing playful satire intended to invert the serious symbols of the American war effort. This targeting of the military occurred during the Christmas season of 1965, when American pilots were planning to drop toy bundles over North Vietnam. The Committee implored Bay Area residents to donate war toys—making it a contest with cash prizes for the best—which would best demonstrate wholesome American values for Vietnamese children. Logistical difficulties dictated that the toy weapons were inauspiciously delivered to Washington aboard buses, but the Pentagon never mentioned the humanitarian toy drops again.[33]

By Richard Nixon's earliest years in office, with the first U.S. troops coming home and television coverage framing American involvement as winding down, the popularity and sale of military toys continued to fall toward pre-1960s levels. Retailers noted parents' clear lack of enthusiasm for, and sometimes outright revulsion toward, "anything khaki." As stores struggled to sell off inventories, prominent manufacturers like Marx began offering toys which had been previously been painted olive drab green in new, garish—nearly psychedelic—colors. In 1970 Hasbro reimagined the G.I. Joe line, in the first of a decade-long series of transformations resulting directly from Vietnam. The fighting soldiers were repurposed into "Adventure Teams" of big-game hunters on safari and scuba divers in search of treasure. Six years later, when combat toys were making a post-Vietnam comeback, the figure was retooled once more, emerging as the modernized Super Joe, a futuristic fantasy warrior—albeit only an eight-inch one, due to rising cost of plastic after the oil shocks—who waged high-tech havoc on alien intruders with laser beams and rocket ships. Gone by this time were his cloth outfits, replaced by a molded uniform, and his authentic military weaponry, supplanted by science-fiction munitions. After a brief furlough between 1978 and 1981, Joe reemerged yet again under the shadow of massive *Star Wars* merchandising. Designed for a new cohort of children with no memories of Vietnam, Joe's otherworldly battlefield exploits against arch-villain Cobra were now thoroughly estranged from the realities and values of military life or identification with the service of fathers, older brothers, or grandpa, with nary a hint of all that unpleasantness from the sixties.[34]

Naturally, the war was most relevant and acutely felt to children who had personal connections with someone serving in Vietnam, directly intertwining the war within their young lives. "My street was my world," one woman said in explaining the role of the sixties in her life, and eventually "it seemed like most of the older teen boys and fathers on my street were off fighting in Vietnam." It is interesting to note, however, that there do not appear to be consistent statistical differences in positive and negative attitudes toward the Vietnam War between those children who knew, or were related, to someone serving compared to those who did not. The only real variation was that the former group tended to wish harder for the war to be over and expressed more hope for a U.S. victory. At church, prayers offered for servicemen from the congregation were voiced more earnestly by these children (sometimes followed by older worshipers' supplications that the fighting end before the younger congregants reached eighteen). In the classroom, although the amount of teaching time spent on Vietnam varied tremendously by school and individual teacher, these students tended to approach war-related assignments more purposefully and with greater sincerity. Schoolchildren without any linkage might disregard such tasks as plotting newsworthy locations with colored push pins on a map of Southeast Asia or reciting last night's television casualty figures for the class, pointing instead to random spots or simply making up the numbers of killed, wounded, and prisoners when called upon. Those who knew someone overseas generally did their homework. And when former high school football stars were killed, normally festive Friday night halftime ceremonies took on a somber tone for everyone.[35]

In the absence of firsthand associations, POW-MIA bracelets (up to six per arm) allowed for the creation of fictive relationships. As one popular aspect of a growing campaign to bring the plight of servicemen listed as prisoner-of-war or missing-in-action to public attention, these commemorative stainless steel and copper bracelets—engraved with a captured or missing man's name, rank, branch of service, and date of loss—gave children "a guy" of their own to wonder about, worry over, and pray for. Beginning in 1970, nearly five million were distributed—Sonny and Cher started wearing them on their *Comedy Hour* show—and they were meant to be worn until the POW or MIA's status had been officially determined or he returned home. Parents and older relatives usually gifted the bracelets to preadolescents, but once on a child's wrist (turned green from the copper version) it engendered considerable pride as an act of performed patriotism. Moreover, the bracelets sentimentalized bonds of protective affection toward a faraway stranger that almost none of these children would ever really know. While hoping every day for a safe homecoming, children eagerly swapped status information with each other. One New Jersey woman still associates the war's end in 1973 with her bracelet, searching the "names of returning POWs" with her friends "to see if 'our guys' had returned," and feeling "elated that 'my guy' had, indeed, come home."[36] Nearly all children took their bracelets off in peacetime, and some mailed them to the repatriated man's family, etiquette dictating that one never send a bracelet before there was a complete accounting. For many, their only "personal" experience with Vietnam remains the vicarious sacrifice of "their guy," and it is his name they rub from the Wall when visiting the Vietnam Veterans Memorial.

If watching adults sweat out the days of a close relative's draft window was unsettling for preadolescents, it paled in comparison to the emotionally charged nature of home life when family members served a tour of duty. "Vietnam was a faraway place that didn't seem to concern me," a Pennsylvania woman explained, "until my oldest brother, right out of college and ROTC, was sent there. Everything changed—the war was brought home, in a big way." For a Michigan woman born in 1960, like so many thousands of others, the disrupting psychological burden of sending brothers to war is the defining imprint of the sixties. "My strongest memories," she wrote to me, "are of my mother dissolving into tears each time she had to put [her two sons] on a plane to serve. I thought my parents were rocks, we never saw them become that emotional . . . [T]his was absolutely crushing for me." Fathers, justifiably proud to have raised sons willing to fulfill their duty, unlike "those long-haired commie hippies," still voiced resentment that their boys might die for nothing. "Just get in there," a Midwestern man recalled his father admonishing a departing brother, "stay low, do your job, shut your mouth, don't be a hero . . . and get home." "My mother was just terrified," an Oregon woman born in 1957 said of her brother's departure. "[S]he tried to put on a brave front, but she was a nervous wreck during his entire tour." For a New Hampshire man born in 1958, the foremost recollection of Vietnam is still the day his brother shipped out to fly medical helicopters. "I was quite upset when he left. I remember spending a lot of time in the school counselor's office that day."[37]

Worry marked the rhythm of family life during those long, unforgettable years. Parents faithfully wrote letters several times a week, if not daily, often with accompanying care packages. Some families dictated conversations about their day, played the piano, and sang into tape recorders, mailing the tapes to the APO (Army Post Office). Whole families anxiously waited for inconsistently delivered correspondence from Vietnam to arrive—sometimes weeks apart—devouring each page in order to glean precious details about their sons' whereabouts and safety. Many mothers kept a large map of Vietnam hanging on the kitchen wall and kept track of their son's stationing throughout the country with a homemade system of stars, circles, and arrows. "I became familiar with all those strange names," the Pennsylvania woman added concerning her brother's absence, "and faithfully watched the news with my parents every day."[38]

Besides the reduced length of service in Vietnam compared to World War II, the greatest difference in regard to family separation between the two wars was television. Network television newscasts afforded households a nightly window into Vietnam, an unprecedented vantage point from which to follow the order of battles, draw a measure of tempered confidence when Viet Cong casualties far outnumbered ours, or, in the most ardent hope of all children, catch a glimpse of loved ones. In turn, television coverage diminished parental censorship. Glued to the set themselves, mothers and fathers found it even more difficult than usual to deflect frank conversations with preadolescent viewers concerning even the most dangerous and scariest aspects of what their brothers or cousins might be going through.

"I'm only 7 years old," a desperate child wrote Lyndon Johnson in December 1967, in a letter that succinctly articulated the troubled thoughts of other little brothers and sisters in that holiday season. "That Chirtmas [sic] coming I should be happy. But Im [sic] not cause our family won't be together. My big brother is in Viet Namn [sic]. I am so scared something will happen to him I pray every night and while I'm praying I can hear mommy crying. Then I get scared. Oh please Mr Johnson please help me not to be scared. You can help me if youll [sic] only bring him home." A woman whose cousin was also in harm's way later recalled, "We said our prayers every night and prayed an extra prayer for all 'The Boys in Vietnam.'" The majority of such prayers were eventually answered; yet, for a sizable number of children the gnawing uncertainty during what one child of the sixties characterized as "one of the most agonizing years of my life" culminated with the worst news imaginable.[39]

A total of 1,400,000 Americans had someone in their family wounded in Vietnam; 275,000 had a family member killed there. A Southern woman born in 1960 found new import and comfort in Peter, Paul and Mary records when her favorite cousin lost his life in Vietnam. "I would play 'Where Have All the

Flowers Gone?' on the stereo," she told me, "and cry and cry and cry." Having
familial involvement in the war may not have had an appreciable impact on
children's views toward Vietnam, but in many cases losing someone shaped
socialization. "It was then," a Northeastern woman discovered, that she came
to feel bitterness not just toward Vietnam, but "that I really began to hate
war."[40]

"My first memory of the effects of 'War'," wrote the daughter of a career
airman stationed at a base in Indiana during 1969, "was at the age of six. There
was a family that lived across the street from us. We used to go over there on
the weekend for homemade ice-cream. When the dad went to Vietnam we
would go with my Dad when he would help the mom with mowing, fixing
house problems, etc. One night while in bed I heard Dad talking about our
neighbor. His wife was notified that her husband had been captured and was
a prisoner of war. I cried a lot during this time because I knew at some time
my dad was going to be deployed. I asked my dad many years later about our
neighbor. He told me, with tears in his eyes, that the man did not survive. The
big shock for him was that I remembered ALL of it."[41]

When daddies went to war, their continued absence deepened this type of
cumulative family crisis, creating a much wider array of psychological and
emotional displacements which tested each member's resilience, adaptability,
persistence, and patience, regardless of age. Since the typical father separation
in the Vietnam War was shorter in duration and more predictable, given a serviceman's predetermined DEROS (Date Eligible for Return from Overseas),
some of the most troubling developmental effects scholars identified in home
front children during World War II either did not appear or were greatly
abbreviated. Despite the recognized need for a father figure in the successful
navigation of early childhood development, there is little indication that paternal separation due to Vietnam, and the subsequent growth of maternal influence in the lives of preschool boys, produced the same level of identification
with mothers which led post-World War II experts to warn of feminizing
tendencies and even sexual identity confusion. Nonetheless, having a father in
Southeast Asia for a year (twelve months for the Army and typically thirteen
months for Marines)—as opposed to the World War II average of thirty-three
months—was a crucial developmental factor, especially in the lives of school-
age children who had known dad before he left. The time spent apart waiting
for DEROS was largely unstructured and improvised. Separation dominated
individual lives as well as the interdependent, transactional nature of familial
relationships in many households.

Some children experienced only the most obvious hardships: loneliness, insecurity, postponement. "My dad served 2 tours of Vietnam," a self-described
mobile Army brat born in 1959 wrote in recounting the day of his father's
departure. "The first time, I was in first grade (so 66/67). I remember family
members were very upset. I didn't understand what was going on other than
people were not happy. I stood up in front of the crowd and said, 'Wow, there
sure will be a lot of tears tomorrow too.'" Virtually all mothers and children
dealt with their unique situations through trial and error, in their own ways
striving to maintain stability and a sense of continuity with subtle modifica-
tions and complex role adjustments to their domestic lifestyles. Some families,
just like some members, coped relatively better or worse. And often these
renegotiations of the family dynamic fed into the era's gendered dialectic concerning the rise of female-headed households, declining male authority, and
women's liberation.[42]

Younger mothers with preschool-age children, married to twenty-
something draftees and enlistees, frequently moved temporarily back into the
refuge of their parents' home for the assistance these familiar surroundings
afforded. Older mothers of school-age preadolescents, married to professional
military men, tended to stay within or near military communities, likewise
for the inherent support system. In either situation, the reallocation of daily
household duties meant that in order to "make the trains run on time" wives
assumed unaccustomed stewardship responsibilities in a dual mother-father
capacity. These behavioral changes on the home front, as unwelcome as they
may have been, hastened the undermining of the Cold War's polarized gender roles and encouraged what feminists would soon refer to as an empow-
ered woman's coming to consciousness. Taking over the household financial
management and budgeting—a real change for previously dependent wives—
obliged some women for the first time to seriously consider the prospect of
employment outside the home or the continuation of an education. Economic
decision-making also routinely involved certain legal issues—selling a car or
signing a lease—which in turn generated friction with the arbitrary limits of a
woman's autonomy. It was frustrating for wives to realize that they could not
make personal property transactions without their husbands because titles and
deeds were in his name.

So too did the scope of women's traditional domestic charge expand.
Still cooking, cleaning, clothing, and running errands for her young children, while overseeing their physical health and social well-being, mothers
also shouldered a more authoritarian role. They laid out codes of conduct,

operating as the family's principal arbiter of disputes and disciplinarian, although many home front children recall their mother wielding the proverbial
threat "wait till your father gets home." These lifestyle changes required profound emotional adjustments, and feelings of satisfaction sometimes mixed
uneasily with mood fluctuations, jumpiness, or dark bouts of depression. Not
infrequently, mothers self-medicated through alcohol or tranquilizers.[43]

As the mother–child relationship quite naturally grew closer and more intense, preadolescents tended to trim their behavioral sails to mom's prevailing
emotional winds. Among the father-related responsibilities children inherited
in his absence, they acquired a heightened awareness, and responsiveness to,
their mother's moods, as well as her emotional needs and demands. Those
younger than nine who were grieving over the separation, but could not
developmentally maintain their sorrow for long periods, might mirror their
mother's behaviors instead of exhibiting their own despair. Older children
reported that they usually chose to suppress their true feelings as a conscious
strategy to not further upset their mother. The strain of adjustment commonly manifested itself in any number of ways, ranging from crying easily, to fear
of the dark, and nightmares to more subtle symptoms like nail biting, shyness,
or social introversion.[44]

"My father was in the Vietnam War for a year and it took a toll on our family," a woman born in 1961 remembered, "and my mother had to get her first
job, which my father wasn't happy about, but she had to feed four kids." The
woman's next recollection speaks to the importance of regular correspondence in helping to inform children's perceptions: "[T]he war was changing
him daily in a bad way, [and] letters from him were full of bitter words, fear
and worry."[45] A Florida man whose father left for Vietnam in 1965, when
he was entering first grade, wrote, "[W]hen I see that military families can
now communicate with soldiers that have been deployed through e-mail and
various other means, I remember that it was not always that easy with us. We
would get a letter from him telling us where he was at that time and then we
would hear on TV that the Viet Cong had attacked or that there was fighting
there, [and] this would worry my mother. But usually he had moved to somewhere else by the time we got the letter."[46]

In the absence of such information, children with fathers overseas wrote the
White House on a regular basis. Hundreds asked Lyndon Johnson if he had
perhaps seen their dad during his surprise visit to Cam Ranh Bay in October
1966. Thousands more mirrored the heartfelt appeal of an upstate New York
girl who wrote, "My father is stationed at Bien Hoa Air Force Base, South

Viet Nam. Mr. President, would it be possible for my daddy to get home for my birthday. It is the only thing in the world I want for my birthday. Please Mr. President, my brothers, Billy 7, Paul 5, Tom 3 think our father is dead and will never come home. It's been such a long, lonesome year. I hope and pray God will help find a peaceful way to end the war in Viet Nam, so my daddy will not have to leave us again."[47]

The red, white, and blue stationery from Vietnam on which soldiers struggled to communicate their experiences—homesick stories of wartime always stopping just short of telling how close they had come to making mom a widow—brought apprehension and concern, but also hopeful expressions of loving you, missing you, and being home for Christmas. Parcels especially lightened the mood, with curiosities and exotic gifts. The most sacred artifacts from the sixties in the lives of countless men and women are the colorful dolls, hand carved animal figurines, and elaborate beaded jewelry which have remained family heirlooms. There were other ways to lighten the mood as well: a Kansan who was four years old when his father was flying helicopters in Vietnam remembered how letters addressed to him—intended to be read to him by his mother—always made direct and loving mention of her even after their marriage had run aground. The pilot usually illustrated these letters with caricatures and humorous drawings showing the illogic of military life, which in the mind of a child mitigated the worry. How bad could things be in Vietnam if wartime was depicted in cartoon form?

Mail could accomplish only so much, though. It was not uncommon for sons and daughters to feel self-conscious about how incomplete their family seemed compared to other more apparently stable homes, and many worked mightily toward filling in the missing pieces. For instance, where departing fathers had left unfinished home improvement projects, children often completed them and other routine maintenance (to varying degrees of success) in order to feel closer to him and win his approval from overseas. Perceptions of dad might also undergo a series of revisions while he was away, with preadolescents mentally fashioning or reconstructing creative scenarios. Thinking back to past bad behaviors which had required punishment from their father conjured up old feelings, making children relive their guilt and shame. While some harbored undeserved resentment for fathers whom they suspected had deliberately chosen to abandon them by going overseas, far more fantasized about him, with glorified imagery out of proportion to reality—the oldest taking to wearing military jackets or emblems of his service—and daydreamed about his idyllic homecoming.

Those progressing developmentally without a father figure sought out surrogate male role models to identify with, usually grandfathers—"I remember
my grandparents being over at the house a lot!" one woman said—but also
uncles, coaches, pastors, scout leaders, and neighbors. For sons and daughters outside the protective culture of a military base, feelings of inadequacy
could be exacerbated by civilian recriminations of the war effort. This was
generally harder on older siblings, because people were more likely to vent
their anti-war frustrations at them for having a father in the war. "We moved
to Indiana . . . to live near family while my Dad was in Vietnam," a woman
born in 1963 told me. "This was the first time I had lived out of the shelter of
military life. I was exposed to people who talked bad about our military and
our president. It made me so angry and sad at the same time. I cried myself to
sleep most nights, worried and scared that my daddy would not come home
to us."[48]

Comparatively speaking, the number of POW/MIA families was rather
small—just under 600 prisoners of war and roughly 1,300 missing in action
when Vietnam ended—yet their experiences are significant considering the
length of separation more closely approximated that of World War II and the
disproportionate amount of attention given them in the public imagination.
Vietnam War prisoners were held for a longer time than in any other American conflict, the average captivity lasting over five years for Navy flyers and
only slightly less for Marines and the Army. This unprecedented length, accentuated by the indeterminate nature of waiting for a prisoner or one listed
as missing, complicated the usual adjustment patterns of families to the absence of father. Mothers and children survived in limbo, not sure if they were
wives, widows, or orphans. Studies detected in some POW/MIA families the
same serious disruptions of healthy psychosexual development in boys found
during the Second World War. In these instances, despairing mothers grew
so dependent on their children that the emotional manipulation they used
to control preadolescents created Oedipal sons whose resultant issues were
frequently worsened by displacement problems when fathers returned.

In the tumultuous lives of POW/MIA children—the majority of whom
were between five and ten years old when dad left—the unknown was always the hardest to bear. Is he alive, how much hope can we realistically have
that he is alive, how might he have died? Fathers were "more remembered
than real," represented around the house by fragments of memorabilia: plastic
models of his aircraft, dress uniforms hanging in the closet, portraits in mom's
bedroom, and encyclopedias bookmarked to Vietnam. Older children with

firsthand recollections of dad endlessly retold a handful of the same cherished stories—about snowball fights, his sense of humor, or bouts of tickling—and concentrated to envision certain traits—eye color and other physical features—which helped define him in their memory. Those too young to recall learned these facts secondhand.[49]

Per official government policy during the Johnson administration, POW/MIA families kept a low profile. The military quietly supplied dependents with confidential information about their missing men, but the political and diplomatic complexity of imprisonment—North Vietnam classified captured airmen as war criminals—left families isolated, viewed as deviants within the military community and enigmas to civilians. It was not until the spring of 1969, when some 2,700 relatives organized together as the grassroots National League of Families of American Prisoners and Missing in Southeast Asia—and Nixon deliberately made the issue more public—that POWs and MIAs came to occupy center stage in the country's convulsive discourse over Vietnam. In the war's last four years, the conflict's unpopularity and associated feelings of disgrace made these predominantly Navy and Air Force pilots and career officers the first, and for a time the only, heroes Vietnam produced. As Americans focused more intently on their imprisonment, the mass media sentimentally framed the thorny geopolitical impasse around how it impacted families, beginning with *Life* and *Look* magazine both highlighting children living without POW fathers in their 1970 Christmas season issues. Thus, semi-orphaned sons and daughters became closely associated in the American mind with the plight of POWs and MIAs, just as the eventual restoration of these incomplete families came to be seen as a metaphor for a fractured country desperate to be whole.[50]

For an estimated twenty thousand orphans, no such reunion was forthcoming. The Vietnam War shattered these young lives, supplanting the normal future they envisioned together as a family with a lifelong, uphill climb to make sense of a father's sacrifice and keep him relevant beyond just storytelling and fading Polaroids. "I remember that day like it was yesterday," a Californian began when recounting the arrival of two Marines in dress blue uniforms—known colloquially as Angels of Death—delivering the official notice that his father, Staff Sergeant Franklin Max Ellinger, had been killed in action. Seven years old in that summer of 1968, with a little brother three years younger, he was sitting on the front steps as the men got out of the military car and walked right past him to knock on the front door. He neither saw nor heard the soldiers' somber conversation with his mother; her scream told the story unmistakably. For the rest of the day, women from their trailer community around Camp Pendleton were in and out with food and condolences. One spent the night with his mother, and the two boys heard her screams again, punctuated with "God no, God no, why?" In the morning she gathered them together for "the talk," all hugging and crying as she explained that "your daddy died in Vietnam." He remembers the funeral in a similar series of vivid recollections: a closed, flag-draped casket, a twenty-one-gun salute, his heart physically hurting. "Mom," he wondered on the drive home, "how come the flags around town aren't flying at half-mast?"[51]

Another former Gold Star child points out that while soldiers killed in wartime have paid the highest price for the country, their orphaned children continue to pay in their own right. In homes too numb for families to effectively talk about their sense of loss, members distanced themselves from death and little was done to actively honor or remember the fallen soldier, either by commemorating his gravesite or even marking his birthday. This was all the more true if mom remarried. Just talking about Vietnam upset adults, so desolate children learned to use that word only sparingly in polite conversation. Isolation and loneliness dominated these childhood experiences, just as resentment, and sometimes outright anger with God, might cloud faith. Replying to the question of what Vietnam meant to her, a San Diego woman born in 1959 whose father had died when she was in the first grade (unrelated to military service), said simply, "I felt very 'different' because all the other kids had both a father and mother at home. [But] as the Vietnam War churned along, more and more kids became like me. I remember when a student wouldn't show up for class for several days, the teacher would tell us that [the student's] father was killed in the war. Be extra nice to him/her when he/she returns.'" Whether privately or as part of more expressive families—those who solemnly observe the date he died—preadolescents yearned for their father's presence in their lives, and with each passing year through adolescence, sought more meaningful understanding of him—not just impersonal statistics, but the subtle particulars and qualities that had made dad uniquely a person.[52]

For widows, the children were his progeny, her husband's living representation, and onto them many mothers placed the immense obligation of carrying on the fallen soldier's name, identity, values, and aspirations. Often, the children placed the same obligation on themselves. "I had to grow up, really faster than I thought I would," the California man, Mike Ellinger, explained to me. "As the oldest, I had to become the man of the house." Already close, the relationship between Mike and his mother, Carol, grew "damn strong" and he credits her with single-handedly being his "backbone." Despite mother and son thinking Vietnam to be a "useless war," she instilled through discipline the same integrity, honesty, and character associated with both parents' beloved Marines (the couple had met in the Corps). Regularly, her parenting style deliberately evoked memories of his father—pointing out the physical resemblance or how much Mike reminded her of him—while also employing paternal lessons from the past. Harkening back to the spanking Mike had once received from his dad for riding his sparkling Stingray bicycle (green with white banana seat) through mud puddles, for instance, served to reinforce respect and care for one's property. When Carol went to college classes, she left Mike in charge of the evening latchkey routine: completing household chores, preparing meals, cleaning the dishes, doing the homework, and getting himself and his brother to bed. It was under her direct guidance in the years after 1968, he says, that he came to really learn "who the Ellingers are." Protecting that legacy also required her faithful nurturing of the natural athleticism and passion for baseball passed down from father to son. On the diamond, with mom in the stands—or working games as the only female Little League umpire around—Mike could transcend the loss, nine innings at a time. He dreamed of being a major leaguer until injuries in high school dictated another career choice. His family's relationship with the Marines suggestion one logical option, and Carol left that decision strictly up to him. But in the end he chose a different path, simply unable to bear the thought of putting her through another military funeral.[53]

Hundreds of thousands more families *were* eventually reunited, and these homecomings created vivid, joyful flashbulb memories with lifelong resonance. "There is not a happier time than when a family member returns from war," a Southern man recalled of his dad's abrupt return. "One day my mother just got a call. It was from my father, he was in New Jersey, he was home." The exhilaration of suddenly seeing their father standing on the porch in khakis or showing up by surprise at school—an intense compression of excitement, relief, and pride—was the most gratifying event in many preadolescents' lives. "I remember watching him walk down the jet gate in full uniform," a woman born in 1959 recalled, "and being so proud to see him." "For the most part, I basically just remember not having a father around for most of my early years," a Vermont woman born in 1965 said of her father's two tours. She recalled "being shy when he came home the second time [1972] and how proud I was of the cake we made for him to welcome the 'boss' home." Regrettably, beyond the immediate warm glow of these reunions, the most important developmental consequences were commonly shaped by the bumpy realities of family restoration in the transitional months and years afterward. Even in well-adjusted households, reintegration often proved to be far more problematic and less fulfilling than veterans, mothers, and children anticipated. As ironic as it might seem, the reorganization strategies which had helped families deal successfully with separation were also what could most adversely affect their readjustment.[54]

Families harbored unrealistic expectations about exactly how, and when, men might be worked back into the domestic fold as dad and husband. Returning servicemen often did not live up to the hero imagery their small children had elaborately built to enshrine them, which could be a jarring and disappointing introduction to the gap between perception and reality. Conversely, veterans brought home their own impractical expectations of their children—concerning deportment, discipline, and hair length—or sought to reclaim the dominant head-of-the-house role more quickly than was comfortable. Those who imposed military-style discipline, especially when mothers had been lenient or grandparents more permissive, fostered particularly stressful child-father relationships. "It was an adjustment for the entire family with him home," a woman born in 1959 said of navigating these new dynamics. "We could push mom much further than dad and had to rein it in with him home." Mothers too might be apprehensive with judgmental husbands, on the defensive when accounting for household management, financial decisions, purchases, or child-rearing practices, and protective of their increased independence in these matters.[55]

Sometimes fathers came back different, physically and/or emotionally. Numerous reminiscences I collected tell of children being more than a little fearful to be around their returned father, usually because he seemed sullen and estranged, or behaved oddly. When men withdrew, reluctant to talk about Vietnam, families often steered conversations clear of the war, a situation pre-adolescents found particularly puzzling. Why would parents remain silent on something as noble as military service, or as honorable as being a Marine? And why did adults frown on expressing pride in your father's soldiering to others outside the family, in effect hiding his achievements? Then there were embarrassing isolated episodes that did not always appear simply quirky at the time. One woman who was ten when her father returned in the late sixties still clearly remembers his reaction to a tornado warning in their town. "Dad thought it was incoming fire and belly crawled across the room until he realized where he was. A few months later, my brother walked up behind dad and tapped him on the shoulder. In an instant, he was flipped over my dad's shoulder on the ground with a foot on his neck. As an adult, one of the things my dad told me about his experiences has really stuck out to me. He said it was hard for him to be around kids again—that [he couldn't assume] they wouldn't have a grenade in their hand. Wow—how sad."[56]

In extreme cases, the development of post-traumatic stress disorder (PTSD) pressed families to the breaking point, with children of the sixties describing their child-father relationships using words such as anguish, torment, turmoil, depression, abusive, controlling, alcoholism, and misfit. A small number point as well to secondary PTSD in mothers and generational PTSD in themselves as key trajectory determinants in their adult inability to appropriately manage friendships and intimate relations.

Even if the number of stereotypically troubled Vietnam veterans can be overstated in American culture—and disputed statistically—most all preadolescents who successfully worked through uncomfortable readjustment periods did so by making some necessary accommodations. Commonly these were changes in appearance (forsaking clothes deemed too trendy), conduct (reintroducing the courtesy titles sir and ma'am), and childhood practices (choosing a quieter form of play), which facilitated family restoration. But when marriages which had failed to reconnect ultimately dissolved in divorce, many sons and daughters who grew up as products of the era's broken homes came to understand their families to have been collateral causalities of Vietnam. The war played an unmistakable role in an upturn of divorces, which more than doubled the country's divorce rate between 1960 and 1980. As Nixon reduced troop levels from the wartime high of 536,100 in 1968 to 475,200 in 1969, the United States broke the yearly record for *number* of divorces that was previously set during another time of demobilization, in 1946. By 1973, with virtually all American troops home, the divorce *rate* likewise topped 1946, and the number of annual divorces surpassed one million for the first time in the nation's history during 1975. "Many of my friends' parents were divorced or single moms with no fathers even in the picture," a Missouri man born in 1962 observed of this trend. "Several people I knew that served in Vietnam divorced multiple times and their kids suffered as a result." Moreover, he detected what is a common belief among his cohort, that transitioning through their parents' Vietnam-era divorce permanently influenced their own life course trajectory pattern in adulthood. "Now take it to the next step: the fact that so many of the children were from divorced families, when they grew up they divorced too, sometimes more than once, even five times. So there was an impact, if not directly, but certainly from a societal perspective."[57]

A Midwestern woman who was eight when her parents divorced articulated this perception quite well: "My parents divorced a few months after my Dad came home, and life changed completely for me. My mother went to work. She became a very bitter woman. We moved a lot, so I never really developed any long-term friendships growing up. She was always looking for the man that would take care of her so she could live the 'right' way. Unfortunately she made several poor choices in her search. She really wanted my siblings and me to be seen and not heard. We didn't talk about our futures, or what we wanted to do in our lives. We had happy times, but when we started developing our own opinions, my mom couldn't handle it. I had very little self-esteem and I mostly read books and did my schoolwork." When pondering what "the sixties" meant from her childhood perspective, she concluded: "Really, the one thing that I remember was Vietnam because we lived it. I didn't see things like the moon landing because they didn't matter much to my mother. I think that if I would've lived with my dad that would've made a difference."[58]

The repatriation of POWs during Operation Homecoming throughout February and March 1973 unofficially marked the end of America's Vietnam War. President Nixon had announced the cease-fire in mid-January, with the Paris Peace Accords formally ending U.S. participation later that month—South Vietnam finally fell to the North in April 1975—but those joyous televised reunions were the only occasion, or cause, for any national celebration. The redemption of these brave men from what diplomat George Kennan described as the "most disastrous undertaking" in the republic's history was the closest thing to finality in Vietnam for America.

Perhaps it is fitting, then, that a large number of home front children consider this historical marker as an appropriate demarcation between childhood and adolescence. "When the war ended, it was no longer on TV," explained a Missouri woman, and "it occurred to me that it was odd because as far as I was concerned for my whole entire life, that had been what was on TV every night. So that was a kind of interesting revelation, I think, on my part." A woman born in 1957 told me that because she lived through her preadolescence concurrently with Vietnam, when the war ended "[i]t was then that my childhood seemed really over, both literally and figuratively." Of course, nothing about Vietnam was ever this clear-cut. The anticlimactic conclusion to the war in early 1973 offered neither satisfaction nor any real closure, but rather a complex suspension of emotion during the remainder of the 1970s, a self-imposed amnesia for Vietnam and veterans that some observers came to associate with a national decline into malaise.[59]

Completion of the Vietnam Veterans Memorial on Washington's National Mall in 1982 started Americans talking about the war again, and with those conversations perceptions began changing. Not so much about Vietnam, but about the soldiers and their families. "The Wall" opened the cultural space necessary for adolescent and adult children of veterans to finally air publicly their simmering private questions about their dad's neglected place in history and whether his service would ever be truly appreciated. Orphans, all but forgotten save by organizations such as Gold Star Wives, confronted new grownup challenges of never getting to know their father adult-to-adult and trying to build intergenerational relationships between his ghost and their own children.

But in looking for developmental results from the Vietnam experience, it appears—from Howard Tolley's contemporary conclusions, which are supported by my research four decades later—that the two most likely issues to be carried into adulthood center on moral uncertainty and issues of trust. Unlike the experience of home front children during World War II, the experience of being socialized to the political and ethical ambiguity of Vietnam carried distinctive developmental implications which weakened naive faith in government while challenging the moral certainty of American culture and society. The Second World War had stamped impressionable home front children with permanent messages about patriotism, democratic principles, and the values of citizenship. Elementary students in the early 1940s were taught what the United States was fighting for and to appreciate the sacrifices required to perpetuate freedom. No comparable curriculum in school or consensus in the general public existed for Vietnam era preadolescents. *Schoolhouse Rock*, CBS's Saturday morning educational series, began airing in 1973, but the "America Rock" historical episodes, the nearest equivalent to the home-front propaganda of World War II, did not start until 1975. However, these episodes did not address the Vietnam War. The U.S. involvement in Vietnam defied the wisdom of Kennedy's once sacrosanct pledge "that we shall pay any price, bear any burden, meet any hardship, support any friend, oppose any foe, in order to assure the survival and the success of liberty." Cold War culture had indeed indoctrinated this generation with comparable absolutes concerning the imperative to prevail over global communism. But in working through the muddled reasoning of why America fought so long in Southeast Asia, children labored to justify stopping communism in an irrelevant place like Vietnam. Abstract explanations like the domino theory were mostly a thin soup. Accordingly, during that period of political socialization and progression of moral development from egocentric preconventional decision making to more decentered conventional ethics, when our lifelong theories of right and wrong are forming, Vietnam instead imprinted children with a tendency toward relativism.[60]

A Tennessee man born in 1961 told a story about a singular memory that, as he said, "sticks out in my mind, but did not register with me at the time as having any historical significance." A neighborhood family friend who joined the Marines out of high school had just returned home, and "sometime later I remember finding all of [his] medals in a garbage can in his parents' backyard. I took the medals home, but later felt guilty for taking them and put them back. I didn't tell my parents that I had found them, but perhaps I should have . . . He came back wounded as well." Today, this self-described product of a conservative Christian home in a very Republican area has experienced "a realization that we probably should not have been involved in the war to begin with. Those that lost their lives in that war died in vain and I am saddened by the useless loss of life and angered by our government's actions during that time period in our country's history." Others, who do not consider themselves politically or socially liberal, but maintain that neither are they particularly pro-military or hawkish, believe their perspectives on war were tempered by how Vietnam touched their family. "Not the politics," a woman born in 1959 clarified, "but the personal toll it took on Americans," especially the "denigration of returning servicemen."[61]

"As I look back with some perspective," a Missourian born in 1956 wrote, "it seems I learned that you cannot simply trust what your leaders say. A person must find out for themselves what is right and wrong. I found it very interesting, the feeling inside of me when I heard a friend's son had died in Iraq. I felt it was a waste of a wonderful young man's life and on some level I felt anger at the parents for 'allowing' their son to be put in harm's way. I was bothered by this unexpected feeling and to be honest felt guilty. I know it was from my Vietnam experience watching both parents and kids 'protecting' themselves from 'unnecessary' war. I guess on some level I feel it is an American's duty to determine what is a 'just' war and an 'optional' war and act accordingly. Has this made me less 'patriotic' or just a less trusting person due to earlier lies?"[62]

The adolescent and young adult baby boomers who questioned Vietnam frequently mention an inability to trust Washington's official proclamations about the conduct of the war—that credibility gap—as the impetus for their personal opposition and eventual disillusionment. A few perceptive preadolescents picked up on this as well, with a number recalling for me that at around ten and eleven years old they too started to become highly skeptical of the nightly body counts. An Oregon woman born in 1957 related the story of this growing suspicion while waiting for her brother to return home. "I remember as the weeks of my brother's tour dragged on," she wrote, "that the Viet Cong's casualties always far outnumbered ours. Even at 11 years old, I found that odd. I watched the news, I read the headlines and heard my family discussing the war, and that graph simply did not make sense to me. While it's entirely possible the VC losses were consistently higher than the U.S., I wondered if someone was playing fast and loose with the figures and maybe padding them a bit."[63]

When a credibility gap finally developed for preadolescents, their distrust seems to have been less about outright government duplicity and more about losing faith in the once romanticized president-as-peacemaker's ability or even willingness to end the war. As with studies from the early 1970s which revealed a marked deterioration of public confidence in government over the last decade because of Vietnam—threatening to "turn off" the baby boom generation to politics—it was Lyndon Johnson and Richard Nixon's failure to bring peace which caused a corresponding corrosion of children's veneration for presidential infallibility and benevolence. Compared to the 1960 findings of political scientists Fred Greenstein and David Easton on political socialization, when elementary school children had almost unanimously held Eisenhower and Kennedy up as the public personification of paternal honesty and goodness, Tolley's surveys in the spring of 1971—well before Watergate—revealed a pervasive view that the chief executive was falling far short of those wondrous qualities. Only 31 percent of students agreed Nixon was doing the right thing in Vietnam, with only 29 percent responding that presidents always told the truth about seeking peace. Overall confidence levels in the president declined the most sharply, to 50 percent in the third grade—meaning half of all ten-year-olds now questioned the president's capabilities—to a predictable 15 percent among more developmentally skeptical eighth graders. Reflecting the Gallup polls the same year, children generally showed no more respect for the president than did adults. Even if Tolley's numbers skewed high, by the early 1970s these political primitives' once unassailable faith in the presidency had clearly suffered. And while adults across the political spectrum told me that they explicitly attribute their views on war to this decline—reflecting deep cynicism, doubt concerning the notion of a just war, or simple pacifism—the likely developmental outcome is more modest. For those growing up in the sixties who reasoned ethically at Kohlberg's conventional level—grappling with the moral abstractions of fairness and justice—the Vietnam War lowered their expectations over the course their life of presidential efficacy, goodwill, and leadership in national collective endeavors.[64]

A rural Missouri man's experience offers a final metaphor for these lessons. "Our neighbor's son was killed a week or so after he was drafted and sent to Vietnam," he wrote the author. "I was upset and worried about his death and the fact that he had to go! But as a child I was more upset that his car sat in a field and fell apart. His parents had bought him a graduation car that 'I wanted': a 1960 black and white, red interior, white top convertible Chevy Impala! It was awesome . . . After [he] was killed, his parents parked the car in the field behind the house and trees eventually grew up through it. Every time I drove by it for years, it became my 'sense of death' reference." This wasted Impala was for him "a sad memorial" to Vietnam, a lasting reminder from a sixties childhood that "Life is not fair!"[65]

CHAPTER EIGHT

Hippies

*. . . they're just kind of in a place until they get adult enough
to have free will enough to choose to be cool on their own.*
Stephen Gaskin, spiritual teacher of the Farm community in Tennessee

THE HALLMARK OF the sixties is conflict: between war and peace, social justice and racism, national interests and individual rights, custodial liberalism
and participatory democracy, young and old, straight and freak, us and them.
Across America a general rejection of the existing systems of authority, and
disobedience to previously respected "superiors" in all their forms, spread like
wildfire in the Vietnam era, dividing the nation as it had not been since the
1860s. As the country grew increasingly polarized on these and other issues,
as many as six million socially conscious activists who chose to take a stand
on the Left staged an "endless pageant of political and cultural protest" in city
streets, public parks, and college campuses, challenging the legitimacy of the
dominant institutions and conventions of Cold War society. Those alienated
and restless baby boomers who enlisted in these largely rights-based battles—
within what is loosely referred to as "the movement"—mobilized to provoke
America into reevaluating itself: to rethink the inconsistencies between American ideals and the reality of the poor, blacks, women, Native Americans,
and homosexuals; reconsider the imperialist status quo versus Vietnamese self-
determination; ponder the relevance of college students; determine who had
the authority to tell free persons right from wrong; and contemplate environmental degradation globally and sexual liberalization locally. In debating,
persuading, and ultimately educating the nation, movement activists sought
resolution of the era's conflicts through meaningful political empowerment
and personal liberation—thus, in their idealistic eyes, making the world a better place.[1]

Again, outside the civil rights struggle, preadolescent children's role in the movement's organized protests was decidedly negligible, with only a few exceptions sprinkled here or there. An eight-year-old did hold a placard with mom at a Sane Nuclear Policy (SANE) rally, and a six-year-old posted handmade "No Littering" notices while clutching a stuffed Smokey Bear in one hand and the latest issue of *Ranger Rick* magazine in the other. And, sure, social imitation encouraged countless children to man the barricades for provincial schoolhouse and neighborhood causes. "As elementary school kids we mimicked what we saw on TV," a Midwestern woman born in 1957 wrote me. "I remember we made picket signs at recess one time just because we felt like protesting when we thought our teacher was giving preferential treatment to a certain kid (we were too naive to realize he came from a broken home and the teacher was just trying to help him out). We just got caught up in the drama of being 'protesters' and got chewed out for it." But few children were actually born into or raised in the pageant of political and cultural protest. The movement's activist lifestyle was simply not conducive to childcare. Besides, from the oppositional New Left political orientation, children were seen as counterrevolutionary and radical parenthood as a waste of time, especially in those years after 1968, which have traditionally been vilified as the "bad sixties," when radicalized militants turned violent.

Two important court cases related to the struggle and dissent over Vietnam did, in fact, broaden children's and students' legal rights. The 1966 *Burnside v. Byars* decision supported freedom of childhood expression, ruling that black Mississippi high school students suspended for wearing buttons reading "One Man One Vote" and "SNCC," after the bodies of Goodman, Cheney, and Schwerner were discovered, had been wrongfully puniéed. Voting rights were a matter of public concern, a circuit court held, and as such students should be allowed to engage in this public discourse. In 1969 the Supreme Court went further, applying First Amendment rights to students for the first time in *Tinker v. Des Moines Independent Community School District*. Four children (two of whom were as young as eight and eleven) of an anti-war Methodist minister father and a mother active in the Women's League for Peace and Freedom had similarly run afoul of school rules against politicized displays, in this instance for wearing black armbands adorned with a peace sign. After a lower court ruled against the Tinkers, the Supreme Court overturned the decision, affirming that civil liberties did not end at the schoolhouse door. Yet both these cases were waged within the legal system by adults on behalf of children, and their outcomes were primarily applicable only to high schools.[2]

Two parallel and often interlocking tributaries of the movement, however, purposefully redefined the postwar, middle-class suburban family and motherhood as central facets of their broader alternative visions: the counterculture's scruffy quest for personal authenticity and, later, second-wave feminism's assault on patriarchy. Counterculturists—hippies, to most—were experimenting with lifestyles and philosophies which elevated the dignity and primacy of the individual in defiance of a dehumanizing culture based on materialism and fear. Hippie parenting therefore involved experimentation in redefining what it means to be a family, a parent, and a child, and then determining, by living according to the new definitions, whether the experiment worked. Although later recognized as the largest utopian movement in U.S. history, the counterculture was never really a social movement as such, but rather an innately fluid gathering of seekers turned on to the same attitudes, tendencies, postures, lifestyles, hedonistic pleasures, and affirmations. Nonetheless, hippiedom—widely sensationalized, but little understood—captured the country's imagination far out of proportion to its relatively limited numbers. After visibly emerging from the underground fringe at San Francisco's Human Be-In festival in January 1967, "flower children" became—for better or worse—the most recognizable shock troops in the movement, a sort of ubiquitous shorthand symbol for all sixties protest, which within a brief couple of years degenerated commercially into cartoonish caricatures of peace, love, and dope. Freaks, as the hippies sometimes identified themselves, were by the same token also perhaps the movement's most threatening elements, precisely because these flamboyantly dressed, long-haired barbarians at the gate fundamentally challenged the very bedrock of what "straight" Americans thought they knew about America.[3]

Grasping the fundamental truth that one could barely make a dent in, let alone overthrow, American society or its political systems, hippies instead dropped out of both, concentrating on openly liberating oneself and then slowly advancing a cultural revolution outward from the individual. For those who tried it, hippie living was about claiming a space, a couple of city blocks or few acres of countryside. There, hippies took the cultural blueprint of the American Dream handed down from the previous generation—grounded in dour puritanical commitments to the Protestant work ethic, rugged individualism, careerism, competition, upward mobility, conformity, and conspicuous consumption—and tore it up. Out of this "great refusal," they fashioned an alternative world where the rules were up for grabs, a counterculture of loosely aligned paisley ghettos, head shops, organic food co-ops, FM radio stations, and underground newspapers.

The Americanization of existentialist philosophy illuminated this path forward. Living solely in the eternal present, hippies made life's meaning through their actions. Or, to put it in a groovier way, they imagined what authentic freedom was and daily lived their gentle values into existence. "Dope" (marijuana, hashish, mescaline, psychedelics) functioned as a requisite tool for deconditioning, for wiping the slate clean—that is, unlearning one's socialization to Cold War culture in order to facilitate a higher consciousness. Dope was understood as sacramental—a ritualistic testimony to one's commitment to an alternative lifestyle—smoked to break down barriers, free inhibitions, and open greater truths. Instead of the drudgery of wage slavery—and all the associated uptight striving, planning, and saving—most self-indulgent and passive hippies kept work to a bare minimum, preferably "cool" labors related directly to pleasure and human needs. Brooks Brothers suits were traded in for faded blue jeans, sandals, and beads. Many adopted what they considered to be simpler and more honest nineteenth-century frontier and Native American aesthetics, with handmade clothing, long dresses, headbands, moccasins, and painted faces. The more politicized sardonically commandeered symbols of the militarized Vietnam era culture, wearing surplus field jackets with rank and insignia while flashing the World War II "V-for-Victory" gesture as a peace sign. Hair was the common denominator for wearing your values— "shoulder length or longer," as the song "Hair" said, beards, or Pancho Villa mustaches.[4]

In rejecting modern life's sterility and rationality, this mellow minority favored intuition, personal experience, and the mystical, preferring a reality where subjective feelings trumped objective social constructions. Localized underground publications with names such as the *Berkeley Barb*, *Vortex*, the *Buffalo Chip*, the *East Village Other*, and the *Whole Earth Catalog* replaced mainstream media as the most trusted sources of news for hippies. But while on one hand, hippiedom celebrated unbridled hedonism—"living for pleasure instead of living according to the punishment-reward system" of straight society, in the words of psychedelic guru Timothy Leary—the self was also subsumed by tribal togetherness. Applying aspects of Zen, Hinduism, and other Eastern religions most applicable to their youthful experience, hippies sought more integrated and cooperative lives within human communities and also within the whole of nature—in sum, living, as nineteenth-century existentialist Henry David Thoreau had suggested, deliberately, not desperately.[5]

Based on the recollections compiled for this study, it appears that hippies were a real curiosity for children growing up comfortably outside the counterculture. Even people from more conservative-minded homes where hippies were vilified and references to them were tightly censored retain an almost obligatory memory of hippies, as if their view of a sixties childhood would be somehow incomplete without one. "Hippies were avoided because of their lifestyle," a representative Arkansas man born in 1961 remembered. "I even got into trouble once for giving a peace sign to my cousin, who my family considered a 'hippie.'" Surely, this inclusiveness stems from hippies being so emblematic of the sixties in popular memory. Even so, there was clearly a certain fascination at work among "straight" children. "I was very impressed with the Beatles and the hippies," explained another Arkansas man, born in 1960. "I wanted to be one when I grew up—a hippie, that is." "As far as the hippie movement, I was too young to join it, but I thought it was cool," a Louisville, Kentucky, woman born in 1959 reminisced. "I let my hair grow as long as I could, and once I put Vaseline in it so it would look like hippie hair (which I suppose was dirty hair). It took a while to wash all of the Vaseline out." Another woman, born in Alabama in 1956, recalled, "My sisters' and my Barbies weren't about fashion. I remember draping something over a chair to make something like a tent and lighting a cone of incense in the middle of it. This was the Ashram, and our Barbies went there to visit the Guru for enlightenment. Unfortunately, our younger sister's doll . . . fell into the incense and got her hair singed off. Sometimes you get enlightenment, sometimes you get your hair burned off."[6]

It is likely that preadolescents recognized kindred childlike qualities in the hippies, or at least a mediated reflection of innocence. Hippies refused to abide by socially fixed demarcations between adulthood maturity and childhood immaturity. Deconditioning, after all, involved shedding adult reasonableness and seriousness and returning to an irreverent and simple childlike state. Acting childish was, in hippiedom, its own virtue. So hippies reveled in weirdness and spontaneous playfulness, dressing up in outlandish costumes and taking zany names—like Wavy Gravy and his Hog Farmers—to blow bubbles and fly kites in joyful performance of humor's very definition: that which elicits amusement and laughter. Their renewed sense of childhood wonder and awe, very much in the magical spirit of J. R. R. Tolkien's Middle Earth or C. S. Lewis's Narnia, was not saddled by adult goals, but rather electrified by childlike dreams.

Of course, certain hippie elements were only distilled down to straight
children through mass media. By 1970, even the *Sears Christmas Wish Book*
showcased longer hair, denim, and more colorful clothing. Television, likewise, played an integral role in "selling" the hippies, and making them safer for
the masses. Consider the thinly disguised Saturday morning dope references
on *H. R.* [Hand Rolled?] *Pufnstuf* and *Scooby–Doo*, with its hippie character
Shaggy, or The Monkees' shanghaiing of the Beatles. The hippie ethic could
also be seen in a couple of prime-time escapist allegories. *Gilligan's Island*, on
CBS from 1964 to 1967, although slightly predating the years of hippiedom,
could still be seen as a story of "castaways" leaving the modern world behind
for a more basic, communal existence. *The Partridge Family* was perhaps a
bit more obvious. Running between 1970 and 1974 on ABC, the show followed the commotion that is kicked up when five fatherless siblings who dress
like hippies, albeit well-scrubbed, form a family rock-n-roll band with their
mother and penetrate suburbia aboard a festively painted school bus, a hippie intrusion into polite society that was invariably tamed within twenty-five
minutes. Despite adult admonishments, from a child's uncritically detached
perspective, hippies did not generally appear to be villainous anarchists. Quite
the contrary, they looked like adult-sized Huckleberry Finns having the time
of their lives. They behaved like so many jovial clowns piling out of psychedelic buses.[7]

In exploring the landscape of childhood within hippiedom, it is important
to remember that the hippie ethic was never monolithic. There were varying
degrees of hippies, and many who identified as a hippie picked and chose the
countercultural elements most conducive or applicable to their lives, frequently just passing through different levels on their journey. Most commonly it
was white, middle-class baby boomers with a little college education taking
the trip, and individual motivations for buying the ticket and the deciding
on the depth of one's immersion are fairly incalculable. Some just *wore* the
counterculture, burning patchouli incense, hanging bead curtains, or sleeping
in water beds. Others drank more deeply from the alternative lifestyle of hedonism, mysticism, organic eating, and yoga. Most who longed to drop out
and live as free people still had to make a living, and so for economic reasons
kept one foot in the straight world, holding down a series of jobs until work
infringed on their freedom. "One knew that one was free," explains religious
studies professor Timothy Miller, "and, within the limits of the mundane
needs of life, lived that way." Only the truly devout managed to change the
content and character of their lives, often in communes.[8]

Just as hippies came in many vibrant hues, hippie parenting sensibilities differed. Hippies agreed that the child-rearing methods in which they had been raised were undesirable, but never really reached a consensus about a suitable replacement. A handful brought rather traditional notions of parenting and child rights to the counterculture, often guided by the same fears and hopes for their children as suburban mothers and fathers. Parents are by nature conservative in a child's eyes, however, and hence, these hippie parents frequently wrestled with an uncomfortable and irreconcilable dichotomy: playing an authoritarian role within a rebellious way of life. Each and every attempt to dictate their preadolescent's behaviors would be seen as evidence that they remained straight. And children could be relied on to point out the inconsistency.[9]

More commonly, though, hippie parents attempted in good faith to channel the same existential and communal vibes into child-rearing which enabled childless adults to freak freely. At the most fundamental level, hippies tested the Cold War meaning of the nuclear family. Was it primarily biological, a corporate and commercial construct, or a collective freely choosing in the moment to share the same living space and values? The hippies understood it to be the latter, and in their reimagining sought to defuse the modern middle-class family's role as the chief socializing agent for the postwar culture from which hippies sought to be deconditioned. Motherhood was a first step, and the counterculture appreciated mothering in the ancient, or at least the nineteenth-century preindustrial, sense. They would be natural, beautiful "earth mothers," in tune with nature and the land, and entrusted with the sacred duty of birthing as many children as possible (birth control was seen as unnatural). Many countercultural ideas about pregnancy, natural childbirth, child-rearing, and breast-feeding—soon to cross-pollinate with second-wave feminism—were, in fact, predicated on the holistic desire to eliminate the artificial boundaries between mind and body, body and spirit, people and people, and people and nature. Straight mothers—alienated and atomized like all straight Americans—gave birth in hospitals, attended by profit-oriented, male doctors, trained in obstetrics and gynecology, using unnatural drugs and tools. Hip mothers, in contrast, increasingly turned to the transcendent experience of natural, woman-centered at-home births attended by female midwives. Child-rearing too, including breast-feeding, was to be integrated within the range of all that makes one human, not carried out by isolated housewives in consultation with proscriptive experts.[10]

Hippie children were all too frequently the outcome of free love meeting haphazard birth control. When the hassle of childcare brought biological fathers down, they habitually "split" for greener pastures. So too did dads and moms commonly (and abruptly) trade in their parental responsibilities when a better offer came along. In the same manner that hippies might quit a good-paying jobs when work began to usurp their "trip," some were thoughtful and engaged parents up until the time their children cramped their lifestyle. Then they disengaged, appearing to some to be selfish and neglectful. "I remember looking forward to my dad coming to pick me up for our biweekly visits and having my heart broke each time he 'forgot' to come," a Missouri woman born in 1969 said of her father, who lived in a blue school bus. "Later, I learned that more interesting things had caught his eye. Very disappointing. He did a great job making me feel like the center of his universe, cutting up fresh fruit for me every morning, but sometimes was just too easily called away."[11]

That being said, hippie parents by and large optimistically and enthusiastically incorporated their sons and daughters into hippiedom's ideals and practices, chiefly because hip parenthood represented a unique opportunity to stop perpetuating society's madness. Turned-on children meant a second chance, the first generation of truly free people and a fresh start toward a utopian future. Seeing in children the original qualities of innocence, openness, and creativity which they were trying to recapture in themselves—untainted by mass commercialized culture—hippie parents spared their children from the suffocating effects of having to grow up by embracing a much purer form of permissiveness than Dr. Spock was ever accused of. They believed family life should develop organically—unstructured and open—without much parental interference, and certainly without a sense of authoritarian hierarchy either imposed, or implied, between parent and child. In a word, children grew themselves up without the stifling *don't*. "If we can preserve what they are now," a hippie dad explained of his free-thinking parenting style in 1969, "keep them free, let every initiative come from them, then ideally we become more like them as they become more like us, and we become one thing, and that's a family." He clarified, "I just want the kids to dig what they're doing here and now. I want the same things for them as I do for me. It seems to me I have to unlearn a whole lot more than learn . . . My education put an obstacle between me and real experience. Whenever a thing is defined, it becomes limited. If a kid picks up an object and doesn't know what it is, it represents unlimited potential. That's creativity."[12]

Thus, hippie childhood was as equally textured as hip adulthood, with just as many degrees of being "turned on." Since the proverbial granola- and tofu-eating hippies were usually less than thirty years old, and most hippie parents entered the hippie life with kids already in tow, hip children (given offbeat nouns and verbs for names) were preschoolers, or at least no more than eight years old. Around the age of five or six, preadolescents in hippie families, from their place of residence in a tiny home, bus, treehouse, geodesic dome, teepee, or isolated commune, began to realize that they were growing up somewhere off the main thoroughfare of American society. Most, however, remember being aware of the ordinary world—with television—which they glimpsed during weekend visits and holidays at grandma and grandpa's house. But, though living in modest simplicity with hardly any durable goods, their homes invariably contained a few toys and books, a stereo, plenty of record albums, maybe a dog-eared *Whole Earth Catalog*, displays of spiritual symbolism, pot growing casually on the windowsill, and perhaps a pet goat or monkey. Function trumped form. Clutter reflected an emphasis on living, not housekeeping. No one worried about what children might break or stain to undermine the resale value of the house. Parents meditated. Groceries came from weekly visits to the co-op. Food was, quite naturally, brown—no white flour or sugar, nothing in a can, nothing frozen, nothing processed, no chocolate. And, in truly unrehearsed fashion, hippie children farted out loud, openly shared in the finer points of profanity, and painted murals on the walls.[13]

Likewise, as Moon Zappa—daughter of musician Frank Zappa—emphasized in her foreword to writer Chelsea Cain's anthology *Wild Child: Girlhoods in the Counterculture*, "clothes were an extension of the imagination, used to name who or what you were for the hour or so you had them on, a dinosaur or a witch or a superhero. Clothes were costumes for putting on shows." There was usually no shortage of freaky folks wandering through your home, either. Zappa, a bicoastal hippie kid born in 1967, wrote, "The men who visited us had patchy beards and bad posture and smelled like B.O. Crouching in the nude near my playthings, they melted brightly colored crayons and made candles out of old milk cartons. Everyone seemed to be unwashed, musky and recently fucked. If they wore clothes, they were flamboyant, mismatched garments with bright colors and crazy patterns that clashed. On the men, clothing always clung to the fleshy parts of their bodies, and drooped and flared where there was hardly any meat on their bones. The women wore tissue paper—thin kerchiefs or dyed, crocheted, doilyesque halters that left nothing to the imagination."[14]

Families traveled on nomadic road trips to experience nature's far-out places and various tribal gatherings (up to, and including, Woodstock), their vehicles filled with only the bare minimum of hippie baggage: sleeping bags, tents, and duffel bags (yet rarely maps). When outlining his own childhood passage toward hippiedom, a California man born in 1964 (and conceived on November 22, 1963, his parents told him) pinpointed the day he and his dad hit the road together in a used bread truck as the crucial first step. Prior to this excursion, the transformation to a hippie lifestyle appeared gradual for him and the other neighborhood children whose parents had made the pilgrimage to the Bay Area (in his family's case, from Long Island, New York, in 1970). His father had dropped out after a hitch in the Navy and was living near the University of California-Berkeley with an interracial deaf couple, which already afforded the son some fairly unusual formative experiences of watching adults of different races smoking marijuana together and communicating through sign language. Although his parents were divorced, mom had a house right next door and sold her handmade tie-dyes on Telegraph Avenue. But things got really weird after his second-grade year, when father and son set off together in an old International Harvester truck—retrofitted with stove and ice box—on what became a five-year, thirty-five state odyssey of crash pads and communes. (He did not begin attending school regularly again until seventh grade.) Constantly in motion and uprooted—living variously with his dad, other adults, or by himself—reading became both his "salvation and education." "Whenever we reached a new town," he told me, "I headed out immediately to the nearest public library to stock up on science-fiction or the local store for Marvel comics."[15]

"Moving is easy when you own almost nothing," another self-professed wild child reflected, "and even easier if things you own are so battered that they become impervious to damage. Everything we possessed had been made by one of my parents or bought secondhand from Goodwill. When I wanted something we couldn't afford (which was most of the time), my parents would do their best to build or sew it. I lusted after pin-striped jeans in third grade, and my mom valiantly sewed me stiff, ill-fitting pink denim jeans (which proceeded to fall off during a ferocious game of Red Rover)."[16]

Moms and dads seemed to be adventurous adult friends running away together as opposed to parents, so accordingly you called them by their first names. "I was taught that no man or woman is above you," Moon Zappa stressed. "Not even a policeman or a president or a pope. I was told these are just jobs. People in the army or the government, or lawyers . . . that's just what they do, not who they are. Authority figures? Ha! Underneath their uniforms and beliefs are flesh and blood humans, same as me. We all answer to something larger than ourselves; therefore, the act of simply calling a teacher or a grownup 'Miss' or 'Mr.' seemed like a ridiculous, arbitrary, socially agreed-upon rule for an agreed-upon order."[17]

"I want the kids to see everything, and I have confidence that things will turn out well," said the hippie father who was interviewed in 1969. "With many people, you have to translate what they say into what they mean. With us, the translation turns out to be the same thing. Our lives are our philosophy. That's where you see it." By definition, and the simple reality of two generations living in close proximity, such autonomy included exposure to the standard countercultural sacraments—rock-n-roll, dope, and sex—at much younger ages than was usually prescribed. Rock-n-roll's bardic nature was renowned for bringing hippies together, listening and talking about ideas. From the surrealistic poetry of Dylan's folk rock to the psychedelic San Francisco sound of the Jefferson Airplane, album-oriented rock and the festival concert experience not only provided the counterculture's soundtrack, but the increasingly uncommercial, message-driven songs also offered hippies music to parent by. "I remember listening to the Beatles' *Let It Be* album for hours on end with my mom," a semi-professional musician told me, citing a causal influence.[18]

A Midwesterner born in 1967 recalled singing along with his mother to Arlo Guthrie's "Alice's Restaurant" and "gathering from her joy the possibilities of living the fantastic values—you can get anything you want and all you need is love—throughout rock-n-roll." Album covers represented the family's collected works of art: the Mamas and the Papas huddled together in a bathtub on *If You Can Believe Your Eyes and Ears*, Big Brother and the Holding Company's *Cheap Thrills*, featuring the drawings of Robert Crumb, and the Byrds' primitive *Sweetheart of the Rodeo* artwork. "There was music, always music," reminisced Chelsea Cain, the editor of *Wild Child* and herself an Iowa hippie born in 1972, "music during big dinners at the long table in the kitchen, music that colored everything (the kitchen was yellow, the house was white, my dress was red), music at night when the dogs would run barking in a pack through the neighbor's fields, listening to Bob Dylan on the porch while my mother taught me the difference between Chile tomatoes and cherry tomatoes in our garden, waking up every morning to music."[19]

Musicians used dope to open the doors of perception through which rock-n-roll evolved in the 1960s, and music and dope were intimately intertwined with the hippie ethic of communalism and cultural rebellion. In fact, dope sales and usage were probably the biggest factors in choosing the location of hippie enclaves. In this regard, there was an important distinction between dope, which expanded your insights into human existence, and "drugs" (cocaine, amphetamines, heroin), which just made you dumb. Marijuana, specifically, occupied such a central place in the hippie lifestyle that preadolescents remember becoming acculturated to its usage very early, seeing and smelling it everywhere. "In 1973-ish, my mom's live-in boyfriend owned a head shop in Albuquerque, New Mexico," a man born in 1967 remembered. "He kept his supplies in our garage. I was rummaging through the inventory one day like a normal six year old and came across 'flavored rolling papers.' I didn't know what a rolling paper was, but I did know what flavored meant. I sat there in the garage and ate them like candy."[20]

Many children partook as equal participants with adults, either passing a joint around the circle or nonchalantly being allowed to smoke within the overall scene. The key for maximizing dope's mind-altering potential, hippies thought, lay in using it positively and sanely, knowing what you were doing and not hurting anyone by paying attention to mind-set and setting. In many hippie families, this appears to have applied equally to adult and child as a matter of course. The California boy on the extended road trip took acid for the first time at the age of eight with his father during a marathon Beatles movie festival. "Dad told me it altered my introverted personality and really made me more outgoing," he recalled. Later in his childhood, when participating with southwestern Native Americans in a peyote ritual, he remembered thinking the powerful effects were particularly impactful on a child's imaginative mind, "introducing him to manifestations of freakish supernatural entities."[21]

"I remember going to the hot springs with my dad in the Sandia Mountains," the New Mexico man wrote, "where all the adults were nude, smoking, and from what I knew of the birds and bees, making babies." Indeed, sex seemed as universal as rock music and dope, which reflected the symbiotic relationship that intentionally existed between the three. Counterculturalists cast off the prudish suburban Victorianism of the 1950s, forgoing the attendant modesty, shame, and guilt they had been socialized to in favor of liberated sexuality. This included more childlike openness and acceptance of nudity. "Every photo of me shows a naked girl-child," one woman explained in *Wild Child* of this preference for a natural physical state, "sometimes with diaper, sometimes without, smudged with dirt and smiling like crazy. There are photos of me naked in tire swings, naked and spread-eagle in old stuffed chairs, naked and sitting on the dirty floor of our little house."[22]

To hippies, sex no longer needed to be confined within a monogamous relationship in the missionary position, with the door locked and lights out, but rather should be spontaneous, expressive, and celebrated. Almost from infancy, preadolescents were not shielded from the natural act of adults mating, or from promiscuity. Even though most were not sexually active, they knew all the details about sex, and all the slang terms for how it got done. "[My mother] drank and fucked like a sailor," revealed one woman in *Wild Child*. "For her birthday, we made her a macramé bell system over her bed that she rang with her toe when she orgasmed." Sometimes it is these sorts of experiences—wandering into an orgy, for example—which have later led to the most consternation and embarrassment over growing up hippie. On one hand, hedonistic behaviors amplified already problematic gender roles. Of all the straight social conventions to be renegotiated, hippie men found paternalism and domesticity hardest to leave behind. In being sexually available to all, women's freedom still looked a lot like subjectification. On the other hand, these behaviors desensitized children and encouraged moral relativism. "Sexual innuendos came fast and furious in our house," the same woman continued. "The randier the joke, the funnier it was. No matter that neither my baby brother nor I knew what the hell we were laughing at. For my tenth birthday, my mom organized a striptease for me and my friends, with bawdy music from *The Sting* and racy nightgowns. I learned to masturbate with my Chatty Cathy. Sex is fun. Sex is a game. Sex is sport."[23]

The idea of alternative "free" schools likewise grew organically from the countercultural ideal of discovery. Founded on the familiar premise that public schools were by nature penal, indoctrinating students with industrial work values which suffocated them under age-graded rules, routines, expectations, and assessments, hip schools—in theory—opened up free spaces where students and teachers learned together. In the collectivist and improvised hippie spirit, free schools operated anywhere, constantly changing location, faculty, and student body, just one step ahead of being shut down by local authorities. (Not the best planners anyway, hippies regularly stumbled when following through on large, multi-step projects.) When these schools were open—and attendance was not mandatory, of course—the deliberately unstructured environments had no real curriculum to speak of, no texts, schedule, or grades. Imagine an all-day recess. Curious students would make discoveries in free play which teachers would grasp as teachable moments.

"Find out what the children are wondering and wonder it," a free school instructor clarified in 1969. The only way to distinguish between student and teacher was by age, since all jumped rope, colored, and sang together. "We're concerned with liberating their imaginations and finding some alternatives to

the middle-class way we were raised," a teacher explained. "Our most important priority is teaching kids to relate to other people." Efficacy was another
matter. Free schools generally broke down in practice, with children milling
about aimlessly and getting into mischief. The lack of structure proved particularly difficult for preadolescents, developmentally and cognitively, as, for
instance, they might fall behind in learning to read. "My parents subscribed
to a theory of education," one free school alumna remembered, "that did not
involve being forced to learn things I wasn't 'ready' to learn—an interesting, if
at times impractical, concept." But it appears many parents chose free schools
for cultural, not academic reasons, anyway. Free schools seem to have been
something of a test over parents' level of commitment to the counterculture,
analogous to trying an open marriage. Parents who had not fully altered their
lives and had sent their children to a free school simply as an antidote to structure were often not comfortable with the level of childhood freedom there. In
these circumstances, parents might supplement free school with home schooling in the evenings over the "three R's" as well as instilling a little discipline.
Most free school students returned to public schools within a year.[24]

Extremely misguided cases existed, however, where free school anarchy
coincided with an unhealthy full-time way of life. In the name of raising preadolescents without "laying uptight adult trips on them," parents turned them
loose on society without oversight or accountability—absolutely no rules, no
boundaries, no bedtime, no chores, no baths or toothbrushes. Eat ice cream
for breakfast, sleep all day, steal, cheat, lie, take overnight trips with strangers, do drugs (and dope), and experiment sexually with other children and/or
adults—the logic being that just like fish in a tank, children would grow to fit
the size of their environment. Yet freedom rationalized selfishness, highlighting inherent shortcomings in the counterculture. While saying they wanted
their children to be so liberated that they no longer needed parents or parenting, what these parents really meant was that if kids were just allowed to be
free enough on their own, then parents could, in good conscience, abdicate
all responsibility for raising them. From this perspective there would be no
reason to make special concessions for subordinating, or even harmonizing,
the parent's own trip with the needs of the children, and certainly no sense in
worrying about how adult behaviors impacted the young.

Inevitably, such parenting styles made for difficult and depressing—not
liberated—childhoods. Exacerbating matters, childhood often unfolded in
adult-oriented households, on urban fringes of the counterculture, where
dozens of hippies might crash for extended periods of time. With little privacy

and few private possessions beyond the clothes on their back—no toys, books, or anything with which to forge an attachment—children living with indifferent, disengaged parents—themselves without jobs or interests beyond the haze of sex and drugs—grew up listless too. They just hung around most of the time, without normal childhood activities and curiosities, in a haze of their own punctuated only by caring for younger siblings. They desperately needed parental attention, but remained emotionally detached from all adults. In public, some tried to give themselves the appearance, and to some extent the trappings, of living a more normal life—going to the movies, skating, or school—yet these facades were difficult to sustain without responsible adults to organize and facilitate. To outsiders, the neglected sons and daughters of hippies could come off as worldly and confident—cool—but in addition to being visibly malnourished, almost all suffered from being developmentally maladjusted. Reckless and jaded, these guarded little loners, without friends their own age, functioned poorly in settings requiring self-motivation. Manipulative with peers and adults, there was also a pronounced tendency to push things too far, stalled as they were in Kohlberg's first stage of moral development, when moral decisions are calculated solely on the chances of getting caught and being punished.[25]

Contemporary observers John Rothchild and Susan Wolf reported in their study *The Children of the Counterculture: How the Life-Style of America's Flower Children Has Affected an Even Younger Generation* that most hippie children they encountered across the country either got lost somewhere in their parents' unworkable fantasies or behaved remarkably normally by middle-class standards. Hippie parents themselves, Rothchild and Wolf were surprised by how well the typical child of the counterculture navigated between home and the outside world. While the perception of the little hippie as a wild child remains deeply entrenched, most preadolescents appeared to Rothchild and Wolf to be fairly well-adjusted, and less obnoxious and self-centered compared to their straight peers. The most obvious outward difference was their confidence in relating with all ages of people in a simple and direct manner, on a person-to-person level. Indeed, with so many adult hippies constantly coming and going along a sort of spiritual network of crash pads and communes, the children almost out of necessity had to overcome any natural inclination toward introversion or shyness. "Whenever we arrived in a new community," one man told me, "the kids already there could be very tribal and not very accepting of newcomers, very Lord of the Flies sometimes, so you had to work to make friends. Adults though were always more inclusive and welcoming than kids." I was "the child who would climb into anyone's lap," one woman remembered, "even if only just introduced, because a friend is a friend regardless of how long the acquaintance."[26]

If hippies did create a new kind of child or childhood, Rothchild and Wolf speculated, they did so in communes, specifically the rural variety. Only there, in a totally new collective dynamic, where the meaning of family was re-introduced to the notion of tribe, were parents operating with the kind of consciousness necessary to reshape the daily adult-child interactions which constituted parenting. While hippiedom developed chiefly in cities and towns, the communal movement spread outward, putting down the most plentiful and deepest roots in the countryside. Unlike earlier communes in American history, which had definite ideological centers—religious, political, or social— hippie communes tended to be freer expressions of dropping out and liv-ing the counterculture ethos. Most of the thousands, if not tens of thousands, which sprang up were ephemeral—lasting a year or two—but they attracted hundreds of thousands of residents and visitors wanting to "live freely without interfering with or being interfered with by the outside world any more than was necessary." But what truly separated the communards living in the vast circuit of sister communes from other hippies was the degree to which com-munal living involved not just integrating one's unique abilities and needs within the common good of the community, but submerging one's ego into the collective heart and mind.[27]

Hundreds of urban communes existed in the Vietnam era, to be sure, but on a continuum of hip, the impact of these less numerous neighborhood col-lectives on children was somewhat more pronounced than being raised in the hippie lifestyle by just your biological parents, yet not quite to the extent experienced by their rural brethren. In urban communes, moms and dads sur-rendered their proprietary parental rights, as all adult communards assumed a hands-on role in nurturing and disciplining other people's children. When a child had a problem, the nearest person was the parent, but the parent wasn't always available. Children, accordingly, spread out their requests for physical needs, attachments, and choice of role models among a number of adults—so much so that it was often difficult to tell which child biologically belonged to which parent. Both generations shared in the responsibilities and duties essential to the urban commune's daily functioning, with wide latitude in choosing routines. Consequently, Rothchild and Wolf noticed a significant difference in children's attitudes toward labor. Whereas preadolescents usu-ally approached the demand to "help out" on a token task with boredom and halfhearted efforts which compelled adults to complete it anyway, signing up for jobs as part of the normal chore rotation gave "work" value, and children took pride in it. The same rules and expectations applied equally to adults and children—no physical violence, no deliberate destruction of property, etc. Failure to pull one's weight and misbehavior disrupted the harmony, and usually fear of disappointing the shared expectations of the commune was a sufficient negative reinforcement. But failing that, isolation could be used as punishment. For instance, when a child forgot to make dinner one night, the group went out for pizza, but left the child behind.[28]

Preadolescents in urban communes paradoxically enjoyed more freedom yet also a more narrowly disciplined life, so to speak, compared to most other children. Never commended for completing a task, neither did they receive individual praise for appearance, intelligence, or athleticism. Little space existed in the collective for being timid and little tolerance for show-offs and attention getters. Boredom, particularly when not attending school, crept in quickly, with more time on children's hands than chores could fill, and no extracurricular activities. Neighborhood playmates rarely came around, because straight parents considered the whole commune thing to be a little too weird. Hippie adults were not intensely preoccupied with their kids—there was no hint of momism—and were more absorbed with their own issues of self-actualization, subordinating children's psychological concerns to the back burner. All this factored into a certain emotional distance between parent and child and also an enhanced ability in children to shield themselves from parental emotional intrusions. Since there was virtually no privacy—often no physical doors or walls—children were privy to the wide spectrum of adult reality at the most intimate level: all the emotional outbursts, altercations, sexual tensions, jealousies, drug freak-outs, breakups, and chaos—adult drama as spectator sport.

And then there were the encounter nights, a weekly communal fixture whereby one and all gathered to air grievances and work out frustrations, usually by democratically passing a "magic" object (as well as dope) to signify who had the floor. Children fully participated, dealing with knotty interpersonal issues as equals with adults in these open forums. As a result, the youngest communards developed, as did many hippie kids, a directness with adults and shed their illusions about honoring parents as anything more than people. Yet, in unraveling the mystery of grown-ups at a particularly young age—conversant with all their parents' shortcomings and peccadilloes—children growing up in urban communes refused to accept the role of sheltered subordinate. Even

those as young as nine tenaciously defended their emotional rights against
perceived parental manipulation and interference, criticizing their mothers
and fathers as peers.[29]

On the isolated rural communes along the back roads of New Mexico,
Colorado, Vermont, Oregon, Washington, and the Ozarks, hippie childhood
unfolded in a more offbeat way still. In taking a vow of poverty to return to
the land, rural communards survived in places called Drop City, Morning
Star Ranch, or New Buffalo on a thin margin, carving out a hard way of
life sustained by gardening, ingenuity, frugality, odd jobs, food stamps, and
imagination. Most resident members—the solid core—tended to be young,
twenty-something women, many of whom were mothers, keeping the collective afloat by handling the daily grind of coordinating cooking and childcare.
Unlike their urban counterparts, where children were often grade-school age
preadolescents with at least some memory of living in their previous nuclear
family, rural communes typically contained preschoolers either born there—
delivered by resident midwives following the *Whole Earth Catalog*'s birthing
section—or with no recollection of life before the commune. Men drifted in
and out, often making for a noticeable lack of couples, so mothers generally
were not around their husbands or whoever the father of her children might
have been. The transient lives of men helped make Vietnam the only worldly
issue which consistently penetrated the communal reality of children, as visiting men shared personal stories of war or how they were staying one step
ahead of the draft.

It is difficult to discuss the approach to parenting in rural communes, since
there was deliberately no attempt to shape preadolescents in any systematic
sense. One might assess straight parenting by how closely children adhered
to the map of their parents' expectations. Communal parents in the remote
country, however, possessed no equivalent map. As Rothchild and Wolf observed, they did not "verbalize their hopes for their children; they do not prepare for their children's future in the accustomed way. If anything, life in the
informal communes denied the future . . . [T]hings progressed in haphazard
fashion and time did not march. Time oozed. The whole sense of the day was
like being on a perpetual acid trip."[30]

Without much parental guidance and less control over development,
growing up became drastically simplified. Communal children could trace
every aspect of their lives back to the source, from their mothers giving birth
and the building of the structures in which they lived to the preparation of
the oatmeal they were served each morning. By contrast, hippies believed,

suburban children were disconnected and had lives that were too neatly com-
partmentalized. Middle-class parents chauffeured their sons and daughters between an ever expanding number of experts and specialists who served the
family's various needs, as if parents did not trust their own instincts about
health, home life, or education. Such an upbringing gave straight children
a sense of dependency and powerlessness. The more holistic view of life and
resourceful do-it-yourself attitude on the commune fostered a sense of agency
in which everybody was a decision-maker, and while each person had a talent
for supporting the collective—carpentry, mechanics, electrical work, plumb-
ing, farming—anyone else could learn them.[31]

In the illogic and pandemonium of the commune, however, children were
not taught to think or reason objectively and thus were never told the rationale behind anything. Adults—here too, the larger group shared parenting
responsibilities—harbored no aspirations that kids should live up to some set
of ideal standards, whether presently or over their life course. Mothers never
appealed to children's morality and sense of guilt as bargaining tools, in no
way admonishing their offspring with abstractions such as "you should know
better than that" or "you should be ashamed of yourself." Discipline, too, was
grounded at the source, and was learn instead in reaction to feelings. If someone, or something, got hurt in any way due to your actions, then you were
in the wrong and should stop doing it. Although mothers tended to be pretty
gruff (all those kids could be a real handful), the punishment fit the crime:
removal for some period from the energy center, the group. Misbehavior was
therefore usually less about ornery calculations and more often just stumbled
into, such as discovering that the freedom to swing your fist ended when it
hit your friend's jaw. And just as adults did not exert impersonal logic-as-
discipline, preadolescents did not shield themselves with defensive arguments,
meaning less back-talking and the kind of tug-of-war which would later re-
quire reconciliation.[32]

Consider a typical day for these innocent primitives. Rising before the
grown-ups, children got dressed by themselves, subsequently looking like
ragamuffins, with dirty faces and uncombed hair, some with pants but no
shirt (or vice versa), clothes on backward, and no shoes. They were actually a
pretty accurate personification of the typical commune's shabby and broken-
down appearance. Functioning effectively as a pack, they milled about, waiting for breakfast, which was a free-for-all akin to feeding hogs at a trough.
Meals were not an occasion to instill manners, and women simply left bowls
of food on a communal table and retreated. Only afterward, as Rothchild and

Wolf observed at one northern California commune, did "grownups reappear
... like keepers after the animals have been let out, and wash down the porch
with a broom and a hose. It was easier to turn on a hose than to convince a
kid not to throw his food."

Because schooling was so haphazard, those old enough to work were often
invited to follow the adults out of the house in the morning to learn experi-
entially (a few communes had cottage industries which financed them), but
kids could decline and just be kids if they wanted. In the absence of organization or planning (few grown-ups even owned a watch), roaming from one
distraction to the next beyond any adult supervision was the only order of the
day for most children. Events simply swept them along like a stream. When
adults went to bathe, they grabbed the nearest kids and took them along, so
the children would at least get washed every couple of days. Hippie attitudes
about social roles held true as well. Since communards viewed all work as
equal, without relative superior or inferior value, children were not socialized
to differentiate themselves based on their talents or aspirations. In the same
way, it would not occur to adults to ask what children wanted to be when
they grew up, and without expectations for their kids, adults rarely expressed
pride in what they accomplished. Storytelling in communes might feature
old world legends, Native American folktales, and astrology, but none of the
Horatio Alger kind of pluck-and-luck narratives. The emphasis rested clearly
on what children were doing right now—just be you.[33]

You could get absolutely filthy playing from sunup to sundown in a
barnyard—or the surrounding countryside, mountains, forests, creeks, and
caves—and hurt, too, climbing among the rusty old farm machinery, slither-
ing under a barbed wire fence, or playing with power tools, knives, and guns.
Even some of the most laid-back hippies found the level of communal child
freedom unnerving. Foraging for food remained one of the few constants for
rural children. Meal times fluctuated in the commune, and women had trouble calculating who might be dropping in to eat at any given point. Adults
were hard-pressed to know if there would be enough food to go around.
With an every-person-for-themselves competition at meal time pitting adult
against adult, adult against child, and child against child, those on the lowest
rungs of the totem pole suffered most of all. Hunger drove children to store up
food like hibernating animals whenever possible, and mothers waged a running battle to keep little hands out of pantries and away from hot stoves. But
through it all, rural women displayed a detachment which reminded Rothchild and Wolf of a seasoned mother of ten, who, having seen it all, is secure

in the knowledge that parental preoccupation with safety does not necessarily make children any safer. Why worry yourself sick trying to filter, cushion, and protect them from life's uncontrollable physical and emotional dangers? Better to let the injuries and near misses fall where they may.

"These mothers did not choose to fight the battles of civilization on the level of dirt and scratches," Rothchild and Wolf concluded. "Dirty kids, bruised kids, a missed meal, a few days without clean teeth, late nights, rough-and-tumble antics were all accepted . . . These children, much younger, were on their own on a physical, survival level." It was a miracle more were not seriously injured or killed, or that there were not more stories of rural commune kids burning down buildings, cutting water lines, and causing general mayhem.[34]

When not engaged in scavenging or play, children seemed to be lost, just waiting around with mystified looks on their faces—like small hitchhikers—for something interesting to happen. On some communes there was plenty of time allotted for music, art, dance, and various games (although hippies frowned on competition). Yet, with no appointments, there were few disappointments. Since nothing was built up—no anticipation or looking forward to any occasion (birthday parties, the circus, a movie night)—rural commune children felt little frustration when events did not pan out. When mothers at the Ranch commune in California decided on the spur of the moment to take their children to a rodeo in a nearby town, their car broke down on the side of the road, and when they finally arrived it was only to find that the rodeo was next week. None of the children fussed, though, over things not working out, because there was no expectation that they would.[35]

Rothchild and Wolf posited that while rural communards were comfortable in having little control over their children's lives, they may, ironically, have actually exercised more control—albeit of a different sort—than suburban parents. For these hippies with no concern for schedules, or for keeping one's room clean, or demanding that rules be followed, control meant "grownups paying attention to kids on a certain emotional level, watching for evidence of immaturity." They "didn't care so much what their children did, as how they behaved while doing it. Knowing the exact physical whereabouts of their children was not a maximum requirement . . . knowing what their children were feeling [was]."[36]

One rural commune, the archetypical Farm community in Tennessee, warrants special attention for its distinctive approach to hip childhood. Under the spiritual teachings of Stephen Gaskin, the Farm was the largest—1,500

residents at its peak—arguably the most influential, and one of the few remaining hippie communes after the Vietnam era. In laying out a rigorous
and austere code for "farmers" to follow—they have been called the Techni-
color Amish—Gaskin also incorporated a codified program for child-rearing
which combined the structure of a religious commune with a secular design
for deliberately modifying children's behavior. Farmers essentially sought a
happy medium between the strictness of how their grandparents had raised
their parents and the prevailing hippie permissiveness in order to rear a moral,
hard-working, honest, and empathetic generation rather than, as they said,
just more sloppy beatniks.

"If you don't teach kids how to be, they'll just all learn," Gaskin asserted.
"What they learn is random, whatever strikes their fancy. On a system of what
looks together. Or what's amusing. Or what might be fun this week." He
continued, "If you're a parent, you have accepted the karma of another human
being who is too young to fend for himself for many years, and for whom you
must be responsible until he is able to fend for himself. If you don't come up
with everything you've got to give him a fair shake, which is an upbringing
that gives him a reliable, accurate idea of the Universe, then you've short-
changed him." In the hippie community, the Farm gained wide acclaim for
its child-rearing practices, attracting dozens of hippie parents daily who were
looking for guidance on how to raise better behaved children.[37]

The philosophy on the Farm emphasized the centrality of children to one's
immortal trip—"We live closer to our kids than square folks do"—believing
them to be in tune with every aspect of adult life on a vibrational (telepath-
ic) level. Farmers, therefore, did not practice birth control and considered
abortions immoral. In fact, a standing offer existed whereby women were
encouraged to use the Farm as an alternative to abortion. Any pregnant
woman would be welcomed, the collective would deliver the baby and care
for the child, and if the mother ever wished to return and claim the youngster, she could. Gaskin's wife, Ina May, pioneered the hippie practice of spiritual midwifery as well. Seeing childbirth as sacramental—delivering the
energy of the life force—Farm midwives preferred to preside over it themselves. "Most doctors aren't compassionate enough to know what it's like to
have a baby," the women argued of why the process could not be entrusted
to men, "and most of them act like they don't know anything about vibes
. . ." Fathers were allowed to be present, but were sometimes sent away if
their bad vibes (not treating the mother right or not respecting the energy)
complicated births.[38]

For the first years, children stayed close to their mothers, as Gaskin did not believe in undermining the family dynamic with commune adults socializing other people's children. Mother and child constituted a basic unit, which the father might choose to be a contributing part of "if he want[ed] to be that cool." As preadolescents got older, though, the three- to five-year-olds attended a roving kindergarten called the Kid Herd, while school-age children split their time between a one-room school—organized well enough around the Tennessee curriculum to earn state accreditation—and apprenticing alongside adults in various agrarian work details. Integrating children into the energy center (where the action was)—even during meditation—was preferable to segregation, although farmers drew the line at kids sharing in dope or sex.[39]

The key, however, to Farm parenting lay in refusing from the beginning to let children be "rip-offs." On the Farm, ripping off meant any negative behavior which interrupted people from "feeling groovy." In other words, children ripped you off when they "stole the show" by selfishly acting out in pursuit of extra attention. Adults too were ripping you off when they hassled you or otherwise became a pain in the ass. And rip-offs were made, not born. If taught to be a rip-off in childhood, you would remain one for life. Thus, farmers expected children of all ages to stay groovy and did not "cop to" (tolerate) being ripped off. Just as when dealing with adults, communards got "straight" (truthful) with children, telling them in plain terms to shape up and stop doing whatever dumb or destructive thing they were up to. Getting straight required parents to put in as much energy as they wanted their children to—yet not negative emotional energy, as anger was considered too "heavy" for kids to deal with. "If you can turn out a kid that's pretty sane, that's heavier than writing a poem," Stephen Gaskin maintained.[40]

Discipline had to be gentle and carried out with compassion. Making children say "yes, sir" or "no, ma'am" was not the point; getting parent and child to recognize each other, and give each other attention, was. Therefore, hollering and spanking were acceptable so long as neither came from a place of anger and parents had a history of playing physically with their children for fun (spanking must not be the only time parents touched their kids, and nonparents should never spank). Likewise, parents trained children to get a handle on their emotions. When children hurt themselves or became afraid, parents did not make a big deal out of it or baby them. Instead they reassured children that not every injury was serious and not all fears were real. Removing offenders from the energy center, not unlike a time-out, was the punishment for the hardest rip-off cases. Parenting, Gaskin advised, was analogous to helping children find their way out of a maze—not by telling them which way led to a dead end, but training them to discover that for themselves. Since the Farm collective operated as a boat, it needed all hands on deck (adult and child) pulling together as one. Gaskin hoped that by straightening out the rip-offs early, "they don't grow up and run away and grow their hair long when they get sixteen or something, or in our case cut it. They'll stay home and grow their hair long, and help you out with the thing."[41]

In practice, though, hippie children, wherever they grew up, did not stay turned-on. Most, it seems, do not consider, or call, themselves hippies, and are even sheepish about using that word when describing their background. While remembering childhood fondly—loving their parents for who they were and appreciating their unorthodox motivations—these sixties children have negotiated a separate peace with mainstream society. "I never really felt like the hippies were my people anyway," one man told me. "I never thought they were my tribe." Nevertheless, it would not be accurate to say that the counterculture failed to leave its imprint on preadolescents, because, hippies were not particularly trying to accomplish anything. They were just experimenting.[42]

Without question, the counterculture's self-righteous naiveté could easily breed irresponsibility and excess. In admitting the infinite into their lives, the saying went, hippies also admitted the chaos. "Our parents offered us a rare freedom to create our lives as we chose," Chelsea Cain stressed. "Those of us who felt safe in this freedom reveled in it, those of us who did not feel safe pined for structure, curfews, limits. Freedom without a safety net can have dire and lasting results." "It always left me with an awful floating feeling," Moon Zappa echoed, " . . . of too much space, of too many choices. I felt very often (and still do) like I was doing a moon walk and my cord came loose from the ship." Many adults told me very matter-of-factly about being "scared straight" by all the bad behaviors they witnessed as children, and expressed a low tolerance now for people who smoke dope to the point where it changes their behaviors. "I was left at a public place when I was a little girl," a woman born in 1969 recalled. "When midnight rolled around, I knew [my father] wasn't coming. I didn't know what to do and didn't have a dime. So I walked. I never wanted anyone to feel that level of fear, shock, and disappointment and decided to maintain a firm level of control from then on."[43]

"I saw a lot of irresponsible behavior in adults," said the California man who took a five-year road trip with his dad. "Once I saw a bookshelf fall right in the middle of a group of stoned-out adults, almost crushing a baby on the floor. Their response was so indifferent to the near-miss tragedy, I realized right there, at eight years old, that I was pretty much on my own in life." When characterizing his relationship with his mother today, the New Mexico man who once ate her boyfriend's rolling papers reflected on how his esteem for her idiosyncrasies has diminished over time. "As a kid, I was proud of her weirdness, but I've become ashamed of it, more intolerant as I got older. Mom has always been that way; I'm the one changing." This is why, he believes, they are not as close now as during his childhood. Maybe, just like those Barbie dolls, sometimes you get enlightenment, and sometimes you just get your hair burned off.[44]

Sandra Eugster, born in 1960 and raised on a Virginia commune explains that while the term "hippie commune" can evoke idyllic freedom and open-mindedness, the actual fact was often disorienting and frightening to a child. As the collective absorbed her nuclear family, the intensity of "growing-up with multiple parents—or none, depending on how you look at it" took a tremendous toll, and the denial of her mother—of which the personal decision to forsake that term of endearment and respect is emblematic—has been irreversible. The experience also led to a lifelong struggle to fit in, or at least pass for normal in mainstream culture. "Maybe it had to do with how often I didn't feel what it seemed I was supposed to feel," Eugster reflects in her memoir *Notes from Nethers*. "My reactions turned out to be off-kilter and hopelessly un-hip. Captive to visionaries, I was in a constant mad scramble to get with the dream. And it was something of a moving target, because I wasn't the dreamer."

> I didn't know that they hadn't themselves necessarily arrived at their espoused states of grace, I just knew that I fell short. Because I occasionally felt judgmental, jealous, or distrustful. I was often resentful and aggrieved, and sometimes I even lied. I *didn't* love and accept everybody, as I was supposed to, I *did* feel competitive . . . I *didn't* feel free and uninhibited when naked with others, even though I was still an "innocent child."' I *longed* for hamburgers and milkshakes . . . And witnessing the home birth was a lot of things, but it wasn't wonderful. Go figure.[45]

Now a counseling psychologist, Eugster ponders "how one extreme breeds the other," believing that after immigrating back into the world, in many ways she grew up to be the opposite of what you would imagine: extremely disciplined and regimented, self-sufficient, private, reserved, and hard to get to know. In seeking to understand such a seemingly counter-intuitive life course, Eugster identifies the basic hippie parenting conundrum. "The wish to return to innocence," she contends, "came with the thought that by removing the barriers between adult and child, the children could be the bridge back to innocence. But the force of nature goes in the other direction, and many children lost their innocence devastatingly early. I often think I was fortunate not to have been molested. But in a sense I was. My exposure to sexual matters was premature, as was my close contact with extreme human peculiarities and, ultimately, the harsh reality of adults doing what was right for themselves as opposed to their charges."[46]

The introduction of sexuality into childhood profoundly damaged untold numbers of children. The "hippies explore[d] sexually taboo terrain," Moon Zappa lamented, "but their children, too young to choose the lifestyle for themselves, suffer the consequences of being exposed to too much stimulus too early on, more than most of us experience in a lifetime." There were "no boundaries, no guidance, no protection. "[N]othing was sacred" another woman, an actress and writer, stressed about her vulnerable girlhood in the counterculture. "What I learned as a child of the sixties—fuck everything that moves and let it fuck you—has definitely shaped my adulthood. My brother and I saw our mother say yes to everyone, so we learned to say yes to everyone, even strangers . . . The free love movement, in practice, set me up for a lifetime of sexual, emotional and physical abuse. I learned that sex is a should. If someone wanted to sleep with me, I let him. It didn't matter—never mattered—if I didn't want to." Considering how attractive the counterculture lifestyle was to predators and charlatans intent on taking advantage of the circumstances, it is perhaps not surprising that both she and her brother were molested by the time they reached adolescence. As an adult, she continues to struggle with trust issues, finding it difficult to get close enough to make real friends or maintain meaningful relationships. "Deep down inside I am conservative," the woman concluded. "I don't like multiple lovers, I only want to sleep with one person. I pretended to separate sex from love, but I was only fooling (and abusing) myself. Sex *was* love for me—a substitute love—not sport, not just fun. Love my body, love me. Simple, easy. Not."[47]

Still, the majority of people who grew up with their hippie parents' "life is short but very wide" approach handled the chaos fairly well, and their experiences with sex and dope seem to be nonissues when functioning in straight society. What is more, many cultural trends in modern America that have decidedly hip origins from the Vietnam era—beyond just the quirkiness or superficial peace and love—have been enthusiastically perpetuated by adult children of hippies. Their lives speak to the expansion of our social imagination and the continued informalization of our culture in clothing, manners, and language. In communicating their core values—introspectiveness, open-mindedness, tolerance uninfluenced by appearances, inclusiveness, and "irreverence toward organizational authority"—they provide strong residual evidence of the individual imperative to define "normal" in one's own life. That these values appear to be so deeply ingrained, and hence difficult to surrender, perhaps makes sense given the timing of moral development in the preadolescent hippie.

Consider the positive effects of the counterculture on a child's changing moral sphere with so much encouragement to progress beyond simple egocentric reasoning and begin thinking of others. Hippie children may well have been socialized to Kolhberg's second level of conventional ethics, when ethical decisions are based on concern for others, well ahead of the developmental age at which this normally occurs around the middle to upper elementary school grades. And hippiedom probably reinforced the tendency to see their young world in synchronization with different perspectives. Timothy Miller, an expert on the hippies and American values, points to numerous places where the "children of hip have tried to work countercultural ideals into the social and physical fabric." operating businesses which specialize in alternative energy or organic living, supporting the decriminalization or legalization of marijuana, contributing to the steady liberalization of sexual mores to include progress toward equal rights for women and gays, promoting environmentalism, plant-based diets, and yoga, living in socially responsible ways with energy-efficient lightbulbs and other earth-friendly products, and promoting community projects like recycling and the reduction of automobile use.[48]

"When I imagine the sixties and seventies," a child of flower children observed, "I am filled with a sad sense that something important has been lost—something that connected people, regardless of their many directions." But often these children see their legacy as an obligation to maintain a sense of balance while continuing to work through the successful and failed lessons of their upbringing. As a young adult, Rain Grimes rebelled by forsaking her childhood influences and conforming. "By the time I was a teenager," the Pacific northwest woman recalled, "I had already lived as a nonconformist and, in some ways, that left me no direction to go but toward conformity. My parents had already fought many battles for me. I was so free to become who I wanted to be that I just wanted to be like everyone else." Only with age has she come closer to full circle, thinking "everything that once felt shameful now seems interesting; I actually enjoy the looks of incredulity from people who did not grow up as I did when I tell my childhood story." "Our parents couldn't shield us from mainstream culture—though many of them tried," Chelsea Cain reflected. "They could simply do their best to pass on the values and beliefs about a difficult, corrupt world. Many of us still struggle with this dichotomy, vainly attempting to be true to each world and betray neither. We may be hippies at home and yuppies in the office. We might want to make pottery and grow organic vegetables and still be drawn to cellphones and Jettas. We struggle to retain the truth of who we are, which many of us find rooted in our childhoods, even as we live in a world that may eschew our alternative beginnings."[49]

"The most maddening thing about me to my wife and friends," the New Mexico man said, "is my total lack of planning. I'm gonna roll with the punches, come up with things spontaneously, not worrying about money, or how it might work out." He believes this attitude to come from the residual hippie in him, as evidenced by his motto for living: "Life is easy, don't make it complicated." Likewise, a man who at eleven years old once hitchhiked back to California with an adult stranger in her twenties and her small child, reflected on how he has made choices to create some of the structure he missed out on as a kid, while still living a bohemian lifestyle characterized in his mind by creativity and flexibility. "I consider myself primed for social changes," he told me of what he thinks are the direct causal links from his hippie childhood. "All the rapid social changes in contemporary times that are unsettling to so many people, I'm hardwired for that already." Chelsea Cain wrote that all the hippie kids she knows "still struggle with questions: questions like when to take on society, and when to go along; when to live in the straight world, and when to abandon the rat race and take a summer off to follow Phish; when to march against clear-cutting-animal-testing-ozone-destroying-special-interests, and when to stay at home and watch [television]."[50]

CHAPTER NINE

Women's Liberation

I have two questions I would like for you to answer. Number One: Why can't women be president? I know it is a tradition for men to be president but can't a tradition change?
Indiana girl to Lady Bird Johnson, February 1966

WOMEN ACTIVISTS HAVE historically proven to be just as uncompromising as men, but due to male resistance, isolation, and intersections of race, class, and marital status, they did not always take to the street to contest their oppression. Throughout the twentieth century, particularly during the period referred to as feminism's "doldrums"—those decades between the first wave of sisterhood surrounding suffrage and the Vietnam era—American women more often than not relied on ingenious and covert tactics for mitigating against patriarchy and a misogynist culture. Even by 1970, when women from the New Left, counterculture, and the civil rights struggle began organizing a separate movement specifically around women's issues—understood as second-wave feminism or, in the more broadly vernacular term, women's liberation—female activism seldom manifested itself as overt physical confrontation with existing political systems or institutions. Instead, feminists changed the sexist culture, and women's social role in it, one individual life at a time. It should come as no surprise, then, that most children of the sixties have not seriously considered the childhood consequences of what is arguably the decade's most far-reaching, sustained, and important "movement." This cohort is conditioned to search their memory for provocative intersections between parochial childhood experience and sixties expressions of public protest. But, as a man born in 1955 wrote, "[I]n a little town of Oklahoma or a suburb of Oklahoma City there wasn't a lot of women's lib and bra burning like you saw on T.V."

By looking for feminism's resurgence only in the crowded, noisy landscape of 1960s political and cultural dissent, this cohort tends to miss the seismic, but disguised, shifts in the very ground beneath them: their own family.[1]

Several years before women's liberationists came to prominence by embracing feminist values, it was working mothers, increasingly those heading single-parent households, who were continuing the redefinition of Cold War, middle-class suburban family life and motherhood initiated by the counterculture. Tangible changes in female behaviors driven by pronounced increases in wage employment for women and the proliferation of divorce and single-parent families created new realities for wives, their husbands, and their children which were wholly out of sync with deeply ingrained *Leave It to Beaver* imagery. Many of these familial trends, considered deviant by 1950s standards, had been in progress for years, but the challenges they posed to tradition only reached a tipping point when a majority of American homes were impacted during the 1960s. Thus, as scholars such as Stephanie Coontz and Arlene Skolnick point out, women's liberation really began, not as a *revolution* against the mainstream so much as an *evolution*, with women starting to rethink the challenging conditions of their work and the nature of their marriage. "The revival of feminism in the 1960s," Coontz argues, "was more response than impetus to women's integration into the labor force," developing hand in hand with women's employment and the rising divorce rate well before female activists articulated feminist ideology or organized their movement sometime around 1970. In tracing second-wave feminism's impact on preadolescents, these historic changes in women's lives are the place to begin, considering that of all sixties phenomena they produced the broadest consequences in the lived experience of childhood. Only afterward did strong and independent-minded moms start disseminating through their imperial practices the notion that daughters should be included in the American Dream. Such reasoning sparked a growing adult awareness of, and sensitivity to, debilitating sexist and patriarchal stereotypes in children's culture, which in turn helped open up new opportunities for girls going forward into the 1970s.[2]

In terms of raw numbers, women's full- and part-time employment rose steadily throughout the postwar years—despite nostalgic misperceptions to the contrary—reaching 22 million in the workforce in 1960 (or roughly 40 percent of American women) on the way toward doubling to 44 million by 1980. Sometime around 1972 the number of women employed outside the home eclipsed the number of housewives. But more powerful demographic trends therein tell a richer story about how jobs outside the home reconfigured family structure and composition. While much of that growth reflects more females who had customarily worked for a wage in the past—those over forty, poorer women, and minorities—married women accounted for the lion's share. In 1950 fewer than one-quarter of all married women were in the labor force, whereas nearly 40 percent were working outside the home in the early 1970s. What is more, a sizeable proportion of women had preadolescents at home, and that figure was likewise rising. Earlier in the Cold War era, married white women's employment history commonly followed a "U-shaped pattern"—that is, they worked until their first childbirth, then quit to stay home full-time for child-rearing, before returning to paid labor only after their youngest children went off to elementary school. In 1950 only 12 percent of those with children under six drew a paycheck. Yet, by the end of the Vietnam War, the fastest gains in labor force participation rates by women occurred among white, middle-class working mothers with preschool and school-age children. During the bicentennial year of 1976, in fact, mothers of young children would actually constitute the majority of women workers. The next year, the Carnegie Council on Children observed, "We have passed a genuine watershed: this is the first time in our history that the typical school age child has a mother who works outside the home."[3]

As the emergent "two wage earner" dynamic became normative, it encouraged other mutually supportive and self-perpetuating renegotiations of marriage and parenthood. For many white, middle-class families, a wife's employment was predicated initially on economic realities, her supplemental income indispensable for achieving and sustaining the family's lifestyle. "It is my understanding that when my parents met and married, it was not my mother's expectation to be the breadwinner," a Michigan woman reflected. "So although my family model included a seemingly independent minded woman, she didn't present her contribution to the family unit in terms that made one think of 'women's liberation.' My mother just did her duty for the family unit. Perhaps the changing role of women in society made my mother's working outside the home less noticeable? My friends' mothers, for the most part, were homemakers, but nobody seemed to think my mother's absence odd." Nonetheless, the longer women worked, the more attractive and rewarding the benefits of working appeared, the more educational achievement was incentivized, and the broader and deeper their life experience and self-confidence. So much so, that wage work held the potential for profoundly reordering family values and the agency to deliberately plot a life course which veered markedly away from the domesticity their own mothers had known. Some boys recall their mothers quietly "starting to shy away from that stay-at-home-wife role," while the more dramatic changes reverberated most loudly with girls. "My mom was always very liberated. She was ahead of her time," a Midwestern woman born in 1958 told me. "My mom was actually the breadwinner of the family for a long time, not that my dad would ever want that repeated. She traveled to Europe with a girlfriend for three weeks, she bought stocks on her own, and worked full time. My dad didn't really have a choice—there was no stopping my mother when she wanted to do something. When I say it, my dad sounds like a big wuss and my mom ran the show, but she was just more *adventurous*."[4]

Although any resultant changes unfolded unevenly and to varying degrees—and were only rarely understood as frontal assaults on orthodox gender roles—more egalitarian decision making between husband and wife was the common result. A Missouri woman born in 1959 emphasized how her mother increasingly found her voice after the money started coming in. "She was traditional in a lot of senses, but once she started working, well, then that was, uh, different," the woman recalled. "She went out with some friends that were out job hunting and she applied and ended up getting the job and everybody else didn't. Then our options grew, things loosened up . . . But as far as mom being liberated, she wasn't, though she didn't hold her tongue about anything . . . I think it was a pretty equal partnership in their marriage after that." Another Missourian, a man born in 1962, remembered similarly that "my mom started demanding that my dad teach her how to drive, she also insisted that he no longer pick up her paycheck [they worked at the same place] . . . It propelled her to initiate and maintain a bit of independence. I am not sure my dad went along with it, but I know my mom started to be more vocal."[5]

Perhaps more significantly, couples negotiated fertility. In spite of the draft's initially positive effects on marriage rates and first-born deliveries to young women in the opening years of the Vietnam War, by 1965 the baby boom had finally cooled off, with birth rates falling precipitously. During this "baby bust," birth rates dropped from 120 births per 1,000 women in 1960 to 60 births per 1,000 women in 1975. In 1965—when the first baby boomers were themselves reaching adulthood—births fell below 4 million for the first time since 1953 and by virtually every measure, fertility did not make an appreciable comeback until the 1980s. It seems that at exactly the same time as the number of children with working mothers rose, the total population of children was in decline, and demographer Landon Jones observed forces at work which operated almost in reverse from those which had produced the boom. Simply put, American women were discovering economically and personally gratifying alternatives to motherhood. Not only did single women in the sixties and seventies choose with more frequency to postpone marriage and/or cohabitate, meaning fewer wives living with husbands during their most fertile years, but married couples moved away from having larger families as well. Unlike the trend in the boom years, Vietnam era parents tended to stop at one or two children, instead of having a third. These shifts certainly reflect conscious family planning choices on the number of children couples wanted and a woman's ability to avert unplanned pregnancies through the contraceptive Enovid, the first hormonal birth control pill, which was licensed in 1960.[6]

Tentative moves toward democratization of housework and child-rearing were likewise set in motion. Increasingly as women worked outside the home, discontent with the burden of their "double day"—paid labor compounded by the hidebound expectation that they also complete the vast majority of unpaid household chores—led couples to reach accommodations that expanded the domestic role for husbands and fathers and also children. "When my mother got a job, my parents got a newer car for my mother to drive, and my sisters had to do more of the housework and cooking," explained a Midwestern man born in 1961. "Pretty much everyone [now had housekeeping to do]—except me. I was the youngest and spoiled rotten. My mom may have done more cleaning, but my dad usually washed the floors, down on his knees scrubbing. Plus he did repairs and maintenance."[7]

While older men usually were more resistant to these adjustments, even minor ones, and more concerned with the opinion of friends and neighbors, younger husbands, who had entered marriage already with a two-income expectation, represented the vanguard of changes that within a generation became relatively commonplace. In regard to baby and childcare, specifically as lone caregivers while mothers were away, fathers' lack of experience in this area was initially the major stumbling block. Many dads conceived of childcare as babysitting, just brief periods of keeping an eye on the kids and addressing their physical needs. Yet with more regular practice, some "husband-sitters" grew into the part, engaging their sons and daughters more frequently with home repair projects, yard work, and trips to the library or zoo.[8]

Again, one of the consistently curious features of sixties childhood is that despite a hesitancy to recognize their mothers as legitimate social actors—nay, activists—many women enthusiastically praise these working mothers for modeling feminist behaviors and values during their earliest preadolescent years which profoundly shaped and colored their lives now as adults and parents. When asked about the influence of women's liberation, a Wisconsin woman born in 1960 responded with: "Ha! Growing up in the rural Midwest—men were the head of the household and that's all there was to it. However, my Mom had (behind-closed-door) talks with my sister and me and expressed her views that *both* the husband and wife in a household work hard to make it work." Speaking for a significant percentage of women, a Kansas woman similarly credited her employed mother with the fact that "[a]s a female, I always expected to work outside the home. I never thought I'd become a housewife." "As a woman," a Georgian woman born in 1956 said, "I always felt like I could be and do whatever I could make happen for myself. My mother was always very independent and self-sufficient. So even though she was of an earlier generation she exemplified women's rights in many ways." From Minneapolis, a woman born in 1964 wrote of her mother, "She was very much a do-it-yourselfer in those days. She dabbled in interior design, she bartended for a while, she was a gourmet cook, and later became a hairdresser and owned her own salon. My friend's moms also worked. One owned a daycare in her home, some were secretaries, one was studying to be an attorney, several were teachers and I had a female doctor. Many of course were in traditional roles, but there is no doubt that my brother and I were given the signal that women could and did do it all."[9]

A St. Louis woman concluded of her mother's impact, "My mother went to work when I was nine years old (out of necessity). It was difficult for her, pay was low, and there were only a few kids going home to empty houses after school. At first, I thought my mom hated working but really she just didn't like not being there for us. She thrived in her new work environment, gained greatly in self-confidence and assertiveness. I witnessed the transformation from meek housewife who kept things nice for her man and family to 'I am woman, hear me roar.' While I sometimes resented having to do chores others had mothers home to do for them, it was obvious that my mom benefited greatly from working (not just monetarily). I knew very early that I could not be happy staying home and being dependent on someone else."[10]

With only so many hours in the day, time on the job meant fewer hours dedicated to motherhood, so one of the principal hardships facing two-wage earners was covering gaps in childcare. Mothers routinely worked part-time or seasonally when the children were small—often in the evenings so one parent would be in the home at all times—and only transitioning to full-time when elementary school began. Studies in the late 1960s found the majority of these preschoolers were cared for during the mother's working hours in private homes—either their own or someone else's—and usually by trusted relatives as opposed to unfamiliar nonrelatives. Only a small fraction attended group facilities like nursery schools initially, although the numbers going to licensed, custodial daycares doubled from 475,000 in 1965 to one million in 1973. For many mothers with older children, though, having their children come home to an empty house after school was unavoidable. "My mother always worked, so it was nothing new to us," a man from suburban Kansas City remembered. "However, we were 'latchkey' kids before the word was invented." The term had actually been in common usage since World War II, but his remarks on the phenomenon's growth reveal the dialectic which took shape concerning the societal and developmental, implications of mother-child separation anxiety and a generation of youth left home alone. "We weren't supposed to tell anyone she worked," he continued. "The principal at our school knew she worked and only our closest friends knew. It wasn't until I was in high school that it became common knowledge. My mother was very afraid she would be ostracized by our friends, neighbors and church families."[11]

Apprehension, and stigma, over latchkey children's potential for delinquency and their susceptibility to a host of developmental maladies ranging from anxiety, timidity, and insecurity to unreasoning fear and other maladjustments increasingly drew public attention toward the nation's mounting shortage of affordable, quality private daycare facilitates. On the heels of a 1964 Department of Labor study which estimated that nearly one million children were left unsupervised for at least part of the day while their mothers worked elsewhere, the call for organized, publicly funded childcare gained traction. Considering the traditional American views of childcare as a family responsibility, rather than a public obligation as in Europe, this debate shaped up to be one of the most contentious of the Vietnam era.

Advocates, led by liberal Democratic Minnesota Senator Walter Mondale and Indiana Representative John Brademas, championed the ambitious Comprehensive Child Development Act, a national network of federally funded, but locally administered, child development centers. This bill, which enjoyed solid women's liberation and civil rights support, as well as backing from the AFL-CIO and educational associations, allocated a hefty $2 billion for community and county centers providing instruction, health care, nutrition, and other social services on a sliding payment basis, with poorer children receiving free care and those from middle-class families charged modest fees. Mondale envisioned the measure—effectively an expansion of Head Start—as the next step toward universal childcare in America. But after passing the Democratic controlled Congress on a bipartisan vote in 1971, the bill was unexpectedly vetoed that December by President Richard Nixon. The veto surprised the bill's supporters because Nixon had already backed the idea of federal spending on childcare for welfare families in his Family Assistance Plan (which was still making its way through Congress), and his administration had helped draft the Comprehensive Child Development Act, but prejudices over collectivized—"communistic"—child-rearing and liberal social engineering apparently carried the day. Nixon said the Mondale bill was fiscally irresponsible, administratively unworkable, and moreover weakened American motherhood by eroding family-centered child-rearing. Some detected strong evidence of the administration's conservative "get tough" campaign directed against the welfare poor. Democrats were unable to override the veto, and as the initiative faded away, proponents could only publically condemned the president as a modern-day Ebenezer Scrooge abandoning Tiny Tim to his fate at Christmastime.[12]

The skyrocketing incidence of divorce in American society and its multiplying effect on single parenthood—disturbing trends which have already been traced in part to the Vietnam War—further intensified, and lent more immediacy to, these childcare issues. By the mid-1970s, as the annual number of divorces topped one million for the first time, the rate of marriages ending in divorce approached 50 percent, basically doubling from 1960 to 1980. This surge was yet another causal factor in the baby bust and illustrates how behavioral changes in women paved the way for attitudinal changes. In the interplay of mutually supportive forces, working women's wider horizons, enhanced self-assurance, and fresh economic prospects of working women increasingly meant that they were also less likely to tolerate unhappy marriages. As the frequency of divorce mitigated the associated scrutiny and ostracization—once formidable deterrents—hundreds of thousands of women chose it as a socially acceptable and financially feasible alternative to a bad marriage, which in turn generated advocacy for "no fault" divorce laws, making divorces easier to acquire.

The number of children involved in divorces soared accordingly, from an estimated 463,000 in 1960 to 630,000 in 1965, reaching 870,000 in 1970 and 1.1 million by 1975, with probably an equal amount dislocated by parental separation each year. Regional variations notwithstanding—figures were higher in the South and West, lower in the Midwest and Northeast—this dramatic upswing represented a threefold increase in the number of American children impacted by divorce between 1956 and 1976. Even though the experience of living in an intact two-parent family remained the standard, divorce became an undisputed fact of life in the 1960s, broadening our definition of family and the domestic context in which childhood played out. Since almost all parents remarried, usually within three years, more children moved in and out of a variety of biological and blended family types. Four out of every ten American children in the era spent at least part of their childhood in a family headed by a divorced, single parent—almost by definition a single mother. Because most divorces took place in the first six or seven years of marriage, children of divorce tended to be preadolescents, and given the prevailing "tender years presumption," courts preferred to award custody of young children to the mother. So prevalent was this judicial doctrine that by the late 1970s the number of female-headed households rose nearly 150 percent, meaning that for every child who resided with a single father, eleven children lived with a single mother. The socioeconomic outcomes proved challenging. Young divorced women and their dependent children—statistically much poorer than two-parent families—experienced a swift decline in their standard of living, due to a single income from comparatively lower-paying clerical and service jobs and to the fact that primary judicial custody was rarely accompanied by adequate child support. In 1972 the poverty line for a female-headed household stood at $4,254. Children represented 36 percent of all white Americans, and 52 percent of all blacks, below this threshold.[13]

Beyond economics, the lived experience of divorce was complicated and perplexing for all involved, even when the marriage had been miserable. Contemporary child experts speculated that two-thirds of all divorces proceeded relatively smoothly for children, and though reactions were extremely individualized, professionals agreed that divorce did not necessarily create problem children. Most preadolescents, it was thought, would eventually turn out well as long as parents put aside personal antagonisms and acted in their best interest. "My parents were one of the first to get divorced in our small town in '72 [and it] carried quite the stigma," a man born in 1967 wrote me. "My mom could hear the whispers when she went to the grocery store. I was the oldest of five and the only one old enough to decide who I wanted to live with. I struggled with that decision but got on the plane when she decided to move from Indiana to California, where my grandparents lived. Got our feet on the ground and moved to Missouri a year and a half later. Learned a lot, close family got even closer, got even more independent, learned how to make friends, stunted development in other areas. All in all, I believe my life is better because of it. I have four siblings and they would say the same thing. It takes a lot to knock me off my pins now. Didn't get married until I was 39 and chose well."[14]

But other studies determined divorce to be a legitimate life crisis for preadolescents—possibly compounded by physical relocation—with the serious potential for distorting normal developmental and psychological progress. "Oh yeah," a woman born in 1959 emphasized, "I forgot to mention that what made it worse was that my mother divorced my dad and then moved across the country to California! That definitely impacted my life!" Socialization issues often stemmed from the altered nature and quality of parental relationships. Children of divorce simply had a smaller window of parental contact each day, with fewer firsthand observations of how a healthy relationship worked and narrow, one-dimensional modeling of gender identification and sex role socialization during their critical developmental years. As a result, people other than parents—day care employees, elementary school teachers, and peers—along with literature and television, rose in relevance as socializing agents. In the home, observant children, no matter the age, instinctively responded to the transformed climate by exhibiting the emotional state of the custodial parent, who themselves was understandably preoccupied with her own anxieties and resentments. Some single mothers compensated for feelings of guilt and shame by submersing themselves in child-rearing, which to a child might appear as overbearing, overprotective, and smothering. Others allowed their feelings of bitterness toward the former spouse to negatively shape their behaviors, while espousing critical appraisals of the opposite sex. More interested in assigning blame than moving forward constructively, such parents might have discouraged their children from accepting the divorce as a positive chance to begin a new life. When single parents did move forward by introducing a new boyfriend or girlfriend into the mix, children could struggle with fresh feelings of jealousy and resentment, seeing the usurper as intruding on their one-on-one relationship with the single parent and jeopardizing the hope for reconciliation. In these homes, preadolescents sometimes spent an inordinate amount of time dwelling on the past, seeming lethargic or mopey, and displaying a diminished appetite for food, school, or play.[15]

The prescriptive literature on the subject of children and divorce proliferated along with the rising rates. One of the earliest and most influential books geared specifically toward children was child psychiatrist Richard Gardner's *The Boys and Girls Book about Divorce* in 1970. Like many experts, Gardner identified open and honest age-appropriate communication between parent and child as key to successfully managing what countless preadolescents re-member as something akin to a civil war. Considering that most substan-tive childhood problems arise when parents were not truthful—intuitively preferring to shelter their sons and daughters from unpleasantness—Gardner cautioned divorced adults about keeping children in the dark or deliberately misleading them. Better to be straightforward—within reason—because (as we have seen with nuclear anxiety) during uncertain times parental half-truths only breed anxiety and mistrust, while honesty fosters security and healthy moral development. Confused children were prone to the blame game as well, assuming for themselves, however, the underserved responsibility for the di-vorce based on specious lines of reasoning. Because mothers and fathers were, after all, infallible, and thus could not conceivably be at fault, shouldering the blame alone made sense. Since many children believed their own misbehavior had caused the split in the first place, they expected their improved conduct would repair it. Those who entertained such misguided fictions often did so for the appearance of control it afforded them and because it kept alive a sense of hope. Instead, the strategy usually only tended to hammer home hard life lessons about how certain situations remained well beyond anyone's control.[16]

Separation issues weighed just as heavily on young minds. From the pre-adolescent view, spouses divorced not only each other, but their children too. In those fragmented families where the noncustodial parent who left home—again, predominantly fathers—was incapable of or disinterested in spending regular and predictable time together, absentee parents and children drifted apart. Despite children's imaginative capabilities to keep the inattentive parent alive in their mind, and their pronounced sense of loyalty and propriety, lone-ly children could feel marginalized, or downright abandoned, often leading them to equate noncustodial parental love with the frequency, punctuality, and duration of visitations. In cases when scheduled visitations were regu-lar, fathers could feel more like entertainers taking their children on a series of amusing "dates" which were unfulfilling for all parties involved, either unduly stressful or leaving youngsters overexcited and exhausted. Without diligent efforts to prevent this creeping estrangement, noncustodial parents risked becoming outliers without substantive influence on their children's development.[17]

Such circumstances tended to lead to periods of overly restless, quarrel-some, overbearing, and possessive behavior in preadolescents. The culture of elementary schools further complicated matters for children of divorce, who measured themselves against their classmates, many of whom lived with both parents. "I think they were first in line to get one," a California woman born in 1959 reflected of her parents' divorce, "which made me quite an oddball . . . and fodder for quite a bit of gossipy 'discussion.'" "I had always grown up hearing how shameful divorce was," echoed a woman born in 1965, "and so it was hard, when my parents divorced, being one of the people I had always been taught to look down on. A good life lesson, I suppose, but I wonder if it's different now that there isn't as much of a stigma."[18]

Educators and experts noted common themes of loss in the artwork of children of divorce—for instance, drawings depicting the search for a missing kite or being lost in the woods and looking for home. Imaginary friends likewise peopled the landscape of these children more regularly, either acting out as "bad" friends responsible for mischief or "good" friends adopting the role of an idealized self. Some preschoolers demonstrated new aversions to playing house, refusing to assume the established roles of mothers and fathers. This challenge to traditional socializing role play raised a red flag among specialists who were already concerned about whether children of divorce would devalue marriage and family, reasoning which might impact their life course by causing them to delay or never marry, or to suffer through multiple failed marriages. Anecdotally at least, dozens of the recollections I collected suggest these concerns were not without some merit. "I know it had an impact," a California man born in 1958 stressed when asked about divorce in his childhood. "I dealt with it. I think I sublimated it a lot. Saw a lot of other people who divorced. Can't even count them. I never got married."[19]

A Pennsylvania woman born in 1960 offered a more comprehensive understanding of how these historical realities which propelled women's liberation resonated causally. She wrote, "I believe one of the reasons I am not married at age 50 is because I instilled in myself that women needed careers to make them complete, and relationships come and go but working proves a point— we have made it into the work force and we are staying. I put career above relationships and now I am rethinking that concept at 50. Was my career path worth giving up a family? It was my choice."[20] Here, in this reflection, lies second-wave feminism's origin story—an appropriate term, given that comic books use it to explain how superheroes gained their powers. It was only after divorced women came to understand how vulnerable their new circumstances left them—casualties in a phenomenon identified as the "feminization of poverty"—that some began embracing feminist attitudes honestly.[21]

"My mother was brought up [to believe] that 'the women stayed at home with the children and the men took care of the finances,'" an Illinois man recalled, but after her divorce she "started to raise three kids by herself, so I guess you could say she was on the ground floor of 'women's liberation.' The impact that this had on our family was having to witness her struggles for equal pay and being protected by law." Together with other working mothers—increasingly college-educated—these were the women whose private renegotiations of their sexually asymmetrical workplaces and gendered divisions of labor at home forged the female consciousness needed to instigate a public movement by the late 1960s, an "ideological revolution," according to Stephanie Coontz, premised on notions of gender equality and work as an essential element in a woman's quality of life.[22]

Betty Friedan's *The Feminine Mystique*, a thought-provoking exposé of the frustrations inherent to American womanhood at midcentury, reverberated among women seeking to avoid re-enacting their mothers' lives. The book's publication in 1963 is widely recognized as the catalyst for second-wave feminism. Like sixties social activism in general, several women's "movements" took root, as opposed to a singular campaign. Leadership remained decentralized, membership highly subjective and permeable, with most localized actions less direct and more discursive. Initially many middle-class, white women were drawn to the moderate political style of the National Organization for Women (NOW), founded in 1966 primarily over dissatisfaction with the reluctance of the Great Society's Equal Employment Opportunity Commission (EEOC) to defend the 1964 Civil Rights Act's prohibition of gender, as well as race, discrimination. With Freidan as its first president, NOW modeled its challenge to sexism on the NAACP's commitment to integration and legalism, working within the system on issues of equality of opportunity. For most of its history, so-called "liberal" feminists functioned as the voice of the women's movement—strengthened by Gloria Steinem's *Ms.* magazine—leading fights over the Comprehensive Child Development Act, affirmative action, the liberalization of state abortion laws stemming from the *Roe v. Wade* Supreme Court decision, and passage of the Equal Rights Amendment (ERA). Their advocacy for Title IX of the Education Amendments of 1972 helped prohibit federally funded high schools and colleges from discriminating on the basis of sex, a landmark move responsible for substantial increases in athletic participation among young women.[23]

While NOW also sponsored mass marches beginning with the Women's Strike for Equality, which brought tens of thousands into the New York City streets during the summer of 1970, a number of women from the New Left, civil rights struggle, and counterculture introduced the "liberation" into the movement with more confrontational and radical points of view. From a visionary core on the East Coast, radical feminist groups such as Redstockings, Cell 16, New York Radical Feminists, and The Furies saw women's liberation as the primary vehicle for undermining male supremacy and capitalism all at once in the New Left's wholesale restructuring of American society. In perhaps the era's most spectacular, and misunderstood, example of their pioneering activism, the New York Radical Women staged a protest at the Miss America pageant in 1968 where participants ceremoniously threw off the yoke of male-defined beauty standards and accoutrements, including bras, girdles, and false eyelashes. And although no bras were actually burnt, in the zeitgeist of the time the media quickly popularized the spectacle as "bra-burning," a not-too-distant cousin of draft card burning. Within a year, the offshoot Women's International Terrorist Conspiracy from Hell (WITCH) followed with demonstrations at a Madison Square Garden bridal fair to "Confront the Whore-Makers," a "zap action" patterned after the satirical, humor-as-protest "Confront the Warmakers" march on the Pentagon carried out in 1967 by Abbie Hoffman and Jerry Rubin's Youth International Party (Yippie).[24]

Yet, despite the many inherent philosophic and strategic differences within the feminist ranks, most women regarded personal experience as the foundation for political action, and, as such, "consciousness raising" groups contained the real power of sisterhood. These informal, grassroots assemblies of women convened around suburban dining room tables, apartment couches, and dorm room floors gave women the autonomous space and time to tease out their own new perspectives on various psychological and cultural constructions: patriarchy and misogyny, stereotypes and feelings of inferiority, nontraditional gender roles, sexual objectification and double standards, domestic violence and rape, sexuality and sexual fulfillment, women's health, independence and careerism. From their dialogues came a myriad of practical, collective solutions in the adult world: healthcare clinics, bookstores and libraries, self-defense classes, battered women's shelters, abortion counseling, and women's studies programs.

In the world of children, many recognized this heightened consciousness through subtle behavioral changes in mom and in passing conversations. A woman in Arkansas recalled the first time a female priest in the Episcopal Church referred to God as "She" in her confirmation class. A surprising number recall their mothers quietly forgoing their Mark Eden Bust Developer or furtively removing dad's cache of *Playboy* magazines from under his side of the bed. A Kentucky woman born in 1963 wrote me, "I remember watching my mom going through labyrinthine rituals of hair and makeup (much worse than today) to get ready for work in the morning. I remember her struggling into a girdle in my very early years, and she laughed about this later in life. She was really, really thin and it was just something that was done. You were a woman? You wore a girdle." When this aspect of the ritual ceased, she said, "I got the sense it was some of the simple things in life that were really liberating. You didn't have to necessarily burn your bra (I heard this a lot), but you were free to express yourself more."[25]

Of all the adaptations, however, none was as impactful for preadolescent children as the feminist dialectics surrounding motherhood. Early feminist repudiations of traditional marriage and motherhood as oppressive institutions of patriarchy had left the movement particularly susceptible to cultural critics who were quick to blame "liberated" women for destroying the family in their selfish abandonment of domesticity. Feminists' reactionary—some called it elitist—anti-motherhood stance also threatened to undermine the movement's nascent solidarity from within by driving a wedge between mothers and childless women. Accordingly, in the late 1960s and early 1970s, practical second-wave feminists rethought this devaluation of motherhood in the abstract, adopting instead a more inclusive view of the liberating potential of motherhood. They still condemned cultural expectations of "mandatory motherhood" and remained apprehensive of the arbitrary limits marriage and motherhood placed on a woman's life choices. But rather than marginalizing mothers for being complicit in their own oppression, the movement embraced women with children with an eye toward improving their individual situations through consciousness raising while simultaneously promoting feminism more broadly through motherhood. Here, in this transcendent female experience—in which men did not share—feminists harnessed what was thought to be best about women: a capacity for nurturing, communication, empathy, intuitiveness, flexibility, and protectiveness.[26]

The celebration of motherhood intertwined with countercultural ideas about authentic "women centered" activities such as childbearing, breastfeeding, and mothering, and thus informed the development of the women's health movement of the early seventies. Women's health was a feminist issue—a matter of self-determination—and as liberationists came to reject the male-dominated and profit-driven medical profession, alternative health organizations—for example, the Boston Women's Health Book Collective, with its classic book *Our Bodies, Ourselves*—came together to educate women who suspected they had been condescendingly left in the dark by doctors about their health and sexuality. Cooperative clinics serving numerous locations similarly provided general medical services for women, with an emphasis on reproductive health. Often, in advocating holistic natural childbirth and midwifery, these facilities cared for feminists and hippies in equal measure.[27]

Like the counterculture, second-wave feminism relied on motherhood's extraordinary potential for socializing children with feminist sensibilities, conditioning them against patriarchy, as a viable means of securing an egalitarian future. Through their child-rearing practices, mothers de-emphasized sex role typing during the toddler years, when children naturally discover the possibilities of sexual identification. When questions invariably arose, it was healthier to satisfy a child's curiosity with the observation that the vagina is simply physically different from the penis, consistently followed with reinforcement about how sexual differentiation is complimentary and without antagonistic connotations of superiority or inferiority. Narrowly defined gender distinctions between what culturally constituted masculinity and femininity—what adults considered stereotypically "boyish" and "girlish"—were similarly minimized as preadolescents developed.

Toward these ends, the *Ladies' Home Journal* examined issues of feminist child-rearing and *Ms.* magazine ran a regular column, "Stories for Free Children," addressing topics of potential interest on divorce, single parenting, and women's lifestyles. (The latter included an illustrated story about a hippie girl named Sylvie Sunflower living on a commune.) Such objectives required vigilantly reorienting parenting styles and expectations on a variety of levels, and avoiding double standards by refraining from complimenting girls solely on their looks or boys on their strength, or exclusively cuddling girls while roughhousing boys. So too were clothing styles reassessed. The era's typically dainty dresses with matching tights, fancy leather shoes, and long hairdos which might encourage girls to think of themselves as passive objects to be admired increasingly fell out of favor in many wardrobes by the 1970s, replaced by informal or unisex blue jeans and sneakers that motivated young ladies to be doers. The same was true with household chores, with boys making beds and vacuuming just as girls mowed lawns and raked leaves.[28]

With these parenting goals, feminist mothers took issue with Dr. Spock's original prescription for thinking about boys and girls as fundamentally different in character and treating them accordingly. Yet, Spock eventually came to endorse the principles of feminist sex role socialization, if not to the same degree. In his regular *Redbook* column and revised editions of *Baby and Child*

Care in the mid-1970s, he cautioned parents on the perceived dangers of raising children without sex distinction, fearing that such a practice jeopardized
the development of healthy sexual identification. Acknowledge the differences, Spock advised, while also allowing children of either sex to freely cross
the boundaries of maleness and femaleness when those societal limits do not
reflect the reality of the individual personality. To avoid stunting their development, quiet boys setting a table with a Worcester Ware Plastic Tea Set
and boisterous girls excavating a ditch with a Tonka dump truck should be
allowed to make those behavioral choices without shame or fear of parental
intolerance and teasing.[29]

Sex role socialization required an awareness of the gender biases and blatant sexism entrenched in children's literature, television, and toys, and the
assiduous promotion of alternative cultural narratives in these mediums.
Mothers sought to raise the consciousness of little girls and boys beginning
with books. The crusade for more representative and realistic portrayals of
females in children's literature is analogous to the trends inspired by the civil
rights movement just a few years earlier, and, in fact, is one facet of the literary "new realism" in the sixties. Prior to the movement, female characters
in children's literature were cast, when at all, in subordinate, home-related
roles that were often insulting and demeaning. When NOW conducted a
two-year study of sex role stereotyping in children's books, it discovered a
ratio of boy-centered to girl-centered stories of 5 to 2 and a ratio of male to
female biographies of 6 to 1. The messages in these books was crystal clear:
while boys led, girls served, destined for the "maintenance of others." Picture
books for nonreaders were some of the earliest socializers, establishing the
basic parameters in children's literature for molding and shaping gendered
ideas in preschoolers. Male characters (including anthropomorphized animals
and vegetables) monopolized titles, central roles, pictures, and storylines, giving the impression that girls were so unimportant that no adult bothered to
write about them. When women appeared, homemaking and motherhood of
course predominated, depicted as an indoor, full-time bore involving inter-
minable cooking, cleaning, child-rearing, shopping, and worry, punctuated
with sedentary stints of recreational knitting or reading. Sure, they cleaned
up messes and gave comforting hugs, but more often than not moms were
restrictive, fearful of activities deemed too dangerous, and scolding nags.
Dads, on the other hand, because of their worldliness, seemed to be the more
fun parent, tackling adventurous tasks in the faith their children were old
enough to handle it.

Equally uninspiring for little girls were the occasional pink collar job opportunities contained within the pages—teaching, typing, and taking temperatures—respectable, to be sure, but requiring lower levels of education, offering few advancements, and affording less prestige than men's jobs. And then there were the vocations that required certain physical attributes, such as stewardess, ballerina, model, or actress. Each cheerful page contained smiling, eager to please role models demonstrating little in the way of intelligence or agency, but capable nonetheless of teaching a lot about dependency and the cultural virtues of suppressing one's sense of self in favor of submissive service. Consider Hallmark's popular *What Boys Can Be* and *What Girls Can Be* picture books. Boys, by comparison, were excited by the prospect of growing up to become firemen, baseball players, policemen, animal trainers, and cowboys—worlds of camaraderie and adventure—or prestigious and skilled doctors, pilots, and astronauts. The pinnacles of *What Boys Can Be* and *What Girls Can Be* were president and mother, respectively.[30]

Storybooks for young readers perpetuated and fortified these distinct sex role prescriptions. In the award-winning 1954 book *The Wheel on the School*, illustrated by Maurice Sendak, a Dutch school girl, Lina, asks, "Can I go, too?" to which a male classmate, Jella, rejoins, "No! Girls are no good at jumping. It's a boy's game . . . girls worry about wet feet and their dresses flying. And they squeal and scream, and then they get scared and go giggly." A male character, Uncle Haskell, in Irene Hunt's 1966 coming-of-age story *Up a Road Slowly*, declares to the heroine, "Accept the fact that this is a man's world and learn how to play the game gracefully."[31] And the song remained the same in both elementary school libraries and classroom textbooks. Math books illustrated boys creating things and earning money, while girls cooked things and spent money. Social studies books showed males as achievers and knowers, explaining the nature of things in response to dumb female questions.

Even the token "tomboy" character proved to be nettlesome. Those females wishing to play the boys' games—exhibiting strength, imagination, or leadership—paid for admittance by renouncing their supposedly feminine characteristics. With no acceptable middle ground, tomboys who wore jeans, played boys' sports, and chose to be unladylike faced teasing and disaffection from both camps. Moreover, literary tomboys usually abandoned their inner potential at some point in order to outgrow this perceived awkward phase and become proper ladies. Alexandra, the spunky, nonconformist whose adventures comprise *A Girl Called Al* by Constance Greene, prefers taking shop to home economics and reads the newspaper, yet by the end of the 1969 book she forgoes her pigtails, loses weight, dresses in pretty clothes, and finds popularity.[32]

Around 1970, though, second-wave feminists began exerting influence over how both daughters and sons learned and internalized the various social changes then under way through alterations of children's media messages. Two vocal groups in particular—Feminists on Children's Media and Women on Words and Images—demanded that publishers offer non-sexist portrayals in children's literature and offer positive images of women's physical, intellectual, and emotional potential in order to launch girls toward full personhood. At home, mothers steered their children toward this new crop of titles, and a few somewhat older ones, featuring females as people in their own right, not superwomen exactly, but just ordinary, identifiable women making it through life under their own steam. Readers became acquainted with characters like Karana, a Native American stranded alone with nothing but her physical skills and wits in Scott O'Dell's *Island of the Blue Dolphin*, published in 1960, and Louise Fitzhugh's precocious *Harriet the Spy* in 1964. Madeleine L'Engle's 1962 *A Wrinkle in Time* introduced headstrong Meg Murry, one of science-fiction's few central girl characters at the time, and Vera and Bill Cleaver created the determined Mary Call, a fourteen-year-old forced to grow up quickly after her dad dies in the 1969 *Where the Lilies Bloom*. *Pippi Longstocking*, the first in a series by Astrid Lindgren that was reissued in 1969, was about the strongest girl in the world, an audacious Swede living with only a horse and monkey, but no parents. And such books were not just for daughters. Gender realism potentially relieved the pressure on boys who had been told to be all that girls were not—fearless, stoic, athletic, and outdoorsy— helping them to avoid increasingly obsolete expectations of adulthood while confidently envisioning alternative paths without automatically being labeled a sissy.[33]

While progress occurred much more slowly than feminists wanted— outmoded books lingered on library shelves for years—children's literature clearly reflected women's concerns throughout the 1970s. In addition to the works of smaller, collective feminist presses in several localized markets, mainstream publishers released a number of more balanced picture books such as *Rain Rain Rivers* in 1969 by Uri Shulevitz, about a little girl's imaginative plans to sail homemade boats, "run barefoot in puddles," and "stamp in warm mud." A trio of 1971 books for emergent readers in kindergarten through third grade presented a boy versus girl battle where girls win (Crosby Bonsall's *The Case of the Scaredy Cats*), a creative girl transforming a box from the trash into a castle and race car (Patricia Lee Gauch's *Christina Katerina and the Box*), and boys and girls playing cowboys, baseball, *and* dolls together, not to mention a dad walking his son to school while mom works in a lab (Betty and Joan Miles's *Just Think!*). For older elementary schoolers, there were biographies of physicist Marie Curie, artist Mary Cassatt, new Israeli Prime Minister Golda Meir, and Shirley Chisholm, the first African American woman elected to the U.S. Congress. In fiction, Marjorie Weinman Sharmat told of a good-natured game of one-upmanship between a boy and girl in the 1971 chapter book *Getting Something on Maggie Marmelstein*. Books traditionally designated as "for girls" were usually just about love and romance, but Alberta Wilson Constant's *The Motoring Millers* from 1969 followed the cross-country exploits of sisters dealing with their father's remarriage in 1910. After the winner of a car race is discovered to be a young lady, Miss Wintergreen, an older woman in the crowd exclaims, "I want you to know that I am highly in favor of your driving in this race. Women should advance their cause in every field." To which Miss Wintergreen responds, "I didn't think about that. I just love to drive. Taught myself on our one-cylinder Trumbull when I was ten."[34]

Given the overwhelming preponderance of females in education, classrooms were also a front line in socialization. True to their collectivist roots in the cultural left, many feminist mothers understood day care to be a communal responsibility and for a time they operated numerous grassroots, cooperative child care centers nationwide. Curriculums were designed to be gender neutral, as were the books, toys, and games teachers chose and the attire students wore. For good measure, facilities sometimes incorporated co-op exchanges for trading in older clothes and materials. Elementary school teachers also became more aware of gender stereotyping—expectations that girls were more verbal and emotional while boys were more aggressive and into math and science—and took subtle steps to reduce it, using less gendered language and not necessarily calling on boys to run the audiovisual equipment or prohibiting girls from carrying heavy items. Teachers and librarians began stocking their shelves, and reading out loud during story time, with books which provided teachable moments for both sexes.

One of the foremost examples of feminist texts incorporated into elementary curriculums was Marlo Thomas's *Free to Be . . . You and Me*. The album, released in 1972, together with a companion illustrated book and one-hour prime-time special on ABC in 1974, featured a collection of children's stories, songs, and sketches—performed by the likes of Thomas, Mel Brooks, Tom Smothers, and Alan Alda—that lightheartedly rethought gender assumptions

with unconventional, and often humorous, happy endings. One of the eighteen tracks, "Ladies First," based on a Shel Silverstein poem, followed a vain
little girl—the very picture of a stereotypically pretty, ornamental female—
through the jungle and into the mouths of tigers, devoured for her shallow-
ness. In a retelling of the Greek myth of Atalanta, a princess refuses to be
married off as a prize—feminists found the passive Disney version of princesses
problematic—and instead consents to wed the suitor who can beat her in a
footrace. The hard-fought race ends in a tie, but instead of submitting to a
romantic happily ever after, the heroine befriends the boy and together the
two seek adventures, living in respectful—as yet unmarried—companionship
grounded in equality. Another tale, "William's Doll," chronicles the efforts of
an otherwise conventional boy to acquire a doll of his own to play with and
care for, a decidedly unconventional masculine representation whose message
was augmented by professional football player Rosie Grier assuring boys that
"It's Alright to Cry" in song.[35]

Vigilant mothers monitored television viewing as well, tuning the set to
programs thought to minimize gender biases and stereotypes. By 1973, this
was becoming easier, as the sixties social climate had rapidly manifested itself
in prime time, a changing of the guard—the "top ten" series in 1973–1974 did
not include a single show from the 1968–1969 "top ten"—which ushered in
an era of more socially relevant programming. "In much the same way that
television transformed the Beatles into the Monkees," popular culture commentator Steven Stark observed of how television domesticated the sixties for
mass consumption, "H. Rap Brown became Linc Hayes of the Mod Squad,
Gloria Steinem became Mary Tyler Moore, and the Vietnam War became
M*A*S*H." Yet in the 1960s, prior to *The Mary Tyler Moore Show*, *Maude*,
or, later still, *Wonder Woman*, such shows were still relatively scarce. So, many
mothers engaged their children in "what-if" conversations about gender roles
on television. Why were there no women MCs on game shows? Why did
female news correspondents only report on stories about household items?
How might the small screen look if women were shown as strong, competent
characters?[36]

Making matters trickier, most of the consistently interesting female characters for preadolescents largely occupied a genre of escapist, fantasy shows
known as "magicom." While these television witches, aliens, and talking cars
may have given the decade a magical quality many sixties children remember, shows such as *Bewitched, I Dream of Jeannie,* and *Gilligan's Island* were
muddled as feminist media texts. Some thought *Bewitched*, running on ABC

from 1964 to 1972, and *I Dream of Jeannie*, on NBC between 1965 and 1970, to be cutting-edge allegories of the early women's rights movement. In both shows, beautiful, desirable blonds endowed with magical powers—triggered by Samantha the witch twitching her nose and Jeannie the genie bobbing her head—tested the boundaries of patriarchy within the safe confines of the sitcom. Yet, others saw in Samantha's abandonment of witchcraft to please her mortal husband, Darrin, and Jeannie's subservience to her astronaut master, Tony Nelson, just two supernatural instances of a tired cliché: clearly superior women curbing their power in order to be accepted into conventional society.[37]

The children who picked up on such mixed signals appear to have tended toward the latter perspective. "The women's lib movement absolutely changed my perception of gender roles; the gender issue was huge for me," a woman born in 1957 outside Washington, D.C., wrote me. "The types of women portrayed in television in the '60s were dismal: cute but dumb (Lucy, Elly Clampett, Laura Petrie), afterthoughts (any female in *Combat!*, *Hogan's Heroes*, *McHale's Navy*, etc.), the Every Mom (June Cleaver, Donna Reed), and the most annoying type: powerful women who voluntarily subjugated themselves—and their powers—to arrogant, fairly unlikable men (*I Dream of Jeannie*, *Bewitched*). Seriously, by the end of the 60s I was rooting for Endora [Samantha's witch mother, who abhorred Darrin]. Wow—I'm even annoyed thinking about it now. Unresolved issues much?"[38]

Saturday morning cartoons reflected fairly accurately most media representations of women. Grossly underrepresented female characters were stereotypically relegated to the roles of wife and mother (Wilma Flintstone), adoring and helpless girlfriend (*Underdog*'s Sweet Polly Purebred and *Dudley Do-Right*'s Nell Fenwick), or witch (*H. R. Pufnstuf*'s Witchiepoo). And while Sweet Polly Purebred was a television reporter and Penelope Pitstop won her share of races on *Wacky Races* and her own *The Perils of Penelope Pitstop* spinoff, feminists found little reason for encouragement. But on this televised landscape largely outside parental oversight, one proto-feminist did emerge in the world of preadolescent viewers during the fall of 1969. Velma Dinkley—"the smart one"—on CBS's *Scooby-Doo, Where Are You?* searched for clues alongside Shaggy, Daphne, and Fred, the three other human members of Mystery Inc. (plus the semi-articulate Great Dane Scooby-Doo), and, while mostly unappreciated, her superior intellect proved decisive in solving each spooky case. In many ways, Velma and her female counterpart, Daphne, represented a cartoon version of the standard dichotomy in female characters, along the same lines as Ginger and Mary Ann on *Gilligan's Island*. For all Daphne's mod beauty and attractiveness to the opposite sex (obviously Fred's love interest), she remained a one-dimensional damsel in distress. The bookish Velma, on the other hand, although frumpy, bespectacled, and socially awkward, had the most depth, and her indispensable intelligence and skills got things done. Despite Fred's masculine claims to leadership, and Daphne's preferential feminine treatment, it was not lost on girls that Velma was the real brains of the outfit. And in this single character, female viewers found an endearing clue about life: that regardless of appearance, being clever—although maybe not the coolest—could take you the farthest.[39]

At the same time that television advertising was reconfiguring the dynamics of toy culture—appealing to children with fantastical toys which could be used as props within their imaginative play—the women's movement contested adult culture to the point where mothers also altered the nature of play, generally through direct consumer action and the preferencing of toys which illuminated feminist-inspired paths toward adulthood. Consequently, mothers helped break down the modern functions of toys as part of the broader changes the toy industry underwent after the Vietnam era's uncertainty. Just as G.I. Joe retreated into the realm of fantasy, most of the girls' playthings which had reinforced gendered vocational themes would soon be supplanted in the 1980s by more innocuous, escapist play with pretend friends like the Care Bears and Rainbow Bright. Since the first decades of the twentieth century, toy culture had been strictly segregated by gender. Toddlers generally received unisex toys, but after about age three the differentiation became more defined. Children's toys were effectively miniatures of the tools adults worked with, and play reinforced the associated sex role stereotypes. With progressively better technology, toys for males functioned as make-believe replicas of men's machinery, training boys for future careers in business, science, industrial production, and soldiering.

Female toys, conversely, gave girls a taste of homemaking and motherhood, paralleling their mother's role in child-rearing with baby dolls and dollhouses, while also acting as mother's little helper with scaled-down versions of grocery stores and kitchen appliances for domestic home management. Baby boomers still engaged these tools of play that were by the 1960s increasingly influenced by the aforementioned developments in television advertising, both in terms of marketing directly to children and product placement. The J. C. Penney's and Sears Christmas catalogues, for instance, sold little box and can sets of name-brand supermarket commodities—Heinz, Hunt's, Del Monte, Green

Giant, Jell-O—and domestic toy titans like Kenner's Easy-Bake Oven came with Betty Crocker mixes. Dolls remained a gift-giving staple as well, especially fashion dolls—Tammy, Crissy, Tressy, and, of course, Barbie—which emphasized clothing, cosmetics, hair, and dress-up play. Surveys showed that while genres such as craft kits (Kenner's Whittle Away and Chip Away) and art kits (Hasbro's Spirograph), along with Tinkertoys, were marketed as unisex, toy makers still aimed Erector sets and chemistry labs nearly exclusively at boys. Seventy-five percent of chemistry sets had only boys on the box, and though the other 25 percent showed boys and girls, none presented just girls. A popular doctor's kit marketed for boys contained a stethoscope, microscope, blood pressure sleeve, and prescription pads. The companion nurse's kit came with an apron, hat, plastic silverware, and tray of plastic hospital food.[40]

Concerned mothers played a prominent role in the "anti-war toy movement" against the militarization of childhood during the Vietnam War, and, together with their allies in Women Strike for Peace, feminist mothers in NOW staged similar public protests against certain types of toys and advertising that were deemed sexist. In November 1971, those two organizations, along with Parents for Responsibility in the Toy Industry, picketed Nabisco headquarters over its subsidiary Aurora's line of classic movie monster plastic models. Chanting "Sadistic Toys Make Violent Boys" and carrying signs reading "Sick Toys Make a Sick Society," the activists took issue with all eight ghoulish kits—Dracula, Frankenstein (by this time with glow-in-the-dark extras), the Phantom of the Opera, and so forth—but targeted two directly: The Pendulum and The Victim. The former, a plastic snap-together torture device, included a barely clothed woman figurine strapped below the swinging pendulum. The female Victim (sold separately) was a likewise scantily clad doll that could be eviscerated under the pendulum, locked in a hanging cage, or menaced by the other monsters in the series. Fearing a boycott against the company, Nabisco quickly discontinued the Aurora series, and with more protests—NOW also picketed the 1971 annual Toy Fair in New York—other toy manufacturers made additional concessions, including Kenner, which began showing girls in traditional male settings in its advertising.[41]

The most substantial changes appear to have played out around seasonal gift-giving. Activist mothers refused to purchase toys like Ideal's short-lived Bizzie Lizzie, a battery powered doll that vacuumed with one hand and ironed with the other. Some tolerated older toys like a walk-in cardboard playhouse, but taught preadolescents to not act out the stereotypes it had historically stood for. Giving gender-neutral toys was a strategic choice. Board games like Clue and Sorry! fostered healthy competition. Those pitched as having a "feminine flair" did not—for example, the Mystery Date Game, The Bride Game, or What Shall I Wear? in which the first player to assemble her date night outfit, complete her wedding arrangements, and purchase a wardrobe won the game. Mothers also deliberately gifted across traditional gender lines, giving a soap-making kit to boys, for instance, or a Handy Andy Tool Set to girls. Many of these choices not only encouraged mixed sex-play—"I was a tomboy, so I played cowboys and Indians with the neighborhood boys. I even received a toy rifle for Christmas one year"—but toys like Sears' Experiments in Aeronautics kit endorsed feminist values as they molded play toward what mothers wanted their daughters to be.

Children's interests were allowed to dictate toy selection and play regardless of sex appropriateness. Remembered one man born in 1958, "My parents obviously didn't feel gender was a factor and if I requested something it was okay, [but] it would be interesting to know though if my brother had requested a Barbie doll if they would have been as forthcoming." Men more so than women, appear to be interested in the finer distinctions between dolls and action figures. "I wasn't allowed to have a G.I. Joe," a Midwesterner told me. "I always thought it was a Vietnam thing. But later [I] learned that it was about boys playing with dolls! Now we get away with it by calling them action figures." "I had a 'Stony' action figure that was a last-minute gift from parents when [a relative] who had asked what to get me refused to buy a G.I. Joe because 'boys should not play with dolls,'" another man recalled, adding, "of course, I later got a G.I. Joe and Captain Action."[42]

For all the layers of meaning attributed to G.I. Joe in boyhood, that other pillar of popular toy culture in the Cold War, Barbie, played an even more powerful role in sixties girlhood. So many women hold cherished Barbie memories, often centered on a specific doll, accessory, or the status they conferred on their owners, that it is tempting to see Barbie's presence as something close to universal. And while some girls imagined a romantic compatibility between the two—"It bugged me that G.I. Joe was so much bigger than Barbie so (in my mind) they couldn't date"—Barbie's relationship with the women's movement was much more nuanced even than the Vietnam War's impact on Joe. Whereas Hasbro's original G.I. Joe succumbed to wartime ambivalence, Mattel never wavered from Barbie's commercial concept. Instead, Barbie's meaning evolved in girl's play culture as the ideal of modern womanhood changed in the 1960s, dependent on what individual girls projected onto her. This is what makes her so special, although it was also the very reason mothers never liked Barbie nearly as much as their daughters did.

While it would be far too simple to characterize Barbie as a feminist, or feminist role model, she nonetheless never invited little girls to become mommies. Thus Barbie reshaped nurturing doll play in America while fomenting a rebellion, perhaps an unconscious one, against domesticity among preadolescent girls. "My sister and I had Barbies and my brother had G.I. Joes," a woman born in 1959 explained to me. "I didn't like to play with baby dolls, they required too much maintenance—changing the diaper, feeding, etc. Barbies could go have a glamorous life without me taking care of them." Such reasoning may have led some girls to feminism later on, but at first, in the early 1960s, Barbie—whose impossibly long legs and exaggerated breasts looked neither childlike nor motherly—tapped into the rebellious teenage lifestyle of older baby boomer sisters, and little girls gravitated toward her as an ideal, "free" teenager. Only by the mid-sixties, as Helen Gurley Brown's *Cosmopolitan* magazine began offering new notions of idealized (sexualized) womanhood, did Barbie start distilling the image of a carefree, unsupervised, sexy single woman down to girls as well. "My Barbie liked boys!" a California woman reflected of this progression. "She traveled to England to date the Beatles, first Paul, who was later dumped for George. Relaxed with Martinis and bubble gum cigarettes. Adored President Kennedy even though her parents were Republicans. She wouldn't be caught dead with Richard Nixon."[43]

This is not to say that Barbie inspired all girls to reject female stereotypes. "Rather," as cultural historian Gary Cross argues, "she prompted them to associate the freedom of being an adult with carefree consumption." Being an eleven-and-one-half-inch cultural screen onto which girls could project their dreams made Barbie a legend. Being the consummate consumer made her a capitalist genius. Many girls embraced the normative gendered world of affluent consumerism the doll represented, and, through inspired daydreams of beauty, dates, and popularity, Barbie taught them about consumption with her seemingly infinite line of accessory props—which dwarfed G.I. Joe's arsenal—ranging from wardrobes to dune buggies, ski cabins, and a United Airlines "Friend Ship" airplane. To remain glamorous and cool, Barbie's environment required continual replenishing with new clothing and playset purchases—all sold separately—that Mattel updated in accord with trends in adult culture. Just like her clothes, even Barbie's crowd of friends reflected the changing times—and Mattel's desire to promote sustained parental spending—with boyfriend Ken in 1961 (updated in 1971 with more contemporary hair), best friend Midge in 1963, younger sister Skipper in 1964, Mod British cousin and friend, Francie and Stacey, respectively, in 1996 and 1968, and African American Christie that same year. In 1967, Mattel offered a trade-in promotion, allowing children to swap their used Barbies for the newer models, not unlike an adult trading in a car. For hundreds of thousands of girls, Barbie represented a future which had little to do with feminist values. "Barbie didn't even think about a career," a woman born in 1957 wrote. "She liked her clothing and Ken! And Ken just liked Barbie." Another woman born in 1957 confirmed, "I never thought of my Barbie as having a career, and yes, it was really all about the clothes."[44]

Probably an equal number of girls, however, rejected the heavy emphasis on materialism and reimagined Barbie along nascent feminist lines. "Barbie was not a fave of mine because she was totally domestic, not a career woman," a Detroit area woman born in 1958 remembered. "She was all about Ken and the clothes." In many homes, as evidenced in dozens of recollections collected for this study, Barbie played out the career aspirations of her young owners, ranging from dentist and architect to Jane Goodall working with chimpanzees, astronaut, and oceanographer. "Barbie did everything, she was superwoman just like my mom," a St. Louis woman born in 1969 recalled, "cooked, cleaned, had kids, a career, the whole ball of wax . . . And she did it extraordinarily well dressed!"[45]

A story from a Missouri woman born in 1962 speaks to Barbie's complicated feminist roles through the eyes of a sixties girl. When four years old, she saw a go-go dancer through the window of a downtown bar. "She danced on the bar and she wore a white bikini," the woman reminisced. "She looked so glamorous to me. There were flashing lights on the bar and as the lights changed, her bikini changed from white to blue to green to yellow. Could life be any better than that? This girl had a job where her clothes actually changed colors!"

Alone in her bedroom at night, the preschooler practiced her own dance moves in front of the mirror until one day, a Catholic nun at the school her older siblings attended questioned her about the future. "I remember one day," she wrote, "one of nuns asked me, 'And what do you want to be when you grow up?' 'I want to be a nun,' I said. I saw her eyes light up, and I quickly added, 'I want to be a nun or a go-go dancer!' thinking, if I can make her eyes light up by telling her I had already made one career choice, imagine how surprised she's going to be when she finds out I have a back-up plan as well! Now, like any little girl, I enjoyed making people's eyes light up just by a little intelligent conversation, so every chance I got, I told anybody who would listen [about] my not one, but TWO career choices! I was so advanced." On the eve of her birthday, she requested a white bikini, but because it was wintertime and swimsuits were out of season, she explained to her mom that a matching bra and panty set would work too. "You are going to be five years old!" came the retort. "'I know,' I said. 'I'm going to need a pair of boots, too!' Mama sighed and Daddy shook his head," the woman wrote. "That year for my birthday, I got a [Barbie] doll and life was good. Of course, I pretended that half the time she was a nun and half the time she was a go-go dancer . . . "[46]

CHAPTER TEN

Conclusions

We were the first mutant flower to grow out of the '60s soil after all.
New Jersey man born in 1956

On Christmas morning 1968, astronaut Jim Lovell confirmed Apollo 8's departure from lunar orbit by signing off with the bombshell revelation, "Roger, please be informed there is a Santa Claus." American children were already breathless, as the night before, on Christmas Eve, Lovell, Frank Borman, and Bill Anders—the first humans to orbit the moon—had enthralled a prime-time television audience—and a global audience of perhaps one billion—with incredible moon and "Earthrise" footage before sending them off to bed by taking turns reading from the Book of Genesis. Apollo 8 was part of the third stage of America's human space flight program, following NASA's Projects Mercury and Gemini. Although John Kennedy did not live to see Gemini, those ten manned flights between 1965 and 1966 had introduced spacewalking and perfected the spacecraft reentry procedures necessary for Apollo. After a deadly tragedy aboard Apollo 1 in early 1967, NASA launched ten more Apollo missions, finally completing Kennedy's odyssey on Sunday, July 20, 1969, just five months before the decade's end.

On that day, as Michael Collins orbited in the command module, Apollo 11 astronauts Neil Armstrong and Edwin "Buzz" Aldrin walked on the moon. Back on Earth, the country paused. You could hear a pin drop from a mile away, with entire neighborhoods falling silent. Inside their homes, families convened that evening, absorbed in the majesty of the grainy televised pictures. *"That's one small step for a man,"* Armstrong triumphantly declared from the ladder, *"one giant leap for mankind." Good morning starshine, the earth says hello,* replied the summer's hit song by Oliver. "My mother made all of us kids stay

up and watch," a Pennsylvania woman who was nine years old that year remembered, "because she said, 'You will never forget what you see tonight.
You will remember this till the day you die.' And she was right."[1] Over the
next three years, ending in December 1972, five other Apollo missions landed
on the moon, prompting countless sleepless nights for children wondering
what the twelve astronauts who explored up there might be doing. To help
them imagine, space toys in all shapes and sizes made a glorious comeback,
ranging from Ideal's S.T.A.R. (Space Travel And Reconnaissance) Team line
to G.I. Joe's Official Space Capsule and Authentic Space Suit, which included
a 45 rpm recording of an orbital flight, but not a Joe.

For some preadolescents, Apollo marked the end of the sixties, while others
thought the Vietnam War's conclusion brought the era to a close for them.
Some historians think the Altamont concert or Manson murders, perhaps Watergate, make for a handier ending. In a study of childhood, however, the
refashioning of American family life under way by the early 1970s, which
substantively disrupted children's environments and experiences, is probably
more accurate. "In the mid-1970s several trends converged to mark the start
of a new phase in childhood's history," historian Steven Mintz observes, as the
traditional, child-centered family once so seemingly permanent was being
replaced with something that more closely resembled the country's current
structure and composition. Some of the historical changes were rooted in the
demographic and economic developments we examined from the 1960s, such
as the significant increases in divorce, single-parent households, mothers in
the workforce, and two-wage-earner families, along with the declining birth-
rates of the baby bust. With the American standard of living having peaked in
1973, declining economic conditions solidified these factors, virtually guaran-
teeing that Americans could no longer afford the typical postwar home life.[2]

Other shifts were attitudinal and ideological, closely identified with the
"Me" Decade. In a country racked by cultural malaise—a crisis of confidence—
following the military defeat in Vietnam, Watergate's scandalous constitutional challenge, an emasculating oil embargo, and maddening stagflation
(double-digit unemployment coupled with double-digit inflation), economically vulnerable Americans in the 1970s faced these new limitations on the
American Dream by turning inward toward more self-oriented approaches to
life. This narcissism translated to more or less adult-centered families compared
to the child-centered nature of Spock's fifties and sixties. Put another way, by
the seventies, the humanistic demand for self-actualization—making decisions
based on what makes you happy—meant parenthood was becoming a lifestyle

choice as opposed to a way of life. For the first time since before the Victorians, the notion of children being more important—or at least as important—as parents ebbed, moving children from the "very center of life to somewhere in its flow," according to social psychologist Elizabeth Douvan. Tendencies such as these appear, in turn, to have disrupted parental conceptions about how best to train their children to pursue an American Dream, which increasingly, as parents saw it, was a target moving further away. But as mounting social anxiety concerning childhood safety—over abduction, molestation, poisoned Halloween candy—bred personal anxieties about children, many parents overcorrected out of fear they had inadequate oversight (there were fewer stay-at-home mothers in the neighborhood during the day). Childhood thus in many ways became overprotected and regimented. Parents circumscribed the geography of childhood, displacing unstructured and outdoor play with adult-organized activities. Consequently, since the 1970s, it can be said that parents have struggled to follow a consistent philosophy, repeatedly responding with confused and contradictory approaches to child-rearing.[3]

While examining the imprints of the historical sixties on the lived experience of children over the course of this study, I have also tried to account for any relative causal effects on various aspects of adult life—how individual childhood perspectives on the 1960s may have influenced later outlooks, values, or careers. Toward this end, I asked respondents to tell me, in the hundreds of self-selected oral histories I collected, "How much, if at all, do you think growing up in the sixties influences how you make sense of contemporary events, politics, wars, and/or life experiences?" I also asked, "Do you ever use your childhood in the 1960s as a standard or lesson in rearing your own children? Put another way, how much, if any, of your sixties experience do you pass on to your children?" From the responses of twenty-first century adults, several common themes came clearly into focus. Once again, one must be careful not to make unsubstantiated generalizations about the links between childhood events and the attitudes and political behaviors of a broad range of people, especially from such a limited sample size. Many internal and external variables must be accounted for along the way. And in reviewing one's life, memory can be a tricky thing, as we constantly and selectively construct meanings and make revisions to past experiences. But that being said, it is safe to say that countless numbers of children born from approximately 1956 to 1970 are convinced that the Vietnam era is a central and enduring organizing feature in their life course. "For the first time," a Florida woman born in 1956 said of reading about my project, "I realized how important that era was, not only to history and the country, but to me personally and how it had impacted my life." "The Sixties," a woman born in 1959 Tennessee underscored, "were really THE defining decade of my life."[4]

Most of the more pronounced examples of how the sixties manifested in children as concrete trajectory changes which were later expressed in the adult years have already been traced. There are, however, also a number of common folk interpretations of the sixties that serve as explanations for adult behaviors to be considered as well. Although people who grew up in the Vietnam era may have a hard time articulating the linkage between historical forces and adult conduct, it is obvious they make meaning of their childhood by organizing value priorities from their memories. Similar to children from other periods of significant social change, for instance the Great Depression or World War II, they use the values recognized from their childhood memories as standards for assessing life experiences. While the adult children of the Depression remained preoccupied with job security and those coming of age in the Second World War kept intensely patriotic feelings of national unity and pride, the children in this study still preference their interpretations of the sixties—those first layers of the developmental onion—when looking at the contemporary world. This is especially true when they see readily applicable circumstances such as the Middle Eastern wars and the election of the country's first African American president. "I suppose my experience of events from that time is essentially nostalgic at this point," a Kentucky woman born in 1963 reflected, "but they do inform my personal worldview in the sense that I can see and *know* that things have changed. I know that I'm hardwired enough from my childhood and my received experience of my parents' and grandparents' lives not to let events, ideas and beliefs go down the Orwellian memory hole as quickly as they seem to today.[5]

"Although it's nostalgic and nice to think of the '60s as the burgeoning of a more enlightened time, which it certainly was in some respects," she continued, "I also think of it as the beginning of our cultural solipsism." Certainly, many like her ground their conservative views in the perceived decline of American in the Vietnam era. "Unlike a number of people who have [contacted you]," an Arkansas woman born in 1957 told me, "I am not a political or social liberal. Contrary to those who embraced the revolution that was the '60s, I see it as dark days in American history. Much of the '60s to my child mind was scarred by the anger that was demonstrated in the protests, the assassinations, the song lyrics, the rebellion, and the fear. I was taught as a child, taught my own children, and still believe today that anger is mostly wasted energy that benefits few. Anger is generally emoted when a person feels inconvenienced, tread upon, or lacking in what he/she believes is deserved. What a waste of time, energy, and life. Even as a child, I recognized the search that people were on during that time . . . I hope that your research turns up a number of people like me who don't believe the '60s were a positive impact on our culture. Rather, I believe it was a downturn in our society's morals/ mores."[6]

Another Arkansas woman, born in 1960, echoed these sentiments. "I have thought a good deal about how growing up in the sixties affected me," she wrote, "and have often thought that the popular conception of the sixties as a time of peace and love does not fit with my childhood perceptions of the world as a place where senseless violence, unjustified war, and political corruption occurred. My own family and neighborhood, in contrast with the nightly news, were safe, peaceful, warm environments, and I think that I grew up with that sense of contrast: the world as potentially chaotic and dangerous, the home and family was secure. I think in some ways I am a more cautious and guarded person 'out in the world' but very at ease with family and friends as a result. I've made conscious efforts to be more open in traveling abroad and embracing new situations, but it doesn't come naturally to me."[7]

"Without question, growing up in the 1960s had a huge impact on my perception of the world and my political philosophy," a self-identified conservative Indiana man emphasized. "From the time I was a child, I have seen the counterculture, and the so-called liberals and progressives populating this country, as my political enemies. Frankly, I have seen them as enemies of the American way of life, enemies of the United States Constitution, and enemies of freedom. On one hand, having been born in 1963, my childhood societal observations were made during the very turbulent second half of the 1960s . . . On the other, my parents and my extended family, excellent role models, adherents to traditional Christian values, patriots all, provided me with an extremely happy and disciplined childhood. Juxtaposing my earliest societal observations against the reality of my childhood probably led me to see politics in starkly black and white terms . . . I believe that having been born in the early 1960s positioned my childhood against a timeline that led to a very polarized view of the American political landscape. I suspect my peers, born five years earlier or five years later, are more prone to believe they see gray where I see a border, clearly and correctly defined, black on one side, white on the other."[8]

Nevertheless, even among conservatives there is usually less certainty when it comes to projecting American military power. In stark contrast to the feelings of national invincibility and unwavering faith in American war efforts carried forward by the children of World War II, sixties children tend to see war as "something not be entered into lightly." "I am conservative, very pro-military," explained the son of a Vietnam veteran born in 1959 and raised in California and Florida, "and do not believe that our military forces should be used carelessly or to solve every conflict on this planet. I believe George Washington was correct when he said that we should remain unencumbered by foreign entanglements."[9]

Others from various points along the political spectrum also expressed their ambivalence over what can be expected from military adventurism. "I definitely think that seeing the events in Vietnam on TV had an effect on me," a Georgia woman born in 1960 pointed out. "I am still pretty liberal and am against the war in Iraq now. Just feel like we are there for the wrong reasons." "I think growing up in the '60s made me skeptical of many things," a Missourian born in 1958 wrote. "I am constantly comparing current events like the Iraq war and the Occupy [Wall Street] movement to what went on in the '60s. I don't like politics and am constantly dissatisfied with the government. All of this is because of my childhood, I'm sure." Speaking for many, a woman whose father had done two tours in Vietnam before she turned ten years old worries over the futility of war. "I look at the current war(s) from the perception of how Vietnam touched my family," she wrote me. "Not the politics, but the personal toll it takes on Americans. I notice how the flags that flew so proudly after 9/11 are gone and how people have moved on to the latest and greatest news item."[10]

The preponderance of those contributing to this study, however, frequently highlighted a shared sense of what one might call an ethic of care, or perhaps the values of Sesame Street. Even the Arkansas woman born in 1957 who thought the sixties were "dark days" concluded by writing, "I do think that, having lived through that era, I am stronger in my moral beliefs and even more adamant that the lives we lead should be positive impacts on others." From very diverse backgrounds, such basic moral reasoning seems to be informed by compassion and a thoughtful tolerance for differences. "I was born in 1958 in Alabama, and was profoundly affected by the '60s, and my thoughts, attitudes, the way I think and act are still deeply affected by that time period," one man wrote me. "Environmentalism, equality of all, Peace and Love are still the core of me." "The '60s represented a time of great special social change," a woman born in Missouri in 1964 echoed. "I try to look at all people and to teach my children to see them as people, male and female, not color, religion, etc. It is natural to gravitate towards the familiar, but [we should] try not to discriminate against those who are different than ourselves. Do not be wasteful, and leave things as you found them. Build up, never tear down." Or, as an Illinois woman passed on to her children, the sixties were about the importance of "the ethics of love, quiet time, imagination, slowing down to think, [and] being there for each other . . . "[11]

"How has growing up in the Sixties made me who I am?" an Alabama woman reflected. "I think that message of 'Peace and Love' got to me. I'm very tolerant, and a firm believer in people 'doing their own thing.' (I really wanted to be a hippie, but I was 11 years old for most of 1967.) I firmly believe in justice, openness and honesty. When Ronald Reagan started talking about the old America he wanted to bring back, I didn't believe there was one. The time I grew into was turbulent, unsteady, with values from the future. I think that people who grew up in the Fifties and earlier may have believed that there was a 'regular' America, frozen in time, with values from the past. These are the people who are more likely to be afraid of change, afraid of Communists under the bed, afraid of people who are different from them. I would hope that the children of the Sixties, who grew up with assassinations, with a series of lies from the government about war, and with the hope of hard-won freedom for all, would be a generation who are tolerant of each other, who respect the past but can live in the moment, and who 'won't be fooled again.'"[12]

Some think that although "far-out ideas do not necessarily work," open-mindedness and flexibility are key. "I think, looking back on that period of time," a Wisconsin woman born in 1960 wrote, "I see the hippies and war protesters as very energetic and passionate young adults. However, in the midst of their passion and energy they may have lacked maturity and wisdom. I would encourage my children not to get so caught up in the excitement of a cause, but to seek out the counsel of someone that has experienced something similar in their lifetime. Too, always remember, with age comes wisdom." "I suspect it influenced me quite a bit," an Arkansas man born in 1961 responded when asked about the sixties influence. "I don't conform to the norm, in fact I am rebellious when it comes to my attitude concerning what other people think about me. I'm me, I am formed by my past, if you don't like me, oh well. I think if I had been ten years older, I would have been the hippie, rebellious toward society. I teach my children to be themselves. Not to conform to someone's idea of how you should live. Be respectful and polite, but at the same time aware of others' underlying intentions." "I think my childhood experiences led to my lifelong fascination with politics," said another man, a Floridian born in 1958, "and an attraction to a profession [newspaper reporter] that would tolerate a degree of questioning authority far beyond what most careers offer. I also think I have gravitated toward career choices that offered a high degree of social consciousness."[13]

As the first children to be socialized into the new realities of racial and gender inclusiveness, they likewise understand themselves to be more willing to embrace social changes. "These events, along with the events I witnessed, affected the way I raised my children," an Illinois man born in 1960 wrote. "I think that my wife and I took all of these events of the '60s and early '70s into consideration and raised our family in a more open and relaxed atmosphere. Our children were always asking questions about the era, as well as current events, and we were able to answer their questions honestly, compared to our parents, [who,] because things were happening so fast, didn't really understand, but just tried to ignore or shield us from everything."[14]

"How has my childhood affected me? I think it made me less fearful of change," a California woman born in 1959 explained. "I grew up with change, between my father's death (and in 1969, my mother's death) and the constant flux of society at that time. I morph and adapt to new things very fluidly. I don't expect things to stay as they are forever. Unlike a lot of people both older and much younger than me, I don't think I had an extended period of childhood 'innocence.' I know that children can die, people get maimed and killed, etc., and it's not because God is displeased with them or they did anything wrong. Bad things do happen to good people, as the adage goes. Again, these early experiences have helped me get over hurdles in my own life. I've always remembered how my mother's simple act of giving some roses to [a] lonely soldier [in a VA hospital] made such a difference to him; now, when I have the opportunity to do some small kindness for someone, I do it gladly. Who knows the impact it will have on that person."[15]

It is true that many harbor vague regrets of having missed out on the more exhilarating aspects of the sixties because of their age. "I love and hate being a child of the sixties," a New Hampshire man born in 1959 mused. "The early boomers, they seemed to have it all—great music, excitement, great sex, hopes/dreams—and gave me a lot to look forward to. But when I was ready to participate and enjoy 'the sixties,' everyone had run out of steam. I was still fired up by the time their passion had turned to apathy." Yet, he, like a number of others, understands this missed opportunity to be a virtue. Their sixties influences are taken to be somehow more pure. Their optimism was spared from the polarization and burnout which tended to disillusion older socially conscious people. "I am now the vice chair of the Dover [New Hampshire] Democrats," the man stressed, "but can't believe that the older baby boomers still say they love the '60s, but some now vote for the GOP. I can't believe how cynical and calculating and hypocritical some boomers are. They've sold out their ideals."[16]

"I was born in 1957 so I am truly a child of the sixties," a West Virginia woman wrote me, "and I do believe what I witnessed had an impact on the adult I have become. I wanted to be older so I could protest the war. So although I was too young to take an active part, my belief system was formed during those years because of what I witnessed. I didn't grow up to be an activist, just someone who hopes to quietly present my way of thinking by how I live. My daughter describes me as gentle. Perhaps that gentleness is a result of growing up amidst the turbulence of the '60s and '70s—both in my home and in the world around me. I believe seeing the events and aftermath of the Vietnam War made me a pacifist, but even more supportive of our troops. Seeing how the soldiers were treated on their return to the U.S. was disgraceful. I believe growing up amidst the civil rights movement made me a more compassionate adult. I feel ashamed for the way Americans treated each other."[17]

"I feel I had great front row seats to something BIG!," a Texas woman born in 1959 reflected. "But I also love that I was a child, rather than at college then," because her hopefulness remained unsullied. And maybe, when it comes to the cultural legacy of the sixties, what distinguishes this cohort is optimistically staying faithful to what they perceive to be the ideals and values they were introduced to in childhood. "I think younger people, born later in the '60s," a Connecticut man born in 1960 wrote, "were more scared than inspired. Me? I still want to make the world a better place and 'teach the world to sing in perfect harmony' on a hillside." "My upbringing during the '60s influences my life every day," a woman born in 1960 in Pennsylvania reinforced. "History tends to repeat itself, and we need to remember what worked and what didn't. There will always be a cause, enemy, issue or problem that seems to have our attention for the moment and someone who believes they have the easy answer. They don't. But we do. We know the right answer, it's the harder right, than the easier wrong. Too many times we just don't want to put forth the effort." "Today, so much needs to be done to bring justice to our hurting world," a Vermont woman born in 1958 said. "I believe that God will give us the grace and strength to 'not grow weary in well-doing.'(Gal. 6:9) I pray that in the spirit of Robert Kennedy, we can still 'dream things that never were and say, why not?'"[18]

NOTES

Chapter One Introduction

1. Steven Mintz, "The Changing Face of Children's Culture," in *Reinventing Childhood after World War II*, ed. Paula Fass and Michael Grossberg, 49.

2. Peter Yarrow and Lenny Lipton, "Puff (The Magic Dragon)," recording, Sterling, 1962.

3. Jacquelyn Dowd Hall, "Disorderly Women: Gender and Labor Militancy in the Appalachian South," in *History of Women in the United States: Historical Articles on Women's Lives and Activities*, ed. Nancy F. Cott.

4. William M. Tuttle, *"Daddy's Gone to War": The Second World War in the Lives of America's Children*, 236, 242; Landon Y. Jones, *Great Expectations: America and the Baby Boom Generation*, 7, 10, 39.

5. Lisa Zhito, email message to author, January 12, 2010.

6. Arthur Marwick, in *Windows on the Sixties: Exploring Key Texts of Media and Culture*, ed. Anthony Aldgate, James Chapman, and Arthur Marwick, 184; Glen H. Elder, John Modell, Ross D. Parke, eds., *Children in Time and Place: Developmental and Historical Insights*, 13, 19, 200–202; Zhito, email message to author, January 12, 2010.

7. Marjorie Randon Hershey and David B. Hill, "Watergate and Preadults' Attitudes toward the President," 723; Fred I. Greenstein, *Children and Politics*, 78, 79, 80; David Easton and Robert D. Hess, "The Child's Political World," 236, 243; Tuttle, *"Daddy's Gone to War,"* 236; Elder, Modell, and Parke, *Children in Time and Place*, 4, 11, 14, 17, 31; Henry Jenkins, ed., *The Children's Culture Reader*, 4.

8. Diane McAlpin, email message to author, January 17, 2010; Bonnie Daws Kourvelas, email message to author, January 23, 2010.

9. Elder, Modell, and Parke, *Children in Time and Place*, 45, 242, 249; Jones, *Great Expectations*, 7, 104, 164; Gary S. Cross, *The Cute and the Cool: Wondrous Innocence and Modern American Children's Culture*, 151; Richard Stengal, "Lost in Time: Too Young for the '60s, Too Old for the '80s," 17.

10. Jones, *Great Expectations*, 7; Mintz, "Changing Face of Children's Culture," 40, 41; Denise Sedlar Dempster, email message to author, January 17, 2010.

11. Elder, Modell, and Parke, *Children in Time and Place*, 13; Elaine Tyler May, *Homeward Bound: American Families in the Cold War Era*, 52, 53, 54; Glen H. Elder, *Children of the Great Depression: Social Change in Life Experience*, 239.

12. Steven Mintz, *Huck's Raft: A History of American Childhood*, 279; Charles E. Strickland and Andrew M. Ambrose, "The Baby Boom, Prosperity, and the Changing Worlds of Children, 1945-1963," in *American Childhood: A Research Guide and Historical Handbook*, ed. Joseph N. Hawes and N. Ray Hiner, 540; Nancy Pottishman Weiss, "Mother, the Invention of Necessity: Dr. Benjamin Spock's *Baby and Child Care*," in *Growing Up in America: Children in Historical Perspective*, ed. N. Ray Hiner and Joseph Hawes, 287.

13. Strickland and Ambrose, "Baby Boom," 538, 540, 541; William Graebner, "The Unstable World of Benjamin Spock: Social Engineering in a Democratic Culture, 1917-1950," 612-29; Mintz, *Huck's Raft*, 279, 282; Jones, *Great Expectations*, 54; Weiss, "Mother," 285, 291.

14. Kenneth Jackson, *The Crabgrass Frontier: The Suburbanization of the United States*, 238, 240, 243, 284; Jones, *Great Expectations*, 43; May, *Homeward Bound*, 104, 162.

15. Jenkins, *Children's Culture Reader*, 21; Strickland and Ambrose, "The Baby Boom," 543; Margaret Mead, "A New Kind of Discipline," 50; Thomas Hine, *Populuxe: The Look and Life of America in the 50's and 60's*, 20, 55.

16. Jones, *Great Expectations*, 47, 139; Mintz, *Huck's Raft*, 298; Erik Barnouw, *Tube of Plenty: The Evolution of American Television, 2nd Revised Edition*; Gerald S. Lesser, *Children and Television: Lessons from Sesame Street*, 80.

17. Elder, Modell, and Parke, *Children in Time and Place*, 196; Richard Louv, *Last Child in the Woods: Saving Our Children from Nature-Deficit Disorder*, 7, 8, 9, 166, 171; Mintz, "Changing Face of Children's Culture," 40, 41, 43.

18. Louv, *Last Child*, 166; Mintz, "Changing Face of Children's Culture," 40; Hal Lifson, *1966! A Personal View of the Coolest Year in Pop Culture History*, 172.

19. Jones, *Great Expectations*, 249; Mintz, "Changing Face of Children's Culture," 43, 44, 45.

Chapter Two John F. Kennedy

1. Letter, Anne Bacqui to the president, January 19, 1961, White House Overflow Files (WHOF), box 83, John F. Kennedy Library (JFKL).

2. Fred I. Greenstein, "The Benevolent Leader Revisited: Children's Images of Political Leaders in Three Democracies," 1371; David Easton and Robert D. Hess, "The Child's Political World," 240.

3. Lawrence Kohlberg, *Philosophy of Moral Development*; Thomas Lickona, *Raising Good Children: From Birth through the Teenage Years*; Marjorie Randon Hershey and David B. Hill, "Watergate and Preadults' Attitudes toward the President," 723; Fred I. Greenstein, *Children and Politics*, 78, 79, 80; Easton and Hess, "Child's Political World," 236, 243; William M. Tuttle, *"Daddy's Gone to War": The Second World War in the Lives of America's Children*; Glen H. Elder, John Modell, Ross D. Parke, eds., *Children in Time and Place: Developmental and Historical Insights*.

4. Greenstein, *Children and Politics*, 46; Fred I. Greenstein, "The Benevolent Leader: Children's Images of Political Authority," 941; Fred I. Greenstein, "The Best-Known American," 15.

5. J. Fred MacDonald, "John F. Kennedy and Television," *Television and the Red Menace: The Video Road to Vietnam*, accessed February 7, 2014, www.jfredmacdonald.com/trm/ivjfk.htm.

6. Steven D. Stark, *Glued to the Set: The 60 Television Shows and Events That Made Us Who We Are Today*, 125.

7. Landon Y. Jones, *Great Expectations: America and the Baby Boom Generation*, 54.

8. Denise Sedlar Dempster, email message to author, January 17, 2010; Tim Stanton, email message to author, January 13, 2010; Easton and Hess, "Child's Political World," 235, 236; David Easton and Jack Dennis, *Children in the Political System: Origins of Political Legitimacy*, 55.

9. Letters, pupils of Grades 2–8, Hyde Park School, to the president, May 20, 1963, Oversized Attachment Files, Box 1116, White House Central Subject Files (WHCF); letter, Mrs. John Dzuroff to the president, June 21, 1961, "D" folder, WHCSF, box 544; letter, Magdalene Perry to the president, April 4, 1961, "B" folder, WHCSF, box 544, JFKL.

10. Greenstein, "Benevolent Leader," 941; Greenstein, "Best-Known American," 16; Greenstein, *Children and Politics*, 45; Robert D. Hess and David Easton, "The Child's Political World," 240, 242; Hess and Easton, "Child's Changing Image," 633, 639, 640, 643.

11. Karen Cooley, email message to author, June 11, 2010; letter, Linda Ciampi to the president, September 11, 1961, "C" folder, WHCSF, box 544, JFKL.

12. Letters, pupils of Grades 2–8, Hyde Park School, to the president, May 20, 1963, Oversized Attachment Files, Box 1116, WHCF, JFKL.

13. Hess and Easton, "Child's Changing Image," 635, 640; Easton and Hess, "Child's Political World," 241.

14. Letter, Joan Rittenbaum to the president, March 5, 1961, WHOF, box 84, JFKL.

15. Letter, Mary Alice McKenzie to the president, May 5, 1961, WHOF, box 83; letter, Judith Ann Tosi to the president, June 14, 1961, WHOF, box 91, JFKL.

16. Easton and Hess, "Child's Political World", 236, 238, 239.

17. Letter, Susan Gordon to the president, March 23, 1961, "G" folder, WHCSF, box 544; letter, Robert McGuiness to Pierre Salinger, February 6, 1961, "ME2" folder, WHCSF, box 544, JFKL; Elder, Modell, and Parke, *Children in Time and Place*, 19.

18. Letter, Mrs. Leonard Loritz to the president, September 20, 1961, "L" folder, WHCSF, box 545; letter, Robert G. Nelson to the president, February 5, 1961, "H" folder, WHCSF, box 544; letter, Julia Healy to the president, January 26, 1961, "H" folder, WHCSF, box 544, JFKL; Tuttle, *"Daddy's Gone to War,"* 115.

19. Letter, Walter Rabel to the president, January 29, 1961, "B" folder, WHCSF, box 544; letter, Mrs. Vernon Copp to the president, February 1, 1961, "C" folder, WHCSF, box 544, JFKL.

20. Letter, Elizabeth Hill Abernathy to the president, January 15, 1962, "H" folder, WHCSF, box 544, JFKL.

21. Marian Hutchings, email message to author, January 22, 2010.

22. Letter, Esther Hayes to the president, February 3, 1961, WHOF, box 83, JFKL.

23. Letter, Kathleen Lentz to the president, January 23, 1961, WHOF, box 83, JFKL.

24. Letter, Lucia Luca to the president, February 14, 1961, WHOF, box 83, JFKL.

25. Letter, Janet Fare to the president, January 25, 1961, WHOF, box 86, JFKL.

26. Letter, Edythe Barlon to the president, January 26, 1961, WHOF, box 84; letter, Peggy Pierce to the president, February 21, 1963, Oversized Attachment Files, Box 1099, WHCF; letter, Karen Nielson to the president, January 23, 1961, WHOF, box 89, JFKL.

27. Letter, Miss Geertsen's 5th grade class to the president, June 5, 1961, WHOF, box 91; letter, Emeline Urban to the president, February 1, 1961, WHOF, box 93; letter, Sandra Teller to the president, February 1, 1961, WHOF, box 93; letter, Judy Epstein to the president, February 1, 1961, WHOF, box 93; Lee C. Lee, *Personality Development in Childhood*, 132–33.

28. Letter, Laury Phillips to the president, January 20, 1961, WHOF, box 84, JFKL.

29. Tom Landrum, email message to author, January 26, 2010; Fred I. Greenstein, "More on Children's Images of the President," 650, 651; David Easton and Jack Dennis, "The Child's Image of Government," 47.

30. Letter, Tim Weinland to the president, January 31, 1961, "W" folder, WHCSF, box 545; letter, Leslie Forbes to the president, November 6, 1962, Oversized Attachment Files, Box 1076, WHCF; letter, Linda Church to the president, February 9, 1961, WHOF, box 96, JFKL; Rob Bellamy, email message to author, February 4, 2010; Hess and Easton, "Child's Changing Image," 644; Easton and Hess, "Child's Political World", 236; Easton and Dennis, "Child's Image of Government," 53.

31. Ted Sorensen, *Kennedy: The Classic Biography*, 358; Arthur Schlesinger, Jr., *A Thousand Days: John F. Kennedy in the White House*, 662.

32. Letter, Maria Mykolenko to the president, April 1961, WHOF, box 96, JFKL.

33. Ada Barnett Stough, "If Children Could Talk to the New President and the New Congress," 3.

34. Robert Dallek, *An Unfinished Life: John F. Kennedy, 1917–1963*, 495, 585; Schlesinger, *Thousand Days*, 662; "Special Message to the Congress on Education, February 20, 1961," accessed February 20, 2014, http://www.jfklink.com/speeches/jfk/publicpapers/1961/jfk46_61.html.

35. "The Federal Government Takes on Physical Fitness," accessed February 21, 2014, http://www.jfklibrary.org/JFK/JFK-in-History/Physical-Fitness.aspx.

36. Letters, 5th grade class to the president, May 25, 1961, Oversized Attachment Files, Box 920, WHCF, JFKL.

37. Letter, the Jetsons to the president, October 14, 1963, "J" folder, WHCSF, box 544, JFKL; Nicholas Schneider and Nathalie Rockhill, eds., *John F. Kennedy Talks to Young People*, 33.

38. Letter, Margaret Ketchum to the president, February 21, 1963, Oversized Attachment Files, Box 1099, WHCF, JFKL.

39. Letter, Marilyn Whitfield to the president, May 24, 1962, "W" folder, WHCSF, box 335, JFKL.

40. "JFK and People with Intellectual Disabilities," accessed February 27, 2014, http: //www.jfklibrary.org/JFK/JFK-in-History/JFK-and-People-with-Intellectual-Disabilities.aspx; "A New Day for the Mentally Retarded," 64.

41. "New Day for the Mentally Retarded," 62, 64; Dallek, Unfinished Life, 490, 491.

42. Maternal and Child Health and Mental Retardation Planning Amendment to the Social Security Act, Statutes at Large, vol. 77, 273 (1963).

43. Martha M. Eliot, "Let's Get Behind the Bold New Program to Combat Mental Retardation in Children," 38.

44. Steve Richardet, email message to author, February 27, 2014.

45. Howard A. Rusk, "A Brighter Future for Disabled Children," 142–45.

46. "The Physically Handicapped in the Regular Classroom," 13–16; "A New Day for the Mentally Retarded," 62, 64; letter, Beth Kindt to the president, February 21, 1963, Oversized Attachment Files, Box 1099, WHCF; letter, Mrs. Ernest Cates to the president, April 2, 1961, "C" folder, WHCSF, box 544; letter, Louis Traas to the president, November 7, 1961, "ME2" folder, WHCSF, box 544, JFKL; Katherine Oettinger, "Opening Doors for the Retarded Child," 68–69.

47. Steve Richardet, email message to author, February 27, 2014.

Chapter Three Space Rockets and Cuban Missiles

1. Tom Landrum, email message to author, January 26, 2010.

2. Ted Sorensen, Kennedy: The Classic Biography, 524, 525, 528; Robert Dallek, An Unfinished Life: John F. Kennedy, 1917–1963, 393; Walter McDougall, The Heavens and the Earth: A Political History of the Space Age.

3. Steve Richardet, interviewed by the American Century Oral History Project, Southeast Missouri State University, November 25, 2013.

4. Steven D. Stark, Glued to the Set: The 60 Television Shows and Events That Made Us Who We Are Today, 139, 140.

5. Tom Landrum, email message to author, January 26, 2010.

6. Erik Barnouw, Tube of Plenty: The Evolution of American Television, 2nd Revised Edition, 308.

7. Dallek, Unfinished Life, 654; Sorenson, Kennedy, 528.

8. Bill Adler, ed., Kids' Letters to President Kennedy, 150; letter, Marion Grabowicz to the president, January 26, 1960 [sic], White House Overflow Files (WHOF), box 89, JFKL.

9. Letter, Mrs. Mike Del Clow to the president, February 28, 1963, "C" folder, White House Central Subject Files (WHCSF), box 544; letter, Gordon Craigo to the president, January 1962, "Com-CZ" folder, WHCSF, box 268, JFKL.

10. Letter, Gorge Mayfield to the president, April 14, 1961, WHOF, box 94; letter, Bill Fromm to the president, February 7, 1962, Oversized Attachment Files, Box 1004, WHCF, JFKL.

11. Steve Richardet, interviewed by the American Century Oral History Project; Rob Bellamy, email message to author, February 4, 2010; Budd Carl Pounds, email message to author, January 14, 2010.

12. Letter and book, Pupils of the 2nd and 3rd grades of Arden School to the president, April 1962, Oversized Attachment Files, Box 1007, WHCF, JFKL.

13. Steve Richardet, interviewed by the American Century Oral History Project.

14. Steven Mintz, "The Changing Face of Children's Culture," in *Reinventing Childhood after World War II*, ed. Paula Fass and Michael Grossberg, 42; Gary S. Cross, *Kids' Stuff: Toys and the Changing World of American Childhood*, v, 153–55, 164, 166, 168; Bill Bruegman, *Toys of the Sixties: A Pictorial Guide*, 111; Thomas Hine, *Populuxe: The Look and Life of America in the 50's and 60's*, 38, 129–31; Barnouw, *Tube of Plenty*, 348, 375.

15. Steve Richardet, interviewed by the American Century Oral History Project; Rob Bellamy, email message to author, February 4, 2010.

16. Dallek, *Unfinished Life*, 392; Sorenson, *Kennedy*, 526–28.

17. "Address at Rice University, Houston," accessed March 27, 2014, http://www.jfk library.org/Asset-Viewer/Archives/JFKPOF-040-001.aspx; Sorenson, *Kennedy*, 528.

18. Letter, Mark Torres to the president, April 14, 1963, WHOF, box 94, JFKL.

19. Cindy M. Sigmon, email message to author, January 26, 2010.

20. Robin Jones, email message to author, January 11, 2010.

21. Linda Godwin, interviewed by the author, Cape Girardeau, MO, May 12, 2014; "Linda Godwin," accessed April 11, 2014, http://columbia-mo.aauw.net/notablewomen /womenfm/linda-godwin/.

22. "Brian Duffy," NASA Oral History Collection, accessed April 11, 2014, http: //www.jsc.nasa.gov/history/oral_histories/DuffyB/DuffyB_6-21-04.htm.

23. "William F. Readdy," NASA Oral History Collection, accessed April 11, 2014, http://www.jsc.nasa.gov/history/oral_histories/ReaddyWF/ReaddyWF_3-20-12.htm.

24. "David A. Wolfe," NASA Oral History Collection, accessed April 11, 2014, http: //history.nasa.gov/SP-4225/oral-histories/wolf.pdf.

25. Steven Craig, email message to author, January 18, 2010.

26. Paul Boyer, *By the Bomb's Early Light: American Thought and Culture at the Dawn of the Atomic Age*.

27. Letters, children of Public School 173 (Flushing, NY) to the president, January 23, 1962, Oversized Attachment Files, Box 1004, WHCF; letter, Gregory Henderson to the president, January 30, 1962, Oversized Attachment Files, Box 1004, WHCF, JFKL.

28. "Atom . . . Bomb . . . Children," 23; Sibylle Escalona, "Children and the Threat of Nuclear War," in *Behavioral Science and Human Survival*, ed. Milton Schwebel, 6, 202; letter, Francis J. McGhee to the president, September 27, 1961, Oversized Attachment Files, Box 974, WHCF; letter, Dale Brooks to the president, February 4, 1962, Oversized Attachment Files, Box 1004, WHCF; letter, Ed Huber to the president, February 7, 1962, Oversized Attachment Files, Box 1004, WHCF; letter, Margot Prussia to the president, February 15, 1962, Oversized Attachment Files, Box 1004, WHCF, JFKL.

29. Letter, Miss Bell's Sixth Grade to the president, October 25, 1962, Oversized Attachment Files, Box 1076, WHCF, JFKL; Sibylle Escalona, *Children and the Threat of Nuclear War*, 6, 9; Escalona, "Children and the Threat of Nuclear War," 217; Benjamin Spock, "Learning to Live in a Troubled World," 26; Denise Sedlar Dempster, email message to author, January 17, 2010.

30. Escalona, *Children and the Threat of Nuclear War*, 6.

31. Dee Ulderich, email message to author, February 6, 2009.

32. Barnouw, *Tube of Plenty*, 367, 373.

33. Escalona, *Children and the Threat of Nuclear War*, 4, 6, 9, 13, 17; "Atom . . . Bomb . . . Children," 23, 24; Judith Viorst, "Nuclear Threat Harms Children," 106.

34. "Olathe Naval Air Station: Administrative History," 1996, National Archives-Central Plains Division, Kansas City, MO.

35. Escalona, "Children and the Threat of Nuclear War," 217; Escalona, *Children and the Threat of Nuclear War*, 10, 11.

36. Escalona, "Children and the Threat of Nuclear War," 217; Escalona, *Children and the Threat of Nuclear War*, 10, 11; Palmer Wilson, email message to author, February 15, 2010.

37. Viorst, "Nuclear Threat Harms Children," 106.

38. Tom Landrum, email message to author, January 26, 2010.

39. James Gates, email message to author, January 15, 2010.

40. Julie Evelsizer, email message to author, January 18, 2010.

41. Lois Dickert, "They Thought the War Was On!" 203; Kathy Lewis, email message to author, February 2, 2010.

42. Ellen Molle Skramstad, email message to author, January 27, 2010.

43. Boyer, *Bomb's Early Light*, 11; Escalona, *Children and the Threat of Nuclear War*, 6.

44. David Kurtz, email message to author, January 18, 2010.

45. This general outline of the Cuban Missile Crisis is based on Don Munton and David A. Welch, *The Cuban Missile Crisis: A Concise History*.

46. "John F. Kennedy Speeches, Radio and Television Report to the American People on the Soviet Arms Buildup in Cuba, October 22, 1962," accessed May 9, 2014, http://www.jfklibrary.org/Research/Research-Aids/JFK-Speeches/Cuba-Radio-and -Television-Report_19621022.aspx; Barnouw, *Tube of Plenty*, 316–17.

47. Tom Duncan Jenkins, email message to author, January 30, 2010.

48. Letter, Alyse Weiss to the president, October 23, 1962, Oversized Attachment Files, Box 1075, WHCF, JFKL.

49. Letter, Joan Horsonsby to the president, October 24, 1962, Oversized Attachment Files, Box 1076, WHCF; letter, Rocco Russomano to the president, October 31, 1962, Oversized Attachment Files, Box 1075, WHCF; letter, Ann Marie Cigna to the president, October 23, 1962, Oversized Attachment Files, Box 1075, WHCF; letters, 3rd grade students from Columbus, OH, to the president, October 25, 1962, Oversized Attachment Files, Box 1075, WHCF, JFKL.

50. Ed Fairbrother, email message to author, January 16, 2010; Chris O'Brien, "Mama, Are We Going to Die? America's Children Confront the Cuban Missile Crisis," in *Children and War: A Historical Anthology*, ed. James Marten, 78–79.

51. Letter, Diane Robinson to the president, October 23, 1962, Oversized Attachment Files, Box 1075, WHCF; letter, Beth Feldman to the president, October 23, 1962, Oversized Attachment Files, Box 1075, WHCF; letter, Susan Shalot to the president, October 29, 1962, Oversized Attachment Files, Box 1075, WHCF, JFKL.

52. Letter, Sandra Karan to the president, October 23, 1962, Oversized Attachment Files, Box 1075, WHCF; letter, Ellen Weinberger to the president, October 23, 1962, Oversized Attachment Files, Box 1075, WHCF; letter, Jeffrey Schoen to the president, October 24, 1962, Oversized Attachment Files, Box 1076, WHCF, JFKL; Escalona, *Children and the Threat of Nuclear War*, 12.

53. Letter, Michael Stephenson to the president, January 23, 1961, WHOF, box 86; letter, Robin Mayers to the president, October 23, 1962, Oversized Attachment Files, Box 1075, WHCF; letter, Carol Jump to the president, October 24, 1962, Oversized Attachment Files, Box 1076, WHCF, JFKL.

54. Letter, Lynn Nimtz to the president, October 24, 1962, Oversized Attachment Files, Box 1075, WHCF, JFKL; Escalona, "Children and the Threat of Nuclear War," 206.

55. Boyer, *Bomb's Early Light*, 355.

56. Viorst, "Nuclear Threat Harms Children," 106.

57. Dickert, "They Thought the War Was On!" 97, 201.

58. Penny Lofton, email message to author, January 14, 2010; Viorst, "Nuclear Threat Harms Children," 106.

59. Escalona, "Children and the Threat of Nuclear War," 201; Milton Schwebel, "Nuclear Cold War: Student Opinions and Professional Responsibility," in *Behavioral Science and Human Survival*, ed. Milton Schwebel, 210–22.

60. Escalona, "Children and the Threat of Nuclear War," 203, 207; Escalona, *Children and the Threat of Nuclear War*, 6; "Atom . . . Bomb . . . Children," 24.

61. Adler, *Kids' Letters*, 154; letter, Michael Kennedy to the president, October 24, 1962, Oversized Attachment Files, Box 1075, WHCF; letter, Belinda Espinoza to the president, October 24, 1962, Oversized Attachment Files, Box 1076, WHCF, JFKL.

62. Spock, "Learning to Live in a Troubled World," 26, 28.

63. Marion S. DeFazio, email message to author, January 27, 2010; letters, 4th graders at Our Lady of Refuge School to the president, October 24, 1962, Oversized Attachment Files, Box 1075, WHCF, JFKL.

64. Spock, "Learning to Live in a Troubled World," 28.

Chapter Four The Assassination

1. Robert A. Caro, *The Years of Lyndon Johnson: The Passage of Power*, 341, 342; Steven D. Stark, *Glued to the Set: The 60 Television Shows and Events That Made Us Who We Are Today*, 149; William M. Tuttle, *"Daddy's Gone to War": The Second World War in the Lives of America's Children*, 3.

2. Erik Barnouw, *Tube of Plenty: The Evolution of American Television, 2nd Revised Edition*, 332; Caro, *Passage of Power*, 341.

3. Judy Dickey, email message to author, November 22, 2011; Roberta Niederjohn, email message to author, January 14, 2010; Jack Zibluk, email message to author, January 18, 2010.

4. Ed Fairbrother, email message to author, January 16, 2010.

5. Steve Richardet, interviewed by the American Century Oral History Project, Southeast Missouri State University, November 25, 2013.

6. Caro, *Passage of Power*, 340, 342, 343; Stark, *Glued to the Set*, 152; Barnouw, *Tube of Plenty*, 332.

7. David Kurtz, email message to author, January 18, 2010; Tim Coleman, email message to author, November 30, 2010.

8. Stark, *Glued to the Set*, 149, 152; Barnouw, *Tube of Plenty*, 333.

9. Barnouw, *Tube of Plenty*, 336.

10. Sarah Frazier, email message to author, January 15, 2010.

11. Robert Dallek, *An Unfinished Life: John F. Kennedy, 1917–1963*, 696; Barnouw, *Tube of Plenty*, 336.

12. Glen H. Elder, John Modell, Ross D. Parke, eds., *Children in Time and Place: Developmental and Historical Insights*, 19.

13. Tom Bohenek, email message to author, January 19, 2010.

14. Julie Barker, email message to author, January 20, 2010.

15. Steve Richardet, interviewed by the American Century Oral History Project.

16. Julie Evelsizer, email message to author, January 18, 2010.

17. Martha Wolfenstein and Gilbert Kliman, eds., *Children and the Death of a President*, 194, 195.

18. Karla Bradley, email message to author, January 19, 2010; Roberta S. Sigel, "An Exploration into Some Aspects of Political Socialization: School Children's Reactions to the Death of a President," in Wolfenstein and Kliman, *Children and the Death of a President*, 47, 49; Wolfenstein and Kliman, *Children and the Death of a President*, xvii, 195, 207; 195; Caro, *Passage of Power*, 343.

19. Sigel, "An Exploration," 49.

20. Carol Bierschwal, email message to author, January 15, 2011.

21. Karen Cooley, email message to author, June 11, 2010; Sigel, 30–56, 145; Caro, *Passage of Power*, 341.

22. Sigel, "An Exploration," 50–52.

23. Sigel, "An Exploration," 55, 62.

24. President Lyndon B. Johnson's Address Before a Joint Session of the Congress, November 27, 1963, accessed June 16, 2014, www.lbjlib.utexas.edu/johnson/archives.hom/speeches.hom/631127.asp.

25. Letter and drawing, Eileen M. Bolabon to the president, June 26, 1965, BAL, Box 38, Name File, WHCF; letter, Emily Buck to the president, November 1, 1966, 6M4a, Letters from School Children, Box 1, Ursa Major School 6th Grade folder, LBJ Library.

26. Letter, Janice Lerro to the president, January 6, 1964, Lerner, Box 153, Name File, WHCF, LBJ Library.

27. Sue Rapone, email message to author, December 9, 2010.

28. Don Wibert, email message to author, January 13, 2010.

29. Dallek, *Unfinished Life*, 696.

30. Sigel, "An Exploration," 53, 55.

31. Randy Karnes, email message to author, April 22, 2010; Rolf Herstad, email message to author, July 20, 2010; Gilbert Kliman, "Oedipal Themes in Children's Reactions to the Assassination," in Wolfenstein and Kliman, *Children and the Death of a President*, 125, 131.

32. Wolfenstein and Kliman, *Children and the Death of a President*, 219, 224, 233.

33. Marya Mannes, quoted in Barnouw, *Tube of Plenty*, 332.

34. Mark Anderson, email message to author, November 27, 2011.

35. Vivian Schwartz, email message to author, December 4, 2011.

36. Sigel, "An Exploration," 66, 67.

37. Kliman, "Oedipal Themes," 119.

38. Sue Rapone, email message to author, December 9, 2010.

39. Wolfenstein and Kliman, *Children and the Death of a President*, 206, 207.

40. Neil J. Salkind, *Theories in Human Development*, 208; Patricia H. Miller, *Theories of Developmental Psychology*, 62; Tuttle, *"Daddy's Gone to War,"* 114.

41. Shelia Dale, email message to author, February 2, 2010; Budd Carl Pounds, email message to author, January 14, 2010.

42. Letter, Florence Alley to Pierre Salinger, January 6, 1964, Alley, Box 100, Name File, WHCF, LBJ Library.

43. Roberta Niederjohn, email message to author, January 14, 2010.

44. Steve Richardet, interviewed by the American Century Oral History Project.

45. Cheryl Tucker, email message to author, January 7, 2010.

46. David Kurtz, email message to author, January 18, 2010.

47. Steve Richardet, interviewed by the American Century Oral History Project.

48. Tom Landrum, email message to author, January 18, 2010; Terry Anderson, *The Movement and the Sixties: Protest in America from Greensboro to Wounded Knee*; Landon Y. Jones, *Great Expectations: America and the Baby Boom Generation*, 7.

49. Penny Lofton, email message to author, January 14, 2010; Mark Lassman-Eul, email message to author, January 11, 2010; Wolfenstein and Kliman, *Children and the Death of a President*, 206; Dallek, *Unfinished Life*, 700.

50. Marion S. DeFazio, email message to author, January 27, 2010.

Chapter Five LBJ and the Great Society

1. President Lyndon B. Johnson's Remarks at the University of Michigan, May 22, 1964, accessed June 26, 2014, http://www.lbjlib.utexas.edu/johnson/archives.hom /speeches.hom/640522.asp

2. Lyndon B. Johnson, *This America*, prologue; Lyndon B. Johnson, *The Vantage Point: Perspectives on the Presidency, 1963–1969*, 73.

3. Steven Mintz, *Huck's Raft: A History of American Childhood*, 321; Paul Conkin, *Big Daddy from the Pedernales: Lyndon B. Johnson*, 209; Ted Sorensen, *Kennedy: The Classic*

Biography, 760; Kriste Lindenmeyer, "Children, the State, and the American Dream," in *Reinventing Childhood after World War II*, ed. Paula Fass and Michael Grossberg, 85.

4. Bill Bruegman, *Toys of the Sixties: A Pictorial Guide*, 79.

5. Letter, David Strunk to the president, November 1, 1966, 6M4a, Letters From School Children, Box School—5th grade folder; letter, Florence Alley to the president, January 6, 1964, Alley, Box 100, Name File, WHCF; letter, Gary Anderson to the president, January 15, 1964, Anderson, Franka, Box 156, Name File, WHCF; letter, Vicki Lerz to the president, May 6, 1964, Lerner, Box 153, Name File, WHCF, LBJ Library.

6. Letter, Douglas J. Storey to the president, January 20, 1965; letter, Steven Long to the president, November 1, 1966, 6M4a, Letters From School Children, Box 1, Roger Park School 4th Grade folder, WHCF, LBJ Library.

7. Letter, Tracy Ann Lert to the president, June 12, 1964, Lerner, Box 153, Name File, WHCF, LBJ Library.

8. Letter, Ellen Lerry to the president, March 8, 1967, Lerner, Box 153, Name File, WHCF, LBJ Library.

9. Letter, Tracy Evans to the president, February 10, 1966, Evans T, Box 135, Name File, WHCF, LBJ Library.

10. Letter, Rebecca Rainey to the president, July 20, 1964, Rainsa, Box 17, Name File, WHCF; letter, Karyl Somerton to the president, September 7, 1964, Somersa, Box 447, Name File, WHCF, LBJ Library; Luci Baines Johnson, *Beatles Stories: A Fab Four Fan's Ultimate Road Trip*, DVD, Directed by Seth Swirsky, Los Angeles, Cinema Libre, 2011.

11. Letter, Ricki Friedman to the president, August 1965, Freidman, Marya, Box 267, Name File, WHCF, LBJ Library.

12. "Message to Congress on America's Children and Youth," February 8, 1967, in James MacGregor Burns, ed., *To Heal and to Build: The Programs of President Lyndon B. Johnson*, 277; Vaughn Davis Bornet, *The Presidency of Lyndon B. Johnson*, 134; Conkin, *Big Daddy*, 228.

13. Johnson, *Vantage Point*, 75; Conkin, *Big Daddy*, 219, 221; Mark Stern, *Calculating Visions: Kennedy, Johnson and Civil Rights*.

14. Mintz, *Huck's Raft*, 321, 322.

15. Barbara Finkelstein, "Uncle Sam and the Children: A History of Government Involvement in Child Rearing," in *Growing Up in America: Children in Historical Perspective*, ed. N. Ray Hiner and Joseph Hawes, 264, 265; Charles Murray, *Losing Ground: American Social Policy, 1950–1980*, 67, 164, 166; Burns, *To Heal and to Build*, 277; "President Johnson's Special Message to Congress: Children and Youth," 20–21; Walter F. Mondale, "What Does Our Country Owe Its Children?" 43–45.

16. Murray, *Losing Ground*, 67, 162, 164; "President Johnson's Special Message to Congress: Children and Youth," 12–13; Conkin, *Big Daddy*, 228; "The Mystery of Rising Relief Costs: Aid to Families with Children," 39–43; Walter Goodman, "A Victory for 400,000 Children: The Case of Mrs. Sylvester Smith," 29, 62, 67, 69, 70, 72; "Here's the Rub: Social Security Bill Restricts AFDC," 16; "The New Welfare: Women and Children Last," 541–42.

17. David Easton and Jack Dennis, "The Child's Image of Government," 52, 53; Johnson, *Vantage Point*, 79; Mark I. Gelfand, "The War on Poverty," in *The Johnson Years, Vol. 1: Foreign Policy, the Great Society, and the White House*, ed. Robert A. Devine, 131; letter, Steve Belka to the president, November 1, 1966, 6M4a, Letters From School Children, Box 1, Roger Park School 6th Grade folder; letter, Gary Cation and Peter Holcomb to the president, April 2, 1965, Cati, Box 141, Name File, WHCF, LBJ Library.

18. Carol Gilligan, *In a Different Voice: Psychological Theory and Women's Development*; Michael S. Katz, Nel Noddings, and Kenneth A. Strike, eds., *Justice and Caring: The Search for Common Ground in Education*; letter, Nancy Friedman to the president, November 9, 1966, Freidman, Marya, Box 267, Name File, WHCF, LBJ Library.

19. Letter and drawing, Rhoda Ann Sorage to the president, June 4, 1968, Box 451, Name File, WHCF; letter, Debra Ann De Suza to the president, November 27, 1967, Dest, Box 152, Name File, WHCF; letter, Florence Alley to the president, January 6, 1964, Alley, Box 100, Name File, WHCF, LBJ Library.

20. Karen Cooley, email message to author, June 11, 2010.

21. Letter, Sharon Cnare to the president, October 20, 1964, Cm, Box 283, Name File, WHCF; letter, Timothy Finn to the president, September 1, 1964, Finn, Q, Box 97, Name File, WHCF, LBJ Library; Hugh Davis Graham, "The Transformation of Federal Education Policy," in Devine, *Johnson Years*, 169.

22. Johnson, *Vantage Point*, 220; Conkin, *Big Daddy*, 230.

23. "President Johnson's Special Message to Congress: Children and Youth," 12; "Now There's a White House Plan for the Nation's Children," 80–81; Andrew L. Yarrow, "History of U.S. Children's Policy, 1900–Present," April 2009, accessed June 13, 2014, http://www.firstfocus.net/library/reports/history-us-childrens-policy:15; Mondale, "What Does Our Country Owe Its Children?" 43–45.

24. Conkin, *Big Daddy*, 221, 230.

25. Yarrow, "History of U.S. Children's Policy"; "Now There's a White House Plan for the Nation's Children," 81.

26. Burns, *To Heal and to Build*, 277; Finkelstein, "Uncle Sam and the Children," 265; "Now There's a White House Plan for the Nation's Children," 80–81.

27. "Remarks at the Signing of the Child Nutrition Act of 1966, October 11, 1966," accessed July 11, 2014, http://www.presidency.ucsb.edu/ws/?pid=27913; Child Nutrition Act of 1966, accessed July 11, 2014, http://www.law.cornell.edu/uscode/text/42/1771; Bertha Olsen, "Will Your Child Eat Lunch at School?" 85; "School Lunches: The Changes Proposed," 9.

28. William M. Tuttle, *"Daddy's Gone to War": The Second World War in the Lives of America's Children*, 117; Glen H. Elder, John Modell, Ross D. Parke, eds., *Children in Time and Place: Developmental and Historical Insights*, 183, 221; Patrick J. McGuinn, *No Child Left Behind and the Transformation of Federal Education Policy, 1965–2005*; Johnson, *Vantage Point*, 206.

29. Remarks on Signing the Elementary and Secondary Education Act, April 11, 1965, accessed July 15, 2014, http://www.lbjlib.utexas.edu/johnson/archives.hom

/speeches.hom/650411.asp; Conkin, *Big Daddy*, 226, 227, 230; Johnson, *Vantage Point*, 208, 210; Graham, "Transformation of Federal Education Policy," 162, 163; Mintz, *Huck's Raft*, 322.

30. Burns, *To Heal and to Build*, 365; Mintz, *Huck's Raft*, 323, 324.

31. Conkin, *Big Daddy*, 227, 228.

32. Annie Lowrey, "50 Years Later, War on Poverty Is a Mixed Bag," A1; "How the War on Poverty Succeeded (in Four Charts)"; Erika Eichelberger, Jaeah Lee, and A.J. Vicens, "How We Won—and Lost—the War on Poverty in 6 Charts."

33. Maya Pines, "Slum Children Must Make Up for Lost Time," 66, 67, 69, 71–76; Mintz, *Huck's Raft*, 322; Johnson, *Vantage Point*, 221.

34. Pines, "Slum Children," 66, 67, 69; Wendy Mazer, "What Head Start Meant to Our Town," 54–55, 111–14; Mintz, *Huck's Raft*, 322; "Project Head Start: The Record after Two Years," 72–74; "Head Start for Children in the Slums," 30–32; Burns, *To Heal and to Build*, 279.

35. "Second Thoughts about a Study," 425–26; "Help for Head Start," 16; "Job Corps, Headstart Reassigned," 400–401; Pines, "Slum Children," 71–76; Debra Kinsbury, email message to author, November 29, 2011; Tracey McCauley, email message to author, November 29, 2012; Mintz, *Huck's Raft*, 322.

36. Mazer, "What Head Start Meant to Our Town," 54–55, 111, 113–14; "Project Head Start: The Record after Two Years," 72–74; "Second Thoughts about a Study," 425–26; "Help for Head Start," 16; "Job Corps, Headstart Reassigned," 400–401; Pines, "Slum Children," 71–76; Johnson, *Vantage Point*, 221; Laurel N. Tanner and Daniel Tanner, "Unanticipated Effects of Federal Policy: The Kindergarten," 49–52.

37. Richard M. Polsky, *Getting to Sesame Street: Origins of the Children's Television Workshop*, 22, 91; Edward L. Palmer and Shalom M. Fisch, "The Beginnings of Sesame Street Research" in *"G" Is for Growing: Thirty Years of Research on Children and Sesame Street*, ed. Shalom M. Fisch and Rosemarie T. Truglio, 4; Joan Ganz Cooney, quoted in Fisch and Truglio, *"G" Is for Growing*, xiii; Gerald S. Lesser, *Children and Television: Lessons from Sesame Street*, 77.

38. John Leonard, "Since the Kiddies Are Hooked: Why Not Use TV for a Head Start Program?," 5, 24–30; Polsky, *Getting to Sesame Street*, viii; Mintz, *Huck's Raft*, 322; Erik Barnouw, *Tube of Plenty: The Evolution of American Television, 2nd Revised Edition*, 348.

39. Polsky, *Getting to Sesame Street*, 3, 13, 65, 90; Leonard, "Since the Kiddies Are Hooked," 26; Lesser, *Children and Television*, 49, 51, 62–74.

40. Lesser, *Children and Television*, 62–74, 223; Palmer and Fisch, "Beginnings of Sesame Street Research," 7.

41. Polsky, *Getting to Sesame Street*, 90; Leonard, "Since the Kiddies Are Hooked," 26.

42. Lesser, *Children and Television*, 38, 39, 85, 86, 92, 93, 99, 125, 126, 130; Polsky, *Getting to Sesame Street*, 22, 91; Mintz, *Huck's Raft*, 323.

43. Mintz, *Huck's Raft*, 323; Polsky, *Getting to Sesame Street*, 107; Lesser, *Children and Television*, 169, 206.

44. Fisch and Truglio, *"G" Is for Growing*, xv; "Sesame Street Report Card"; Lesser, *Children and Television*, 210, 223–25.

45. Fisch and Truglio, *"G" Is for Growing*, 141.

46. Keith W. Mielke, "A Review of Research on the Educational and Social Impact of Sesame Street," in Fisch and Truglio, *"G" Is for Growing*, 93; Aletha C. Huston, Daniel R. Anderson, John C. Wright, Deborah L. Linebarger, and Kelly L. Schmitt, "Sesame Street Viewers as Adolescents: The Recontact Study," in Fisch and Truglio, *"G" Is for Growing*, 132, 141; Mintz, *Huck's Raft*, 323; Lesser, *Children and Television*, 177; Katie Zezma, "How Did We Get to Sesame Street? Via LBJ's Great Society," accessed July 29, 2014.

Chapter Six The Southern Struggle for Civil Rights

1. "President Lyndon B. Johnson's Special Message to Congress: The American Promise," March 15, 1965, accessed June 17, 2015, http://www.lbjlibrary .org/lyndon-baines-johnson/speeches-films/president-johnsons-special-message-to -the-congress-the-american-promise/.

2. Ben H. Bagdikian, "Negro Youth's New March on Dixie," 18; Ellen Levine, ed., *Freedom's Children: Young Civil Rights Activists Tell Their Own Stories*, 74; Terry Anderson, *The Movement and the Sixties: Protest in America from Greensboro to Wounded Knee*.

3. Robert Coles, *Children of Crisis: A Study of Courage and Fear*, 71, 142, 321; Robert Coles, "Racial Identity in School Children," 56.

4. Jordana Y. Shakoor, *Civil Rights Childhood*, 95–97, 132; Coles, *Children of Crisis*, 61, 63, 337, 338.

5. Shakoor, *Civil Rights Childhood*, 80; Coles, *Children of Crisis*, 63, 64, 349; James Baldwin, quoted in Rebecca de Schweinitz, *If We Could Change the World: Young People and America's Long Struggle for Racial Equality*, 121.

6. De Schweinitz, *If We Could Change the World*, 122; Robert Coles, "Civil Rights Is Also a State of Mind," 33; Coles, "Racial Identity," 68; Coles, *Children of Crisis*, 339, 341.

7. Coles, *Children of Crisis*, 66.

8. Ibid.

9. Levine, *Freedom's Children*, 2, 5, 13, 15; de Schweinitz, *If We Could Change the World*, 76, 181; Shakoor, *Civil Rights Childhood*, 97.

10. Shakoor, *Civil Rights Childhood*, 90, 159; Coles, *Children of Crisis*, 342, 344, 345.

11. De Schweinitz, *If We Could Change the World*, 76; Levine, *Freedom's Children*, 3; Coles, *Children of Crisis*, 342, 344-45.

12. Karen Cooley, email message to author, June 11, 2010.

13. Shakoor, *Civil Rights Childhood*, 151–54, 165; Coles, "Racial Identity," 57; Coles, "Civil Rights is Also a State of Mind," 45.

14. Katherine Davis Fishman, "Children in the Line of March: Question of Involving Children in Social and Political Issues," 99; Coles, *Children of Crisis*, 62, 67, 71, 322, 337, 352, 367; Coles, "Racial Identity," 68.

15. Coles, *Children of Crisis*, 48, 50, 62, 65, 336; Kenneth B. Clark and Mamie P. Clark, "Racial Identification and Preference in Negro Children," in *Readings in Social Psychology*, ed. Eleanor E. Maccoby.

16. Coles, *Children of Crisis*, 51.

17. Coles, "Civil Rights is Also a State of Mind," 33; Coles, *Children of Crisis*, 67, 68.

18. Coles, "Civil Rights is Also a State of Mind," 35, 45.

19. Margaret Anderson, "Clinton, Tenn.: Children in the Crucible," 12, 48; Coles, *Children of Crisis*, 59, 68–70, 322.

20. Wilma King, *African American Childhoods: Historical Perspectives from Slavery to Civil Rights*, 168; Audrey Edwards and Craig K. Polite, *Children of the Dream: The Psychology of Black Success*, 2.

21. King, *African American Childhoods*, 157, 166; Coles, *Children of Crisis*, 178, 319, 329; de Schweinitz, *If We Could Change the World*, 192, 198; Coles, "Racial Identity," 69; Bagdikian, "Negro Youth's New March on Dixie," 16.

22. De Schweinitz, *If We Could Change the World*, 194, 195, 210, 233; Shakoor, *Civil Rights Childhood*, 113; Levine, *Freedom's Children*, xii; King, *African American Childhoods*, 168.

23. Shakoor, *Civil Rights Childhood*, 130; Levine, *Freedom's Children*, 16, 35; Vincent Harding, quoted in Shari Goldin, "Unlearning Black and White: Race, Media, and the Classroom," in *The Children's Culture Reader*, ed. Henry Jenkins, 137.

24. Shakoor, *Civil Rights Childhood*, 176; Levine, *Freedom's Children*, 4, 16.

25. King, *African American Childhoods*, 166, 167.

26. De Schweinitz, *If We Could Change the World*, 4, 86, 91, 103–18, 135, 142; Goldin, "Unlearning Black and White," 136.

27. Fishman, "Children in the Line of March," 92, 99; de Schweinitz, *If We Could Change the World*, 87, 120, 152, 181, 192, 204; Coles, *Children of Crisis*, 82.

28. Anderson, "Clinton," 12; King, *African American Childhoods*, 157; Dorothy Sterling, *Tender Warriors*, 66; Goldin, "Unlearning Black and White," 137, 138, 145; de Schweinitz, *If We Could Change the World*, 87, 205; Coles, *Children of Crisis*, 107.

29. Sterling, *Tender Warriors*, 26, 66; Goldin, "Unlearning Black and White," 138, 145; Coles, *Children of Crisis*, 108; Shakoor, *Civil Rights Childhood*, 92.

30. Coles, *Children of Crisis*, 106, 110, 120, 121; "Thirteen Years after 1954: Negro Pupils in the South," 77, 80; Anderson, "Clinton," 12, 45; Levine, *Freedom's Children*, 39.

31. Ruby Bridges, *Through My Eyes*, 14, 16, 20, 48, 50, 52.

32. King, *African American Childhoods*, 162, 163; Coles, *Children of Crisis*, 49, 77, 80.

33. King, *African American Childhoods*, 158, 160; Anderson, "Clinton," 12, 48–55; Goldin, "Unlearning Black and White," 142, 143; Ian Stevenson, "People Aren't Born Prejudice," 40; de Schweinitz, *If We Could Change the World*, 123, 129.

34. Coles, "Racial Identity," 54, 56, 57; Stevenson, "People Aren't Born Prejudice," 104.

35. Coles, *Children of Crisis*, 52, 56, 57, 61; Bridges, *Through My Eyes*, 52.

36. Paul Goodman, "Children of Birmingham," 242–44; de Schweinitz, *If We Could Change the World*, 239.

37. Henry Hampton and Steve Fayer, eds., *Voices of Freedom: An Oral History of the Civil Rights Movement from the 1950s through the 1980s*, 134; King, *African American Childhoods*, 166; Levine, *Freedom's Children*, 95, 96, 184.

38. Levine, *Freedom's Children*, 95, 96, 134.

39. "John F. Kennedy's Report to the American People on Civil Rights, 11 June 1963," accessed on August 12, 2015, www.jfklibrary.org/Asset-Viewer/LH8F_0Mz-v0e6Ro1yEm74Ng.aspx.

40. Martin Luther King's "Eulogy for the Martyred Children," September 18, 1963, accessed on August 11, 2015, kingencyclopedia.stanford.edu/encyclopedia/document-sentry/ doc_eulogy_for_the_martyred_children/; King, *African American Childhoods*, 167.

41. Hampton and Fayer, *Voices of Freedom*, 173, 174; Coles, *Children of Crisis*, 321.

42. John Dittmer, *Local People: The Struggle for Civil Rights in Mississippi*, 244, 257, 259–61, 269; Levine, *Freedom's Children*, 113, 114, 123; Hampton and Fayer, *Voices of Freedom*, 185.

43. Levine, *Freedom's Children*, 116, 120, 123.

44. Ibid, 117, 118.

45. Ibid, 123–25, 127, 128.

46. Ibid, 119, 121, 122.

47. Ibid, 128, 137.

48. Ibid, 121, 122, 126, 127.

49. David Nevin, "Struggle That Changed Glen Allan," 108–11; Dittmer, *Local People*, 284, 368, 369, 370.

50. Nevin, "Struggle That Changed Glen Allan," 108, 111; Dittmer, *Local People*, 371, 375.

51. Dittmer, *Local People*, 371, 373, 375, 382; Nevin, "Struggle That Changed Glen Allan," 108, 110, 111.

52. Hampton and Fayer, *Voices of Freedom*, 217, 219; Levine, *Freedom's Children*, 149–54, 191.

53. Levine, *Freedom's Children*, 151–54.

54. Levine, *Freedom's Children*, 144, 153, 155, 156; Hampton and Fayer, *Voices of Freedom*, 219, 228–29, 240.

55. Hampton and Fayer, *Voices of Freedom*, 240; Levine, *Freedom's Children*, 157, 158.

56. Hampton and Fayer, *Voices of Freedom*, 240; Levine, *Freedom's Children*, 157, 158.

57. "What Can We Tell Our Children? Views of a White Southern Mother and a Negro Mother," 25.

58. "Thirteen Years After," 77; Rita Kramer, "Desegregation—After School," 47; Mel Watkins, "White Skins, Dark Skins, Thin Skins," 127, 129, 137, 138; "The Revolution since Little Rock," 95–107; Glen H. Elder, John Modell, Ross D. Parke, eds., *Children in Time and Place: Developmental and Historical Insights*, 17.

59. Watkins, "White Skins," 127, 129, 138; Kramer, "Desegregation," 47.

60. William Van Deburg, *New Day in Babylon: The Black Power Movement and American Culture, 1965–1975*; Shakoor, *Civil Rights Childhood*, 201.

61. James M. Curtis, *Rock Eras: Interpretations of Music and Society, 1954–1984*.

62. "The All-White World of Children's Books," 63–65, 84, 85; "*Stevie*: Realism in a Book about Black Children," 54–58; Liz Gant, "That One's Me! New Books for Black Children Mirror Their World," 52, 54; Jane Granstrom and Anita Silvey, "A Call for Help: Exploring the Black Experience in Children's Books," 395–404; King, *African American Childhoods*, 172.

63. Julie Vesper Sapp, email message to author, January 13, 2010.

64. "What Can We Tell Our Children?" 8, 19; "1960s and 1970s Survey Results," May 2007, Johnson County Museum, Shawnee, KS; James W. Clarke and John W. Soule, "How Southern Children Felt about King's Death," 40; Levine, *Freedom's Children*, 171.

65. John Mathews and Ernest Holsendolph, "The Children Write Their Own Postscript: Reactions to Rioting," 63, 66, 68, 73–75; Alex Poinsett, "Ghetto Schools: An Educational Wasteland," 52–57; Robert Coles, "Children of the American Ghetto," 17–19.

66. Tracye Ann Matthews, "'No One Ever Asks What a Man's Place in the Revolution Is': Gender and Sexual Politics in the Black Panther Party, 1966–1971," 90; Coles, "Children of the American Ghetto," 17; Coles, "Civil Rights is Also a State of Mind," 32, 33.

Chapter Seven The Vietnam War

1. James Marten, *Children for the Union: The War Spirit on the Northern Home Front*, 4; Steven Mintz, *Huck's Raft: A History of American Childhood*, 118, 120, 127, 130, 132, 255.

2. George C. Herring, *America's Longest War: The United States and Vietnam, 1950–1975*.

3. Lawrence M. Baskir and William A. Strauss, *Chance and Circumstance: The Draft, the War, and the Vietnam Generation*, xi, 7; Landon Y. Jones, *Great Expectations: America and the Baby Boom Generation*; Marianne P. Bitler and Lucie Schmidt, "Birth Rates and the Vietnam Draft," 566.

4. Baskir and Strauss, *Chance and Circumstance*, 6, 9, 15, 22, 23.

5. Andrea Kutinova, "Paternity Deferments and the Timing of Births: U.S. Natality during the Vietnam War," 351, 352, 359, 361, 364; Baskir and Strauss, *Chance and Circumstance*, 22, 30, 31, 33, 282; Bitler and Schmidt, "Birth Rates and the Vietnam Draft," 566–69; Jones, *Great Expectations*, 108.

6. Jessica Wilmarth, email message to author, March 21, 2010; Anna B. Gray, email message to author, January 11, 2010; Carol Bierschwal, email message to author, January 15, 2010; Melvin Small, *Covering Dissent: The Media and the Anti-Vietnam War Movement*, 1, 17.

7. Erik Barnouw, *Tube of Plenty: The Evolution of American Television, 2nd Revised Edition*, 380, 399, 401; Gerald S. Lesser, *Children and Television: Lessons from Sesame Street*, 81; "Television-The First Television War," accessed January 28, 2015, http://www.americanforeignrelations.com/O-W/Television-The-first-television-war.html.

8. Kathy Cornett Smalley, email message to author, May 29, 2014; Roberta Niederjohn, email message to author, January 14, 2010; Debbi Goodier, email message to author, April 20, 2010; Bart Greenwalt, email message to author, December 9, 2011; Howard Tolley, Jr., *Children and War: Political Socialization to Internal Conflict*, 32–34, 90.

9. Eileen Mulvihill Harmon, email message to author, January 14, 2010; Lisa Zhito, email message to author, January 12, 2010; letter, Randy Roth to the president, November 1, 1966, 6M4a, Letters from School Children, Box 1, Ursa Major School 4th Grade folder; letter, Anthony Allgood to the president, January 24, 1968, Alley, Box 100, Name File, WHCF, LBJ Library.

10. James Marten, ed., *Children and War: A Historical Anthology*, 5; Tolley, *Children and War*, 39, 128; letter, Richard Friedman to the president, March 28, 1966, Freidman, Marya, Box 267, Name File, WHCF; letter, Tina Quick to the president, November 5, 1967, Conn L-R, Box 366, Name File, WHCF, LBJ Library.

11. Tolley, *Children and War*, 6, 37, 38, 61, 68, 70, 95, 126, 127.

12. Neil J. Salkind, *Theories in Human Development*, 208; William M. Tuttle, *"Daddy's Gone to War": The Second World War in the Lives of America's Children*, 114.

13. Letter, Karen Wilber to the president, November 1, 1966, 6M4a, Letters from School Children, Box 1, Roger Park School 6th Grade folder; letter, Randy Paul Allgaier to the president, February 28, 1968, Alley, Box 100, Name File, WHCF; letter, Tommy Evans to the president, March 19, 1966, Evans T, Box 135, Name File, WHCF, LBJ Library; Tolley, *Children and War*, 36, 39.

14. Karen Cooley, email message to author, June 11, 2010; Tuttle, *"Daddy's Gone to War,"* 45; letter, Glenn Anderson to the president, February 27, 1968, Anderson, Franka, Box 156, Name File, WHCF; letter, David Giliam to the president, November 1, 1966, 6M4a, Letters from School Children, Box 1, Roger Park School 5th Grade folder, LBJ Library; Budd Carl Pounds, email message to author, January 14, 2010; Steven Peel, email message to author, January 17, 2010.

15. Tolley, *Children and War*, 63, 75.

16. Barnouw, *Tube of Plenty*, 380, 401, 402; Steven D. Stark, *Glued to the Set: The 60 Television Shows and Events That Made Us Who We Are Today*, 169, 171.

17. Tolley, *Children and War*, 63–67, 99, 109, 116, 117; Anna B. Gray, email message to author, January 11, 2010; Palmer Wilson, email message to author, February 14, 2010; Jack Zibluk, email message to author, January 17, 2010.

18. Cara Sroges, email message to author, March 4, 2010; letter, Paul Friedman and Dean Ballard to the president, January 10, 1967, Freidman, Marya, Box 267, Name File, WHCF, LBJ Library; Tolley, *Children and War*, 41, 42, 67, 87

19. Cyndi Fitzpatrick, email message to author, January 18, 2010; Jan Dempsey, email message to author, February 15, 2010; Julie Barker, email message to author, January 20, 2010.

20. Cindy Lehto, email message to author, July 15, 2010.

21. Letter, Charlene DeStefano to the president, July 22, 1964, Dest, Box 152, Name File, WHCF, LBJ Library; Susan Doyle, email message to author, June 22, 2010.

22. Tom Paxton, "What Did You Learn in School Today?" recording, Chrysalis One Music, BMG Rights Management US, LLC., 1962.

23. Diane McAlpin, email message to author, January 17, 2010; Paula Moomey-Ivey, email message to author, June 26, 2010; Anna B. Gray, email message to author, January 11, 2010.

24. Staff Sergeant Barry Sadler and Robin Moore, "The Ballad of the Green Berets," recording, RCA, 1966.

25. Anonymous, email message to author, January 31, 2010; Steve Richardet, interviewed by the American Century Oral History Project, Southeast Missouri State University, November 25, 2013.

26. Carol Andreas, "War Toys and the Peace Movement," 84, 85, 89; Barnouw, *Tube of Plenty*, 376.

27. Gary S. Cross, *The Cute and the Cool: Wondrous Innocence and Modern American Children's Culture*, 156, 157; Gary S. Cross, *Kids' Stuff: Toys and the Changing World of American Childhood*, 175, 176; Andreas, "War Toys," 96.

28. "War Talk and War Games," 21; Andreas, "War Toys," 84, 85; Barnouw, *Tube of Plenty*, 374, 375.

29. Sue Adams, email message to author, February 11, 2010; Michelle Ferrari, *Reporting America at War: An Oral History*, 140.

30. Judy Dickey, email message to author, November 22, 2011; Cross, *Cute and the Cool*, 157; Cross, *Kids' Stuff*, 177.

31. "War Talk and War Games," 20–23; Andreas, "War Toys," 91, 94–96; Benjamin Spock, "Playing with Toy Guns: Effects of Warlike Games and Toys on Children," 24–32.

32. Letter, Brian Williams to the president, July 7, 1967, Box 324, Name File, WHCF, LBJ Library.

33. Andreas, "War Toys," 87, 92–96, 98; "Incident at Fort Dix: Picketing of Armed Forces Day War Ceremonies for Children," 809.

34. Barnouw, *Tube of Plenty*, 441; Andreas, "War Toys," 87; Cross, *Cute and the Cool*, 157; Cross, *Kids' Stuff*, 177, 187, 191, 203, 205; Richard O'Brien, *The Story of American Toys*, 204, 211.

35. Amy Rider, email message to author, February 10, 2010; Tolley, *Children and War*, 75.

36. Sue Bailey, email message to author, March 3, 2012.

37. Marion S. DeFazio, email message to author, January 27, 2010; Jan Allman, email message to author, June 23, 2010; Richardet, interviewed by the American Century Oral History Project; Cindy Lehto, email message to author, July 15, 2010; Daniel P. Gmyrek, email message to author, January 15, 2010.

38. Marion DeFazio, email message to author, January 27, 2010.

39. Letter, Cathy to the president, December 16, 1967, Catholica, Box 141, Name File, WHCF, LBJ Library; Marion DeFazio, email message to author, January 27, 2010.

40. Jones, *Great Expectations*, 118; Cindy Lehto, email message to author, July 15, 2010.

41. Cheryl Hunsell, email message to author, December 7, 2012.

42. Hamilton McCubbin, Edna J. Hunter, Philip J. Metres, Jr., Edna J. Hunter, and John A. Plag, eds., *Family Separation and Reunion: Families of Prisoners of War and Servicemen Missing in Action*, 50, 66; Tuttle, *"Daddy's Gone to War,"* 216, 217, 226, 237; Karen Cordell, email message to author, February 6, 2010; Natasha Zaretsky, *No Direction Home: The American Family and the Fear of National Decline, 1968–1980*.

43. McCubbin, et al., *Family Separation*, 28, 29, 41, 211.

44. Ibid, 34, 40.

45. Diane Blankenship, email message to author, May 13, 2010.

46. Melvin Merchant, email message to author, March 14, 2010.

47. Letter, Patricia Finnell to the president, February 10, 1965, Finn, Q, Box 97, Name File, WHCF, LBJ Library.

48. Cheryl Hunsell, email message to author, December 7, 2012; Karen Cordell, email message to author, February 6, 2010; McCubbin, et al., *Family Separation*, 40, 44, 67, 68, 70, 154.

49. McCubbin, et al., *Family Separation*, 13, 46, 47; "A Celebration of Men Redeemed," 13, 14; "Memories of Divided Families," 36–43; Karen Thorsen, "A Campaign to Get a Husband Home," 32; Zaretsky, *No Direction Home*, 55.

50. Zaretsky, *No Direction Home*, 32, 38, 43, 52, 54, 55.

51. Michael Ellinger, interviewed by Joel P. Rhodes, Cape Girardeau, MO, May 8, 2015.

52. Roberta Niederjohn, email message to author, January 14, 2010; *Gold Star Children*, DVD, JRB Communications, LLC, 2013.

53. Michael Ellinger, interviewed by Joel P. Rhodes; McCubbin et. al., *Family Separation*, 165, 215.

54. Melvin Merchant, email message to author, March 14, 2010; Susan Hammond, email message to author, February 18, 2010; Karen Cordell, email message to author, February 6, 2010.

55. Tuttle, *"Daddy's Gone to War,"* 89, 215, 217, 218.

56. Karen Cordell, email message to author, February 6, 2010.

57. Doug Tarwater, email message to author, March 19, 2010.

58. Jones, *Great Expectations*, 214, 216; Cheryl Hunsell, email message to author, December 12, 2010.

59. Denise Dowling, email message to author, February 20, 2010; Anna B. Gray, email message to author, January 11, 2010; "A Celebration of Men Redeemed," 13.

60. Tuttle, *"Daddy's Gone to War,"* 115, 116; Marten, *Children for the Union*, 4.

61. Joe Mode, email message to author, January 15, 2010; Cindy M. Sigmon, email message to author, January 26, 2010; Karen Cordell, email message to author, February 6, 2010.

62. Anonymous, email message to author, January 31, 2010.

63. Cindy Lehto, email message to author, July 15, 2010.

64. McCubbin, et al., *Family Separation*, 203; Tolley, *Children and War*, 62, 64, 65, 68, 130.

65. Steven Craig, email message to author, January 18, 2010.

Chapter Eight Hippies

1. Terry Anderson, *The Movement and the Sixties: Protest in America from Greensboro to Wounded Knee*, i.

2. Anna B. Gray, email message to author, January 11, 2010; Steven Mintz, *Huck's Raft: A History of American Childhood*, 328–32.

3. William Hedgepeth, "Hippies as Parents: What Kind of Children Are the New People Raising?" 69; Timothy Miller, *The Hippies and American Values*; Peter Braunstein, "Forever Young: Insurgent Youth and the Sixties Culture of Rejuvenation," in *Imagine Nation: The American Counterculture of the 1960s and '70s*, ed. Peter Braunstein and Michael William Doyle, 251; Theodore Roszak, *The Making of a Counterculture: Reflections on the Technocratic Society and Its Youthful Opposition*.

4. Miller, *Hippies and American Values*, xiv, 1, 3, 96; Braunstein, "Forever Young," 254; Tom Engelhardt, *The End of Victory Culture: Cold War America and the Disillusioning of a Generation*.

5. Miller, *Hippies and American Values*, 101.

6. David Finley, email message to author, November 20, 2012; Denise Sedlar Dempster, email message to author, January 17, 2010; Julie Evelsizer, email message to author, September 18, 2010; DJ Thomas, email message to author, January 7, 2010.

7. Braunstein, "Forever Young," 252, 254, 257, 260; Miller, *Hippies and American Values*, 46, 102; Steven D. Stark, *Glued to the Set: The 60 Television Shows and Events That Made Us Who We Are Today*, 155, 157, 158, 174.

8. Miller, *Hippies and American Values*, 94.

9. John Rothchild and Susan Wolf, *The Children of the Counterculture: How the Life-Style of America's Flower Children Has Affected an Even Younger Generation*, 12, 37, 51.

10. Lauri Umansky, *Motherhood Reconceived: Feminism and the Legacies of the Sixties*, 25–27, 32, 52, 53, 55, 56.

11. Jeanie Rhodes, interviewed by Joel P. Rhodes, Cape Girardeau, MO, February 8, 2016.

12. Hedgepeth, "Hippies as Parents," 71, 72, 74; Umansky, *Motherhood Reconceived*, 25–27, 55.

13. Rothchild and Wolf, *Children of the Counterculture*, 5, 7.

14. Moon Zappa, in Foreword to *Wild Child: Girlhoods in the Counterculture*, ed. Chelsea Cain, xv, xiv, 8.

15. Richard La Rosa, interviewed by Joel P. Rhodes, Cape Girardeau, MO, March 2, 2016.

16. Rain Grimes, "Fear of a Bagged Lunch," in Cain, *Wild Child*, 94.

17. Rothchild and Wolf, *Children of the Counterculture*, 8; Zappa, in Foreword to *Wild Child*, xvii.

18. Kirk Knoll, interviewed by Joel P. Rhodes, Cape Girardeau, MO, January 27, 2016.

19. Hedgepeth, "Hippies as Parents," 70, 71; Chelsea Cain, *Wild Child*, xxi.

20. Kirk Knoll, interviewed by Joel P. Rhodes; Miller, *Hippies and American Values*, 1, 3.

21. Richard La Rosa, interviewed by Joel P. Rhodes.

22. Kirk Knoll, interviewed by Joel P. Rhodes; Grimes, "Fear of a Bagged Lunch," 94; Umansky, *Motherhood Reconceived*, 25–27.

23. Elizabeth Shè, "Free Love Ain't," in Cain, *Wild Child*, 54.

24. Hedgepeth, "Hippies as Parents," 72; Rothchild and Wolf, *Children of the Counterculture*, 12, 15, 20, 23, 28, 36; Grimes, "Fear of a Bagged Lunch," 95.

25. Rothchild and Wolf, *Children of the Counterculture*, 15, 17, 21, 26, 33.

26. Richard La Rosa, interviewed by Joel P. Rhodes; Rothchild and Wolf, *Children of the Counterculture*, 9, 52, 54, 192, 193, 195; River Light, "Ghosts," in Cain, *Wild Child*, 154; Miller, *Hippies and American Values*, 77, 78.

27. Miller, *Hippies and American Values*, 74, 76, 80.

28. Rothchild and Wolf, *Children of the Counterculture*, 54, 58, 61, 63, 74, 195.

29. Ibid, 66, 69, 70, 74, 77.

30. Ibid, 79, 81, 128, 192.

31. Ibid, 124, 198, 203.

32. Ibid, 199, 200, 201.

33. John Poppy, "Child of the Commune," 34, 36; Rothchild and Wolf, *Children of the Counterculture*, 84, 89, 114, 185, 193, 198, 199.

34. Rothchild and Wolf, *Children of the Counterculture*, 87–89.

35. Ibid, 89, 90, 94, 194.

36. Ibid, 196.

37. Stephen Gaskin, *Hey Beatnik, This Is the Farm Book*, no page numbers; Rothchild and Wolf, *Children of the Counterculture*, 147, 178.

38. Ina May Gaskin, *Spiritual Midwifery*.

39. Gaskin, *Hey Beatnik*, no page numbers; Rothchild and Wolf, *Children of the Counterculture*, 182, 183.

40. Gaskin, *Hey Beatnik*, no page numbers.

41. Ibid.

42. Richard La Rosa, interviewed by Joel P. Rhodes; Braunstein, "Forever Young," 260.

43. Cain, *Wild Child*, xxiv; Zappa, Foreword to *Wild Child*, xvii; Jeanie Rhodes, interviewed by Joel P. Rhodes.

44. Richard La Rosa, interviewed by Joel P. Rhodes; Kirk Knoll, interviewed by Joel P. Rhodes.

45. Sandra Eugster, *Notes from Nethers: Growing Up in a Sixties Commune*, 3, 4, 5, 6, 127, 128.

46. Eugster, *Notes from Nethers*, 313, 316, 317; Angela A. Aidala, "Communes and Changing Family Norms: Marriage and Lifestyle Choice among Former Members of Communal Groups," 311–38.

47. Zappa, Foreword to *Wild Child*, xviii; Shè, "Free Love Ain't," in Cain, *Wild Child*, 55–60.

48. Zappa, Foreword to *Wild Child*, xixi; Rothchild and Wolf, *Children of the Counterculture*, 99, 103, 194; Miller, *Hippies and American Values*, 111, 117, 120, 121; Eugster, *Notes from Nethers*, 312, 317.

49. Cecily Schmidt, "Common Threads," in Cain, *Wild Child*, 130; Rain Grimes, "Fear of a Bagged Lunch," 100; Cain, *Wild Child*, xxiv.

50. Kirk Knoll, interviewed by Joel P. Rhodes; Richard La Rosa, interviewed by Joel P. Rhodes; Cain, in Wild Child, xxiv, xxvi, xxvii.

Chapter Nine Women's Liberation

1. David Arthur Machiran, email message to author, December 6, 2010.

2. Arlene Skolnick, *Embattled Paradise: The American Family in an Age of Uncertainty*, 78, 81, 98, 106, 120; Stephanie Coontz, *The Way We Never Were: American Families and the Nostalgia Trap*, 154, 167; Glen H. Elder, John Modell, and Ross D. Parke, eds., *Children in Time and Place: Developmental and Historical Insights*, 180, 181; Glen H. Elder, *Children of the Great Depression: Social Change in Life Experience*, 7.

3. Coontz, *Way We Never Were*, 156, 161, 162, 166; Skolnick, *Embattled Paradise*, 108; Natasha Zaretsky, *No Direction Home: The American Family and the Fear of National Decline, 1968–1980*, 11; Landon Y. Jones, *Great Expectations: America and the Baby Boom Generation*, 192.

4. Coontz, *Way We Never Were*, 162; "1960s and 1970s Survey Results," May 2007, Johnson County Museum, Shawnee, KS; Elizabeth Douvan, "The Age of Narcissism, 1963–1982," in *American Childhood: A Research Guide and Historical Handbook*, ed. Joseph N. Hawes and N. Ray Hiner, 590, 591, 595, 596; Diane Krumm, email message to author, November 12, 2010; Cara Sroges, email message to author, January 20, 2010.

5. Coontz, *Way We Never Were*, 162, 166–68; Skolnick, *Embattled Paradise*, 108, 110; Leslie Tiller, email message to author, February 20, 2010; Isaiah Laster, email message to author, November 23, 2011.

6. Elizabeth Waldman and Robert Whitmore, "Children of Working Mothers, March 1973," 50, 52; Jones, *Great Expectations*, 222, 228, 231–34; Paula S. Fass, "The Child-Centered Family? New Rules in Postwar America," in *Reinventing Childhood after World War II*, ed. Paula Fass and Michael Grossberg, 13.

7. Gary Davis, email message to author, December 10, 2011.

8. Louis Weeks, "Father Takes Care of Baby," 60, 61; Douvan, "Age of Narcissism," 595, 596.

9. Dee Anne Smelcer, email message to author, November 28, 2010; Cathy Pentz, email message to author, January 16, 2010; Vesna Plakanis, email message to author, January 14, 2010; Douvan, "Age of Narcissism," 595.

10. Laura Rexroat, email message to author, December 5, 2010.

11. "1960s and 1970s Survey Results," Johnson County Museum; T. Berry Brazelton, "Your Toddler: When Both Parents Work," 88, 120; Eleanor Limmer, "When

Mother Goes Away," 42, 43, 68; "What Every Mother Owes Her Child and Herself," 134.

12. Walter F. Mondale, "What Does Our County Owe Its Children?" 43–45, 114–15; "Child Care Veto: Day-Care Plan," 23–24; "Spirit of Christmas Present: Nixon's Veto of Children's Programs," 291–92; Steven Mintz, *Huck's Raft: A History of American Childhood*, 358; Limmer, "When Mother Goes Away," 68.

13. "Monthly Vital Statistics Report, Advance Report, Final Divorce Statistics, 1976, From the National Center for Health Statistics," accessed December 2, 2015, http://www.cdc.gov/nchs/data/mvsr/supp/mv27_05sacc.pdf; Josef E. Garai, "Children of Divorce," 47; Waldman and Whitmore, "Children of Working Mothers, March 1973," 50, 55; John F. McDermott, "Divorce from 3 to 6," 99; "Divorce: Its Effect on Children," 12–14; Zaretsky, *No Direction Home*, 11; Jones, *Great Expectations*, 247; Coontz, *Way We Never Were*, 166, 167, 182, 183; Skolnick, *Embattled Paradise*, 121.

14. Jerry Wirth, email message to author, March 19, 2010.

15. Nancy G. Meredith, "When Parents Divorce," 44, 84, 85; Richard Gardner, "If Your Parents Are Getting Divorced," 93, 95, 98; Richard A. Gardner, "The Boys and Girls Book about Divorce," 118–21; Connie Fulks Wineland, email message to author, March 19, 2010; "Dialogue with Mothers: Helping Children Accept Divorce," 26; Benjamin Spock, "How Divorced Parents Can Help Their Children Adjust," 33, 41.

16. "Child's Guide to Divorce," 63; Gardner, "If Your Parents," 98.

17. Spock, "How Divorced Parents," 34; Robert Goldscheider, "Not Only on Sunday: Divorced Fathers and Their Children," 40, 47.

18. Connie Fulks Wineland, email message to author, March 19, 2010; Katherine Owsley Long, email message to author, January 11, 2010.

19. Jones, *Great Expectations*, 247; "Divorce: Its Effect on Children," 12; McDermott, "Divorce from 3 to 6," 99, 102; Brazelton, "Your Toddler," 120; Katherine Owsley Long, email message to author, January 11, 2010; John Delmos, email message to author, July 28, 2010.

20. Roseann Cadau, email message to author, January 19, 2010.

21. Coontz, *The Way We Never Were*, 167.

22. Dave Minner, email message to author, April 5, 2010; Lauri Umansky, *Motherhood Reconceived: Feminism and the Legacies of the Sixties*, 14; Coontz, *Way We Never Were*, 154, 162, 163, 166–68.

23. Winifred Brienes, *Young, White, and Miserable: Growing Up Female in the Fifties*, 12; Umansky, *Motherhood Reconceived*, 14.

24. Alice Echols, *Daring to Be Bad: Radical Feminism in America, 1967–1975*.

25. Ashley, email message to author, March 21, 2010; Jennifer Horne, email message to author, January 18, 2010.

26. Umansky, *Motherhood Reconceived*, 3, 16, 32, 34, 35, 39, 42, 43, 45, 103, 110, 115, 119; Coontz, *Way We Never Were*, 149, 150.

27. Umansky, *Motherhood Reconceived*, 52, 60, 62, 63.

28. Brazelton, "Your Toddler," 120; Margaret M. Conant, "Learning to Be a Boy, a Girl, or a Person," 18–21; Benjamin Spock, "Should Girls Be Raised Like Boys?" 24, 26, 28; "Parent's Guide to Sex Education."

29. Lynn B. Iglitzin, "A Child's-Eye View of Sex Roles," 23–25; Spock, "Should Girls," 28.

30. "A Feminist Look at Children's Books," 236; Lenore J. Weitzman, Deborah Eifler, Elizabeth Hokada, and Catherine Ross, "Sex Role Socialization in Picture Books for Preschool Children," 1125, 1131, 1134, 1135–37, 144, 145; John Stewig and Margaret Higgs, "Girls Grow Up to Be Mommies: A Study of Sexism in Children's Literature," 236, 239, 240, 241; Sally Allen McNall, "American Children's Literature, 1880-Present" in Hawes and Hiner, *American Childhood*, 401; Umansky, *Motherhood Reconceived*, 20, 43; Elder, Modell, and Parke, *Children in Time and Place*, 200.

31. "A Feminist Look at Children's Books," 237; Weitzman et al., "Sex Role Socialization," 1125, 1143; Meindert DeJong, *The Wheel on the School*, 10; Irene Hunt, *Up a Road Slowly*, 31.

32. "A Feminist Look at Children's Books," 236–38; Weitzman et al., "Sex Role Socialization," 1138; Conant, "Learning to Be a Boy," 19; Constance Greene, *A Girl Called Al.*

33. Carol Jacobs and Cynthia Eaton, "Sexism in the Elementary School," 20–22; "A Feminist Look at Children's Books," 235, 236; Diane Gersoni Stavn, "Reducing the Miss Muffett Syndrome: An Annotated Bibliography," 32, 33; Leslie Paris, "Happily Ever After: Free To Be . . . You and Me, Second-Wave Feminism, and 1970s American Children's Culture," in *The Oxford Handbook of Children's Literature*, ed. Julia Mickenberg and Lynne Vallone, 525, 526.

34. Stavn, "Reducing the Miss Muffett Syndrome," 33; "A Feminist Look at Children's Books," 236, 239, 240; Uri Shulevitz, *Rain Rain Rivers*, 8; Alberta Wilson Constant, *The Motoring Millers*, 91.

35. Paris, "Happily Ever After," 520, 521, 527, 529, 530, 531, 533; Umansky, *Motherhood Reconceived*, 43, 46, 47, 49; Jacobs and Eaton, "Sexism in the Elementary School," 22.

36. Steven D. Stark, *Glued to the Set: The 60 Television Shows and Events That Made Us Who We Are Today*, 154, 155, 158, 174.

37. Erik Barnouw, *Tube of Plenty: The Evolution of American Television. 2nd Revised Edition*, 430, 431.

38. Diane McAlpin, email message to author, January 17, 2010.

39. Jan Sinnott, "Zap! Bam! Pow! Chauvinist Children's Culture," 12.

40. Gary S. Cross, *Kids' Stuff: Toys and the Changing World of American Childhood*, 52, 67, 69, 71, 79, 80, 147, 157, 158; "A Report on Children's Toys and Socialization to Sex Roles," 56.

41. Nancy Lyon, "More Than Child's Play," 54–55, 98; Cross, *Kids' Stuff*, 187, 191.

42. Lyon, "More Than Child's Play," 55; Cross, *Kids' Stuff*, 183, 186; Nancy Northway, email message to author, March 19, 2010; Robin Machiran, email message to

author, December 6, 2010; Roy Griffaw, email message to author, September 26, 2011; Rob Bellamy, email message to author, February 4, 2010.

43. Gary S. Cross, *The Cute and the Cool: Wondrous Innocence and Modern American Children's Culture*, 155, 156; Cross, *Kids' Stuff*, 172, 173; Eric Rand, "Older Heads on Younger Bodies," in *The Children's Culture Reader*, ed. Henry Jenkins, 382, 383, 388; Karen Cordell, email message to author, February 6, 2010; Dee Mercier Van Valkenburg, email message to author, July 7, 2010; Mary Rogers, *Barbie Culture*.

44. Cross, *Kids' Stuff*, 173, 175; Eileen Mulvihill Harmon, email message to author, January 14, 2010; Diane McAlpin, email message to author, January 14, 2010.

45. Nancy Northway, email message to author, March 19, 2010; Deborah Steffens-Hotop, email message to author, September 14, 2010.

46. Deby Lyn Doerhoff, email message to author, May 3, 2010.

Chapter Ten Conclusions

1. Sue Rapone, email message to author, January 16, 2010.

2. Paula S. Fass, "The Child-Centered Family? New Rules in Postwar America," in *Reinventing Childhood after World War II*, ed. Paula Fass and Michael Grossberg, xii, 2; Steven Mintz, *Huck's Raft: A History of American Childhood*, 334; Natasha Zaretsky, *No Direction Home: The American Family and the Fear of National Decline, 1968–1980*, 11, 197; Henry Jenkins, ed., *The Children's Culture Reader*, 22.

3. Zaretsky, *No Direction Home*, 138, 190; Steven Mintz, "The Changing Face of Children's Culture," in in Fass and Grossberg, *Reinventing Childhood after World War II*, 45, 46; Elizabeth Douvan, "The Age of Narcissism, 1963–1982," in *American Childhood: A Research Guide and Historical Handbook*, ed. Joseph N. Hawes and N. Ray Hiner, 604; Arlene Skolnick, *Embattled Paradise: The American Family in the Age of Uncertainty*; Landon Y. Jones, *Great Expectations: America and the Baby Boom Generation*, 251; Fass, "Child-Centered Family?" 2, 14.

4. Debbie Allen, email message to author, January 13, 2010; Sarah Frazier, email message to author, January 15, 2010.

5. Glen H. Elder, *Children of the Great Depression: Social Change in Life Experience*, 6, 15, 74, 150, 152, 153, 184, 258, 259, 267; Ashley, email message to author, March 21, 2010.

6. Ashley, email message to author, March 21, 2010; Cindy M. Sigmon, email message to author, January 26, 2010.

7. Jennifer Horne, email message to author, January 18, 2010.

8. Robert Kring, email message to author, December 5, 2012.

9. Melvin Merchant, email message to author, March 14, 2010.

10. Cyndi Fitzpatrick, email message to author, January 18, 2010; Judy Dickey, email message to author, November 22, 2011; Karen Cordell, email message to author, February 6, 2010.

11. Cindy M. Sigmon, email message to author, January 26, 2010; Budd Carl Pounds, email message to author, January 14, 2010; Debbie Zisser, email message to

author, November 7, 2011; Marsha Louise Cravens, email message to author, October 7, 2014.

12. Julie Evelsizer, email message to author, January 18, 2010.

13. Dee Anne Smelcer, email message to author, November 28, 2010; David Finley, email message to author, November 20, 2012; John McCosh, email message to author, January 16, 2010.

14. Tim Coleman, email message to author, November 30, 2010.

15. Roberta Niederjohn, email message to author, January 14, 2010.

16. John Dowd, email message to author, July 7, 2010.

17. Julie Barker, email message to author, January 20, 2010.

18. Kate Killian, email message to author, January 31, 2010; Jack Zibluk, email message to author, January 18, 2010; Sue Rapone, email message to author, January 16, 2010; Jan Dempsey, email message to author, February 15, 2010.

SELECTED BIBLIOGRAPHY

Adler, Bill, ed. *Kids' Letters to President Kennedy*. New York: William Morrow, 1961.

Aidala, Angela A. "Communes and the Changing Family Norms: Marriage and Life-Style Choice among Former Members of Communal Groups." *Journal of Family Issues* 10:3 (1989): 311–38.

Aldgate, Anthony, James Chapman, and Arthur Marwick, eds. *Windows on the Sixties: Exploring Key Texts of Media and Culture*. London: I. B. Tauris, 2000.

"The All-White World of Children's Books." *Saturday Review* 11 Sept. 1965.

Anderson, Margaret. "Clinton, Tenn.: Children in the Crucible." *New York Times Magazine* 2 Nov. 1958.

Anderson, Terry. *The Movement and the Sixties: Protest in America from Greensboro to Wounded Knee*. New York: Oxford Univ. Press, 1995.

Andreas, Carol. "War Toys and the Peace Movement." *Journal of Social Issues* (Jan. 1969): 84–89.

Appleton, Hillary, and Russell Connor. *"Sesame Street" Revisited*. New York: Russell Sage, 1975.

Appy, Christian. *Working Class War: American Combat Soldiers & Vietnam*. Chapel Hill: Univ. of North Carolina Press, 1993.

Ariès, Philippe. *Centuries of Childhood: A Social History of Family Life*. New York: Vintage, 1962.

Arterton, F. Christopher. "The Impact of Watergate on Children's Attitudes toward Political Authority." *Political Science Quarterly* 89:2 (June 1974): 269–88.

"Atom . . . Bomb . . . Children." *Newsweek* 20 Nov. 1961.

Bagdikian, Ben H. "Negro Youth's New March on Dixie." *Saturday Evening Post* 8 Sept. 1962.

Bane, Mary Jo. *Here to Stay: American Families in the Twentieth Century*. New York: Basic Books, 1976.

Barnouw, Erik. *Tube of Plenty: The Evolution of American Television. 2nd rev. ed.* New York: Oxford Univ. Press, 1990.

Baskir, Lawrence M., and William A. Strauss. *Chance and Circumstance: The Draft, the War, and the Vietnam Generation*. New York: Vintage, 1978.

Berman, Paul. *A Tale of Two Utopias: The Political Journey of the Generation of 1968.* New York: Norton, 1996.

Bernard, Jessie. "Note on Changing Life Styles, 1970–1974." *Journal of Marriage and Family* 37 (Aug. 1975): 582–93.

Bernstein, Robin. *Racial Innocence: Performing American Childhood from Slavery to Civil Rights.* New York: New York Univ. Press, 2011.

Beschloss, Michael. *The Crisis Years: Kennedy and Khrushchev, 1960–1963.* New York: HarperCollins, 1991.

———. *Taking Charge: The Johnson White House Tapes, 1963–1964.* New York: Simon & Schuster, 1998.

Biskind, Peter. *Seeing Is Believing: How Hollywood Taught Us to Stop Worrying and Love the Fifties.* New York: Holt, 2000.

Bitler, Marianne P., and Lucie Schmidt. "Birth Rates and the Vietnam Draft." *American Economic Review* 102:3 (2012): 566–69.

Bornet, Vaughn Davis. *The Presidency of Lyndon B. Johnson.* Lawrence, KS: Univ. Press of Kansas, 1984.

Botstein, Leon. "The Children of the Lonely Crowd." *Change* 10 (May 1978): 16–20.

Boyer, Paul. *By the Bomb's Early Light: American Thought and Culture at the Dawn of the Atomic Age.* Chapel Hill: Univ. of North Carolina Press, 1994.

Brandwein, Ruth A., Carol A. Brown, and Elizabeth Maury Fox. "Women and Children Last: The Social Situation of Divorced Mothers and Their Families." *Journal of Marriage and the Family* 36 (Aug. 1974): 498–514.

Braunstein, Peter. "Forever Young: Insurgent Youth and the Sixties Culture of Rejuvenation." In *Imagine Nation: The American Counterculture of the 1960s and '70s,* ed. Peter Braunstein and Michael William Doyle. New York: Routledge, 2002.

Braunstein, Peter, and Michael William Doyle, eds. *Imagine Nation: The American Counterculture of the 1960s and '70s.* New York: Routledge, 2002.

Brazleton, T. Berry. "Your Toddler: When Both Parents Work." *Redbook* Oct. 1974.

Bremner, Robert, ed. *Children and Youth in America: A Documentary History.* Vol. 2. Cambridge: Harvard Univ. Press, 1971.

Bridges, Ruby. *Through My Eyes.* New York: Scholastic, 1999.

Brienes, Winifred. *Young, White, and Miserable: Growing Up Female in the Fifties.* Boston: Beacon, 1992.

Bruegman, Bill. *Toys of the Sixties: A Pictorial Guide.* Akron: Cap'n Penny, 1992.

Burner, David. *Making Peace with the 60s.* Princeton: Princeton Univ. Press, 1996.

Burns, James MacGregor. *To Heal and to Build: The Programs of Lyndon B. Johnson.* New York: McGraw-Hill, 1968.

Cain, Chelsea, ed. *Wild Child: Girlhoods in the Counterculture.* Seattle: Seal Press, 1999.

Caro, Robert. *The Years of Lyndon Johnson: The Passage of Power.* New York: Vintage, 2012.

Carter, Amy, and Ryan L. Teten. "Assessing Changing Views of the President: Revisiting Greenstein's Children and Politics." *Presidential Studies Quarterly* 32:3 (Sept. 2002): 453–62.

"A Celebration of Men Redeemed." *Time* 19 Feb. 1973.

Chafe, William H. *The Paradox of Change: American Women in the Twentieth Century.* New York: Oxford Univ. Press, 1991.

"Child Care Veto: Day-Care Plan." *Time* 20 Dec. 1971.

"Child's Guide to Divorce." *Time* 26 Oct. 1970.

Clark, Kenneth B., and Mamie P. Clark. "Racial Identification and Preference in Negro Children." In *Readings in Social Psychology*, ed. Eleanor E. Maccoby. New York: Holt, 1958.

Clarke, James W., and John W. Soule. "How Southern Children Felt about King's Death." *Trans-Action* Oct. 1968.

Coles, Robert. "Children of the American Ghetto." *Harper's* Sept. 1967.

———. *Children of Crisis: A Study of Courage and Fear.* Vol. 1. Boston: Little, Brown, 1967.

———. *Children of Crisis: Selections from the Pulitzer Prize-Winning Five-Volume Children of Crisis Series.* Boston: Little, Brown, 2003.

———. "Civil Rights Is Also a State of Mind." *New York Times Magazine* 7 May 1967.

———. "Racial Identity in School Children." *Saturday Review* 19 Oct. 1963.

Collins, Gail. *When Everything Changed: The Amazing Journey of American Women, from 1960 to the Present.* New York: Little, Brown, 2014.

Conant, Margaret M. "Learning to Be a Boy, a Girl, or a Person." *PTA Magazine* March 1972.

Conkin, Paul. *Big Daddy from the Pedernales: Lyndon B. Johnson.* Boston: Twayne, 1986.

Constant, Alberta Wilson. *The Motoring Millers.* New York: Thomas Y. Crowell, 1969.

Cook, Thomas D., Hillary Appleton, Ross F. Conner, Ann Shaffer, Gary Tamkin, and Stephen J. Weber. *"Sesame Street" Revisited.* New York: Russell Sage, 1975.

Coontz, Stephanie. *The Way We Never Were: American Families and the Nostalgia Trap.* New York: Basic Books, 1992.

Corcoran, Mary. "The Economic Consequences of Marital Dissolution for Women in the Middle Years." *Sex Roles* 5 (March 1979): 343–53.

Cott, Nancy. *The Grounding of Modern Feminism.* New Haven: Yale Univ. Press, 1989.

Crawford, Vicki, Jacqueline Rouse, and Barbara Woods, eds. *Women in the Civil Rights Movement: Trailblazers and Torchbearers, 1941–1965.* Bloomington: Indiana Univ. Press, 1993.

Cross, Gary S. *The Cute and the Cool: Wondrous Innocence and Modern American Children's Culture.* New York: Oxford Univ. Press, 2004.

———. *Kids' Stuff: Toys and the Changing World of American Childhood.* Cambridge: Harvard Univ. Press, 2001.

Curtis, James M. *Rock Eras: Interpretations of Music and Society, 1954–1984.* Bowling Green: Bowling Green State Univ. Popular Press, 1987.

Dallek, Robert. *Lone Star Rising: Lyndon Johnson and His Times.* New York: Oxford Univ. Press, 1992.

———. *An Unfinished Life: John F. Kennedy, 1917–1963.* New York: Back Bay, 2003.

David, Jay, ed. *Growing Up Black.* New York: William Morrow, 1968.

Davis, Flora. *Moving the Mountain: The Women's Movement in America Since 1960.* Champaign: Univ. of Illinois Press, 1991.

Davis, Jeffrey. *Children's Television, 1947–1990.* Jefferson, NC: McFarland, 1995.

Davis, Michael. *Street Gang: The Complete History of Sesame Street.* New York: Penguin, 2009.

Dawson, Richard E., and Kenneth Prewitt. *Political Socialization: An Analytic Study.* Boston: Little, Brown, 1967.

Degler, Carl. *At Odds: Women and the Family in America from the Revolution to the Present.* New York: Oxford Univ. Press, 1980.

DeJong, Meindert. *The Wheel on the School.* New York: HarperCollins, 1954.

deMause, Lloyd, ed. *The History of Childhood.* New York: Psychohistory Press, 1974.

Demos, John. *A Little Commonwealth: Family Life in Plymouth Colony.* New York: Oxford Univ. Press, 1970.

———.*Past, Present, and Personal: The Family and the Life Course in American History.* New York: Oxford Univ. Press, 1986.

de Schweinitz, Rebecca. *If We Could Change the World: Young People and America's Long Struggle for Racial Equality.* Chapel Hill: Univ. of North Carolina Press, 2009.

Devine, Robert A., ed. *The Johnson Years, Vol. 1: Foreign Policy, the Great Society, and the White House.* Lawrence: Univ. Press of Kansas, 1987.

"Dialogue with Mothers: Helping Children Accept Divorce." *Ladies' Home Journal* Feb. 1972.

Dickert, Lois. "They Thought the War Was On!" *McCall's* April 1963.

Dittmer, John. *Local People: The Struggle for Civil Rights in Mississippi.* Champaign: Univ. of Illinois Press, 1994.

"Divorce: Its Effect on Children." *PTA Magazine* Oct. 1972.

Dornbusch, Sanford M., and Myra Strober, eds. *Feminism, Children, and the New Families.* New York: Guilford, 1988.

Douvan, Elizabeth. "The Age of Narcissism, 1963–1982." In *American Childhood: A Research Guide and Historical Handbook*, ed. Joseph N. Hawes and N. Ray Hiner. Champaign: Univ. of Illinois Press, 1985.

Easton, David, and Jack Dennis. *Children in the Political System: Origins of Political Legitimacy.* New York: McGraw-Hill, 1969.

———. "The Child's Image of Government." *Annals of the American Academy of Political and Social Science* 361 (Sept. 1965): 40–57.

Easton, David, and Robert D. Hess. "The Child's Political World." *Midwest Journal of Political Science* 6:3 (Aug. 1962), 229–46.

Echols, Alice. *Daring to Be Bad: Radical Feminism in America, 1967–1975.* Minneapolis: Univ. of Minnesota Press, 1989.

Edwards, Audrey, and Craig K. Polite. *Children of the Dream: The Psychology of Black Success*. New York: Doubleday, 1992.

Egendorf, Arthur. *Healing from the War: Trauma and Transformation after Vietnam*. Boston: Houghton Mifflin, 1985.

Eichelberger, Erika, Jaeah Lee, and A.J. Vicens. "How We Won—and Lost—the War on Poverty in 6 Charts." *Mother Jones* 8 Jan. 2014.

Elder, Glen H. *Children of the Great Depression: Social Change in Life Experience*. Chicago: Univ. of Chicago Press, 1974.

———. "Hard Times in Women's Lives: Historical Influences across Forty Years." *American Journal of Sociology* 88 (1982): 241–69.

———. *Life Course Dynamics: Trajectories and Transitions, 1968–1980*. Ithaca: Cornell Univ. Press, 1985.

———, John Modell, and Ross D. Parke, eds. *Children in Time and Place: Developmental and Historical Insights*. New York: Cambridge Univ. Press, 1994.

Eliot, Martha M. "Let's Get Behind the Bold New Program to Combat Mental Retardation in Children." *Parents Magazine* April 1963.

Elkin, Frederick, and Gerald Handle. *The Child and Society: The Process of Socialization*. New York: Random House, 1972.

Engelhardt, Tom. *The End of Victory Culture: Cold War America and the Disillusioning of a Generation*. New York: Basic Books, 1995.

Escalona, Sibylle. *Children and the Threat of Nuclear War*. New York: Child Study Association of America, 1962.

———. "Children and the Threat of Nuclear War." In *Behavioral Science and Human Survival*, ed. Milton Schwebel. Palo Alto: Science and Behavior Books, 1965.

Espenshade, Thomas J. "The Economic Consequences of Divorce." *Journal of Marriage and the Family* 41 (Aug. 1979): 615–25.

Eugster, Sandra. *Notes from Nethers: Growing Up in a Sixties Commune*. Chicago: Academy Chicago, 2007.

Evans, Sara. *Personal Politics: The Roots of Women's Liberation in the Civil Rights Movement and the New Left*. New York: Vintage, 1979.

Eyerman, John, and Andrew Jamison. *Music and Social Movements: Mobilizing Traditions in the Twentieth Century*. New York: Cambridge Univ. Press, 1997.

Farber, David. *The Age of Great Dreams: America in the 1960s*. New York: Hill & Wang, 1994.

Farrell, James J. *The Spirit of the Sixties: The Making of Postwar Radicalism*. New York: Routledge, 1997.

Fass, Paula S. "The Child-Centered Family? New Rules in Postwar America." In *Reinventing Childhood after World War II*, ed. Paula Fass and Michael Grossberg. Philadelphia: Univ. of Pennsylvania Press, 2011.

———, and Michael Grossberg, eds. *Reinventing Childhood after World War II*. Philadelphia: Univ. of Pennsylvania Press, 2011.

"A Feminist Look at Children's Books." *Library Journal* 15 Jan. 1971.

Ferrari, Michelle. *Reporting America at War: An Oral History*. New York: Hyperion, 2003.

Figley, Charles, and Seymour Leventman, eds. *Strangers at Home: Vietnam Veterans since the War*. New York: Praeger, 1980.

Finkelstein, Barbara. "Uncle Sam and the Children: A History of Government Involvement in Child Rearing." In *Growing Up in America: Children in Historical Perspective*, ed. N. Ray Hiner and Joseph Hawes. Champaign: Univ. of Illinois Press, 1985.

Fisch, Shalom M., and Rosemarie T. Truglio, eds. *"G" Is for "Growing": Thirty Years of Research on Children and Sesame Street*. Mahwah, NJ: Erlbaum, 2000.

Fishman, Katherine Davis. "Children in the Line of March: Question of Involving Children in Social and Political Issues." *New York Times Magazine* 7 Nov. 1965.

Forman-Brunell, Miriam. "Barbie in LIFE: Life of Barbie" (Object Lesson). *Journal of the History of Childhood and Youth* 2:3 (Fall 2009): 303–11.

Fried, Richard M. *The Russians Are Coming! The Russians Are Coming!: Pageantry and Patriotism in Cold-War America*. New York: Oxford Univ. Press, 1999.

Friedenberg, Edgar Z., ed. *The Anti-American Generation*. Chicago: Aldine, 1971.

Gallup, George H. *The Gallup Poll: Public Opinion, 1935–1971, Vols. 1 and 2*. New York: Random House, 1972.

Gant, Liz. "That One's Me! New Books for Black Children Mirror Their World." *Redbook* Aug. 1972.

Garai, Josef E. "Children of Divorce." *Parents Magazine* March 1973.

Gardner, Richard. "If Your Parents Are Getting Divorced." *New York Times Magazine* 22 Nov. 1970.

———. "The Boys and Girls Book about Divorce." *Harper's Bazaar* Feb. 1971.

Gaskin, Ina May. *Spiritual Midwifery*. Summertown, TN: Book Publishing Co., 1977.

Gaskin, Stephen. *Hey Beatnik, This Is the Farm Book*. Summertown, TN: Book Publishing Co., 1974.

Gersoni Stavn, Diane. "Reducing the Miss Muffett Syndrome: An Annotated Bibliography." *Library Journal* 15 Jan. 1972.

Gilligan, Carol. *In a Different Voice: Psychological Theory and Women's Development*. Cambridge: Harvard Univ. Press, 1982.

Gitlin, Todd. *The Sixties: Years of Hope, Days of Rage*. New York: Bantam, 1993.

Goldin, Shari. "Unlearning Black and White: Race, Media, and the Classroom." In *The Children's Culture Reader*, ed. Henry Jenkins. New York: New York Univ. Press, 1998.

Goldscheider, Robert. "Not Only on Sunday: Divorced Fathers and Their Children." *Parents Magazine* May 1974.

Goodman, Paul. "Children of Birmingham." *Commentary* 1 Sept. 1963.

Goodman, Walter. "A Victory for 400,000 Children: The Case of Mrs. Sylvester Smith." *New York Times Magazine* 25 Aug. 1968.

Gordon, Linda. *Woman's Body, Woman's Rights: A Social History of Birth Control in America*. New York: Penguin, 1977.

Gordon, Michael, ed. *The American Family in Social-Historical Perspective*. New York: St. Martin's, 1973.

Graebner, William. "The Unstable World of Benjamin Spock: Social Engineering in a Democratic Culture, 1917–1950." *Journal of American History* 67 (Dec. 1980): 612–29.

Graham, Hugh Davis. "The Transformation of Federal Education Policy. In *The Johnson Years, Vol. 1: Foreign Policy, the Great Society, and the White House*, ed. Robert A. Devine. Lawrence: Univ. Press of Kansas, 1987.

Granstrom, Jane, and Anita Silvey. "A Call for Help: Exploring the Black Experience in Children's Books." *Horn Book Magazine* Aug. 1972.

Greene, Constance. *A Girl Called Al*. New York: Viking, 1969.

Greenstein, Fred I. "The Benevolent Leader: Children's Images of Political Authority." *American Political Science Review* 54:4 (Dec. 1960): 934–43.

———. "The Benevolent Leader Revisited: Children's Images of Political Leaders in Three Democracies." *American Political Science Review* 69:4 (Dec. 1975): 1371–98.

———. "The Best-Known American." *Trans-Action* (Nov. 1966): 13–17.

———. *Children and Politics*. New Haven: Yale Univ. Press, 1969.

———. "More on Children's Images of the President." *Public Opinion Quarterly* 25:4 (Winter 1961): 648–54.

Grimes, Rain. "Fear of a Bagged Lunch." In *Wild Child: Girlhoods in the Counterculture*, ed. Chelsea Cain. Seattle: Seal Press, 1999.

Grossman, Andrew. *Neither Dead nor Red: Civil Defense and American Political Development during the Early Cold War*. New York: Routledge, 2001.

Halberstam, David. *The Children*. New York: Random House, 1998.

Hampton, Henry, and Steve Fayer. *Voices of Freedom: An Oral History of the Civil Rights Movement from the 1950s through the 1980s*. New York: Bantam, 1990.

Hareven, Tamara, ed. *Transitions: The Family and the Life Course in Historical Perspective*. New York: Academic, 1978.

Hareven, Tamara, and Andrejs Plakans, eds. *Family History at the Crossroads: A Journal of Family History Reader*. Princeton: Princeton Univ. Press, 1987.

Hareven, Tamara, and Barbara Trepagnier. *Families, History and Social Change: Life Course & Cross-Cultural Perspectives*. Boulder: Westview, 1999.

Harrison, Cynthia. *On Account of Sex: The Politics of Women's Issues, 1945–1968*. Berkeley: Univ. of California Press, 1989.

Hawes, Joseph N. *Children between the Wars: American Childhood, 1920–1940*. New York: Twayne, 1997.

———, and N. Ray Hiner, eds. *American Childhood: A Research Guide and Historical Handbook*. Westport, CT: Greenwood, 1985.

"Head Start for Children in the Slums." *American Education* Dec. 1964.

Hedgepeth, William. "Hippies as Parents: What Kind of Children Are the New People Raising?" *Look* 15 July 1969.

Heineman, Kenneth J. *Campus Wars: The Peace Movement at American State Universities in the Vietnam Era*. New York: New York Univ. Press, 1993.

"Help for Head Start." *PTA Magazine* April 1967.

Henriksen, Margot A. *Dr. Strangelove's America: Society and Culture in the Atomic Age.* Berkeley: Univ. of California Press, 1997.

"Here's the Rub: Social Security Bill Restricts AFDC." *Newsweek* 15 Jan. 1968.

Herring, George C. *America's Longest War: The United States and Vietnam, 1950–1975.* Philadelphia: Temple Univ. Press, 1979.

Hershey, Marjorie Randon, and David B. Hill. "Watergate and Preadults' Attitudes toward the President." *American Journal of Political Science* 19:4 (Nov. 1975): 703–26.

Hess, Robert D., and David Easton. "The Child's Changing Image of the President." *Public Opinion Quarterly* 24:4 (Winter 1960): 632–44.

Hess, Robert D., and Judith V. Torney. *The Development of Political Attitudes in Children.* Chicago: Aldine, 1967.

Hine, Thomas. *Populuxe: The Look and Life of America in the 50's and 60's.* New York: Knopf, 1986.

Hiner, N. Ray, and Joseph Hawes, eds. *Growing Up in America: Children in Historical Perspective.* Champaign: Univ. of Illinois Press, 1985.

Hodgson, Godfrey. *America in Our Time: From World War II to Nixon, What Happened and Why.* New York: Vintage, 1976.

Hoffman, Lois W., and Martin L. Hoffman, eds. *Review of Child Development Research.* Vols. I and II. New York: Russell Sage, 1966.

Holt, Marilyn Irvin. *Cold War Kids: Politics and Childhood in Postwar America, 1945–1960.* Lawrence: Univ. Press of Kansas, 2014.

"How the War on Poverty Succeeded (in Four Charts)." *New Yorker* 14 Jan. 2014.

Hulbert, Ann. *Raising America: Experts, Parents and a Century of Advice about Children.* New York: Knopf, 2003.

Hunt, Irene. *Up a Road Slowly.* Chicago: Follett, 1966.

Huston, Aletha C., Daniel R. Anderson, John C. Wright, Deborah L. Linebarger, and Kelly L. Schmitt. "Sesame Street Viewers as Adolescents: The Recontact Study." In *"G" Is for Growing: Thirty Years of Research on Children and Sesame Street*, ed. Shalom M. Fisch and Rosemarie T. Truglio. Mahwah, NJ: Erlbaum, 2000.

Iglitzin, Lynn B. "A Child's-Eye View of Sex Roles." *Today's Education* Dec. 1972.

"Incident at Fort Dix: Picketing of Armed Forces Day War Ceremonies for Children." *Christian Century* 19 June 1968.

Jackson, Kenneth. *The Crabgrass Frontier: The Suburbanization of the United States.* New York: Oxford Univ. Press, 1985.

Jacobs, Carol, and Cynthia Eaton. "Sexism in the Elementary School." *Today's Education* Dec. 1972.

Jamison, Andrew, and Ron Eyerman. *Seeds of the Sixties.* Berkeley: Univ. of California Press, 1994.

Jaros, Dean, Herbert Hirsch, and Frederic J. Fleron, Jr. "The Malevolent Leader: Political Socialization in an American Sub-Culture." *American Political Science Review* 62:2 (June 1968): 564–75.

Jenkins, Henry, ed. *The Children's Culture Reader*. New York: New York Univ. Press, 1998.

———, Tara McPherson, and Jane Shattuc, eds. *Hop on Pop: The Politics and Pleasures of Popular Culture*. Durham: Duke Univ. Press, 1998.

"Job Corps, Headstart Reassigned." *Science News* 26 April 1969.

Johnson, Lyndon B. *This America*. New York: Random House, 1966.

———. *The Vantage Point: Perspectives on the Presidency, 1963–1969*. New York: Holt, Rinehart and Winston, 1971.

Jones, Landon Y. *Great Expectations: America and the Baby Boom Generation*. New York: Ballantine, 1981.

Katz, Michael S., Nel Noddings, and Kenneth A. Strike, eds. *Justice and Caring: The Search for Common Ground in Education*. New York: Teachers College Press, 1999.

Kelley, William E., ed. *Post-Traumatic Stress Disorder and the War Veteran Patient*. New York: Brunner/Mazel, 1985.

King, Wilma. *African American Childhoods: Historical Perspectives from Slavery to Civil Rights*. New York: Palgrave Macmillan, 2005.

Kliman, Gilbert. "Oedipal Themes in Children's Reactions to the Assassination." In *Children and the Death of a President*, ed. Martha Wolfenstein and Gilbert Kliman. Garden City, NY: Doubleday, 1965.

Kline, Stephen. *Out of the Garden: Toys and Children's Culture in the Age of TV Marketing*. London: Verso, 1993.

Kohlberg, Lawrence. *Essays on Moral Development, Vol. 2: The Psychology of Moral Development*. New York: Harper & Row, 1984.

———. *Philosophy of Moral Development*. New York: Harper & Row, 1981.

Kramer, Rita. "Desegregation—After School." *New York Times Magazine* 31 May 1964.

Krassner, Paul. *Confessions of a Raving, Unconfined Nut: Misadventures in the Counterculture*. New York: Simon & Schuster, 1994.

Kutinova, Andrea. "Paternity Deferments and the Timing of Births: U.S. Natality during the Vietnam War." *Economic Inquiry* 47:2 (1 April 2009): 351–64.

Lasch, Christopher. *The Culture of Narcissism: American Life in an Age of Diminishing Expectations*. New York: Norton, 1978.

Lee, Lee C. *Personality Development in Childhood*. Monterey, CA: Brooks/Cole, 1976.

Leonard, John. "Since the Kiddies Are Hooked: Why Not Use TV for a Head Start Program?" *New York Times Magazine* 14 July 1968.

Lesser, Gerald S. *Children and Television: Lessons from Sesame Street*. New York: Random House, 1974.

Levine, Ellen, ed. *Freedom's Children: Young Civil Rights Activists Tell Their Own Stories*. New York: Avon, 1993.

Lickona, Thomas. *Raising Good Children: From Birth through the Teenage Years*. New York: Bantam, 1994.

Lifson, Hal. *1966! A Personal View of the Coolest Year in Pop Culture History*. Chicago: Bonus, 2002.

Lifton, Robert Jay. *Home from the War: Vietnam Veterans: Neither Victims nor Execu-tioners*. New York: Simon & Schuster, 1973.

Light, River. "Ghosts." In *Wild Child: Girlhoods in the Counterculture,* ed. Chelsea Cain. Seattle: Seal Press, 1999.

Limmer, Eleanor. "When Mother Goes Away." *Parents Magazine* Dec. 1971.

Lindenmeyer, Kriste. "Children, the State, and the American Dream." In *Reinventing Childhood after World War II*, ed. Paula Fass and Michael Grossberg. Philadel-phia: Univ. of Pennsylvania Press, 2011.

———. *The Greatest Generation Grows Up: American Childhood in the 1930s*. Chicago: Ivan R. Dee, 2007.

Lipsitz, George. *Time Passages: Collective Memory and American Popular Culture*. Min-neapolis: Univ. of Minnesota Press, 1990.

Loss, Archie. *Pop Dreams: Music, Movies, and the Media in the 1960s*. Fort Worth: Harcourt Brace, 1999.

Louv, Richard. *Last Child in the Woods: Saving Our Children From Nature-Deficit Dis-order*. New York: Algonquin, 2008.

Lowenberg, Peter. *Decoding the Past: The Psychohistorical Approach*. Berkeley: Univ. of California Press, 1996.

Lowrey, Annie. "50 Years Later, War on Poverty Is a Mixed Bag." *New York Times* 5 Jan. 2014.

Lyon, Nancy. "More Than Child's Play." *Ms.* Dec. 1972.

Maccoby, Eleanor E., ed. *Readings in Social Psychology*. New York: Holt, 1958.

Macunovich, Diane J. *Birth Quake: The Baby Boom and Its Aftershocks*. Chicago: Univ. of Chicago Press, 2002.

Maddox, William S., and Roger Handberg. "Presidential Affect and Chauvinism among Children." *American Journal of Political Science* 23:2 (May 1979): 426–33.

Marling, Karal Ann. *As Seen on TV: The Visual Culture of Everyday Life in the 1950s*. Cambridge: Harvard Univ. Press, 1996.

Marten, James. *Children for the Union: The War Spirit on the Northern Home Front*. New York: Ivan R. Dee, 2004.

———, ed. *Children and War: A Historical Anthology*. New York: New York Univ. Press, 2002.

Marwick, Arthur. *The Sixties: Cultural Revolution in Britain, France, Italy, and the Unit-ed States, c. 1958–c. 1974*. New York: Oxford Univ. Press, 2000.

Masnick, George, and Mary Jo Bane. *The Nation's Families: 1960–1990*. Boston: Auburn, 1980.

Mathews, John, and Ernest Holsendolph. "The Children Write Their Own Post-script: Reactions to Rioting." *New York Times Magazine* 2 June 1968.

Matthews, Tracye Ann. "'No One Ever Asks What a Man's Place in the Revolution Is': Gender and Sexual Politics in the Black Panther Party, 1966–1971." Ph.D. diss., University of Michigan, 1998.

May, Elaine Tyler. *Homeward Bound: American Families in the Cold War Era*. New York: Basic Books, 2008.

Mazer, Wendy. "What Head Start Meant to Our Town." *Parents Magazine* Oct. 1969.

McClarnand, Elaine, and Steve Goodson, eds. *The Impact of the Cold War on American Popular Culture*. Carrollton: State Univ. of West Georgia, 1999.

McClary, Andrew. *Toys with Nine Lives: A Social History of American Toys*. New York: Linnet, 1997.

McCubbin, Hamilton, Edna J. Hunter, Philip J. Metres, Jr., Edna J. Hunter, and John A. Plag, eds. *Family Separation and Reunion: Families of Prisoners of War and Servicemen Missing in Action*. Washington: U.S. Government Printing Office, 1974.

McDermott, John F. "Divorce from 3 to 6." *New York Times Magazine* 22 Oct. 1967.

McDougall, Walter. *The Heavens and the Earth: A Political History of the Space Age*. New York: Basic Books, 1985.

McGuinn, Patrick J. *No Child Left Behind and the Transformation of Federal Education Policy, 1965–2005*. Lawrence: Univ. Press of Kansas, 2006.

Mead, Margaret. "A New Kind of Discipline." *Parents Magazine* Sept. 1959, 50.

"Memories of Divided Families." *Life* 4 Dec. 1970.

Meredith, Nancy G. "When Parents Divorce." *Parents Magazine* Jan. 1971.

Meyerwitz, Joanne, ed. *Not June Cleaver: Women and Gender in Postwar America, 1945–1960*. Philadelphia: Temple Univ. Press, 1994.

Mickenberg, Julia, and Lynne Vallone, eds. *The Oxford Handbook of Children's Literature*. New York: Oxford Univ. Press, 2011.

Mielke, Keith W. "A Review of Research on the Educational and Social Impact of Sesame Street." In *"G" Is for Growing: Thirty Years of Research on Children and Sesame Street*, ed. Shalom M. Fisch and Rosemarie T. Truglio. Mahwah, NJ: Erlbaum, 2000.

Miller, James. *Democracy Is in the Streets: From Port Huron to the Siege of Chicago*. Cambridge: Harvard Univ. Press, 1994.

Miller, Patricia H. *Theories of Developmental Psychology*. San Francisco: Freeman, 1983.

Miller, Timothy. *The Hippies and American Values*. Knoxville: Univ. of Tennessee Press, 2011.

Milner, Murray. *Freaks, Geeks, and Cool Kids: American Teenagers, Schools, and the Culture of Consumption*. New York: Routledge, 2006.

Mintz, Steven. "The Changing Face of Children's Culture." In *Reinventing Childhood after World War II*, ed. Paula Fass and Michael Grossberg. Philadelphia: Univ. of Pennsylvania Press, 2011.

———. *Huck's Raft: A History of American Childhood*. Cambridge: Harvard Univ. Press, 2006.

———, and Susan Kellogg. *Domestic Revolution: A Social History of American Family Life*. New York: Free Press, 1988.

Mondale, Walter F. "What Does Our Country Owe Its Children?" *Parents Magazine* May 1972.

Morrow, Robert W. *Sesame Street and the Reform of Children's Television*. Baltimore: Johns Hopkins Univ. Press, 2006.

Mueller, John E. *War, Presidents, and Public Opinion*. New York: Wiley, 1973.

Munton, Don, and David A. Welch. *The Cuban Missile Crisis: A Concise History*. New York: Oxford Univ. Press, 2007.

Murray, Charles. *Losing Ground: American Social Policy, 1950–1980*. New York: Basic Books, 1984.

Murray, John P. *Television and Youth: 25 Years of Research and Controversies*. Boys Town, NE: Center for the Study of Youth Development, 1980.

"The Mystery of Rising Relief Costs: Aid to Families with Children." *U.S. News & World Report* 8 March 1965.

Nevin, David. "Struggle That Changed Glen Allan." *Life* 29 Sept. 1967.

"A New Day for the Mentally Retarded." *McCall's* March 1964.

"The New Welfare: Women and Children Last." *Commonweal* 8 Sept. 1967.

"Now There's a White House Plan for the Nation's Children." *U.S. News & World Report* 20 Feb. 1967.

O'Brien, Richard. *The Story of American Toys*. New York: Abbeville, 1990.

Oettinger, Katherine. "Opening Doors for the Retarded Child." *New York Times Magazine* 12 May 1963.

Olsen, Bertha. "Will Your Child Eat Lunch at School?" *Parents Magazine* Sept. 1966.

Ossian, Lisa. *The Forgotten Generation: American Children and World War II*. Columbia: Univ. of Missouri Press, 2011.

Palmer, Edward L., and Shalom M. Fisch. "The Beginnings of Sesame Street Research." In *"G" Is for Growing: Thirty Years of Research on Children and Sesame Street*, ed. Shalom M. Fisch and Rosemarie T. Truglio. Mahwah, NJ: Erlbaum, 2000.

"Parent's Guide to Sex Education." *Parents Magazine* April 1964.

Paris, Leslie. "Happily Ever After: Free to Be . . . You and Me, Second-Wave Feminism, and 1970s American Children's Culture." In *The Oxford Handbook of Children's Literature*, ed. Julia Mickenberg and Lynne Vallone. New York: Oxford Univ. Press, 2011.

Paterson, James T. *America's Struggle against Poverty, 1900–1985*. Cambridge: Harvard Univ. Press, 1986.

Patterson, Anita Haya. *From Emerson to King: Democracy, Race, and the Politics of Protest*. New York: Oxford Univ. Press, 1997.

Perlstein, Rick. *Before the Storm: Barry Goldwater and the Unmaking of the American Consensus*. New York: Nation Books, 2009.

"The Physically Handicapped in the Regular Classroom." *NEA Journal* Dec. 1964.

Pines, Maya. "Slum Children Must Make Up for Lost Time." *New York Times Magazine* 15 Oct. 1967.

Poinsett, Alex. "Ghetto Schools: An Educational Wasteland." *Ebony* Aug. 1967.

Polsky, Richard M. *Getting to Sesame Street: Origins of the Children's Television Workshop*. New York: Praeger, 1974.

Poppy, John. "Child of the Commune." *Saturday Review* 5 Feb. 1972.

"President Johnson's Special Message to Congress: Children and Youth." *PTA Magazine* March & April 1967.

"Project Head Start: The Record after Two Years." *U.S. News & World Report* 19 June 1967.

Rand, Eric. "Older Heads on Younger Bodies." In *The Children's Culture Reader*, ed. Henry Jenkins. New York: New York Univ. Press, 1998.

"The Revolution since Little Rock." *Life* 29 Sept. 1967.

Rhodes, Joel P. *The Voice of Violence: Performative Violence as Protest in the Vietnam Era*. Westport, CT: Praeger, 2001.

Rogers, Mary. *Barbie Culture*. London: Sage, 1999.

Rorabaugh, William. *Berkeley at War: The 1960s*. New York: Oxford Univ. Press, 1989.

Roszak, Theodore. *The Making of a Counterculture: Reflections on the Technocratic Society and Its Youthful Opposition*. Garden City, NY: Doubleday, 1969.

Rothchild, John, and Susan Wolf. *The Children of the Counterculture: How the Life-Style of America's Flower Children Has Affected an Even Younger Generation*. Garden City, NY: Doubleday, 1976.

Rowe, John Carlos, and Rick Berg. *The Vietnam War and American Culture*. New York: Columbia Univ. Press, 1991.

Rupp, Leila, and Verta Taylor. *Survival in the Doldrums: The American Women's Rights Movement, 1945 to the 1960s*. Princeton: Princeton Univ. Press, 1987.

Rusk, Howard A. "A Brighter Future for Disabled Children." *Parents Magazine* Nov. 1965.

Salkind, Neil J. *Theories in Human Development*. New York: Van Nostrand, 1981.

Schlesinger, Arthur, Jr. *A Thousand Days: John F. Kennedy in the White House*. Boston: Houghton Mifflin, 1965.

Schmidt, Cecily. "Common Threads." In *Wild Child: Girlhoods in the Counterculture*, ed. Chelsea Cain. Seattle: Seal Press, 1999.

Schneider, Nicholas, and Nathalie Rockhill, eds. *John F. Kennedy Talks to Young People*. New York: Hawthorne, 1968.

"School Lunches: The Changes Proposed." *U.S. News & World Report* 28 March 1966.

Schwebel, Milton, ed. *Behavioral Science and Human Survival*. Palo Alto: Science and Behavior Books, 1965.

"Second Thoughts about a Study." *Science News* 3 May 1969.

"Sesame Street Report Card." *Time* 16 Nov. 1970.

Shakoor, Jordana Y. *Civil Rights Childhood*. Jackson: Univ. Press of Mississippi, 1999.

Shulevitz, Uri. *Rain Rain Rivers*. New York: Farrar, Straus & Giroux, 1969.

Sigel, Roberta S. "An Exploration into Some Aspects of Political Socialization: School Children's Reactions to the Death of a President." In *Children and the Death of a President*, ed. Martha Wolfenstein and Gilbert Kliman. Garden City, NY: Doubleday, 1965.

Sinnott, Jan. "Zap! Bam! Pow! Chauvinist Children's Culture." *Off Our Backs* 1:7 (1970): 12. College Park: Univ. of Maryland Archives.

Sitkoff, Harvard. *The Struggle for Black Equality, 1954–1980.* New York: Hill & Wang, 1981.

Skolnick, Arlene. *Embattled Paradise: The American Family in the Age of Uncertainty.* New York: Basic Books, 1991.

Skolnick, Peter L., Laura Torber, and Nikki Smith. *Fads: America's Crazes, Fevers, and Fancies from the 1890s to the 1970s.* New York: Thomas Y. Crowell, 1978.

Slotkin, Richard. *Gunfighter Nation: The Myth of the Frontier in Twentieth Century America.* New York: Atheneum, 1992.

Small, Melvin. *Covering Dissent: The Media and the Anti-Vietnam War Movement.* New Brunswick: Rutgers Univ. Press, 1994.

Sorensen, Ted. *Kennedy: The Classic Biography.* New York: Harper Perennial Political Classics, 2009.

Spigel, Lynn, and Michael Curtin, eds. *The Revolution Wasn't Televised: Sixties Television and Social Change.* New York: AFI/Routledge, 1997.

"Spirit of Christmas Present: Nixon's Veto of Children's Programs." *Commonweal* 24 Dec. 1971.

Spock, Benjamin. *The Common Sense Book of Baby and Child Care.* New York: Duell, Sloan & Pearce, 1946.

———. "How Divorced Parents Can Help Their Children Adjust." *Redbook* March 1971.

———. "Learning to Live in a Troubled World." *Redbook* Aug. 1964.

———. "Playing with Toy Guns: Effects of Warlike Games and Toys on Children." *Redbook* Nov. 1964.

———. *Raising Children in a Difficult Time.* New York: Norton, 1974.

———. "Should Girls Be Raised Like Boys?" *Redbook* Feb. 1972.

Stark, Steven D. *Glued to the Set: The 60 Television Shows and Events That Made Us Who We Are Today.* New York: Free Press, 1997.

———. *Meet the Beatles: A Cultural History of the Band that Shook Youth, Gender, and the World.* New York: HarperCollins, 2005.

Sterling, Dorothy. *Tender Warriors.* New York: Hill & Wang, 1958.

Stern, Mark. *Calculating Visions: Kennedy, Johnson and Civil Rights.* New Brunswick: Rutgers Univ. Press, 1992.

Stevenson, Ian. "People Aren't Born Prejudice." *Parents Magazine* Feb. 1960.

"*Stevie*: Realism in a Book about Black Children." *Life* 29 Aug. 1969.

Stewig, John, and Margaret Higgs. "Girls Grow Up to Be Mommies: A Study of Sexism in Children's Literature." *Library Journal* 15 Jan. 1973.

Stough, Ada Barnett. "If Children Could Talk to the New President and the New Congress." *Parents Magazine* Dec. 1960, 3.

Strickland, Charles E., and Andrew M. Ambrose. "The Baby Boom, Prosperity, and the Changing Worlds of Children, 1945-1963." In *American Childhood: A*

Research Guide and Historical Handbook, ed. Joseph N. Hawes and N. Ray Hiner. Champaign: Univ. of Illinois Press, 1985.

Tanner, Laurel N., and Daniel Tanner. "Unanticipated Effects of Federal Policy: The Kindergarten." *Educational Leadership* Oct. 1973.

Taylor, Ella. *Prime-Time Families: Television Culture in Postwar America*. Berkeley: Univ. of California Press, 1991.

"Thirteen Years after 1954: Negro Pupils in the South." *Ebony* April 1967.

Thorsen, Karen. "A Campaign to Get a Husband Home." *Life* 29 Sept. 1972.

Tischler, Barbara, ed. *Sights on the Sixties*. New Brunswick: Rutgers Univ. Press, 1992.

Tolley, Howard, Jr. *Children and War: Political Socialization to Internal Conflict*. New York: Teachers College Press, 1973.

Tuttle, William M. *"Daddy's Gone to War": The Second World War in the Lives of America's Children*. New York: Oxford Univ. Press, 1993.

Umanksy, Lauri. *Motherhood Reconceived: Feminism and the Legacies of the Sixties*. New York: New York Univ. Press, 1996.

Unger, Irwin. *The Best of Intentions: The Triumph and Failure of the Great Society under Kennedy, Johnson, and Nixon*. New York: Doubleday, 1996.

U.S. Bureau of the Census. *Historical Statistics of the United States, Colonial Times to 1970, Part 1*. Washington: U.S. Government Printing Office, 1975.

U.S. Congress. Senate. Subcommittee on Children and Youth of the Committee on Labor and Public Welfare. *Hearings before the Subcommittee on Children and Youth. American Families: Trends and Pressures, 1973*. 93rd Cong. 2nd Sess. 24–26 Jan. 1974. Washington: Government Printing Office, 1974.

Van Deburg, William L. *New Day in Babylon: The Black Power Movement and American Culture, 1965–1975*. Chicago: Univ. of Chicago Press, 1992.

Viorst, Judith. "Nuclear Threat Harms Children." *Science News Letter* 16 Feb. 1963.

Waldman, Elizabeth, and Robert Whitmore. "Children of Working Mothers, March 1973." *Monthly Labor Review* (May 1974): 50–52.

"War Talk and War Games." *PTA Magazine* Jan. 1968.

Watkins, Mel. "White Skins, Dark Skins, Thin Skins." *New York Times Magazine* 3 Dec. 1967.

Weeks, Louis. "Father Takes Care of Baby." *Parents Magazine* Feb. 1971.

Weiss, Nancy Pottishman. "Mother, the Invention of Necessity: Dr. Benjamin Spock's *Baby and Child Care*." In *Growing Up in America: Children in Historical Perspective*, ed. N. Ray Hiner and Joseph N. Hawes. Champaign: Univ. of Illinois Press, 1985.

Weitzman, Lenore J. *The Divorce Revolution: The Unexpected Social and Economic Consequences for Women and Children in America*. New York: Free Press, 1985.

———, Deborah Eifler, Elizabeth Hokada, and Catherine Ross. "Sex Role Socialization in Picture Books for Preschool Children." *American Journal of Sociology* (May 1972): 1125–45.

"What Can We Tell Our Children? Views of a White Southern Mother and a Negro Mother." *Redbook* May 1964.

"What Every Mother Owes Her Child and Herself." *Ladies' Home Journal* June 1966.

Whitfield, Stephen. *The Culture of The Cold War*. Baltimore: Johns Hopkins Univ. Press, 1996.

Wolfenstein, Martha, and Gilbert Kliman, eds. *Children and the Death of a President*. Garden City, NY: Doubleday, 1965.

Wrightman, Lawrence. "Parental Attitudes and Behaviors as Determinants of Children's Responses to the Threat of Nuclear War." *Vita Humana* 7 (1964): 178–85.

Zappa, Moon. Foreword to *Wild Child: Girlhoods in the Counterculture,* ed. Chelsea Cain. Seattle: Seal Press, 1999.

Zaretsky, Natasha. *No Direction Home: The American Family and the Fear of National Decline, 1968–1980*. Chapel Hill: Univ. of North Carolina Press, 2007.

Zelizer, Viviana A. *Pricing the Priceless Child: The Changing Social Value of Children*. Princeton: Princeton Univ. Press, 1985.

Zezma, Katie. "How Did We Get to Sesame Street? Via LBJ's Great Society." *Washington Post* 22 May 2014.

INDEX